Lord of the Dance

SUNY Series in Buddhist Studies
Matthew Kapstein, Editor

Lord of the Dance

The Mani Rimdu Festival in Tibet and Nepal

Richard J. Kohn

State University of New York Press

Published by
State University of New York Press, Albany

Printed in the United States of America

For information, address State University of New York Press,
90 State Street, Suite 700, Albany, NY 12207

Production by Michael Haggett
Marketing by Patrick Durocher

Library of Congress Cataloging-in-Publication Data

Kohn, Richard J., 1948–
Lord of the dance : the Mani Rimdu Festival in Tibet and Nepal / Richard J. Kohn.
p. cm. — (SUNY series in Buddhist studies)
Includes bibliographical references and index.
ISBN 0-7914-4891-6 (alk. paper) — ISBN 0-7914-4892-4 (pbk : alk. paper)
1. Mani Rimdu Festival. 2. Buddhism—Nepal—Steng-chen-dgon (Monastery : Thyångboche, Nepal)—Rituals. 3. Dance—Religious aspects—Buddhism. 4. Tantric Buddhism—Rituals—Texts. 5. Rñiṅ-ma-pa (Sect)—Rituals. I. Title. II. Series.

BQ5720.M28 K64 2001
294.3'436'095496—dc21 00-055622

10 9 8 7 6 5 4 3 2 1

To Jack

Contents

Part III In Conclusion

Tables

Photographs

Mural, Thubten Chöling Printing House, artist: Kapa Par Gyaltsten of Pangkarma, ca. 1970, front cover

Lord of the Dance *Maṇḍala*, ca. 1950, back cover

Illustrations

Map

Foreword

I first met Rick Kohn in New York in 1978, as he was about to depart for Nepal to begin fieldwork for his Ph.D. dissertation. His proposed research concerned aspects of the temporary art created for ritual use in Tibetan Buddhism. I had recently returned from Nepal, and he wished to inquire about conditions for research in Solu, to the south of the Mount Everest region. I could not have imagined then, nor, indeed, could Rick, that his work would result a decade later in the fullest cinematographic and textual documentation of a major Tibetan ritual cycle yet achieved.

Rick's sumptuous 16 mm documentary film, *Lord of the Dance, Destroyer of Illusion* (1985), has been widely appreciated since its first release. Known only to a relatively small number of specialized scholars, however, is his thousand page dissertation, *Mani Rimdu, Text and Tradition in a Tibetan Ritual,* completed in 1988 at the University of Wisconsin. The film and the thesis both describe the Mani Rimdu festival celebrated annually at several of the Sherpa monasteries of Nepal. Because the festival had been often attended by trekkers and anthropologists, and indeed had been the topic of two previous books, one may suspect that it was already very well known. Rick showed us, however, that the Mani Rimdu festival remained poorly described and largely misunderstood. Its history, religious significance, and the elaborate ritual cycle in which the few days of public festivity are embedded had never been properly examined. In fact, even the public masked dances, for which the Mani Rimdu was best known, had been in important respects misdescribed.

As Rick clearly recognized, the religious arts of Tibet, including masked dance, painting and sculpture—which have much impressed Western observers owing to their fantastic imagery, profound symbolism, and splendid color and ornamentation—are almost entirely subservient to one great art form, the Buddhist tantric ritual. Without analyzing the ritual, its structure and syntax, the individual products of Tibetan art are little more than disconnected artifacts; or, to use an image that is more appropriate to the present subject matter (where the ritual "liberation" of the *lingka* is of central concern), they are like the limbs of a sacrificial victim that lay lifeless apart from the body that once animated them. Though always deeply engaged in the study of Tibetan art, both in its temporary and enduring manifestations, Rick therefore chose to study the Mani Rimdu as an organic whole, a living ritual body at whose heart was the living lama and the *maṇḍala* he created. Rick's film and thesis in effect developed as the ethnographic equivalent of a biological life history.

Throughout the abundant annotations to his work, and in his bibliography, Rick refers to a very wide range of previous research on Tibetan Buddhism. It is clear, however, that within this field one conversation partner looms particularly large, namely, the brilliant pioneering scholar, René de Nebesky-Wojkowitz. The latter's encyclopedic work on the *Oracles and Demons of Tibet,* and his important and difficult explorations of Tibetan sacred dance, were not, however, models that Rick emulated in any simple sense. He saw these, rather, as important points of departure, platforms upon which to erect his own intricate *maṇḍala*-palace of inquiry. Significant, too, in this regard, was the background provided by Ferdinand Lessing's great study of the *Yung-ho-kung* Tibetan temple complex in Beijing and by Stephan Beyer's pathbreaking researches on *The Cult of Tārā.*

The two large volumes of Rick's dissertation included a thorough descriptive analysis of the rituals of the Mani Rimdu, and complete translations of the corpus of liturgical texts that guide and accompany these rites. Rick's approach was, to be sure, emphatically descriptive. Though interested in theoretical reflection on a wide range of pertinent issues—including the analysis of ritual, the role of visual documentation in ethnographical research, and the methodology of translation—Rick believed that in the final analysis ritual performance spoke for itself. The ethnographer's role in some respects paralleled that of the accomplished critic, whose task was not so much to attempt to supply a definitive interpretation of the performance, but rather to assist the viewer in discovering just what there was to see, and to suggest some of the many avenues of possible understanding. As a result, Rick's work suggests an elaborately detailed study of an opera, supplying descriptions of its history, the dramatis personae and the various theatrical functions and roles, together with a thorough synopsis of the events in the drama, and, finally, the libretto itself.

Rick and I began to discuss prospects for the publication of the thesis not long after he had completed it. He soon reached the conclusion that, while the work as a whole might serve as a reference to specialists, an abridgement complementing the film would provide a useful introduction to Tibetan religious performance for those more broadly interested in Buddhism and in the study of ritual. Rick completed a preliminary version of the text in 1994, largely on the basis of the first volume of his dissertation. Before he could complete a final revision, however, tragedy struck and Rick was forced to turn his energies to battling the illness that ultimately claimed his life in May of this year. With the remarkable courage he summoned up throughout his struggle, Rick finished work on the manuscript just two months before his passing. It has been my responsibility and my privilege to see his book through the press.

I am profoundly grateful to Marianne Betterly-Kohn for her thoughtful encouragement throughout the preparation of Rick's book. Thanks, too, to Benjamin Bogin for generously assisting in the compilation of the index, and to the editorial staff of the State University of New York Press for their care at every stage of production.

Matthew T. Kapstein
Editor, SUNY Series in Buddhist Studies
The University of Chicago
September 2000

Preface

In 1978, I set off for the Himalayas to begin a project called "Temporary Art in Buddhist Communities of Nepal." It was a study of three media that had been largely ignored by students of Tibetan art: sculpture of butter and dough (*gtor ma*), paintings of sand (*rdul mtshon dkyil 'khor*), and ritual constructions of thread (*mdos*). Although in America over the past few years, a demonstration of sand painting or even dough sculpture has become practically obligatory for museum exhibitions of Tibetan art, in 1978 it was difficult to even find photographs of them.

Such art was made for ritual, and, once in the field, it became apparent that a meaningful study would have to include their ritual context. To narrow my focus, I not only decided to concentrate on a single ritual, but also I began to shop around for one rich in temporary art. My search led me to the Mani Rimdu festival at Chiwong Monastery. At that time, Mani Rimdu was one of the few, if not the only regularly scheduled ritual in Nepal to use a sand *maṇḍala*.

And I was hooked. The *maṇḍala* was magnificent, the tormas diverse. The festival was enchanting. Above all, the people there were unbelievably kind and helpful. One man whom I had barely met, the well-known Sherpa painter Oleshe, presented me with his entire collection of rare Tibetan xylographs pertaining to the ritual.

If the festival was fascinating, it was also unknown, despite the fact it had been written about before. Of Mani Rimdu's eighteen days, only three had been even partially described. With no knowledge of the Tibetan language, previous writers had ignored the hundreds of pages of texts used in the rituals. Of this rather large corpus, only two short prayers—less than a dozen pages, had been translated into any Western language. Even so, their translation was merest coincidence and their connection to the festival was not known.

The deeper I went into the rituals, the more entranced I became by the beauty of their religious concept, their structure and, often, of their literary style. Beyond the individual rituals, there was another dimension of form—the interplay of each element with the others and the grand architecture of the festival as a whole. This interplay became a major focus of my research.

As I worked on, a crucial fact became apparent, one of a practical nature. Mani Rimdu was so big that it could not be used as a means to any other end. It was a study in and of itself.

I reflected on the works that had first inspired my research—Ferdinand Lessing's monumental plan to study the rituals of each chapel of *Yung-Ho-Kung;* David Snellgrove's organic account of how Buddhists use ritual and art in *Buddhist Himālaya;* Stephen Beyer's compendious study of the rituals belonging to *The Cult of Tārā,* and through them, of the structure of Tibetan ritual itself. As far-reaching as these pioneering works were, a niche still was left—a comprehensive study of a major Tibetan festival and the function of ritual in it.

My initial object in seeking out Mani Rimdu had been a wise one—to limit my project to reasonable dimensions. Now, with the ambition and naïveté of a fledgling fieldworker, in a stroke I had converted my project into a juggernaut of research that was to roll for nearly a decade.

Such a work could not have been accomplished without much help, and I am happy to have this chance to thank those who have contributed their faith, their expertise, or their financial support to this project.

The research was begun with the generous support of the Fulbright-Hays Doctoral Dissertation Research Abroad Fellowship program of the Department of Education.

I was able to return to Nepal for another eighteen months through the kindness of the Social Science Research Council and American Council of Learned Societies. Without the help of this program, funded by the Ford Foundation and the National Endowment for the Humanities, the project could never have been brought to completion.

There are some who can never be thanked enough. Lama Trulshik Rinpoche, Chant Leader Ngawang Tsundru, and the monks and nuns of Thubten Chöling, Chiwong and Thami Monasteries, opened their homes to me, their heritage and their hearts. Mani Rimdu is their tradition and this book is theirs.

Nor is there any way to repay the kindness of my first teacher and graduate advisor at the University of Wisconsin, Geshe Lhundup Sopa. Without the solid background in Buddhist Studies that he gave his students, it is doubtful that the guardians of the Mani Rimdu tradition would have been willing to entrust their precious legacy to me; without his innate patience, this book would not have been accomplished.

Special thanks also go to Lama Tharchin, who gave endless hours of guidance through the convoluted byways of Mindroling ritual. All those who are his students are fortunate to have such a teacher and friend.

A great debt of gratitude is due to His Majesty's Government of Nepal and the Research Division and Centre for Nepal and Asian Studies at Tribhuvan University in Kathmandu. Their enlightened policies ensure the continuation of an international effort to record and preserve the diverse and remarkable culture of their beautiful land.

As a side effect of the open atmosphere that they have created for scholars, the city of Kathmandu itself has become one of the world's great institutes of Asian Studies and the collegial atmosphere among researchers there is one of the many pleasures of field work in Nepal. The colleagues, Nepali and Western who throughout the evolution of this project have given advice, encouragement, and intellectual stimulation are too numerous to catalogue here. Some of them are (in alphabetical order): Dr. Barbara Aziz; Pandit Baidya Ashakaji Bajrcarya; Professor Dor Bahadur Bista of Tribhuvan University; Mr. Keith Dowman; Mr. Hugh R. Downs; Professor David N. Gellner; Dr. Harka Gurung; Mr. Hubert Ducleer; Fr. John Locke, S.J.; Mr. Kalsang Namgyal; Professor Bruce Owens; and Professors Christoph von Fürer-Haimendorf, David Snellgrove, and Tadeusz Skorupski of the School of Oriental and African Studies at the University of London.

Special thanks are due to Dr. Michael Oppitz, director of the Ethnographic Museum at the University of Zurich. All of us to whom he has opened his library, his home, and his mind are enormously fortunate. A friend like him is good to have and hard to find.

Nepal was an ideal place for my study in many ways. In its astounding cultural diversity, it preserves analogs of each side of the Tibetan cultural family tree. Here we find medieval Indian tantracism (among the Newars of Kathmandu) side by side with classic Siberian shamanism (among the Magar of West Nepal and others). On occasion, I have looked to either Newar Buddhism or to shamanism to illuminate an aspect of Mani Rimdu. Without the advice of experts in each field such as Pandit Bajracarya, Dr. Gellner and Fr. Locke on the one hand and Dr. Oppitz on the other, such comparative studies would have hardly been possible.

I owe considerable gratitude to the United States Educational Foundation in Nepal, the United States Information Service, and the American Embassy in Kathmandu. They provided help and hospitality that made my work easier and my stay in Nepal more pleasant.

I also give my thanks to Ms. Sabine Lehmann and the management and staff of the Vajra Hotel in Kathmandu for providing shelter and friendship on many occasions when I stumbled raw and disheveled out of the mountains; and to Mr. Charles Thomas for his generous hospitality and for the use of his wonderful library.

Doctor Mark Tatz also deserves special mention here; with the heroism of a true *bodhisattva*, he undertook the task of reviewing the manuscript of my dissertation and offering his intelligent and insightful comments. Professor Matthew Kapstein of the University of Chicago also deserves my thanks for encouraging me to transform that dissertation into this book.

Thanks also to Keith Dowman of Kathmandu for permission to reproduce the Sherpa artist Oleshe's line drawing of 'Gyur med rdo re from his "The Nyingma Icons."

My most heartfelt thanks go to my family who never lost faith through long years of watching this project unfold. Last but never least, I thank Franz-Christoph Giercke of Sky Walker Productions, who with a wave of his wand let me share the results of this long and arduous work with thousands of people around the world.

To the others unnamed who have contributed help, advice and inspiration, thank you.

Sources and Methodology

This book brings together several types of information on ritual practice—literary sources, works of art, and ethnographic data. The methodology is similarly manifold. For the ritual texts, the first step was translation. Later, each work was checked, often line by line, with one or more experts in the ritual.

The visual arts form a very special part of the festival. Lord of the Dance and the other deities of Mani Rimdu are portrayed on the walls of monasteries and on scroll paintings belonging to their lamas. Some works of art—miniature paintings on cloth, *maṇḍalas* painted of sand, and sculpture molded from barley flour dough and colored butter—are not only made specifically for rituals, but also play a precisely defined role in them. Artworks in Tibet are often based on texts, and in a sense, form a visual commentary on those texts. My approach here has been the mirror image of traditional art history; I was less concerned with what Mani Rimdu could tell us about the art of Solu Khumbu than with what that art could tell us about Mani Rimdu.

The methods of the ethnographic research were participant observation and interview. I attended eleven performances of Mani Rimdu, eight of them from beginning to end. At the same time, I studied the performance with ritual experts such as the Chant Leader of Thubten Chöling. Whenever possible, I correlated my notes and sketches with the texts on site.

Throughout the process, I photographed the rituals and the implements used in them. From time to time, these photographs were also used as primary data. In later stages, I was able to consult material from my film *Lord of the Dance/Destroyer of Illusion* in a similar fashion.[1]

Ritual texts form the script of Mani Rimdu. The rituals that the texts describe are series of recitations and guided visualizations designed to have a direct and immediate emotional impact on those who practice them as well as long-term spiritual benefits. The tradition itself states that an intense emotional experience, or at least the physiological accompaniments of one, while not to be confused with the final goal, is a sign of meditative success. The hair on one's head and body stands on end; tears come to one's eyes.

Insofar as a meditator's mind is free from distraction—and a mind free from distraction is a meditator's goal—at the moment of practice, the ritual is the very content of his mind. By repetition, the rituals are designed to shape and condition his mental world. Short of clairvoyance, a sympathetic reading of ritual gives us a uniquely direct insight into the mind of a Tibetan or Sherpa monk. If we let ourselves fall under their spell, even as lovers of literature, we can begin to appreciate the emotional satisfactions of the life of a Buddhist meditator.

The image of Buddhist meditation we have had in the West is of a rather abstract and chilly affair. Whatever merit this stereotype may possess for other types of practice, it is certainly not the case in the tantric tradition to which the rituals of Mani Rimdu belong. Those with any lingering doubts on this matter are referred to the self-empowerment ritual, where, having visualized himself as the god, the meditator imagines that

> The red letter *hrīḥ* in the heart of this body of mine that has become that of the Lord of the Dance Great Compassion, burns like a butter lamp. Its shining light stimulates the gods of the *maṇḍala* to project countless forms from their minds—bodies and syllables, symbols which blaze in a mass of beams of light, which come helter-skelter like rain and snow, like a blizzard. They enter through [my] pores and fill [my] body completely to the brim. Bliss blazes unbearably.[2]

The structure of this book evolved into two parts.

The first contains a few brief remarks on various aspects of the ritual in general. It provides an overview of some of the questions raised by a complex Buddhist cultural performance such as Mani Rimdu.

The heart of the book, part two, contains the bulk of the ethnographic and analytic material. It consists of a day-by-day account of the progress of the festival based on field observation and interview, interwoven with key passages drawn from the texts.

The informants who contributed their knowledge to this book were for the most part monks of Thubten Chöling and Chiwong monasteries and experts on, or at least participants in the festival. Villagers were also consulted as was appropriate, although to a far lesser extent. Many of the latter came from Junbesi, a large village midway between the two monasteries. Others were from a variety of villages in Solu-Khumbu.

The principal informants were:

H. E. Trulshik Rinpoche (Zhva lde'u 'Khrul zhig Rin po che XI, Ngag dbang blo bzang mdo ngag bstan 'dzin), abbot of Thubten Chöling. As spiritual heir to Abbot Ngawang Tenzin Norbu of Rongphu Monastery, Trulshik Rinpoche has long been the spiritual leader of the Everest region and the leading expert on Mani Rimdu and on the god Lord of the Dance. Trulshik

Rinpoche's incarnation lineage descends from an eighteenth-century Lharam Geshe (Doctor of Divinity with Highest Honors) named Guyang Lodetsel (Gu yangs blo bde rtsal), who was from the great Geluk Monastery of Drepung. Though trained in the rival Geluk Order, he became a disciple of the famous Nyingma saint Jigme Lingpa ('Jigs med gling pa, 1730–98) and then "became (i.e., reached the enlightened state of) a Heruka." Guyang Lodetsel is said to have performed many marvelous feats (*rdzu 'phrul*) before the age of ten. In more recent years, Trulshik Rinpoche XI had been the main disciple of H. H. Dilgo Khyentse Rinpoche, who, until his own death in 1991, had become leader of the Nyingma Order at the death of H. H. Dudjom Rinpoche in 1987. Trulshik Rinpoche has represented the Nyingma Order several times at Kālacakra initiations given by H. H. the Dalai Lama.[3]

Ven. Ngawang Tsundru (Ngag dbang brTson 'grus), Chant Leader (*dbu mdzad*) [pron. "umze"] of Thubten Chöling. The principal rituals that comprise Mani Rimdu are also done outside of the festival; many of them are performed more often at Thubten Chöling than at Chiwong. A superb Umze as well as an excellent teacher, Ngawang Tsundru knows every aspect of their performance in detail.

Ven. Sang Sang Tulku, Ngawang Jimi (Sang sang sprul sku Ngag dbang 'jigs med), incarnation of the father of the previous Trulshik Rinpoche and the disciple of the present one. A member of a Kagyü incarnation lineage, he was educated at Rumtek Monastery. At the time of my research, he had for

Trulshik Rinpoche, flanked by monks of Thubten Chöling and Chiwong, Chiwong 1982

a number of years acted as Diamond Master at Thubten Chöling. Recently, he built his own monastery in Nepal.

Ven. Lama Tsedrub Tharchin (Bla ma Tshe sgrub Thar phyin), a hereditary lama (*sngags pa*) of the Repkong lineage in Amdo province. Among Lama Tharchin's many areas of expertise, is detailed knowledge of the major protector ritual of Mani Rimdu, the *Playful Ocean,* which he learned from his teacher Kusho Gyurme (sKu zhabs 'Gyur med a.k.a. 'Gyur med rdo rje).[4] Kusho Gyurme traveled with Dudjom Rinpoche, later head of the Nyingma Order, when he was young; the two men were at Mindroling together. According to Lama Tharchin, Kusho Gyurme was equally famous as an expert on ritual as the illustrious Nyingma hierarch. Lama Tharchin is in possession of his notes on the *Playful Ocean.* Since he is not a member of the Rongphu/ Solu-Khumbu subtradition, I frequently checked his exegeses with Trulshik Rinpoche. In nearly every case they agreed. In recent years, Lama Tharchin has been in Northern California, where he has a established a flourishing retreat center.

Ven. Tengpoche Rinpoche, Ngawang Tenzin (Ngag dbang bsTan 'dzin), is abbot of the Khumbu monastery famous for its Mani Rimdu traditions.

Ven. Thami Rinpoche, Ngawang Shedrup Tenpai Gyaltsen (Ngag dbang Bshad sgrub bstan pa'i rgyal mtshan), abbot of the other Khumbu monastery that performs Mani Rimdu.

Head Monks, the Ven. Ngawang Pintsok and the Late Ven. Ngawang Tsokdruk of Chiwong Monastery; Ven. Ngawang Yönten, and the monks of Chiwong Monastery.

The Monks of Thami Monastery.

Among those who contributed valuable information in the earlier stages of this research were Mr. Lobsang Chönjor, then of dGa' ldan chos pa'i gling Monastery in Kathmandu, and Khenpo Lobsang Gendun Rinpoche, its late abbot; and Penyima of Mendokpalgye, Solu, who was Chant Leader of Chiwong in the late 1960s.

About the Translations

Ritual is aimed at affect. In the translations, I have tried to give a feeling of the text as well as its sense. Wherever possible I give an English equivalent for a Tibetan word or phrase rather than relying on a transcription of the Tibetan or a reconstruction of the Sanskrit. This method extends to names of deities and classes of spirits. Thus, for example, rDo rje sems dpa' (Vajrasattva) is Diamond Mind Hero; *srin po*, ghoul; *gnod byin*, Malefactor/Benefactor; and *klu*, Serpent Spirit. A ghoul might make an English speaker shiver; a *srin po* or a *rākṣasa* would leave him equally cold. In some cases, Sanskritization seemed particularly ill-advised; Tibet had *srin po* and *gnod byin* before it had heard of the *rākṣasa* and *yakṣa* of India; in Solu as in Tibet itself, *klu* worship may antedate the advent of Buddhism. In proposing English equivalents, I have followed the mythological and etymological formulations of my informants. Although sometimes disputable as etymology, they are invaluable as ethnography.[5]

In the analytical sections of this book, where aesthetics were of less concern, Sanskrit equivalents are used more freely. Mantras and other Sanskrit material included in the Tibetan text are given verbatim. If the Sanskrit of the texts is corrupt, it is fairly systematic and those wishing to explore the transliteration system of the Mindroling *gter ma* tradition will find the primary data undisturbed.[6]

A Note on Secrecy

It is best to deal with issue of secrecy at least briefly here at the outset. Our own main ritual text, the *Lord of the Dance Manual,* advises the initiate:

> Now, you will enter this great *maṇḍala.*
> You will give birth to wisdom.
> Since you will gain the highest true achievement thereby,
> Do not speak to those who do not see.[7]

More recently, His Holiness the Fourteenth Dalai Lama has written,

> If the secret mantra is practiced openly and used for commercial purposes, then accidents will befall such a practitioner, even taking his life, and conditions unfavorable for generating spiritual experience and realizations in his continuum will be generated. With other books it is not too serious to make an error, but with books of Mantra it is very serious to err either in explanation or in translation. Furthermore, if the fault of proclaiming the secret to those who are not ripened is incurred, there is danger that instead of helping, it will harm. There are many stories of people who have begun treatises on Mantra but have been unable to complete their lifespan and others whose progress was delayed through writing a book on mantra.[8]

If this seems in a dire vein, we should remember that traditionally the tantra system has promised death, madness, and hell to those that abuse it. According to many authorities this danger is not so much mystical as it is simply practical. Stephen Beyer put it neatly in *The Cult of Tārā.* Although referring specifically to the protector cult, his words could be as easily applied to the tantra as a whole:

> All these objects of monastic rituals . . . are powerful deities who symbolize currents of cosmic force to be tampered with only at one's own peril. They constitute the monastic cult because they are best left to the ritual experts. It is not that their cult is particularly secret, just as there is nothing esoteric about the workings of a television set; but in both instances the forces involved are too potent to be played with by a layman, and in both instances the same warning applies.[9]

The monastery that was the source of the Mani Rimdu rituals was particularly secretive, even among guardians of tantric traditions. According to at least one informant, this was not necessarily an advantage:

> At Mindroling they were very secretive. The Lord of the Dance rituals have three commentaries: *Accompanying Methods, The Precious Lamp* and *The Light which Illumines Suchness*. None of them alone is sufficient to understand how to perform the ritual. On top of this, there are even other commentaries, like the single folio on how to complete the *lingka*.
>
> Even these commentaries hide things. For example, when discussing drawing the lines of the *maṇḍala*, *Accompanying Methods* calls the directions "fire, ghoul," etc. They would also abbreviate things [so that they would not be understood], such as just saying do the "suppression of the gnomes" or "cleanse." So no one ritual text is complete. They made things so complicated that people would just give up after a few tries. I think this was stupid.
>
> Mindroling did this with many of its practices. They never even told other monasteries everything. Now that Mindroling is gone, this seems like a mistake. Had they been more open, their traditions would be alive. Now, except for Thubten Chöling and what little there is in India—in Dehra Dun, with Khyentse Rinpoche, and some others—there are none at all.

This opinion goes some way perhaps in explaining why these texts, long held secret, were entrusted to my shaky (although suitably shaking) hands. Sang Sang Tulku advanced another explanation of secrecy and its revelation; one that neatly, and with defensible orthodoxy, sidesteps the problem:

> In the past tantra was kept a secret, not to be shown to anyone without initiation. But there are some things that are naturally secret. Even if you show them to someone else, they will not see; even if you explain them, they will not understand.[10]

If some "declassification" of secret material was implicit in my research, we should remark that this is not a new phenomenon. Originally, tantric dance was, and, as we shall see, in some places, still is only practiced behind closed doors. Even the seemingly innocuous and readily available Perfection of Wisdom Sūtras are said to have been guarded as secret when they were first introduced to the human world.

Be that as it may, I was careful to receive permission to translate the texts that follow from Trulshik Rinpoche, the guardian of the Mani Rimdu tradition. When the translations were nearing completion, I asked for specific permission to publish them. To him, the issue was long since settled. "Why else would you translate them?" was his somewhat puzzled reply.

Abbreviation Key

AM *Accompanying Methods*. (Thugs rje chen po bde gshegs kun 'dus kyi cho ga'i lhan thabs snying po'i mdzas rgyan zhes bya ba).

BO *Burnt Offering*. (Zab lam bde gshegs kun 'dus kyi sbyin sreg gi cho ga 'dod don myur 'grub ces bya ba.)

BP *Biographical Prayer*. (gTer chen chos kyi rgyal po'i rnam thar gsol 'debs zhal gsungs ma.)

D Das, *Tibetan-English Dictionary.*

DP *Daily Practice*. (Thugs rje chen po'i rgyun khyer zab lam snying po'i dril ba).

E Edgerton, *Buddhist Hybrid Sanskrit Dictionary.*

EL *Erasing the Lines*, from *Notes on the Practice* (NP).

GC Geshe Chodrak's Dictionary

GW *Guardians of the Word* (bKa' srung = Thugs rje chen po bde gshegs kun 'dus kyi cho ga dang 'brel bar srung ma spyi dang bye brag gi mchod gtor 'bul ba'i ngag 'don gyi rim pa).

Jä Jäschke, *A Tibetan—English Dictionary.*

ICSR *Inviting the Colored Sand to the River.*

LIS *The Light which Illumines Suchness*. (Thugs rje chen po bde gshegs kun 'dus kyi sgrub thabs rnam bshad de kho na nyid snang ba'i 'od ces bya ba).

LT Lama Tharchin.

MIO *Mountain Incense Offering*. (Ri bo bsang mchod).

MV *Mahāvyutpatti*

NL Ngawang Lemen, Trulshik Rinpoche's servant.

NP *Notes on Doing the Complete Ritual Practice of Great Compassion.* (Thugs rje chen po'i sgrub mchod dkyus ma tsam gyi phyag len zin bris). *bDe kun*, vol. *Wu.*

NY Ngawang Yonten, monk of Chiwong Monastery

NW Nebesky-Wojkowitz, *Oracles and Demons of Tibet.*

PL *Precious Lamp* (Rin chen sgron me).

PO *The Playful Ocean.* (bsTan skyong pa'i dam can po rnams kyi phrin las dngos grub kyi rol mtsho zhes bya ba).

QBB *Quickly Bestowing Blessings.* ('Dir snang zin med kyi bya ba dang sgrib lus skye bar zlos pa'i rabs mdor bsdus tshigs su bcad pa byin rlabs myur 'jug ces bya ba bzhugs so.)

RP *Religious Practice* ([sMin gling] Chos spyod kyi rim pa thar lam rab gsal zhes bya ba.).

RT Rinchen Tsering, assistant to Lama Tharchin in the early 1980s.

SST Sang Sang Tulku.

SO *Condensed Torma Ritual for the Sworn Ones in General.* (Dam can spyi'i gtor ma'i cho ga nyung ngur bsdus pa).

S/P *Site/Preparation Ritual.* (Thugs rje chen po bde gshegs kun 'dus kyi sa chog dang/sta gon gyi ngag 'don dkyus gcig tu bkod pa).

SWT *Sky Walker Torma Offering.* (mThun mtshams mkha' 'gro gtor 'bul).

TCU Thubten Chöling Umze, Ngawang Tsundru.

TE *Torma Empowerment.* (Thugs rje chen po bde gshegs kun 'dus kyi gtor dbang gi mtshams sbyor ngag 'don bdud rtsi'i nying khu zhes bya ba).

TPT *Three-Part Torma Ritual.* (Chos spyod kyi rim pa thar lam rab gsal zhes bya ba las/gTor ma cha gsum gyi rim pa.) In RP.

TR Trulshik Rinpoche.

UB *The Practice of Union of the Blissful Great Compassion Arranged in Ritual Form.* (Thugs rje chen po bde gshegs kun 'dus kyi sgrub thabs chog khrigs zab lam gsal ba'i nyin byed ces bya ba). Short Title: *Union of the Blissful Manual* (bDe gshegs kun 'dus las byang).

Part One

Orientations

1

Introduction

This book describes a complex Tibetan festival in light of its performance and texts. It also looks at the works of art used in the festival and at the festival itself as a work of art.

The Mani Rimdu festival is performed in the Sherpa and Tibetan monasteries of Solu-Khumbu District in the Everest region of Nepal. These institutions, like nearly all the monasteries in Nepal outside of the Kathmandu Valley, belong to the Nyingma order of Tibetan Buddhism.

Among all the ethnic groups of Nepal, the Sherpas are perhaps the best known, on account of their exploits as mountaineers. Nepal, however is not their original home. The first Sherpas came from Khams, the eastern province of Tibet, around 1533.[1] Western scholars agree that the Sherpa's religious beliefs are, in the words of Christoph von Fürer-Haimendorf, the pioneer of Sherpa ethnography, "basically those of Tibetan Buddhism."[2] In Mani Rimdu, it would be difficult to make any distinction of belief and practice according to ethnic lines. Indeed, the festival at Chiwong is performed by Sherpas and Tibetans working in partnership.

Despite the Sherpas' long tradition of Buddhist faith, large monasteries are a recent innovation in Solu-Khumbu. Whatever antiquity local tradition ascribes to them, the largest monasteries in the region—those which perform Mani Rimdu—were all built within the last seventy-five years.[3]

Although often casually identified as a "Sherpa festival," Mani Rimdu began at Rongphu Monastery in Tibet. This institution on the north face of Everest was an influential force in the efflorescence of Sherpa monastic culture earlier in this century.

Like much of Rongphu practice, most of the rituals that comprise Mani Rimdu find their source at Mindroling Monastery, the great Nyingma center of central Tibet. In a way, Rongphu served as a substation in the transmission of the Mindroling lineage, collecting and reassembling its traditions and then sending them over the Nangpala pass to the monasteries of Solu-Khumbu just a few days journey south.

In present day Solu-Khumbu, Mani Rimdu is performed at three Sherpa monasteries: Chiwong, Thami, and Tengpoche, and in a somewhat different form at Thubten Chöling, a monastery founded by refugees from Rongphu. Participants at each of the Sherpa monasteries often maintain that their version of festival is identical to the others', although if pressed, they will admit to certain differences. These variations often shed light on the processes by which Tibetan rituals are formed and we will examine them as they arise.

Mani Rimdu belongs to a genus of Tibetan rituals known as *ril sgrub* (pill practices) [pronounced ril-drup]. The name Mani Rimdu is the Sherpa pronunciation of the Tibetan term *maṇi ril sgrub* (the practice of *maṇi* pills). The species of *maṇi*-pill rituals, which are dedicated to the god Avalokiteśvara, is not unique to the Everest region. A short *maṇi*-pill text, simply called *"Mani Rimdu Ritual"* (*Maṇi ril sgrub gi cho ga*), was collected in China by W. W. Rockhill in the 1880s. A *maṇi ril sgrub* was performed at "Shih-fang-t'ang, to the west of Hsi-huang-ssu, outside the north wall of the city" of Beijing.[4] Today, the Dalai Lama himself performs a *maṇi ril sgrub*. Our Mani Rimdu, although a variety of the larger species, has its own texts and traditions.

To give an idea of the scope of the festival, a few statistics are in order. Mani Rimdu lasts up to eighteen days, although in some monasteries and some years it may be a few days shorter. In that time, several hundred hours are devoted to ritual practice. Eliminating the considerable repetition involved, over fifty hours of unique ritual are performed. The core of thirty-odd liturgical texts total over two hundred folios. There is, in addition, a considerable amount of material committed to memory: commonly used mantras, invocations and exhortations, daily prayers and so on. Four commentaries on the ritual of the main deity are known. The commentaries range in length from eleven to two hundred twenty-six folios.

In interpreting this Himalayan mass of data, I have always sought to first understand how the participants in the festival themselves perceive it. This has been amplified with reference to the indigenous commentaries and then with reference to other authorities and traditions, Tibetan and foreign.

As to be expected with such a long and complex event, Mani Rimdu covers much cultural ground. Many of the subjects we shall discuss are already known to Western scholarship in one form or another and to one extent or another. René de Nebesky-Wojkowitz, for example, has written at length on the cult of the protector deities and on Tibetan sacred dance; Stephan Beyer, on the structure of tantric ritual. For more than four decades, the late Rolf Alfred Stein argued persuasively on the influence of the "nameless religion" on Tibetan Buddhist praxis.

That contemporary Tibetan Buddhism and in particular the practices of the Nyingma sect were influenced by indigenous beliefs and practices which in turn bear striking similarities to shamanic cults across northern and central Asia, seems both obvious and is by now well documented, at least from a structural viewpoint if not an historical one. Both Nebesky-Wojkowitz and Stein devote a whole chapter to the subject, and Helmut Hoffmann, Mircea Eliade, and Robert B. Ekvall treat it at length. Recently, Geoffrey Samuel dedicated an entire book to this thesis.[5]

In Mani Rimdu, we will see several such parallels, but for all its traces of pre-Buddhist belief and practice, Mani Rimdu is preeminently a Buddhist celebration. In its visionary dramaturgy, we can see the core principles of the Buddhist religion worked out. As with all tantric practice, indeed all of Mahāyāna Buddhism, its inner goal is to incarnate wisdom and compassion on earth.

The main rituals of Mani Rimdu belong to the most profound system of Tibetan meditation, the *anuttarayoga* class of tantra. In terms of philosophical view, they are said to embody the view of *rdzogs chen*, the Great Perfection or Great Fulfillment system.

In this book, topics specific to the tantras arise on nearly every page. I have tried to deal with them in as straightforward a manner as possible, without attempting a general disquisition on the subject. Those interested in exploring Tibetan tantra can refer to a growing body of sound scholarship on this profound and fascinating subject.[6]

With the Great Fulfillment system, we face special difficulties. Given its secrecy among the Tibetans of the Nyingma sect who are its chief exponents, it may never be wholly open to public view. This book could not even begin to fill such a tremendous void. Happily, among my sources were Buddhist yogis fully versed in the Great Fulfillment system. Whenever the material veered in that direction or towards the equally difficult subject of the yoga of channels and winds, I endeavored to eke out enough information to make the translation clear even in the absence of a full exegesis.

If the individual parts of Mani Rimdu do not reveal any startlingly new realms of investigation, its very breadth gives us a certain advantage. In it, we can see principles that other scholars have remarked in a general context function in the particular.

This breadth also affords the opportunity to consider previously isolated cultural elements in juxtaposition, interacting in the living context of a contemporary cultural performance. We can, for example, compare the tongue of the magic dagger to the tongue of the gods; the central pole of the dance court to the central pole of the offering cake to the spine of a yogi; the weight of a cobblestone to the weight of Mount Meru.

The importance of these correspondences transcends the superficial fascination of coincidence or the delights of etiological speculation. By examining them, we are able to see recurrent elements in outwardly different events, and having understood their structure, predict unknown features of incompletely explained rituals. Even in a cultural system as self-conscious and as vocal as Tibetan Buddhism, structure speaks where the tradition itself remains silent.

As Mircea Eliade remarked:

> We compare or contrast two expressions of a symbol not in order to reduce them to a single, pre-existent expression, but in order to discover the process whereby a structure is likely to assume enriched meanings.[7]

Within the breadth of the Mani Rimdu festival, some structures occur again and again like *leitmotiven* in a Wagner opera. Thus, we will return several times to such themes as movement through a tube, the descent of light, the rainbow cord, the world tree, and the cosmic sheep.[8] Each new context will suggest new aspects of the symbol, enriching its connections and meaning.

The purpose of the work before you is primarily descriptive. If in addition to the analyses sketched above, there is a thesis here, it is a rather simple one. The job of a monk is largely ritual and meditation, and ritual and meditation have satisfactions of their own.

These emotional and if you will, aesthetic satisfactions cannot be overemphasized, nor does one have to be a Buddhist or meditator oneself to appreciate them. No one who has sat in the dark recesses of the chapel as Mani Rimdu is performed can be insensible to the mood the rituals create. No one who has sat with the monks during a break in the session and seen their faces, still enrobed in the quietude of meditation, could doubt that the effect of ritual on those who perform it is profound.

A part of the affective dimension of the ritual lies in the liturgy itself, and can be appreciated without the sonorous music and the rhythm of the chants. Buddhism has ever described itself as a method of overcoming suffering and finding a transcendent happiness and peace. Tantric rituals, these small worlds within which a meditator acts as if he has already reached his goal, bring their own share of joy, even if it is only a fleeting shadow of a greater joy to come.

To perform an elaborate ritual complex such as Mani Rimdu is to participate in the creation of an elaborate work of art, and the joy of a professional meditator practicing his art can be understood, at least in part, if we consider the satisfactions of more familiar arts. Like a symphony or opera, a major ritual has its movements and motives, its structures and parallels, its changes of theme and emotion.

As with the *leitmotiven* of Wagner or variations on a theme by Bach, the repetition with variation of a symbol structure itself has a function. Structural parallels that students of religion find of intellectual interest have aesthetic impact and emotional resonance for those who participate in the ritual.

The socioeconomic benefits of being a monk are obvious and have been noted often enough. Joy, hard to prove and impossible to quantify, sometimes eludes ethnographers. In a sense, however, to suggest, as has often been done, that the major advantage to being a monk is economic or social is as vulgar as it would be to suggest that Vladimir Horowitz was only in it for the money. The virtuoso meditator like the virtuoso musician is the one who participates the most fully in his art, the one for whom there is the least "difference between the dancer and the dance."

If the performance of a ritual is an art, it is also a craft. Tormas must be carefully sculpted of barley-flour dough and butter, a sand *maṇḍala* drawn neatly and with precision. The liturgy should be clear, well-ordered and crisply performed. Like other craftsmen, the ritualist is proud of his professional skills.

Once, after I had been a regular visitor to the monastery for several years, the manager of Thubten Chöling invited me to photograph the Lord of the Dance rituals performed at his monastery. When I objected that in the darkness of the chapel, I would have to use a lamp whose bright flash might disturb the monks at their prayers, he replied, "No, you come tonight. You bring your lamp and take pictures. We want people in foreign lands to know that the monks of Thubten Chöling do things right."

The true medium of the arts of meditation and ritual is the human heart. The final counsel of the rituals of Mani Rimdu is that we regard the Earth as paradise and all those that inhabit it as gods. As Trulshik Rinpoche once wrote in a poem addressed to a group of visitors from the Kharta region of Tibet:

> If your mind is pure, everyone's a Buddha.
> If your mind is impure, everyone's ordinary.
> We all wander *saṁsāra* by the power of impurity.
> Learn to purify your perceptions, People of Kharta![9]

This is not an insight unique to tantra or even to Buddhism. The Gospel of Luke states that:

> The kingdom of God cometh not with observation: neither shall they say, lo here! or lo there! for, behold, the kingdom of God is within you. (17:20–21)

A similar impulse was given tongue in a shamanic context by the Native American mystic Black Elk. Having traveled in a vision to the world-tree at the center of the universe, he remarked, "but anywhere is the center of the world."[10]

For Eliade, this is a fundamental principle of human religiosity:

> This means that everywhere in the cosmos archaic man recognizes a source of the magico-religious sacred, that any fragment of the cosmos can give rise to a hierophany, in accordance with the dialectic of the sacred.[11]

The archaic, of course, should not be confused with the ancient. It is alive and well. Hierophanies, at least small ones, are not that hard to find:

> . . . you look at the clock and it is only five minutes from eternity; you count the objects on the mantelpiece because the sound of the numbers is a totally new sound in your mouth, because everything new and old, or touched and forgotten, is a fire and a mesmerism. Now every door of the cage is open and whichever way you walk is a straight line toward infinity. [12]

As Joseph Campbell observed in the introduction to the *Historical Atlas of World Mythology*, "the first function of mythology is to waken and maintain in the individual a sense of wonder and participation in the mystery of this finally inscrutable universe."[13]

It is this sense of wonder, perhaps, that distinguishes the human race. In it, as odd a couple as an American novelist and a Tibetan mystic can meet. As the Great Perfection yogis say, *rig pa*, the awareness of a Buddha, is an everyday sort of mind. It can be found everywhere.

2

The Gods

Each of Mani Rimdu's many heterogeneous rituals invokes its own panoply of deities. These range from high tantric tutelaries (*yi dam*), the embodiments of great universals, on one end of the spectrum, to the deities of the mountains, rocks, and streams of Solu-Khumbu on the other. In the broad ground between these extremes, we find ancient gods of India and of Tibet pressed into service as defenders of the Buddhist faith. In addition, there is the typical assortment of other high-ranking spirits from Tathāgatas to Sky Walkers. Below them all swirl hosts of semidivine and demonic agencies of every sort and description.

In this section, we discuss the central deity of Mani Rimdu and the gods who form his immediate entourage. Their enormous numbers prohibit us from lavishing this attention on the festival's full pantheon, although a general discussion of the protectors and notes on specific lesser figures will be found later.

The main deity, Lord of the Dance, sits at the center of the *maṇḍala*. In his heart, dwells the fierce deity Hayagrīva. Within Hayagrīva's heart in turn, rests the abstracted entity known as the Contemplation Hero. Surrounding the main deity on the four petals of a lotus sit the Sky Walkers of the four families. Beyond them, in the doors of the *maṇḍala* palace, stand four animal-headed goddesses known as the Four Sorceresses.

LORD OF THE DANCE

The full name of Mani Rimdu's chief deity (*gtso bo*) is Union of the Blissful/Lord of the Dance/Great Compassion (bDe gshegs kun 'dus Gar dbang Thugs rje chen po). Both the written and oral traditions, however, usually refer to him by only part of this unwieldy name, either Union of the Blissful (bDe gshegs kun 'dus, abbreviated 'bDe kun'), or Lord of the Dance Great Compassion (Gar dbang Thugs rje chen po).[1]

Western scholars first noted the presence of Lord of the Dance in Solu-Khumbu in 1957. In a description of the murals at Chiwong in *Buddhist Himālaya*, David Snellgrove gave an excellent short description of the deity, his entourage, and a bit of his history.[2] In name, Union of the Blissful has something in common with the more widely known Union of the Secret Ones, (gSang ba 'dus ba, Ssk. Guhyasamāja). For Snellgrove, Union of the Blissful, like Guhyasamāja, is "one of those anonymous entities, who is chosen to represent the notion of essentially-impersonal reflectively-personalized buddhahood."[3] All the personal deities, *yidam*, need to have a certain degree of anonymity so that they can serve for a meditator as a vision of himself in the enlightened state. A mirror that already held a strong image would not be a mirror. The declared corporate nature of Guhyasamāja and Lord of the Dance polishes this depersonalized reflectivity to a high gloss.

Different deities are associated with different levels of tantric practice. Trulshik Rinpoche identifies Lord of the Dance as a Highest Yoga Tantra (*anuttarayogatantra*) form of Avalokiteśvara, the *bodhisattva* who embodies the compassion of all the Buddhas throughout space and time. Lord of the Dance practices are particular to Mindroling Monastery in Central Tibet and come from *gter ma*, hidden texts, discovered in the seventeenth century by its abbot.

Lord of the Dance is red in color and has four hands. The first two hands clasp a *vajra* before his chest in folded palms. He holds a rosary of miniature red lotuses between the thumb and forefinger of his second right hand as if he were counting them.[4] His second left hand holds a full-sized red *utpala* lotus.

The expression on his face is at once peaceful and wrathful (*zhi khro*). He smiles, but his eye-teeth show. His forehead furrows slightly. He wears a golden crown with five diadems. He has three eyes.

He is seated in the diamond, or as we call it, "lotus," posture. His consort Secret Wisdom Mother (gSang ba ye she yum) sits facing him on his lap.[5]

"The notion that Avalokiteśvara might be regarded as the primordial deity, the point of departure for a unique theogony" Matthew Kapstein observes, "was introduced into Tibet no later than the ninth century with the translation into Tibetan of the *Kāraṇḍavyūha-sūtra*."[6]

Avalokiteśvara has been considered the special patron deity of Tibet since at least the twelfth century.[7] His primacy as a deity for Tibetans, though, seems to begin in the eleventh century, with the pandit Atīśa and others. This denoted a crucial shift in the intellectual history of Tibet. In the words of Snellgrove and Richardson, it marked the change "from dependence on an accepted Buddhist symbolic arrangement to devotional allegiance to a divine being conceived as a god in the Hindu pattern . . . a change [that] begins to characterize all Tibetan Buddhist practice."[8]

By the time the *Maṇi bKa' 'bum*, the fount of later Avalokiteśvara lore, appears in the twelfth to thirteenth centuries, it had become firmly established, "that Avalokiteśvara was the patron deity of Tibet" and the King Srong btsan sgam po was "the very embodiment of Avalokiteśvara, [and] the founder of *Buddhadharma* in his formerly barbarian realm."[9]

By this time, the fame of Avalokiteśvara was spread throughout popular culture by strolling maṇipa, initiates who made a profession of reciting Avalokiteśvara's mantra, *oṁ maṇi padme hūṁ*, for the benefit of the populace.[10] Later, the cult of Avalokiteśvara becomes so widespread that his mantra can be heard on every lip and be seen in every hand, spinning inside well-worn *maṇi*-wheels. On the *maṇi*-walls that dot the landscape, Tibetan Buddhists engrave his mantra into the very bedrock of the Himālayas.

The physical description of Lord of the Dance has many similarities to the white four-armed deity that is the most common form of Avalokiteśvara in Tibet. Indeed, our tradition states that the name *Lord of the Dance* Great Compassion itself differentiates him from the ordinary four-armed Avalokiteśvara who it calls *"Prince* Great Compassion" (Jo bo Thugs rje chen po). The great twelfth-century compendium of Buddhist iconography, the *Sādhanamālā*, calls the white four-armed Avalokiteśvara Ṣaḍakṣari-Lokeśvara, "Lord of the Six Syllables." Ṣaḍakṣari-Lokeśvara is the form associated by the *sādhana* with the *Kāraṇḍavyūhasūtra* and, as his name suggests, with the six-syllable mantra, *oṁ maṇi padme hūṁ*.[11] He is the canonical deity most closely related to Lord of the Dance. Ṣaḍakṣari is said in Tibet to be the specific form of Avalokiteśvara that incarnates as the Dalai Lama.[12]

Although generally similar, the two gods differ in details of consort, color, facial expression, and dress and ornamentation. The contents of the hands also show minor differences. White Avalokiteśvara's first pair of hands display the same *mudrā* as that of Lord of the Dance, but are either empty or hold a wish-granting jewel. His second pair of hands holds a white lotus rather than a red one, and an ordinary rosary, rather than a rosary (that is to say, garland) of flowers.

"There were, however," states Matthew Kapstein, "other important developments of Avalokiteśvara in Tibet. The Rgyal ba rgya mtsho (Jinasāgara) form of the deity, the *yi dam* of the Karmapas which had been introduced by Ras chung in the twelfth century, offers the closest iconographic precedent among them to the Smin gling Lord of the Dance, and was familiar to, and propagated by Gter bdag gling pa himself."[13]

The name Lord of the Dance conjures a number of images. Ironically, most of them are misleading to one extent or another. For example, although the god is associated with the "dance festival" of Mani Rimdu, there is no intrinsic connection between Lord of the Dance and dance festivals.[14]

Lord of the Dance also occurs as an epithet in the names of yogis. The great lexicographer Sarat Chandra Das defines *gar gyi dbang po* as "a yogi or ascetic engaged in meditation."[15] One of our own texts, in fact, calls 'Gyur med rdo rje, the founder of the Lord of the Dance tradition, Padma gar dbang "Lotus Lord of the Dance."[16]

Some Nyingma texts call Padmasambhava, the progenitor of their school, "Padma gar dbang thod 'phreng rtsal."[17] Indeed, Padmasambhava's biography lists Lotus Lord of the Dance (Pad ma Gar gyi dbang phyug) among the forms of Padmasambhava that illumine the myriad worlds beyond the borders of the Saha universe.[18]

According to Lama Tharchin, *gar dbang* means *sprul sku*—"tulku"—emanation or incarnation; or *sku tshab*, "physical representative." He glosses the term as *sprul pa'i rol gar kyi dbang phyug*, master of the dance of incarnation.

For Trulshik Rinpoche, the epithet indicates Lord of the Dance's connection with *anuttarayogatantra* and is unrelated to its use in the names of yogis. In another interview however, he explains "Lord of the Dance" much as Lama Tharchin defined it, that is, as indicating Avalokiteśvara's power to incarnate in each of the six realms of living beings. This theme is often illustrated in the Buddhist cosmographical paintings known as "wheels of existence" (*srid pa'i 'khor lo, bhavacakra*), where a standing figure of Avalokiteśvara is placed in each realm. In this regard, we might say that the term "Lord of the Dance" refers to the creativity or adaptability of Avalokiteśvara's compassion—the power which allows him to incarnate in whatever form will best allow him to help a given class of living beings.

For many of us, the epithet Lord of the Dance immediately calls another deity to mind—the Hindu god µiva or Mahādeva (Tib. Lha chen). Interestingly enough, the Mindroling texts themselves link the two gods.

According to the *Playful Ocean*, Mahādeva arises "From the play of Lotus Lord of the Dance Compassion,/In the body of a worldly protector in order to tame the hard to tame," and "following the orders of great glorious Lord of the Dance," he guards the places where Lord of the Dance's *maṇḍala* resides.[19] Elsewhere, the text places Lord of the Dance at the head of the lineage of lamas that have enjoined vows upon Mahādeva.[20]

Speaking of Lord of the Dance, David Snellgrove, the first scholar to study Buddhism in Solu-Khumbu stated rather boldly that,

> Although originally a form of µiva, this divinity was accepted into Buddhism as one of the many forms of Lokeśvara. He therefore becomes a special manifestation of Avalokiteśvara.

In the last hundred years there has been discussion among scholars of whether or not µiva and Avalokiteśvara have a common source, as even the names Iśvara (The Lord) and Avalokita-Iśvara (The Lord who Looks Down) would suggest. Reviewing the evidence in her *Introduction à l'Étude d'Avalokiteçvara*, Marie Thérèse de Mallmann concludes: "If there exist undeniable analogies between Avalokiteśvara and µiva, they do not go back to the ancient period, textually and iconographically, they do not seem to appear before the tenth century or later."[21] Giuseppe Tucci, in his critique of de Mallmann, however, notes that the famous seventh-century Buddhist traveler Hsuan Tsang observed that to the people who dwell at the foot of Mount Potala, Avalokiteśvara's paradise, the god sometimes appears "in the aspect of Pāśupata Tīrthika or of Maheśvara."[22]

Of course, no matter when the connection between the two deities originated, it is still significant. As Snellgrove observed, "the popularity of Avalokiteśvara in Tibet is presumably to be explained by the popularity of this divinity (known as Lokeśvara and popularly confused with µiva) in the Himalayan region in general."[23] In any event, our texts, which first saw the light of day in the late seventeenth century, are hardly likely to put an end to the debate.

The Kathmandu Valley of Nepal is, of course, the home of the Newars, whose living tantric Buddhist tradition is closest to that of Tibet. The Newars also worship a form of Avalokiteśvara called "Lord of the Dance." This god, known to the Newars as Narteśvara, Padmanarteśvara, or Natsyadeo is important to their cult practice and occurs in several forms.

In the Newar *dikṣa*, or initiation ceremony, Padmanarteśvara must be worshipped and serenaded. The form of Padmanarteśvara here is eight-handed, holding a *vajra* to the crown of his head and in one of his left hands, a bell. In the initiation, the *vajrācārya* (Diamond Master) who presides at the ceremony is said to instruct the disciple in how to use these instruments in the manner of Padmanarteśvara. Each of the god's other six hands holds a lotus, corresponding to a syllable of his mantra, *oṁ ma ṇi pad me hūṁ*. He tosses these lotuses into each of the six realms of rebirth, symbolizing that the initiation closes the doors of the six rebirths to the initiate.[24]

Of course, all forms of Avalokiteśvara are associated one way or another with the six realms.[25] In light of Trulshik Rinpoche's comment, however, it is interesting that Newars associate this specific form of Avalokiteśvara with the six realms and in such an important context.

In newer times, Newars also depicted Padmanarteśvara in the temples of the Kathmandu Valley. One form figures in the Minath Temple in Patan, which is situated across the street from the important Patan Macchendranath Temple and is associated with it. Padmanarteśvara is portrayed no less than three times here: on the *toraṇa* of the temple, in a small bas-relief on the support of the large temple bell, and on the *toraṇa* of another building in the temple complex.[26] According to contemporary Newar scholar Dr. Ashakaji Bajracarya, Padmanarteśvara's presence on the *toraṇa* indicates "that they do tantric work there" in general, adding that Padmanarteśvara showed himself in the form of

Jatadhari Lokeśvara, a.k.a. Minath.[27] The form of Padmanarteśvara shown at the Minath Temple is the closest in appearance to the form we associate with Hindu depictions of µiva as Nāṭarājā, "Lord of the Dance" or "King of the Dance." This form, balanced on one foot, haloed by a circle of swaying arms, seems to epitomize all the grace of dance. Indeed, it is only when we count his eighteen hands and notice that each holds a lotus, that we know that we are not looking at a statue of µiva Nāṭarājā himself.[28]

If, curiously, there is no indication from Tibetan sources connecting Padmanarteśvara with dance (other than his presence along with *'chams* in a festival less than a century old), the same is not true among the Newars. For them Padmanarteśvara is the embodiment of dance, and, as Natsyadeo, is evoked by dancers and/or non-dancing priests whenever they perform the dance of the Aṣṭamātṛkā, the powerful autochthonous goddesses of the Kathmandu Valley. The very first act of the Asṭamātṛkā dance is the song of Padmanarteśvara and the display of his picture.[29]

On the occasion of the dance, a buffalo is sacrificed to the shrine of Natsyadeo, a small triangular niche in the temple wall. Dr. Bajracarya notes that, in theory, Narteśvara should not have blood sacrifices, only offerings of the five ambrosias. He adds, however, that it is evident that the beneficiary of the sacrifice is Narteśvara since the mantra used by the *Gubaju* officiating at the sacrifice is "oṁ nama narteśvarāya."[30]

According to British Anthropologist and authority on Newar Buddhism David Gellner, each of the old neighborhoods or *tole* of Kathmandu has its own shrine to Natsyadeo. The singers of religious songs (*bhajan*) sacrifice there, and often the shrine itself is decorated with buffalo horns. Buddhists identify the god of these shrines as Narteśvara; Hindus as Mahādeva Nāṭarājā.[31]

Kalamandapa, a contemporary Newar dance group in Kathmandu, incorporates a short *sādhana* of Padmanarteśvara in its adaptations of traditional *cārya* dance.[32]

> Hail to Padmanarteśvara
>
> —Hail to him who gives the Secret Mantra by means of the power of bliss.
> —He is the very form of all understanding and all knowledge.
> —He is the Lord who practices the eightfold meditation.
> —All hail to him the giver of all yogic success.
>
> Refrain:
> —He creates the whole universe for himself with his yogic mind.
> —He instructs this universe with his enlightened mind.
> —He has freed himself from the snare of illusion and gives happiness to all.
> —To such a true teacher I continually bow my head in respect.

Above, we saw that although Narteśvara is a peaceful deity, as Natsyadeo the Newars worship him with blood like a Bhairab, a wrathful one. In the Tibetan tradition, Lord of the Dance is classed as a *zhi khro* deity. When applied to a single deity, this term indicates a god who is both peaceful and wrathful at the same time. Iconographically, this is indicated by the god's face: he smiles, but with bared fangs.

The term *zhi khro* also applies to a class of deities and rituals. The *zhi khro* tradition invokes two separate groups of deities, one peaceful and one wrathful. The cult of the peaceful and wrathful deities is widespread in Solu-Khumbu and is the most popular ritual cycle at Sherpa monasteries. One work of the *zhi khro* cycle has become quite well-known in the West as *The Tibetan Book of the Dead.*

In *zhi khro* ritual, the peaceful deities emanate from main deity Samanthabhadra's head and the wrathful deities from his heart. Lord of the Dance emanates from his throat.[33] This equivocal position, being neither wholly with the peaceful nor with the wrathful deities, but somehow with both or between both is a recurrent image.

Snellgrove noted in *Buddhist Himālaya* that Lord of the Dance was ". . . the special *yi dam* of the Rongphu lamas and therefore both of Rongphu and Jiwong (Chiwong) Monasteries."[34] At present however, aside from his annual presence at Mani Rimdu (and his cameo appearance in the *zhi khro* cycle), the god is not worshipped on a regular basis at Chiwong or any other Sherpa Monastery.[35]

Quoting "his informants," von Fürer-Haimendorf correctly identified Lord of the Dance, who he styled "Ku-wang Thu-je-chembu," both as a form of Avalokiteśvara and as "'the god of Mani-rimdu.'"[36] Unfortunately, later writers on the festival ignored this facet of von Fürer-Haimendorf's auspicious beginning to the anthropology of the Sherpa.

Half a century earlier, Austine L. Waddell claimed that the cult of Union of the Blissful Lord of the Dance, Great Compassion was important at Pemayangtse (Tib. Padma yangs rtse; Sik. Pemiongchi) Monastery in Sikkim.[37] He also mentioned, without giving its title, that novices there were given examinations on a forty-page book of the "magic circles" of that god.[38] Pemayangtse was, up until recently at least, Sikkim's most important Monastery.[39] Since it was modeled on Mindroling, we should not wonder at the importance of Lord of the Dance there.[40] In 1895, Waddell noted that "until a few years ago [Pemayangtse] was in the habit, of sending to Min-dol-lin its young monks for instruction in the higher discipline and ritual."[41] The present state of the Lord of the Dance cult in Sikkim is yet to be explored.

Since he is a Mindroling deity, one would expect to find Lord of the Dance at the refugee resettlement of that monastery in India at Dehra Dun. Trulshik Rinpoche actually asked after his favorite deity when he visited Mindroling Trichen, the hierarch of Mindroling, a number of years ago. Mindroling Trichen replied that he no longer has any disciples studying Lord of the Dance, nor is the ritual practiced at his monastery. According to Trulshik Rinpoche, although before his death in 1991, Dilgo Khyentse Rinpoche would give the Lord of the Dance initiation, he did not teach the practice. Mindroling itself suffered severe damage at the hands of the Chinese, who among other things burned all of the monastery's books and printing blocks. Although by 1993, some religious practices had begun to reestablish themselves there, it is unknown whether Lord of the Dance is among them. Thus, unless a tradition flourishes in Sikkim or elsewhere, Trulshik Rinpoche at present may be its sole exponent.

Whatever its vicissitudes in other places and other times, the cult of Lord of the Dance is definitely on the upswing in the Solu-Khumbu district of Nepal. Since its destruction by the Chinese in 1959, Rongphu has been reborn in Solu-Khumbu as Thubten Chöling. As he was at Rongphu, Lord of the Dance is the main *yi dam* at the new monastery.[42] Backed by the prestige of its abbot, Trulshik Rinpoche, in the past several years Lord of the Dance has been not only the most frequently practiced deity at Thubten Chöling, but also the one most frequently requested at the annual mass initiations held there. Of the approximately one hundred candidates each year, some 80–90 percent have sought initiation in the *maṇḍala* of Lord of the Dance.[43] As Trulshik Rinpoche's influence increases in the Nyingma order, Lord of the Dance is sure to spread beyond the confines of the Everest Region.

The main text of Mani Rimdu is the Union of the Blissful *Manual.* When he composed it in 1897, Ngawang Tenzin Norbu (Ngag dbang bstan 'dzin nor bu) wrote that his new edition followed "along the lines of the way it is done at Orgyan Mindroling," but was "revised in order to conform to what appears in the great *Precious Treasure Trove* (*Rin chen gter mdzod*)."[44]

There are four commentaries to the Lord of the Dance practice: 'Gyur med rdo rje's own *Accompanying Methods;* and no less than three by his younger brother the Translator Dharmaśrī: *Notes on the Practice of the Entire Accomplishment Worship of Great Compassion*, *The Precious Lamp*, and the massive *Light which Illumines Suchness.* There is no commentary on Mani Rimdu per se, but the one considered most relevant to the festival is the *Precious Lamp.*

The Lord of the Dance cycle possesses a sizable literature aside from the texts used in Mani Rimdu. One Mindroling collection is some four inches thick.

THE HORSE-HEADED ONE

In the tantras it is not uncommon to find that one deity lives inside the heart of another. Often two such deities are specified, a Wisdom Mind Hero (*ye shes sems dpa'*), and within *his* heart, a Contemplation Hero (*ting nge 'dzin sems dpa'*). Sometimes these "heroes" have a non-anthropomorphic physical form. The Vajrasattva meditation found in the preliminary practices of the Lord of the Dance *Manual*, for example, specifies that atop the moon in the deity's heart, there is "a vajra marked with a *hūṁ*."[45]

In the Lord of the Dance ritual, the Wisdom Mind Hero is rTa mgrin [pronounced Tamdrin; Ssk. Hayagrīva], a fierce deity associated with the Lotus Family in general and with Padmasambhava and Avalokiteśvara in particular.

The name Hayagrīva originated in the Indian purāṇas, and is sometimes translated as "Horse-Necked One." According to R. H. van Gulik's excellent monograph, however, the deity's name would be more accurately rendered as the Horse-Headed One.[46] Although the name Hayagrīva was often originally an epithet of Viṣṇu, "about A.D. 500, the Northern Buddhists in India venerated Hayagrīva as Vidyārāja, and as an aspect of Avalokiteśvara." Hayagrīva became prominent throughout East and central Asia as a god of horses per se. The horse god is, of course, as Mircea Eliade points out, a typical shamanic deity.

> The courser is pre-eminently the shamanic animal; the gallop and dizzying speed are traditional expressions of "flight", that is of ecstasy.[47]

In the *Manual*, Hayagrīva is also known as Excellent Horse Heruka (rTa mchog Heruka) or Glorious Steed (rTa mchog dpal), and as King of Wrath (Khro ba'i rgyal). He is referred to as a primordial god (*gnyug ma'i lha*), one who has always been a god, as opposed to a recent apotheosis.

The *Manual* praises him saying—

> Although you waver not from reality's peace,
> The savage fury of your terrifying form blazes like fire!
> Wrathful King! Blood drinker! Glorious Steed!
> Your raging laughter! I praise you! [17b5]

In addition to being known for his fearsome neighing laugh, Hayagrīva is also known for his Horse's Dance, in which the god is called upon to fulfill his vow to "dissolve the three worlds in the objectless realm."[48] Although called a "dance," it is part of the liturgy the monastic assembly recites in its seats each day of Mani Rimdu. In the Site Rituals and during the masked dance, however, the Horse's Dance becomes a dance in fact as well as in name.[49]

Although meditators visualize Hayagrīva living within Lord of the Dance's heart, painters show Hayagrīva standing immediately below him. The *Manual* describes him as holding "a lotus garland and a lotus," like Lord of the Dance himself. Unlike Lord of the Dance, however, Hayagrīva's "form rages fury."[50] In paintings, we can see iconographic details not found in the *Manual*. Some of these are common to one or more of the many other forms of the god, some are unique to the Lord of the Dance *sādhana*.

As elsewhere, Hayagrīva here has a small, green, neighing horse's head protruding from the top of his head. He is red in color as befits a god of the lotus family. He has one face. His three round, bulging eyes and flame-like bushy eyebrows are typical of fierce deities. His fanged mouth gapes and his nose wrinkles with anger. As the text states, he has two hands which hold a lotus and a rosary of lotuses. He has a crown of skulls and a garland of freshly severed heads. He is cloaked with a human pelt, an elephant skin, and a silken ribbon. He wears a tiger-skin skirt.

Hayagrīva's consort, naked but for a leopard-skin skirt, is light red in color. She has one face and two hands. Her right hand holds a chopper and circles her consort's neck. Her left holds a skull in the typical pose, near to his face as if offering it to him. Her right leg is stretched out parallel to his and her left leg wraps around his waist.

In addition to his evocation as a member of the *maṇḍala*, we also find Hayagrīva in other parts of the Lord of the Dance ritual. Some of these contexts are generalized, are rôles he performs in many *sādhanas*. The first such rôle is as the Expeller of Demons.

> May I instantaneously blaze as Excellent Horse *Heruka*
> Radiant with almost unbearable fury, like the fire at the end of the world! [6b4]

In this guise, the meditator bribes, cajoles, and threatens the obstructive spirits gathered in the place of meditation to "in haste itself, go away." If the troublesome demonic forces do not obey, the meditator declares—

> I will project a host of wrath
> And diamond weapons from my mind! [7.4]
>
> Your bodies and voices like unto fine powder
> Will be shattered! That is sure. [7.5]

Hayagrīva is also invoked in the next section of the ritual, "Defining the Borders."[51] Here he is the King of Wrath who builds the diamond pavilion that will keep out the obstructive forces he has just expelled.

THE CONTEMPLATION HERO

Just as Hayagrīva dwells with the heart of Lord of the Dance, the Contemplation Hero (*ting 'dzin sems dpa'*) dwells within Hayagrīva's heart. In the words of the *sādhana*—

In his heart, meditate the Contemplation [Hero],
A clear red letter *hrīḥ*, blazing light.[52]

Although in general, meditational deities have a "seed" syllable (*sa bon*) in their hearts, and here that syllable is the same as the Contemplation Hero, the two terms are not necessarily synonymous. Other *sādhanas*, for example, identify the Contemplation Hero as an object marked with a syllable rather than a syllable itself.[53]

AMITĀBHA

The Tathāgata at the head of the Lotus Family is Amitābha, the Buddha of Boundless Light. Painting and meditation make this metaphor concrete. *Thangka* painters place a small image of Amitābha atop Lord of the Dance's head and meditators visualize him floating there.

On my crown, the head of the family, Boundless Light,
Dressed as an incarnation, holds the life vase. [10b1]

According to later Buddhist theory, every Buddha has three bodies: a Body of Truth (*dharmakāya*), a Body of Enjoyment (*saṁbhogakāya*), and an Emanation Body (*nirmāṇakāya*). The text indicates that Amitābha here is in his *nirmāṇakāya* form. This is implied by the monk's robes in which he is dressed in paintings of Lord of the Dance. His name in Tibetan may also hint at this. According to some, the name Boundless Light (Tib. 'Od dpag med) specifically indicates the *nirmāṇakāya* form of the deity while Infinite Illumination (sNang ba mtha' yas) refers to his *dharmakāya* form.

SECRET WISDOM MOTHER

Lord of the Dance's consort, Secret Wisdom Mother (gSang ba ye shes yum), is portrayed in two forms. Normally, she is shown as we have already seen her, seated on Lord of the Dance's lap in sexual union with him. Her head is thrown back in the ecstatic pose typical of consorts and some solitary Sky Walkers (*mka' 'gro ma; ḍākiṇī*). She has four arms. The first pair, flung around the god's neck, holds a chopper and a skull bowl. The second right hand brandishes a sword high in the air. The second left holds a *vajra*-tipped *khaṭvāṅga* staff at waist level.

More elaborate paintings also show Secret Wisdom Mother standing alone in the lower right quadrant of the canvas. In this form, she is somewhat fiercer than when she is in union with Lord of the Dance. She dances on a small humanoid figure, bearing her weight on her left leg, which is slightly bent. Her right leg is drawn up, with the heel almost touching her "secret place."

When she is in union with Lord of the Dance, Secret Wisdom Mother wears a crown of lotuses and a long garland of lotuses about her neck. When she is alone, the crown is of ornamented skulls and the necklace of freshly severed human heads. She holds the chopper and skull just below chest level.

Snellgrove identifies this goddess simply as the red *ḍākiṇī* or as "Pāṇḍaravāsinī, the goddess who is regularly assigned to the lotus family."[54] Pāṇḍuravāsinī or Pāṇḍaravāsinī appears in the *Mañjuśrīmūlakalpa*, an early tantric work, as one of the half-dozen goddesses who surround Avalokiteśvara.[55] Later, these goddesses are distributed as consorts to the five families of Tathāgatas. The standard Sanskrit iconography, the *Sādhanamālā*, specifically gives this name to the consort of the Two-Armed Padmanarteśvara.[56] By the time of Tsongkhapa, Avalokiteśvara is considered the "lord . . . of the lotus lineage" and Pāṇḍaravāsinī, its "mother."[57]

Our texts however, do not use the name Pāṇḍaravāsinī. Instead, they invariably call Lord of the Dance's consort Secret Wisdom Mother. Judging from the mantra they give her, *oṁ dhumaghaye namaḥ svāhā*, her name would be "Dhumaghaya," although that name points to a source other than Sanskrit.

Secret Mother's treatment is precisely similar to that of Nairātmyā in the Hevajra cycle, Vajrayoginī in the Cakrasaṁvara, Viśvamātā in the Kālacakra, and, most significantly, Sarvabuddhaḍākiṇī in the Jinasāgara-Avalokiteśvara. Most important *gter-ma* cycles have both a *yab-ka* and *yum-ka*, focusing upon the two consorts respectively.[58]

One thing, however, sets Secret Wisdom distinctly apart—we find a ḍākiṇī of the same name in another Nyingma text, the biography of Padmasambhava.[59] The biography calls her the "highest of *ḍākiṇīs*" and gives her other names as Ḍākiṇī "Sun-Moon Achievement," Sūryacandrasiddhi (mKha 'gro nyi zla dngos grub) and "Queen of Karma" (Las kyi dbang mo che). It is she who Padmasambhava meets in the great cemetery of Secret Play (gSang chen rol pa) where he received the secret name of Skillful Skull Rosary (Thod phreng rtsal).

Padmasambhava prostrates to the *ḍākiṇī*, praises her as his guru, and asks her for outer, inner, and secret empowerments.[60] Transforming Padmasambhava (who has taken his form of Dorje Drolö) into the syllable *hūṁ*, she swallows him. Then,

> Outwardly his body became like that of the Buddha Amitābha,
> and he obtained the [em]power[ment]s of the Knowledge Bearer of
>   Life (*tshe yi rigs 'dzin 'grub pa'i dbang rnams*).
> From the blessing of being within her body,
> Inwardly his body became that of Avalokiteśvara

and he obtained the [em]power[ment]s of the meditation of the Great Seal.
He was then, with blessings, ejected through her secret lotus,
and his body, speech, and mind were thus purified from mental defilements.
Secretly his body became that of Hayagrīva, Being of Power,
and he obtained the power of binding the haughty gods and demons to vows (*dregs pa'i lha 'dre dam la 'dog dbang thob*).[61]

This empowerment within the body of the *ḍākiṇī* is a feature of the highest yoga tantra, and occurs in the Lord of the Dance ritual as well, as does the theme of a goddess devouring and subsequently giving birth to a practitioner.[62] This episode in the biography raises Lord of the Dance's consort from the ranks of the quotidian *ḍākiṇīs* (if that adjective could ever be truly applied to any of these celestial figures). It is Secret Wisdom Mother that gives Padmasambhava his spiritual rebirth as the theophany of the Lotus family deities who are not only crucial to the Lord of the Dance tradition, but central to Padmasambhava's role in the spiritual history of Tibet. Thus, our obscure ritual resonates with the deepest chords of Nyingma mythology.

THE ENTOURAGE

The Four Sky Walkers

Arrayed around Avalokiteśvara in the *maṇḍala* on the four petals of a lotus are the *ḍākas* belonging to the four families of Buddhas. Each embraces his respective *ḍākiṇī*. The names *ḍāka* and *ḍākiṇī* mean "Sky Walker." They are celestial beings who traverse the sky of wisdom with the grace of a bird in flight. So common are the Sky Walkers as representatives of the Buddha families that the text takes scant notice that there are four instead of the normal five. The "Praise" section, for instance, lauds them as follows:

You who make the five wisdoms real, and make use of the five poisons—
Who purify the aggregates and appear in the five families—
Bodies that unite bliss and emptiness indivisibly!
I praise the host of Sky Walkers of the five families! [18.2]

The text seems to imply that Lord of the Dance himself should be taken as the fifth Sky Walker. In that case he would take the place of the *ḍāka* of the fifth family, the Tathāgata family, which is normally headed by Vairocana. Since Lord of the Dance is of the lotus family, in his *maṇḍala* that family is represented twice while the Tathāgata family is ignored. Variant patterns such as this are common in Tibetan iconography, particularly in systems that were formulated before the present-day comprehensive schema coalesced.[63]

The passage quoted above expresses the symbolism of the *ḍāka/ḍākiṇīs* and of the five families in general. They are the agencies which transform the flawed world of *saṁsāra*, with its gross aggregates and virulent poisons, into the perfect world of *nirvāṇa*. Seen another way, they reveal the intrinsic perfection of this imperfect world.

As the *Manual* states:

> I have long since spontaneously achieved
> The five Buddhas' Body, Speech and Mind;
> The five poisons purified and the five wisdoms
> Indivisible from them . . . . [UB 11b3]

Trulshik Rinpoche explains that the five poisons are purified in becoming one with the five wisdoms. His list, below, differs somewhat from Snellgrove's systematization in *Buddhist Himālaya*.[64]

THE PASSIONS PURIFIED

Passion Purified	*Wisdom*	*Tathāgata*	*Constituent*
stupidity purified *gti mug rnam par dag pa*	truth realm wisdom *chos dbyings ye shes* =	Imperturbable *Mi 'gyur mi bskyod*	Body *sku*
anger purified *zhe dvang rnam par dag pa*	mirror wisdom *me long ye shes* =	Illuminator *rNam par snang mdzad*	Speech *gsung*
egotism purified *nga rgyal rnam par dag pa*	equanimitous wisdom *mnyam nyid ye shes* =	Jewel Born *Rin 'byung*	Mind *thugs*
desire purified *'dod chags rnam par dag pa*	discriminating wisdom *sor rtog ye shes* =	Endless Illumination *sNang ba mtha' yas*	Intelligence *yon tan*
envy purified *phrag dog rnam par dag pa*	active wisdom *bya grub ye shes* =	Success *Don yod grub pa*	[Activity *'phrin las*]

The Four Sorceresses

One of the more interesting, complex and enigmatic classes of deities in the Lord of the Dance cycle is the group of goddesses known as the *phra men ma* [pronounced "tra-men-ma"]. The *phra men ma*, whose name I have translated as Sorceresses, stand as guards in the doorways of Lord of the Dance's *maṇḍala*.[65] Each belongs to one of the Buddha families: Diamond Sorceress, Jewel Sorceress, Lotus Sorceress, and Action Sorceress.

The four Sorceresses have other things in common as well. Each has the body of a beautiful young woman and the face of an animal: a raven, a pig, a dog, or an owl. "Each of them," the text tells us, "holds a *khaṭvāṅga* in her left hand. Each is naked and dances ecstatically."[66] They dwell, the ritual avers, in "the fortress of the strict word and vow!"[67]

In a passage particularly dense with meaning, the *Manual* equates the Sorceresses with several realms of Buddhist tantric thought.

> I praise you, great glorious attendants,
> Sorceresses who actually are the four immeasurables!
> Magicians! Masters of the four actions—
> Who perfect the acts which summon, tie, bind and intoxicate! [18.3]

Commenting on this, *The Light which Illumines Suchness* states that the Sorceresses are "the substance of the four immeasurables" (*tshad med bzhi'i dngos gzhi*).[68] It further correlates the four immeasurables (compassion, love, joy, and equanimity), the four acts, and the four Sorceresses' hand implements.

As if this were not a tight enough knot of symbolism, the empowerment section of the *Manual* associates the Sorceresses with the four types of action: pacifying, extending, magnetizing, and destroying. Similarly, the long commentary (LIS 127.1) explains that they are called "Magicians" or "Miraculous Ones" (*rdzu 'phrul*) because "the play of their unstoppable magical illusions, which are of the nature of the four acts of pacification, etc., tames [beings]."

To unravel every strand of this skein of symbolism and to trace it to its historical source, even were it possible, would be beyond our purpose. It is interesting, however, to look at a few points on some of the threads, as clues to the nature of these fascinating and complex figures.

The goddesses' seed syllables—*jaḥ hūṁ baṁ hoḥ*; their implements—the hook, lasso, chain, and bell; and their actions of summoning, tying, binding, and maddening are all of a piece. This symbolic complex is recalled whenever a spiritual entity is summoned into a real or imagined object. Thus, throughout the ritual they are used when the malevolent Spying Ghosts are drawn into an effigy, and equally when the Wisdom Beings are invited to inhabit the meditator during creation stage yoga. In either case, a yogi recites the syllables, making the *mudrā* symbolic of each implement in turn, and imagines that he has performed the requisite action with regard to the entity invoked.

In the Lord of the Dance *Manual*, these mantras and *mudrās* are applied to the tutelary deity and his entourage in the "entreaty to stay" that follows the "invitation of the wisdom circle."[69]

Hūṁ. I beg you to stay, indivisible,
Like water poured into water,
In this great self-emergent *maṇḍala*,
In these gods emanated by inconceivable concentration!

jaḥ hūṁ baṁ hoḥ samayatiṣṭha together!

The ninth-century lexicon, the *Mahāvyutpatti*, lists only one of our goddesses, Vajrāṇkuśī (rDo rje lcags kyu ma), Diamond Hook Woman.[70] The symbology of the summoning hook and so on, however, predates the formulation of the tantra transmitted to Tibet, as we can see by its presence in the proto-tantric Shingon system of Japan.

THE FOUR SHINGON EMBLEMS[a] 四明

action	*tool*
summoning	hook
leading	cord
firmly holding	lock
resultant joy	bell

[a]Soothill 176.

In dealing with Sorceresses themselves, let us first summarize the attributes that the Lord of the Dance *Manual* gives to them.

THE FOUR SORCERESSES

maṇḍala	*quarter*	*family*	*color*	*face*	*action*	*tool*		*seed*	*immeasurable*
pacifying	east	Diamond	white	raven	summon	hook	*ankuśa*	*jaḥ*	compassion
extending	south	Jewel	yellow	pig	tie	lasso	*pāśa*	*hūṁ*	love
magnetizing	west	Lotus	red	dog	bind	chain	*sphoṭa*	*baṁ*	joy
destroying	north	Action	green	owl	madden	bell	*ghaṇṭa*	*hoḥ*	equanimity

The origin of the *phra men ma* seems to be at least as complicated as their function. It is likely that they coalesce many different traditions of mythology and of symbology. Some of these traditions are that of animal-headed goddesses in general, that of directional goddesses, and that of door-goddesses.

Figures with the heads of animals and human bodies are one of the oldest features of world religion.[71] In India, numbers of animal-headed goddesses were worshipped in circular temples, often surrounding a central image of µiva.[72] In central Asia, we sometimes see a bird-headed goddess associated with spiritual rebirth of a shaman. According to the Yakut,

> . . . each shaman has a Bird of Prey Mother, which is like a great bird with an iron beak, hooked claws, and a long tail. . . . At the shaman's spiritual birth . . . the bird . . . cuts the candidate's body to bits, and distributes them among the evil spirits of disease and death. Each spirit devours the part of the body that is his share; this gives the future shaman power to cure the corresponding diseases. After devouring the whole body the evil spirits depart.[73]

There is of course, an entire school of Tibetan Buddhist meditation, called *"gcod"* or "cutting off," which models itself on the self-sacrifice of the shaman. In *gcod*, the meditator repairs to a lonely and frightening spot and visualizes cutting his own body to bits and feeding it to the ravening demons who haunt the place. This, it is said, is an extraordinarily effective means of "cutting off" one's own ego-attachment.

There are also structural similarities between the birth of a shaman and the crucial act of Buddhist tantricism, the meditations of creation-stage yoga, or, as it might be even more literally translated "the stage or process of giving birth." In the creation process, the *maṇḍala* is the place where the initiate is reborn as the god, where it is revealed that, for those with pure perceptions, the world is paradise and all beings are divinities.

How then do the Sorceresses guard the *maṇḍala's* door? As the commentary says, the Sorceresses *are* the four immeasurables. In tantric terminology, the four immeasurables are the "pure aspect" of these outwardly ferocious symbolic beings. It is fitting that when one enters the *maṇḍala*, one is reborn as an enlightened being with immeasurable love, immeasurable compassion, immeasurable joy and immeasurable equanimity. This immeasurable vision is the gateway to the pure vision of the world as divine. Like the Yakut Bird of Prey Mother dismembering the body of the future shaman, the four immeasurables dismember the initiate's discordant habits of perception, so that he may experience a spiritual rebirth.

As the *ḍākiṇī* of Padmasambhava's biography devoured the great guru only to give him spiritual rebirth from her own womb, the iconography of the Sorceresses, with their heads of beasts and birds of prey and their bodies of naked women, suggests that they perform a similar function for those who enter the *maṇḍala* whose doors they guard.[74]

There is, of course, also a larger Tantric Buddhist tradition of animal-headed goddesses. Some of these are obviously Indian in origin. Others may be of Tibetan or central Asian origin.[75] The Lion-headed goddesses of the Tibetan pantheon are quite well known, both as independent figures and in the entourage of the goddess µridevī.[76] A bird-headed *yoginī* is found, for one, in the entourage of Cakrasamvara.[77] Perhaps most famous, and certainly the most numerous, are the animal-headed goddesses of *The Tibetan Book of the Dead*. These deities arise on the twelfth day of the *bardo*, the state between death and rebirth.[78] Some of these goddesses are summarized in the chart below.

By their position and their function as guards, the Sorceresses can also be called simply *"sgo ma,"* or "door women." Some traditions, such as the Union of the Precious Ones and Vajrakīla, however, have both *phra men ma* and *sgo ma* and keep the two categories separate.[79] In the preceding chart, in cases where two categories of animal-headed goddesses exist in a single *sādhana*, I have concentrated on those associated with the *maṇḍala* doors. Although their heads may differ, wherever they are specified, the direction, hand-implement and body color of the door goddesses agree with those of the Sorceresses of the Lord of the Dance cycle.

ANIMAL-HEADED GODDESSES OF THE FOUR DOORS

	Lord of Dance	*Book of Dead*[a]	*Samvara*[b]	*Precious*[c]	*Vajrakīla*[d]	*Four-Hand*[e]
E	raven	cuckoo	horse	horse	raven	vulture
S	pig	goat	boar	boar	owl	owl
W	dog	lion	lion	lion	stag	crow
N	owl	serpent	wolf	serpent	yak	*khyung*

[a] Fremantle and Trungpa, *The Tibetan Book of the Dead,* 1975: 67. There are, of course, many animal-headed goddesses in the *Book of the Dead.* These four are the Goddesses of the Doors.

[b] Lessing's diagram is somewhat obscure as to the deities' directions. I have reconciled them in my list according to their names and colors. Despite their names, Vajra Hook, and so on, in Lessing's *sādhana* all these goddesses seem to have the same hand implements: a skull drum (l.) and a "magic wand" (r.). See Lessing, *Yung-Ho-Kung,* 1942: 131.

[c] Union of the Precious Ones, from Snellgrove, *Buddhist Himālaya,* 1957: 232, listed in the chart are the four gate keepers. Snellgrove does not specify their directions. I have assumed for the chart that his list is in standard order. The *sādhana* also gives a list of eight *phra men ma* with the heads of a lion, tiger, fox, wolf, vulture, eagle, crow, and owl.

[d] Nebesky-Wojkowitz, *Tibetan Religious Dances,* 1976: 92, 98. These are the "gate guards" from the "dance notes" (*'chams yig*) of Vajrakīla translated by Nebesky-Wojkowitz. Interestingly, though, they are identified not as *phra men ma*, which the *'chams yig* gives separately, but as four different classes of spirit: a Malefactress/Benefactress (*gnod sbyin mo, yakṣi*), a Terrifier (*'jigs byed*), an Ambrosia (*bdud rtsi*), and a Killer (*gsod byed*), respectively. Nebesky-Wojkowitz also notes that "according to the only eye-witness account of a Vajrakīla dance so far available, these four *sgo-ma* are supposed to be bird-headed."

[e] Cf. Nebesky-Wojkowitz, *Oracles and Demons,* 1956: 46–47. The animal names in Tibetan are: *bya rgod, 'ug pa, khva ta,* and *khyung.* Nebesky-Wojkowitz notes that there are eight goddesses in the entourage of Ye shes mgon po phyag bzhi pa rGva lo'i lugs, and their directions are reversed from the normal "Buddhist" order: E, W, N, S, SE, SW, NW, NE.

In the *Sādhanamālā*, we find the parts of the household door: the lock, keys, planks, and curtains each personified as a goddess.[80] More germane to our discussion, however, are the two goddesses found portrayed on the traditional door curtains of the secret *pūjā* room of a Newar temple.[81] They are called simply "Kākāsyā" and "Ūgyāsyā." As the names indicate, they have the head of a raven and an owl respectively. Kākāsyā is blue and Ūgyāsyā is green. Both are in standing posture and have four arms. The upper two hold a skull bowl.[82] The lower pair holds a *khaṭvāṅga* (r.) and a *ḍamaru* (l.).

Door goddesses seem to belong to the broader category of directional goddesses. Directional goddesses can be found in the *Niṣpannayogāvalī*, written in the late eleventh or early twelfth century,[83] and the *Vajratārā-sādhanam*. The roughly contemporaneous *Sādhanamālā* gives a list of six directional goddesses, four of which correspond with the door goddesses of the Lord of the Dance *sādhana*. Although, once again the heads differ—here they seem all to be human—the other aspects are constant.

THE GODDESSES OF DIRECTION[a]

quarter	*color*	*face*	*tool*	*name*
east	white	?	hook	Vajrāṇkuśi
south	yellow	human	lasso	Vajrapāśi
west	red	human	chain	Vajrasphoṭā
north	green	?	bell	Vajraghaṇṭā

a From Bhattacharyya, *Indian Buddhist Iconography*, 1958: 258, 297–299. In Bhattacharyya's translation *ankuśa* is goad and *paśa* noose. The last two goddesses in the set of six, Uṣṇīṣavijayā and µumbhā, clearly have little in common with the other four, and were added to make the four directions six. Bhattacharyya, Ibid., 1958: 293 gives blurry pictures of statues of Vajrapāśī (fig. 193) and Vajrasphoṭā (fig. 194) from a Beijing collection. They are both shown with human heads. The other two undoubtedly follow suit.

As we have noted, in the *Book of the Dead*, the Sorceresses form a separate category from the door women. Indeed, in the chart of door goddesses above, the heads of the goddesses of *Book of the Dead* are in every case different from those of the Lord of the Dance door goddesses. However, goddesses similar to those of the Lord of the Dance Sorceresses can be found among the many other groups of animal-headed goddesses enumerated in the *Book of the Dead*. As might be expected, most of them belong to the category of Sorceresses.

THE EIGHT SORCERESSES OF THE HOLY PLACES IN THE BOOK OF THE DEAD

direction	*name*	*color*	*face*	*right hand*	*left hand*
east	Siṁhamukhā	"wine"	lion	crossed at breast	
south	Vyāghrīmukhā	red	tiger	crossed pointing downward	
west	µrgālamukhā	black	fox	razor	entrails
north	µvānamukhā	dark blue	wolf (dog?)	hold corpse to mouth	
southwest	Kaṁkamukhā	dark red	hawk	flayed skin over shoulder	
southeast	Gṛdhamukhā	pale yellow	vulture	shoulder: corpse / hand: skeleton	
northwest	Kākamukhā	black	raven	sword	skull cup
northeast	Ūlumukhā	dark blue	owl	vajra	sword

The one type missing from the list is a sow-headed goddess. She does, however, turn up elsewhere in the *Book of the Dead* as Vārāhī, one of the six *yoginīs* of the northern quarter. Vārāhī is, of course, a Hindu deity of considerable antiquity. The form found in the *Book of the Dead* holds a "noose of teeth," a detail which agrees more with our "Binding Woman" than with other descriptions of Vārāhī.[84]

Francesca Fremantle and Chögyam Trungpa identify the *phra men ma* as the *piśācīs* of India, a kind of demon "somewhat less terrible than the *rākṣasa*."[85] The *Mahāvyutpatti* (4756), however, translates *piśāca*, as *sha za*, carnivore, and lists them among the Hungry Ghosts. In the *Sādhanamālā*, *piśācī* occurs as an epithet of the goddess Parṇaśabarī. According to Bhattacharyya, this indicates that "she was regarded as one of the demi-gods, half human, half divine."[86] Like other members of the Indian demon class, the name *piśāca* may have originally belonged to a tribal group long ago demonized by the more centrally located architects of Indian culture.

What clues can the lexicographers provide for the etymology of the term *phra men ma*? A *phra men ma* would be a woman who performs *phra men*, which H. A. Jäschke defines as "sorcery, witchcraft." Geshe Chodak says that *phra men pa*, a masculine form of the word, is "applied to demonesses and to those who are both sky walkers and demonesses, and also to semi-divine ghouls" *('dre mo zer ba dang mkha' 'gro dang 'dre mo gnyis yin pa la'ang zer ba dang lha min srin po la'ang zer/)*. He defines *phra men ma* as *sha za 'gro* (carnivorous beings). Trulshik Rinpoche however, states unequivocally that they are "like goddesses. . . . They are not demonesses (*'dre mo*)."[87]

According to Trulshik Rinpoche, the term *phra men* refers to deities with a human body and an animal's head in general. *Phra men ma* refers to the female of the type. Because they bring about heterogeneous appearances, they can be called "apparitions."[88] When I tell Trulshik Rinpoche about Das' definition of *phra men* as "magical forecasts," he says that the term has nothing to do with telling the future, but rather with a kind of direct perception (*mngon shes*). He emphasizes that the *phra men ma* are the guardians of the gates and in reality (*don du*) the four immeasurables.[89]

The name *phra men ma* can be also applied to living women, but in a sense that is less than divine. John Ardussi and Lawrence Epstein, in their discussion of "The Saintly Madman in Tibet," refer to them as a type of witch related to the *bdud mo* and the *gson 'dre*. Characteristically, they are "pious women who spend all their time in prayer and other religious activities, but whose thoughts turn evil and unconsciously harm other people."

> Alternating with violent and aggressive behavior, the victims are characterized by autistic withdrawal from their environment, loss of speech, and occasional episodes of hyperphagia and coprophagia. In terms of social relations this seems to symbolize two types of anti-

> social acts, withdrawal from interaction and eating too much or too many horrible things. Witches are always depicted as cannibalistic, and at their gatherings they are supposed to gorge themselves on human and animal corpses.[90]

It is interesting to note that however different they are from their divine namesakes in the Lord of the Dance *maṇḍala*, Ardussi and Epstein's human *phra men ma* have at least one area of similarity. The *phra men ma* goddesses have strange animal-like faces; human *phra men ma* have strange animal-like eating habits.

Based on the testimony of their informants, Ardussi and Epstein categorize these women "in a preliminary fashion" as schizophrenics.[91] Curiously, this identification of *phra men ma* as mad-women brings us back to the Indian *piśācī*.[92] In classical times, the *piśāca* demons gave their name to a form of marriage. Of all the supernatural models for marriage, it was considered the lowest. In the words of A. L. Basham, it "can scarcely be called marriage at all—the seduction of a girl while asleep, mentally deranged, or drunk."[93]

In this, it is well to remember that one of the hallmarks of tantricism on both sides of the Himalayas is the identification of the saint with the madman and of the sexual, and in particular the sexually degraded and dangerous, with the divine.

Poetically at least, the borderland between the abnormal and the supernormal is a vague one. To embody immeasurable compassion, immeasurable love, immeasurable joy, and immeasurable equanimity is abnormal by ordinary human standards. To embody that promiscuously ecstatic union with existence, which the Sky Walker and the Sorceress suggest with their spread legs and their faces transformed by abandon, transformed even into the faces of animals, is by worldly standards deranged.

3

Deity Yoga

One of the earliest and most fundamental concepts of Buddhism is that of the path—that religion has a goal and that there is a means to reach that goal. In the introduction, we remarked that a sense of wonder, a vision however fleeting of the world as divine, is part of our common human heritage. In the context of tantric yoga, this vision is not left to chance or an arbitrary grace. It is cultivated by a process of meditation.

Each day the participants in Mani Rimdu meditate that:

> The world outside becomes a divine palace.
> Its inhabitants are perfected as the gods of the circle.
> Sounds that resound are the mantra's own sound.
> The mind's memories and thoughts are the Body of Truth. [UB 18.5]

The type of meditation in which one visualizes oneself as a god and the world as paradise has two stages: the process of creation (Tib. *bskyed rim;* Ssk. *utpattikrama*), often translated as the generation stage; and the process of perfection (*rdzogs rim; niṣpannakrama*) or stage of completion or fulfillment. The process of perfection continues the efforts of the creation process. It makes the yogic vision of the creation process real.[1]

Without attempting a general *excursis* on the subject of tantric meditation, it would be well to mention some of the special features belonging to the tradition at hand.

The creation process is commonly divided into three parts: self-creation (*bdag bskyed*), visualizing oneself as the deity; creation in front (*mdun bskyed*), visualizing the deity floating in space before one; and creation in the flask (*bum bskyed*), visualizing the deity in a flask of holy water.[2]

According to Trulshik Rinpoche, in the New Translation Schools the three are performed separately. In the Nyingma, however, they can be done all at once. This simultaneous method, he adds, is easier. Although the sequential method can also be used, it is more difficult inasmuch as that which is visualized (*dmigs bya*) is more extensively developed.

Thus, in the Nyingma school there are three systems of *bskyed rim:* (1) meditating on the deity as the self, in front and in the flask all at once (*bdag mdun bum gsum gcig char bsgom pa*); (2) meditating on them separately (*bdag mdun bum gsum so sor bsgom pa*); (3) a system where, before the recitation, the creation of the deity passes from oneself into the creation in front like one lamp lighting another (*me rim btab lta bu phye ba'i bsgom pa*).

In each case, the creation process has three aspects.[3]

1. visualizing the form of the god clearly (*rnam pa gsal ba*)
2. keeping in mind the purity of the form (*rnam pa dag par dran ba*)
3. assuming the ego of the deity (*lha'i nga rgyal 'dzin pa*)

The deities visualized such as Lord of the Dance belong to the class known as *yi dam* (Ssk. *iṣṭadevatā*). *Yi dam* has most often been translated as tutelary deity, although recently the term personal deity has been used. It is said that a *yi dam* is the very form in which a meditator will attain Buddhahood. This concept may give a clue to the origin of the term. In Tibetan, *yi dam* is related to the word for promise or pledge (*dam tshig*). The underlying concept seems to be either that the *yi dam* is the deity to which one is pledged, or that it is the form in which one promises to become a Buddha, a provisional image of one's potential Buddhahood.[4] Other deities of the pantheon are merely worshipped; the *yi dam* is the god one strives to become.

The tutelary deities of the tantric pantheon have little in common with the gods of other traditions. For the most part, they lack the personality of Jehovah or the mythological / biographical details of the Greek or Hindu gods. They are not creators of the universe. In keeping with their role as ciphers of an eternal vision, the tutelary deities are oddly static.

What the *yi dam* have instead of biographies are "pure attributes." The commentaries, for example, explain that Lord of the Dance's clasped hands are the union of method and wisdom, and that they clasp a *vajra* because wisdom and method are bound as of one taste with the indivisible diamond of bliss.[5]

Lord of the Dance, then, is pure. He does not have a body of flesh and blood, but a pure body. On his level of being, it is said that even the causes, which would result in a gross body of flesh and blood subject to death and decay, are totally absent. Having a pure body means that Lord of the Dance's hands are not *like* the union of wisdom and method, they *are* the union of wisdom and method.

In "recollecting the purity" of the deity, the meditator calls these pure attributes to mind in detail. Thus, when he has re-created himself as the deity, his hands are not flesh and blood, but wisdom and method and so on. This refinement of the creative self-image dissolves the basis of demonic pride. In the language of deity yoga, it is said to be the antidote to becoming a *rudra* instead of a god.[6]

We might speculate that this functions in an analogous way to early Buddhist (or "Hīnayāna" in Tibetan parlance) meditations on the *skandhas* and similar schemes for analyzing the human condition. The Hīnayāna philosophers enjoin us to analyze the components of our body and mind. In so doing, they say we will find no real basis for our feeling of selfhood; the feeling that drags us helpless through the disasters of *saṁsāra*. In recollecting the "purity of the form," we remember the individual characteristics of the deity. Like the *skandhas*, each in itself is an unsuitable resting place for a sense of ego, or in this case a feeling of demonic pride. Between them, nothing can be found on which the towering edifice of such an error might be built.

The third aspect of the creation process is assuming the deity's ego. This is the thought "I am the deity." This "divine pride" is often considered to be the most crucial aspect of the creation process. It is sometimes said that we should not think that we are just imagining that we are the deity. The deity is more like what we really are than our normal self-image is. In Buddhism, our normal self-image is by definition a total illusion. As the contemporary Tibetan historian of religion, Khetsun Sangpo has put it,

> These substitutions are not false visualizations. It is not a matter of first thinking your surroundings are ordinary and then replacing them by something that is fantastic but false. You are to conceive them as having been this way from the very beginning and that you are identifying their own proper nature. Your senses normally misrepresent what is there, but through this visualization you can come closer to what actually exists.[7]

This identification of the mind as such (*sems nyid*) with Buddhahood is for the Nyingma school not only the crux of the tantric vision, but also its defining feature. As Dudjom Rinpoche points out, citing the *Heruka Galpo,*

> Through the causal vehicle of dialectics
> Mind-as-such is meditated upon as the cause of buddhahood.
> Through the resultant vehicle of mantras
> Mind-as-such is meditated upon as buddhahood.[8]

If the deities of Buddhism (and its concept of reality) are quite different from the deity (and concepts of reality) of the Judeo-Christian tradition, one aspect of man's relation to the divine is constant. That is faith. The *Playful Ocean* declares:

> O body which is as pervasive and pure as imperceptible space,
> Although we cannot perceive [you] to invite [you], or pray that you come,
> We pray you play wisdom's illusion and come
> From the realm of compassion itself, which is purified as the body of truth.[9]

No matter how a deity is construed, it takes faith for a human being to invoke an unseen god.

Faith in unseen powers is fundamental to cultural milieu of Solu-Khumbu. It is common to the highest lama and to the lowliest villager. It underlies every aspect of Mani Rimdu. Once, when discussing with Trulshik Rinpoche the merits of the *maṇi* pills that are at the heart of Mani Rimdu, I brought the conversation around to faith. The power of faith is a common theme in Tibetan culture, and their myths and theories on the subject sometimes come close to our notion of the placebo effect. Nevertheless, when I asked him if the efficacy of the pills was dependent on the faith of the person who takes them, his answer was simple and direct: "No. If you give the pills to a dog, the dog will gain the merit."

From this perspective, it is not the power of faith that is at issue here, but the power of blessing (*byin rlabs*).

4

The Sworn Protectors

The *maṇḍala* of the central deity is surrounded by protective circles of lotuses, cemeteries, diamonds, and flames. His divine assembly, as pictured in the visionary paintings known as *tshogs zhing* is surrounded by circles of protective deities. This section will provide an introduction, albeit a brief one, to the protector rituals that form so important a part of Mani Rimdu.

The protector deities worshipped during Mani Rimdu fall into two main groups. The first is the Great Protectors, high gods of the Indian pantheon accorded at least sometimes with great spiritual advancement and always with great supernatural powers. The gods of the second group are more parochial, for the most part, they are Tibetan deities of lower rank. In the Mindroling tradition, these are called the "followers" (*rjes 'brang*) of the Great Protectors.

The Great Protectors have an equivocal aspect. On the one hand, they are often addressed as pure Buddha-like beings.

> Although from the Truth Realm, you display the body of a glorious
>   Blood Drinker,
> Originally, you are pure. We propitiate you
> With progress on the paths of creation and fulfillment,
> Such as the yoga that recognizes that you are indivisible
>   from our own minds! [PO 43.3]

Or,

> Hūṁ! Without straying from the realm of total purity,
> Out of compassion, you teach in a body of wrath.
> May we propitiate you, great powerful hero,
> Heruka, who has vanquished the demon army! [PO 43.5]

Or, again

Hrīḥ! Come here, bearer of the diamond of every Conqueror's speech,
Great God brother and sister, who rise
From the play of Lotus Lord of the Dance Compassion,
In the body of a worldly protector in order to tame the hard to tame! [PO 45b6]

On the other hand, the protectors are called *dam can*, "sworn ones" bound by promises extracted by powerful magicians and yogis. Often these promises are construed to be oaths to benefit the world rather than harm it following their ferocious inclinations.

The liturgy lists many boons that the protectors should bestow from increasing crop yields to replenishing "yogis' degenerate and broken vows!" [PO 47b5]. The typical short list is found in the ceremony of the Virtuous One, a form of Mahākāla:

Glorious Diamond Great Black One, Lord of Hosts, brother and sister and entourage—transgress not the words and advice of the root and lineage Lamas! Protect the Buddhas' teaching! Praise the grandeur of the [Three] Jewels! Defend the rule of the Virtuous Community and religion! Cure the ills of the world! Increase sentient beings' benefit and pleasure! Be a friend who helps Yogis! Complete the Mantra Holders' work! Subdue the enemy of anger! Vanquish harmful Obstructors! In particular, pacify all outer, inner and secret opposing conditions; increase and expand conducive conditions—the panoply of good we wish for; and act to bring success to each and every highest and ordinary true achievement, for all those who participate in this vow! [8b6]

According to Lama Tharchin, the protectors' specific promise is to manifest in this world compassionately to protect religion and beings. He puts an unexpected spin on the issue, however. Without such promises, he ventures, the protectors might not manifest at all.

Such a concept is implicit in the act of invoking the protectors. There is always the suggestion that if those performing the ritual did not invoke the deity in question, he would simply fail to appear and thereby default on his contract. Often their liturgy makes this explicit, as in this passages from the liturgy Virtuous One:

Hūṁ! I am a knowledge bearer and an achiever.
I dwell in the holy. I am attracted to the gods.
You are a guardian, a possessor of magic powers.

Long ago, under the gaze of the Great Glorious One,
You swore to guard the teaching.
If I, the yogi, now invoke
Your strict promise,
By the power of your vow, I pray you come! [PO 41.3]

If such a promise is sign of an equivocal nature, it is in part a type of equivocation that the tradition ascribes to the Buddha himself. On the one hand, a certain logic argues that in his infinite compassion, a Buddha is incapable of doing other than helping beings. The tradition itself, however, constantly belies this. According to the legendary accounts of the life of the Buddha, after his enlightenment µākyamuni despaired of communicating to mortals his insight in all its subtlety. Only after the god Brahmā urged him, did he consent to remain on Earth to teach. Similarly, in the "Seven-fold Service" used in nearly every Tibetan ritual, the practitioner says,

Buddhas that long for *nirvāṇa*,
I beseech you to stay for an ocean of æons!
I urge you to turn the wheel of religion
Molded to the minds of those to be trained![1]

Like human religious practitioners who daily invoke their faith in the three jewels and their resolve to attain enlightenment, in the rhetoric of their rituals at least, the protectors need to constantly reaffirm their vows of compassion.

Others take a more dire view of the protectors and their potential danger. Some believe that it can be harmful to begin propitiating a deity if one will not persist in his ritual service. Tibetan physicians examine their patients urine for signs of divine affliction. "For instance, perhaps one was showing devotion and making propitiation for some time to that 'god' and then stopped . . . disturbance in this square indicates harm at the hands of such a figure."[2]

According to Robert B. Ekvall, ". . . there is not much evidence to show that conversion to Buddhism is regarded as necessarily final or enduring: CHos sKyong may perhaps backslide."[3] Ekvall gives a mythological justification for this unreliability.

In the prologue to the Gesar epic, Padmasambhava is shown as concerned and greatly grieved because, although in time past he had bound the gods of the land by an exercise of magic repeated twice—here the Bon number appears—that subjugation was losing its force. Because the thaumaturgic tour de force had not been repeated thrice—here the Buddhist number appears—the native gods were stirring anew in rebellion, and someone was needed to reconvert or reconquer the demons of the Land of the Snows.[4]

Propitiation of the protectors is an area in which monks can display the professionalism that is the result of their lifelong dedication to ritual service. This service creates a relationship with these dangerous unseen forces that borders on intimacy.

> Bhyoḥ! Great Cemetery Goddess,
> Raise your body from your cemetery home!
> Come to this place with a loving heart,
> The yogis longingly pray.
> Mother whose play is the very appearance of wisdom,
> Cemetery Goddess, Raise your body
> From the vast, unutterable, unchanging realm!
> Come here, for the time has come! [PO 28.5]

As we shall see, this relationship with the protectors and the skill in handling them contributes to the monks value as a community resource.

Some European authors have regarded the protector deities as a projection of violent psychological forces.[5] Others, including some of our finest scholars, have tended to dismiss the very concept of propitiation from Buddhism altogether, along with other elements that they deem "superstitious" or "unorthodox," and more extraordinary, to claim that "learned" Tibetans do likewise. Even Ferdinand Diederich Lessing, the totemic ancestor of all of us who would study Tibetan ritual, was not immune, and wrote:

> The idea [of "untimely death"] springs from the same root as the view, so common among so-called primitives, that death and illness are not natural, but the work of pernicious demons and their baneful witchcraft. Our author rejects such a view. Nevertheless he admits, or *seems to admit*, the possibility of interference with the life process by some outside power. Learned lamas, it is true, adhere personally to more philosophical theories, but at the same time they compromise with the needs of the populace. This attitude of theirs finds support in the Scriptures which say that the Buddha himself adjusted his methods to the conceptual amplitude of his audience.[6] (*italics mine*)

In Solu-Khumbu, I never heard any such suggestion coming from a Tibetan or Sherpa. Even were the implicit concept of this sort of socially systemic deceit not inherently unpleasant, mercifully, it is unnecessary in this case. The propitiation of protectors is too fundamental to Tibetan culture to conceive of as merely tolerated in a credulous peasantry by an artful and condescending, if benign, elite.

To the people of Solu-Khumbu, propitiation is not just an advisable activity, but an essential one. Everyone can give a story of how a bad sign was dealt with, or a calamity averted by propitiating the relevant protector. Villagers who quite literally have never heard the word *sūtra* or its Tibetan equivalent, *mdo*, have an easy familiarity with the term *skang gso* (propitiation).

The monastic elite comes from the same villages and the same families.[7] As monks, their involvement with the cult of the protectors increases dramatically. In Solu-Khumbu, protector rituals form an important part both of a monk's professional duties and of his private religious practice. There is nothing to suggest that belief in the protectors or any other supernatural entities decreases or is vitiated by the monastic experience. If anything, it increases. To the Sherpa monk, disbelief in the protectors is nearly unimaginable, especially in anyone interested in religion.

> Monk One: You probably don't believe in the Followers, do you?
> Ethnographer: *(silence)*
> Monk One: *(with a troubled look)* But you surely believe in the Great Protectors, don't you?
> Ethnographer: *(silence)*
> Monk Two: *(in the nick of time)* Of course he does!

Of course, Tibetan theologians are no strangers to subtle psychological interpretation. Wondering if any of our own scholars' theories might find their cognates in higher Tibetan intellectual circles, I made protectors and propitiation the topic of an interview with H. H. the Dalai Lama. Surely, if we were to find Lessing's "learned lama," it would be here in the apartments of this man revered by all of Tibet for his learning as well as for his saintliness. What His Holiness said is of sufficient moment to summarize at some length.[8]

Q. What is the nature of the Sworn Protectors of Religion (*dam can chos srung*)?

> A. Tibetan Buddhism has two aspects. On the one hand there is a strict causal system. On the other hand, there is a great multiplicity of gods. Some people in Tibet think that the Protectors are almost like creator gods [but this is not the case].
>
> In general there are two types of causes: the fundamental cause and helping causes. [The classical example used in explaining causation is a potter making a pot.] In this example, the fundamental cause is the clay, and the additional causes are the instruments, the

potter, etc. that create the pot. Without clay, no matter how good the instruments, no pot can be made.

It is on the level of helping causes that the Protectors can be useful. No one but you yourself can change your basic karma [which is the fundamental cause of your future], but as to when it will ripen and which aspect, the protectors can make adjustments.

Q. What is the purpose of propitiation (*bskang gso*)?

A. In the phrase *bskang gso*, *bskang ba* means "to satisfy", as in satisfying a desire (*'dod pa bskang ba*), or satisfying the mind (*thugs bskang ba*). *gSo ba* means "to repair", to make up for a past offense of word or deed, to repent or confess (*bshags pa*). Thus, *bskang gso* is satisfying the Protectors and making up for past offenses. It puts them in a favorable frame of mind if you later need a favor from them. It is like giving a party for a rich and powerful man, or apologizing to him if you have offended him.

In *bskang gso*, offerings are given, but they may be insufficient. They must be augmented by mentally created offerings. All the offerings must be cleansed by meditation and mantras, otherwise the gods may not be able to use them.

The beings of the spirit world cannot be perceived by the ordinary mind. They can sometimes be perceived in a semi-conscious state, such as when falling asleep. Otherwise, it is necessary to have one-pointedness of mind in order to perceive them. Many people do *bskang gso* just thinking of their stomachs, they do not do it one-pointedly. This is cheating. It is a waste of time, a waste of effort, and a waste of money.

The spirit world has so many different races—*dmu*, *rgyal po*, *btsan*. Sometimes, I think they must have race relations problems. (*laughter*). Also some protect Buddhism, and others are against Buddhism, so, like people, they also have ideological conflicts.

Even in my sketchy account, this interpretation is sophisticated and at the same time imbued with Buddhist philosophical principles. What it does not do, however is explain away the protectors or devalue their propitiation.

Early Western writers on Buddhism called that religion atheistic and praised it as "the religion of common sense." But just as Lessing's concept of a "learned lama" is an ethnocentric one, the concept of Buddhist atheism is imbued with our own cultural heritage and limited by it.

For us, the antipodes of religiosity have been the absolute monotheism of the ancient Near East and its derivatives, and a more recent but hardly less absolute rationalism. It is true that Buddhism is atheistic in the sense that it does not center on a demiurge or Creator of the Universe similar to that of Judaism, Christianity, or Islam. However, as we gain more data on the beliefs of living Buddhists, it seems clear that none of them live in the peculiarly empty cosmos of the modern West, with a cold infinite void above and only Earth below.

THE PLAYFUL OCEAN AND THE FOLLOWERS

The rituals of the Great Protectors are found in a text called the *Playful Ocean of True Achievement* (*dNgos grub rol mtsho*). Like nearly all the ritual texts of Mani Rimdu, the *Playful Ocean* originated at Mindroling Monastery. The *Playful Ocean* is quite similar to the main protector ritual of the Dudjom lineage, the *Phrin las rnam rol*, *The Play of Ceremony*. Sometimes the two texts correspond word-for-word. Lamas familiar with both traditions, such as Trulshik Rinpoche and Lama Tharchin, will refer on occasion to the Dudjom text to check a sticky passage of the *Playful Ocean*.

Our edition of the *Playful Ocean* is printed at Thubten Chöling from blocks carved at Rongphu. Available from the Library of Congress, the *Playful Ocean* and the *Followers* are among the few Mani Rimdu texts found in American libraries.[9]

According to the commentarial tradition of the *Precious Lamp* (*Rin chen sgron me*), the protector ritual to be used in connection with Lord of the Dance is the *Guardians of the Word* (*bKa' srung*), a short text centering on Great God (Lha chen). Great God, Mahādeva of the Indians, is considered by the tradition to be an emanation of Lord of the Dance and the special Guardian of the Word of his teachings.

Although the *Guardians of the Word* focuses on Mahādeva, it alludes to all the gods of the *Playful Ocean*, albeit briefly. Thus, the use of the longer text is a natural elaboration of the basic form of the ritual. The *Playful Ocean* is, in fact, the protector ritual usually used at Thubten Chöling when performing the rituals of Lord of the Dance. Presumably, it became a fixed part of Mani Rimdu when the festival was first codified by Ngawang Tenzin Norbu.

In Mani Rimdu, the first of the daily protector rituals is "Blessing the Offerings."[10] The first chapter of *Playful Ocean*, the Yoga of Self is only necessary when the *Playful Ocean* is performed on its own. It is not used in Mani Rimdu, since the function of creation or generation of the tutelary deity has already been fulfilled by the maṇḍala of Lord of the Dance.[11]

It is possible to spread the performance of the *Playful Ocean* over several days, worshipping a few deities each day. In such a case, the practitioners must issue a "General Invitation of the Defenders of Religion," so that the full complement of deities will be invoked each day. During Mani Rimdu, the monks of Chiwong use the passage by that name in the *Guardians of the Word*, because of the connection of that text to the Lord of the Dance rituals.

When the *Playful Ocean* is performed alone, a similar interpolation may be drawn from 'Gyur med rdo rje's *Condensed Torma Ritual for the Sworn Ones in General* (*Dam can spyi'i gtor ma'i cho ga nyung ngur bsdus pa*). The two ceremonies are so similar that it was only after considerable thought that experts unequivocally specified that the *Guardians of the Word* should be used in Mani Rimdu rather than the *Condensed Torma Ritual.*

The *Playful Ocean* addresses nine different deities. Four are types of Mahākāla; two can be classed as types of the Goddess, Devī; the remainder are heterogeneous. An addendum for Long Life Woman, a deity associated with Rongphu, brings the number to ten. The ten protectors of the Mindroling / Rongphu tradition are summarized in the following chart.[12]

TYPOLOGY OF THE GREAT PROTECTORS

	Mahākāla		*Devī*		*Other*
1	Virtuous One	5	Mantra Guardian	6	Great God
2	Four-Handed One	9	Cemetery Grandmother	7	Planet Demon
3	Neuter			8	Son of Renown
4	Four-Faced One			10	Long Life Woman

Long Life Woman is at the head of a group of goddesses known as the Five Long Life Sisters. According to the texts, these native Tibetan goddesses were converted to Buddhism on no less than three occasions: first, by the Achievement Yoginīs in the Singhala cemetery; second, by Padmasambhava at Khalarongo; and last by Milarepa at Chubar.[13]

Ngawang Tenzin Norbu of Rongphu composed this ritual for the mountain goddess whose home was so close to his monastery, basing it on prayers written by the great Kagyü poet Pemakarpo (Padma dkar po)—a lama of Milarepa's lineage. Thus, although the Long Life Sisters are worshipped elsewhere in Tibet, our text belongs exclusively to Rongphu and its satellites.

The *Playful Ocean* is an anthology assembled by 'Gyur med rdo rje from the separate practices of nine separate deities. Today, editions of the individual rituals of at least some members of the group are still found. Presumably all of the texts existed as independent units before the collection was made.

The organizing principle underlying the anthology is simple. It is structured to facilitate practice. To understand the organization of the *Playful Ocean*, we must first briefly examine its structure from the viewpoint of a single protector ritual.

The process begins with the preliminary practices necessary to embark on the main meditation. The first is the yoga of self, in which the meditator remakes himself as the tutelary deity. Without the power of the tutelary, an ordinary man dare not approach the great and powerful protectors. Another necessary preliminary is the blessing of the various offerings. In a sense this parallels the first act: just as an ordinary man cannot approach the protectors, an ordinary offering cannot satisfy them. Both the offering and the one who offers must be infused with a higher power.

Next comes the actual practice, which can be divided into nine parts. The first is the basic ceremony (*'phrin las*) (1) for the deity, the visualization of the deity and his entourage. Typically, the basic ceremony also includes an invitation, a plea to stay, placing the god under oath, a salutation, and a general offering.

Following this, the torma is offered (2) with an elaborate mantra. The deity is then praised (3),[14] and his own mantra recited (4). Now comes the propitiation (*bskang ba*) (5) of the deity per se, a special set of offerings to fulfill his desires and satisfy his mind.

A confession (6) follows the propitiation. In the *Playful Ocean*, some deities such as Virtuous One and Great God, have their own special confessions. The next section brings us to the point of the exercise—requesting action toward the desired goal (7).[15] Finally, the torma is then fed to the deity (8), and the concluding rituals performed (9).

This model holds for shorter propitiation rites as well as for longer ones. Thus, we can see its basic elements in the "General Invitation" of the *Guardians of the Word*, and in the shortest of all of our protector rituals, Ngawang Tenzin Norbu's two folio *Unelaborated* (*sPros med*). As these rituals demonstrate, when worshipping more than one protector, it is the practice to first invoke all the deities concerned, then to give each his offering in turn, praise him and so on. When a group of deities each of whom has a separate text is worshipped, the practitioner will flip from manuscript to manuscript to achieve the same effect.

The *Playful Ocean* in a sense does this for him. It disassembles the Mindroling protector rituals and collates them so that the practitioner need not flip cumbersomely between nine separate volumes. With the tenth deity, Long Life Woman, the original process can still be seen. Not among the nine Mindroling protectors, when she is worshipped the monks must continually flip between her text and the *Playful Ocean*.

If the liturgies of the *Playful Ocean* are heterogeneous in origin, they are also heterogeneous in structure, style, and mood. "The Ceremony for the Glorious Protector, The Four-Faced One," has its own introduction and is prefaced by a passage written in the mysterious "symbolic alphabet of the Sky Walkers," unintelligible to ordinary mortals. As Trulshik Rinpoche puts it, each syllable of this alphabet speaks volumes to those with eyes to see.[16]

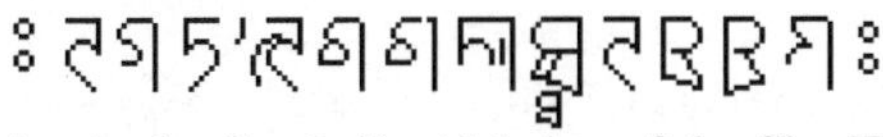

Inscription in the Symbolic Alphabet of the Sky Walkers (*mkha' 'gro brda' yig*) heading "The Ceremony for Four-Faced One" (PO 16.2)

Some of the rituals invite the gods with onomatopoeic verse (e.g., Planet Demon, f 25.4), others do not. Some have elaborately categorized offerings with separate verses for ordinary, secret, medicine, *rakta,* and torma offerings (e.g., Great God, f 22.5 ff.). Others (e.g., Son of Renown, f 27b4) content themselves with a single generic verse. Virtuous One (2.7.2.1, f 49.2 ff.) and Great God (2.7.2.2, f 49b3 ff.) alone among the protectors have their own confessions. These confessions are included when its god is worshipped and excluded when he is not.

The mood of the various prayers varies with the deity invoked. The ithyphallic Great God with his voluptuous consort Umādevī clinging to his shoulder is propitiated in a sensuous mood. The propitiation of the fearsome Four-Handed Mahākāla is appropriately violent and gruesome. Its imagery, whose *fleurs* are always *mal,* is enough to make Baudelaire blanche—

> Your drink—vicious heart's-blood swirls like an ocean;
> Your bath—maddening poison blood violently shimmers;
> Flowers of the five senses burst into blossom;
> Human meat smolders; smoke banks in clouds;
> Butter lamps of human grease blaze like apocalyptic fires;
> Ambrosial blood-clot perfume billows wave after wave;
> A gruesome supper shimmers with flesh, blood and bone;
> Turbulent roaring music quakes the three planes.
> Gladdened and sated by this offering,
> This inconceivable cloud of inner cemetery offerings,
> Grant us enlightenment and magic power! [12b6]

If, in the *Playful Ocean*, the style of the rituals differs considerably from one deity to another, both in terms of literary merit and apparent age, the *Followers* anthology is even more heterogeneous.[17]

One prayer from the *Followers*, "The Worship Cloud for the God of the Plain," stands out from the rest in several respects. First, as an exercise in liturgical style, it is of the first rank. Second, it is written in the first person, and the voice is that of Padmasambhava. Third, as if to give stylistic evidence to back up this attribution, the prayer has a particularly ancient ring to it, unique among the liturgies of Mani Rimdu.[18] Even a brief passage evokes a host of antique Tibetan literary devices, such as repetition, a preoccupation with genealogy, a taste for turquoise, and a love for the contours of the land of Tibet—

> Name the body god's father—
> He is 'O te gung rgyal.[19]
> Name the body god's mother—
> She is the One-Winged Turquoise Bird (g.Yu bya gshog gcig).
> Name the body god himself—

He is Ya hud god of the Cruel Ones.
Name the country in which you dwell—
It is 'Dam bshod snar mo.[20]
A wild throne of shimmering green turquoise,
Verdant in summer, verdant in winter too.[11b1]
The country in which you dwell is delightful to experience.
You adore it! [It is] the country of the gods! [11b2]

God of the Plain or God of the Plateau (*Thang lha*) is in himself an intriguing deity. He figures in early Tibetan mythology and divination and is mentioned in the Dunhuang manuscripts.[21] Despite his name, he is often considered a mountain god.[22]

Part of our text commemorates God of the Plain's conversion to Buddhism. René de Nebesky-Wojkowitz puts this event in a familiar mythic context; the same story is told of many of Tibet's autochthonous deities:

> A legend relates that this mountain god was once an adversary of Buddhism. When the Buddhist missionary Padma Sambhava came to Tibet, Nyen-chen Thang-la tried to block the saint's path with mists and snowstorms. But Padma Sambhava succeeded in breaking the mountain god's opposition and converting him into a protector of the Yellow Doctrine.[23]

From a literary viewpoint, the *Playful Ocean's* propitiation sequences in particular are poetry in a very dark key.

> Out of the empty realm, the sky before me becomes a raging tangle of blood and clots—Malaya, the volcanic island of blazing meteoric iron. In this horrifying, chilling place, at the hub of a great palace of graveyard play, atop a lotus and a sun, the syllable HUM sits on the corpses of a man and a horse. It becomes a chopper marked with a HUM, which changes into the Glorious Protector of Wisdom, Virtuous One, the Great Black One. He is in the form of a diamond ghoul: body blue-black; short and stocky and thick of limb. He is radiant as a hundred thousand suns.
>
> One face, two hands, three eyes has he. He grins, face aglow and his fangs drip blood. His tongue rolls and clacks fiercely on his palate. His nose wrinkling in anger, snorts out hurricanes. His three eyes, round and red, roll back in rage. His dark brown hair, beard and eyebrows stand on end, and blaze with a great star's light. [5b5]

The protector rituals are a trove of information about the odd corners of Tibetan culture. The liturgy, among other things, serves as a catalogue of cultural artifacts real and mythical. During the propitiation, in addition to the "normal" peaceful and wrathful offerings, such as offering water of "vicious heart's-blood" or "tempest tossed fat-specked blood" [45.1], the worshippers offer a variety of magical implements. Among these are soul-stones, life-wheels, secret images, mantra tags, murderous blades, meteorite thunderbolts, and copper needles [42b5].

The beribboned arrow is, of course, present. This ancient artifact, typical of the "nameless religion" of Tibet and of Siberian shamanist culture appears in the propitiation in various forms. Four-Handed One [42b3] and Cemetery Grandmother [48b3] each receive a vulture-feathered arrow hung with multicolored silks; Four-Faced One, "an arrow of heroic bamboo, beribboned with strips of tiger and leopard skin and multicolored silk."[24]

Hearts are a common item: bastard's hearts and life-hearts are offered on one occasion [42b5], a knifed heart on another [43.6]. Sometimes one magic device is filled with a variety of others. Four-Faced One, for example, receives a "fallen hero's heart" stuffed with "images, mantra tags, a life-wheel and soul-stone" [44b3]. Four-Handed One gets "The heart of a hero slain in battle / Filled with a life-wheel with no mistakes / A triangular natural image-stone, [and] a bastard's heart." Cemetery Grandmother gets a bastard's heart filled with her life-wheel [48b3].

Nor are hearts the only vessel to be so used. The container may be a horn, or in the case of Great God, a phallic vessel [46b6].

Black animals are offered to all forms of Mahākāla. The offering to Four-Handed One is a striking example of the theme.

> The black horse, bedecked with ornaments, gambols like the wind.
> The shaggy bull yak is as majestic as a thunderhead.
> The demon sheep has a white rump and a curling iron horn.
> The black bear-like dog trots following tracks of blood.
> The black bird with the thunder-iron beak swoops and soars.
> Birds and beasts of prey pounce on the life of enemies and obstructors. . . . [42b1]

Such images are found in art as well as literature. On the wall outside of the protector room of the Junbesi village temple, is a painting of such a "display" *(spyan gzigs),* [pronounced *chensik*]. Contemplating this dark herd, one recalls the cave paintings that are man's earliest religious art and is reminded of the animal cults that antedate other religions in Asia as elsewhere in the world.[25]

It is as literary tropes, however, that these images are perhaps the most familiar, at least in post-diaspora Tibet. A group of monks from Namgyal Monastery visiting the "Wisdom and Compassion" exhibition at the Asian

Art Museum of San Francisco stood rapt before a *spyan gzigs* painting. "Oh," one exclaimed, "there is the sheep with the curling iron horn," as the other monks huddled around him to identify images that they knew from texts but had never before seen depicted.

As we have noted, with so many deities to worship it is often impractical to complete the *Playful Ocean* and the *Followers* in a single day. For Mani Rimdu a system of rotation is used which spreads the worship of the protector over four days.

PROTECTOR RITUAL SCHEDULE[a]

Great Protectors

DAY 1	*DAY 2*	*DAY 3*	*DAY 4*
Virtuous One	Four-Handed	Neuter	Four-Faced
Great God	Great God	Great God	Mantra Guardian
Cemetery God	Son of Renown	Planet	Great God
Long Life Woman	Cemetery God	Cemetery God[b]	Cemetery God

[a] Chart, copied from ms. attributed to Trulshik Rinpoche in the possession of the Diamond Master of Chiwong, 1983. First six lines of chart, minus interpolation of Cemetery God (Dur lha, i.e. Dur 'khrod lha mo) in type three days (see next note) agrees with TCU's account. Tengpoche Rinpoche's oral account of the Protector Rituals at his monastery tallies exactly with the chart. 5/28/83.

[b] In 1984, the Chiwong Konyer checked my chart and inserted Cemetery God here, this was confirmed by observation at Thami Monastery the following spring.

THE FOLLOWERS

DAY 1	*DAY 2*	*DAY 3*	*DAY 4*
Lion Face	30 Governors	Dagger Guardians	Medicine Ladies
Medicine Ladies	Medicine Ladies	Medicine Ladies	King [Pehar]
Good Diamond	Good Diamond	Good Diamond	Good Diamond
Demon/Stern/Serpent God of the Plain[c]	Furious Haughty One	Steadfast Women	Stern One

[c] Added from new Chiwong Umze's manuscript.

In addition to the liturgy of the specific deities, the general parts of the *Playful Ocean* also must be recited. Thus, each day of Mani Rimdu, the monks devote several hours to propitiating the protectors.

The protector rituals also form a crucial part of the Mani Rimdu's sacred dance tradition. The entire *Playful Ocean* is performed each day of the dances. On the day of the masked dance, this makes for an exhausting marathon of ritual that begins long before dawn and does not end until close to midnight.

5

History: The Lord of the Dance Rituals

On Friday, August 23, 1680, 'Gyur med rdo rje, a.k.a. sMin gling gter chen, the great Treasure Revealer (*gter ston*) of Mindroling Monastery, publicly removed thirteen scrolls of yellow paper (*shog ser*) from a cave at Sha 'ug stag sgo in the Mon county of Tibet. They were the hidden texts (*gter ma*) of the Lord of the Dance rituals.[1]

'Gyur med rdo rje (1646–1714), the last of the forty-eight *gter ston* prophesied in the *Padma thang yig*, was a younger contemporary of the Fifth Dalai Lama, Ngag dbang blo bzang rgya mtsho (1617–1682).[2] It is said that when 'Gyur med rdo rje was a young man, the Dalai Lama was his teacher, and that when 'Gyur med rdo rje became older, the roles were reversed. This relationship between the founder of Mindroling and the most prominent representative of the Gelugpa order is less surprising when we note that the Fifth Dalai Lama was born in a Nyingma family.[3] In 1676, just four years before the discovery of the Lord of the Dance *gter ma*, the relatively small institution of Mindroling was established as "an important monastic teaching center."[4] Basking in the prestige of the Great Fifth, Mindroling became the most influential Nyingma Monastery in Central Tibet.[5]

It is said that through his relationship with 'Gyur med rdo rje, the Dalai Lama was inspired to bring monastic dance to the Gelugpa sect, which had shunned it up until then. The fifth Dalai Lama became one of the main exponents of the Mindroling Dance traditions.[6]

As we have already mentioned, Lord of the Dance strongly resembles the white four-handed form of Avalokiteśvara that Tibetans believe incarnates on earth as the Dalai Lama. Given the close relationship between the discoverer of the Lord of the Dance text and the Fifth Dalai Lama, it is possible that this resemblance is more than coincidental.

'Gyur med rdo rje, Father of the Lord of the Dance Tradition

It is well within the bounds of what Tibetans consider "skillful means" for a lama to tailor a religious practice for a powerful patron. One can easily imagine 'Gyur med rdo rje creating a meditation for his spiritual friend that honored him by playing in a poetic way with his identity of Avalokiteśvara. This, in fact, appears to have been the case. Tulku Thondup, in his excellent survey of the *terma* tradition, asserts that the Great Fifth "was one of the main receivers of this tradition."[7]

Lord of the Dance, moreover, is a variation on the Avalokiteśvara theme that is particularly "Nyingma" in style.[8] Thus, such an act would at once refer to the Great Fifth's secret Nyingma sympathies and deepen the already close bond between the two men.

The tradition might discount such speculation—or credit it to the serendipity of karma—at least in so far as it implies that 'Gyur med rdo rje consciously crafted the tradition to suit his illustrious disciple. Lord of the Dance is, after all, a "treasure" teaching: 'Gyur med rdo rje discovered it, he did not invent it. Part of the raison d'être of treasures is their ability to suit themselves to changing times and circumstances. If Lord of the Dance seems miraculously appropriate to his circumstances, it is nothing to wonder at in a milieu that is by nature miraculous.

If, however, 'Gyur med rdo rje had drawn a spiritual connection to strengthen a personal and political alliance, and moreover, cited a hidden text as a justification for so doing, it would not be a unique case either in Tibetan history, or even in his own time. It is, in fact, just what the Great Fifth himself seems to have done to honor one of his teachers, Blo bzang chos kyi rgyal mtshan (1570–1662). The Dalai Lama declared him to be an incarnation of Avalokiteśvara's celestial teacher Amitābha, and in so doing instituted the office of Panchen Lama. The decision was based, in part, on a *terma* that the Dalai Lama himself published.[9]

According to Trulshik Rinpoche, among the many *yi dam* of Mindroling and among the many treasures that 'Gyur med rdo rje discovered between his twenties and his death, Lord of the Dance was not the most well-known, nor the most frequently practiced. Lord of the Dance practices rather, occupied a special position at Mindroling. Considered the best of all of 'Gyur med rdo rje's many treasures, like a precious possession they were kept hidden; revealed but occasionally and to a select few. Trulshik Rinpoche likens this to not showing one's treasury to others or to the United States not sharing its nuclear secrets.

The Lord of the Dance traditions were brought from Mindroling to Rongphu Monastery by its great abbot, Ngawang Tenzin Norbu. Lord of the Dance became his *yi dam,* and hence the *yi dam* of his monastery and of his principal disciple, the present Trulshik Rinpoche.[10]

It was Ngawang Tenzin Norbu who, using the Lord of the Dance rituals (which he had edited into their present form) as a basis, founded the Mani Rimdu festival that is practiced in Solu-Khumbu today.

Although Mindroling practices form the basis of the liturgy, in creating the dances Ngawang Tenzin Norbu was more eclectic. According to Trulshik

Rinpoche, his teacher took the basis of the *'chams* from bZhad Monastery in gTsang province (gTsang bzhad dgon pa byang). To this, he added some dances from Mindroling such as the Cymbal Dance (*rol 'chams*) and his own changes and innovations.

The story of the transmission of the Lord of the Dance tradition is one of fluctuations and reversals, even ironies. A small cult at the influential monastery of Mindroling, Lord of the Dance becomes a large cult at the small monastery of Rongphu. Its most elaborate ritual, Mani Rimdu, is imported to Nepal, where the festival prospers, but the cult languishes. At the Sherpa monasteries where Mani Rimdu is performed, the festival is the only occasion Lord of the Dance rituals are practiced.

A key to understanding many of these vicissitudes—and the vicissitudes of many a deity, Tibetan and otherwise—is the sponsorship of a charismatic leader. Under the ægis of Ngawang Tenzin Norbu, Lord of the Dance prospered at Rongphu. Now, with the sponsorship of Trulshik Rinpoche, he flourishes at Thubten Chöling.

Without active sponsorship the situation is different. We have already spoken of Trulshik Rinpoche's informal survey of the state of Lord of the Dance teachings and practices in the early 1980s. In the refugee establishments of India, the cult of Lord of the Dance barely exists.[11] Books on Lord of the Dance are equally scarce. Not finding *The Light which Illumines Suchness*, the major Lord of the Dance commentary in Dharamsala, Trulshik Rinpoche presented one of his few remaining copies to H. H. the Dalai Lama. Presumably, the Lord of the Dance tradition has died out in Tibet. Thus, unless the tradition that Waddell discovered in nineteenth-century Sikkim is still alive there, the cult of Lord of the Dance does not exist outside of the Solu-Khumbu district of Nepal.[12]

Given the vastness of the Tibetan pantheon, the secrecy of the Lord of the Dance tradition at Mindroling, and its restriction to that inaccessible monastery and others under its sway, it is small wonder that the deity largely escaped the notice of foreign observers. Previous references, where they exist, are scanty.

THE SPREAD OF MANI RIMDU

Unhappily, Trulshik Rinpoche no longer is in possession of the records which fix the exact date of the first Mani Rimdu at Rongphu. In his estimation, it began there between 1907 and 1910 and moved to Solu-Khumbu about 1940.[13] Tengpoche was the first monastery in Nepal to perform the festival. Two to three years later, Chiwong gave its first performance. Only many years later did Mani Rimdu come to Thami.

Trulshik Rinpoche's recollections are in basic agreement with data collected by Luther Jerstad and Christoph von Fürer-Haimendorf. According to

Jerstad's sources, the first Tengpoche Mani Rimdu was performed in 1938.[14] The first complete Thami performance was in 1950, although the festival without the dances is said to have performed there since 1940 or 1942.[15]

At Rongphu, Mani Rimdu was performed in the fourth month. It was one of two dance festivals held at that monastery. The shorter (*mdor 'dus*) *'chams*, consisting of a *gtor rgyab* dance and a Golden Libation (*ser skyems*), was performed in the twelfth month.[16]

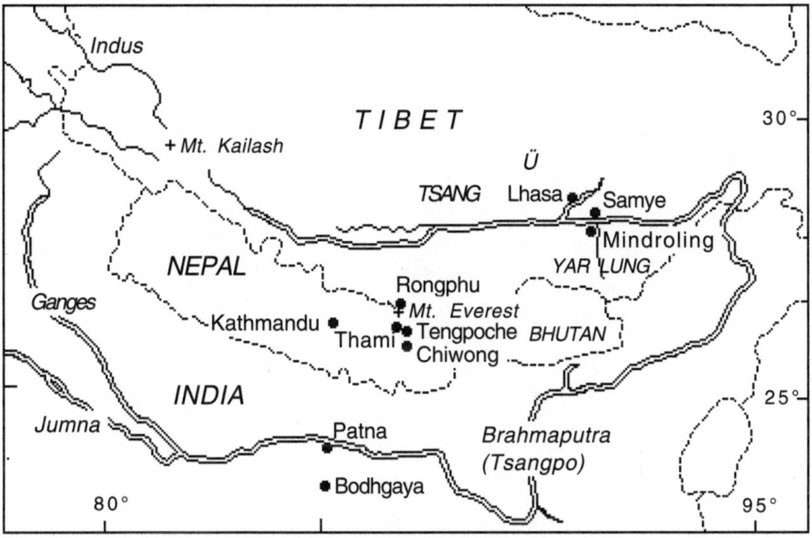

Himalayan Region[17]

6

Tibetan Religious Dance

Mani Rimdu has often been described as a "dance-drama."[1] Although, as we will see, this appellation is simplistic to the point of error, Mani Rimdu does certainly contain dance.[2]

The standard study of Tibetan sacred dance (*'chams*) is René de Nebesky-Wojkowitz's *Tibetan Religious Dances*. At the time of his research in the 1950s, Nebesky-Wojkowitz felt that it would be "premature to attempt now to undertake a profound analysis" of the subject of the origin of *'chams*. This situation has not changed in the past decades.

As Nebesky-Wojkowitz rightly suggested, one would need to first unravel the "two components" of "original Tibetan spiritual concepts and practices of Indian Tantracism."[3] This book can not hope to even begin such a task: the traditions of Mani Rimdu are too far removed from their ultimate Tibetan sources to satisfy even half of the bargain. We can, however, cast a passing glance at each side of the family tree of Tibetan sacred dance, and in the process, discuss a few of the problems that research in this field must confront.

Were we to seek the lost Indic antecedents of *'chams*, one place to look would be Kathmandu. There, the Vajrācārya, the priestly caste of Buddhist Newars, have their own tradition of sacred dance. Much of *cārya* dance is still performed in the inner recesses of Kathmandu's *bahals* (Ssk. *vihāra*), hidden from uninitiated eyes. Often, it is performed at night.

Even the most casual examination of *cārya* dance reveals elements reminiscent of Tibetan *'chams*. Some of its movements, for example, resemble the curious hopping gait of certain Tibetan dance steps. As Kathmandu is the last bastion of the type of Indian tantricism that spread to Tibet, it is likely that *cārya* dance is a granduncle if not a direct ancestor of much Tibetan dance. If it is possible to finally answer the question of Newar influence or analogs, it will only be after studies are made closely comparing the choreography and liturgy of Tibetan dance and its relatives. It is to be sincerely hoped that someone undertakes such a study before the traditions involved disappear.

Although the early history of religious dance in Tibet is still obscure, there is "sporadic evidence" to suggest that the heroes of Tibet's early bardic songs (*sgrung*) were portrayed in masked dance.[4] Ritual dances ushered in the New Year in Tibet as early as the period of the kings, and continue to do so today.[5]

The succeeding phases of the development of Tibetan ritual dance are not any clearer than the earlier ones. This is perhaps because, like the *cārya* dance of the Newars, *'chams* was originally performed in secret, at night, and barred to the uninitiated.[6]

The first Buddhist sect to perform the *'chams* in public were the Nyingma. This apparently initially received opposition from other sects, particularly the Sakya, although they, too, eventually began to perform the sacred dance for a general public.[7]

Perhaps the earliest performance of a *'chams* dated by Tibetan historians was that of the monk Lhalung Pelki Dorje, who was disguised as a lay tantric (*sngags pa*) in 842 C.E.[8] This occasion is remembered not for its importance in the history of Tibetan dance, but because Pelki Dorje used his performance of the black hat dance as a ruse to assassinate the apostate King Langdarma.

The sacred dance reached the Gelugpa tradition during the time of the fifth Dalai Lama (1617–1682).[9] Thus, as we have already suggested, *'chams* as a national phenomenon in Tibet can be laid at the door of the same remarkable figure who introduced the secret texts of Lord of the Dance to the world—the Great Fifth's Nyingma *guru* —Orgyan gTer bdag gling pa, a.k.a. 'Gyur med rdo rje.[10] It has been suggested that the famous treatise on sacred dance (*chams yig*) attributed to the Fifth Dalai Lama was in its final form actually ghost written by 'Gyur med rdo rje.[11]

It is no surprise, then, to learn that even in later times, 'Gyur med rdo rje's monastery, Mindroling was known for the lavish scale of its dances. One of these had over one hundred roles—and costumes and masks for each.[12]

Tibetan Buddhist dance today contains what is evidently pre-Buddhist material, but how similar the present tradition is to those that existed before the introduction of Buddhism to Tibet is uncertain. Such pre-Buddhist Tibetan elements as we find could have easily crept in at a later point.[13] The New Year's dancer of the royal period, for example, had little in common, in appearance at least, with the dancers of Mani Rimdu.

> On this occasion a costume was worn which vividly recalls the dress of the shamans. It was white, the hair of the head was rolled up and

held together by silver bands, protected by a turban bearing an image of a *khyung*. . . .[14]

If it is difficult to find an early precursor of *'chams* from which we might trace a clear line forward to the present, it is equally perilous to attempt to reconstruct ancient *'chams* from existing traditions. In Mani Rimdu we see some of the flexibility that makes hard and fast determination of the origin of the tradition problematic.

A good example of this is found in the dance of the local protectors—gods who are pre-Buddhist in type, if not pre-Buddhist chronologically. At Chiwong and Thami, the dance portrays Shar lung, the local god of Rongphu Monastery. At Tengpoche, the dance and the costume are identical, but the character is identified as a completely different deity, an even more parochial spirit, Zur ra rva skyes.

Even were we to assume that as an individual deity Shar lung is historically pre-Buddhist, which is by no means proven, it would be wrong to assume out of hand that the dance of Shar lung is a pre-Buddhist survival. In certain basic features, Shar lung's dance is similar to dances featuring more Buddhistic figures. The dance of Dorje Drolö (rDo rje gro lod), a manifestation of the Buddhist saint Padmasambhava, for example, also features a single deity preceded by two heralds. The action of both dances is also similar; the deity is given a chair and fed part of the feast offerings.

Into this equation, we must factor the ability of one deity to replace another. Just as Shar lung was not the last deity to occupy the leading rôle of this dance, there is no reason to assume he was the first. Given the similarities between the dances of Dorje Drolö and Shar lung, in the absence of historical data it is difficult to say whether we are looking at the survival of a pre-Buddhist performance in Buddhist guise in the former case, or a Buddhist dance tradition with some pre-Buddhist trappings in the latter.

With Zur ra rva skyes we are close enough to the source to understand his presence. The deity of a hidden valley of Khumbu, Tengpoche Rinpoche found him more relevant to his monastery than Shar lung, the god of Rongphu on the other side of Everest.[15]

Similarly, although other traditions of Tibetan sacred dance center around the god Vajrakīla, the Mani Rimdu dances, like the festival as a whole are based on the meditations on Lord of the Dance.[16] Here, once again the history is recent and clear. By all accounts, this innovation was the work of Lama Ngawang Tenzin Norbu, Abbot of Rongphu and seminal figure in the religious life of the Everest region of the last generation.

Like most things Tibetan, *'chams* has its own literary tradition. As Nebesky-Wojkowitz stated in *Oracles and Demons of Tibet*, however, such works "are extremely rare":

> The printing blocks are generally kept under seal, and copies of these texts may be printed only with the permission of the church authorities, which is difficult to obtain.[17]

Nebesky-Wojkowitz's *Tibetan Religious Dances* contains the first translation of a Tibetan dance book (*'chams yig*). This is an extraordinary asset for all those who would study *'chams*, and parallels to many features of the Mani Rimdu dances can be found in this work.

As far as Mani Rimdu itself is concerned, there is said to be no true *'chams yig* specific to the festival.[18] The closest thing to one, and that not very close, is a one or two folio "counting book" (*grangs ka*). According to one source, even this counting book is not in ordinary use at Chiwong, and the monks learn to count their steps through oral instruction.[19]

A traditional explanation of the genesis of *'chams* is that they originate in the visions of a lama. In the words of the Vajrakīla dance book,

> Especially the precious teacher (*Guru Rinpoche*) *Chos kyi dbang phyug*, the *zhabs drung Rin chen phun tshogs* of *'Bri khung* monastery and many other "discoverers of treasure books" (*gter bton*) went in their dreams to the *Zangs mdog dpal ri*. Here, having seen the performance of various dances, they kept in mind the manifold body positions they had observed and also the wonderful apparitions utilizing these for the practice of dancing.[20]

Mani Rimdu is no exception to this rule. Tengpoche Rinpoche states that Ngawang Tenzin Norbu saw the dances in meditation. He adds more prosaically, if somewhat contradictorily, that the Mani Rimdu dances "are a mixture of types from several different monasteries."[21]

Innovation and flexibility have not always been tolerated in Tibetan dance. The early eighteenth-century dance book cited above discusses an innovation of an earlier contemporary in the following terms.

> The master (*bdag po*) *sNgags 'chang* from the *Sa skya* monastery inserted into the *Phur pa smad las kyi 'chams* the Dance of the Owners of the Cemetery (*Dur khrod bdag po'i 'chams*) in order to present a new spectacle.... Perhaps it is correct—but the lamas living before his time did not practice the dance in this way, and, since he inserted this figure newly, it is not suitable to be included in the *'chams*. Nowadays, some priests not knowing anymore the way of practicing correctly the rites of Secret Mantras perform the dance as they think is suitable only to gain food and in this manner they deceive people. They think that the *'chams* is just like an ordinary play and spectacle,

and the common words which the above lama said without thinking made obvious the foolishness of his utterances.[22]

As if this were not enough, the authors of the dance book expatiate further on the subject in the concluding verses:

Those who have given up the true way of practicing this dance and have introduced their own style which is without origin,
In accordance with their imagination—such dancers could just as well perform the dance in the middle of a market.
These are people who lower the Great Secret Doctrine.[23]

The dance book here makes a categorical distinction between a valid source of inspiration (visionary dreaming) and an invalid one (imagination). It should be noted though that whether a specific innovation is praised or excoriated is often a matter of the prestige of the innovator and the eye (and/or sectarian affiliation) of the beholder. Stringent purism is standard in criticism of rivals, sectarian and otherwise.

Certainly, we should not expect innovation per se to be prized in a system where doctrines are verified by tracing them to an historical or a celestial Buddha. The visions of a noted yogi, however, are considered direct contact with the ultimate source of the tradition. No one has ever criticized Ngawang Tenzin Norbu for his rôle in founding Mani Rimdu.

Whatever *'chams* may have been in 1712 when the critique we cited was published, in Solu-Khumbu today religious dances are considered largely as a spectacle.

Some of the clerics who perform Mani Rimdu perceive this aspect of the festival to be a fault. To them, a spectacle lacks the virtues that characterize serious religious practice. Others, while not finding fault specifically with Mani Rimdu, believe that *'chams* in general has fallen from its golden age. One learned lama explained that although it is said that in ages past even the smallest gesture of the *'chams* had a meaning, nowadays, the meanings are forgotten.[24] In a smaller time frame, monks from Rongphu often claim that today's Mani Rimdu is but a pale shadow of the original festival of their homeland.

The ritual object most closely associated with the dance is, of course, the mask. In many places in the world, and Tibet is one of them, masks are held to have an inherent power, even a resident spirit.

It is said that when the seventh Karmapa saw the mask of the Mahākāla Yeshe Gonpo called "the Black Sumbha," he saw the deity in person.[25]

Pa nam dga' dgong, a Gelugpa monastery located between Gyantse and Shigatse, possessed an ancient *'chams* mask of the *yakṣa* Jinamitra, "alleged to possess supernatural qualities." Pregnant women came to see the mask "to ensure easy delivery. The principal dancer, shortly after donning the mask, is supposed to fall into a state similar to strong intoxication."[26]

In donning the mask, the dancer dons the persona of the mask. In this way, the mask defines the job of the actor or the shaman at a basic level. In the words of the eccentric Tibetan saint and folk hero Drukpa Kunlek: "They say that they are the body of Mahākāla."[27]

For Eliade, there is "a 'law' well known to the history of religions: *one becomes what one displays*. The wearers of masks *are* really the mythical ancestors portrayed by their masks."[28]

Such a conception is not alien to tantric dance. The masks of the Aṣṭamātṛkā dancers of the Kathmandu Valley are believed to possess a life of their own. As an emblem of this, they undergo a full set of Newar lifecycle rituals, from birth rites to death rites.[29]

Among the Newars of present-day Kathmandu, dancers are often considered possessed by the gods that they portray. If a dancer attacks a spectator, as they sometimes do when someone has violated the sanctity of the occasion, the assailant is restrained passively if at all. The community excuses him as possessed by the god and therefore not in control of his actions.[30]

On yet another level, the mask can be taken as a symbol for the way in which human beings assume roles in their day-to-day lives. Although this concept parallels certain currents in tantric thought, it is not an interpretation found within the tradition. The rich world of symbolism often associated with the mask is either absent in Mani Rimdu, or so totally submerged as to be nearly so. Mani Rimdu is full of instances of men assuming a divine persona, but this is done in a liturgical context and irrespective of dance and mask, the god assumed is *always* Lord of the Dance.[31]

However strange it might seem at first glance to don the mask of one god and yet imagine you are another, there is a logic to it. Since, as the fruit of Tantric yoga, one will achieve enlightenment in the form of one's chosen deity, from a strict standpoint, a yogi only assumes the identity of a god of the personal deity class (*yi dam; iṣṭadevatā*). Thus, if you ask, as I did of Trulshik Rinpoche, whether there is any self-creation (*bdag bskyed*) for the dance, the reply will come, "no, only the normal self-creation of Lord of the Dance in the daily ritual." The gods of the dance, with the exception of Dorje Drolö, who is a form of Padmasambhava, are Sworn Protectors and *not* gods a yogi seeks to become.[32]

Further, as the *Playful Ocean* makes clear, "ritual dance, and music and dance with hand gestures . . . carefully, brilliantly done" are a propitiation of the protector deities. Propitiation of the protectors, as the *Playful Ocean* makes abundantly clear, is only undertaken while visualizing oneself as the *yi dam*.[33]

With ritual logic thus militating against it, it is somewhat surprising to read in Nebesky-Wojkowitz's translation of the Vajrakīla dance book that "the dancer has to imagine himself to be whichever deity he represents and he should bear a proud and steadfast manner,"[34] or that "the art of keeping one's mind in the proper attitude—the meditation upon the deities represented in the dance has to be carried out in a clear manner and without distraction."[35] Fortunately for our theory, the interpretation that the dancer must visualize himself as the character he portrays belongs to Nebesky-Wojkowitz, not to the dance book. The Tibetan text merely states in the first case that the dancer "should firmly grasp the ego of the deity in question,"[36] and in the second "the mental art is to act inseparably from the ego and clear appearance of the creation stage deity."[37] According to internal evidence, then, the Vajrakīla dance book confirms the data that we have collected—"the deity in question" is likely none other than "the creation stage deity," the personal deity appropriate to the festival rather than the deity portrayed in any given dance. As the dance book tells us, "the wonderful *mudrā*-dance [is] done in connection with the *bskyed rim* meditation."[38] *bsKyed rim* meditation is by definition visualization of oneself as a deity of the *yi dam* class.

Trulshik Rinpoche, in fact plainly states that there is no self-creation of the characters of the dance. Instead,

> There is a reason, a necessity to each of the dances. For example, for the Golden Libation, we offer a golden elixir to the lama, the *yi dam*, the *ḍākiṇīs* and the protectors. There is no other meditation or way of thinking, except for the necessary reason. In general, however, during all the rituals from the Site Rituals on, one should think of one's body as the god (Lord of the Dance), speech as the mantra, and mind as *dharmatā*.[39]

If, in Mani Rimdu, the only god to possess the dancers is Lord of the Dance, that is not to say that Tibet has no tradition of possession by protector gods. The well-known Tibetan oracles, in fact, do just that. Interestingly, the rhetoric used to describe the possession of an oracle similar to that used in part of the creation process yoga. The god Pehar descends upon the oracle of Nechung (*lha 'bab*) just as the wisdom beings descend upon the creation process yogi (*ye shes 'bab*).[40]

Nevertheless, yogic theory aside, questions of whether other *'chams* traditions recognize possession by protector deities, or whether in the case of the masks such as "the Black Sumbha" cited above, possession by the deity is transferred from the mask to its wearer, will only finally be determined by investigation of those specific traditions. The lifetime career of a monk may be meditation, but during the days of the dance his job is as an actor. Even if, in a strict tantric sense the dancers do not visualize themselves as the gods portrayed in the dance, in a looser sense, they may. Like actors everywhere, the dancers of Mani Rimdu imagine they are the characters they portray.[41]

Actors in the West have their own culture, and a framework in which to describe their experience. Mani-Rimdu notwithstanding, the cultural framework of the Sherpa lacks a theatrical tradition and its language of theory. As Trulshik Rinpoche's comments imply, the theoretical structure of creation process yoga does not explain the assimilation of character in the dance. The data available so far suggests that at Chiwong, the performers are left pretty much to their own devices.

The one dance book that has been translated mainly describes steps, *mudrās* and ritual actions. Occasionally, however it directs the dancer to simulate an emotion. Thus, we read "act . . . as if frightened" (*bred tshul gyi*) or "act as if unable to look at the corpse." Sometimes these directions become quite specific: "In order to act as if being in doubt and wanting to see if the corpse is dead or not, one lifts the heels slightly and raises oneself somewhat upward."[42]

When an actor is really in character, an audience can see it. On the day of the "dance rehearsal," it becomes clear that best Sherpa performers portray their characters effectively without the aid of elaborate costumes or masks, or the underpinning of an elaborated performance theory.

7

The Officiants

Most of the Mani Rimdu rituals are performed by the entire monastic assembly, or at least as many of them as are necessary and/or available at a given time. The texts often refer to the assembly as the "two center rows," the *gzhung gral gnyis*.[1] The term refers to the two long benches that form the center of the typical monastic assembly hall (*'dus khang*). The right hand row is headed by the Chant Leader (*dbu mdzad*). It is he who initiates the prayers and keeps the rhythm going. He is also the conductor of the monastery orchestra, leading the musicians with his cymbals.

At the head of the left hand row is the seat of the monastery's most important functionary, the Diamond Master. It is he who performs the key ritual operations and gives instructions to the chant leader. Some rituals, such as the preparation of the *lingka*, or the site ritual for the Burnt Offering, are performed by the Diamond Master alone.

The title Diamond Master (Tib., *rdo rje slob dpon;* Ssk., *vajrācārya*) is ambiguous. It refers to both the officiant of a given ritual and the monastic functionary who normally performs that task. It also indicates the perfect tantric teacher, one who can, in the words of the liturgy, blow "the auspicious conch of religious teaching" for his disciples "in harmony with their varied inclinations."[2]

Among the Buddhist Newars of Kathmandu, where the indigenous monkhood was secularized centuries ago, the function of Diamond Master became hereditary and Vajrācārya, a family name.

According to Trulshik Rinpoche, in large monasteries in Tibet such as Mindroling, the lama rarely performed day-to-day ritual tasks, and the position of Diamond Master was assimilated to that of Diamond Deputy (*rdo rje rgyal tshab*).

At a medium-sized monastery, like Rongphu or Thubten Chöling however, the lama who heads the monastery (and who is usually the incarnation of the previous head of the monastery) often performs the duties of Diamond Master himself, although an official by that name may also be present. At Thubten Chöling, for many years Sang Sang Tulku has been the official Diamond Master. At Chiwong, which has no incarnate lamas, the position goes to the senior monk, who is invested with a small ceremony.

At a small monastery the Diamond Master performs other functions that would be the job of a separate official at a larger institution. In the literature, we sometimes read of *'chams dpon* (dance masters). At Chiwong the job of instructing the monks in dance goes to the Diamond Master.

In our context, the Diamond Master of a ritual is normally the official by that name; he belongs to the monastery performing the ritual. Because of the ambiguity of the rôle, however, this is subject to change. Chiwong has no resident lama of its own at present. When Trulshik Rinpoche arrives at Chiwong for Mani Rimdu, or when Sang Sang Tulku is there alone, as ranking lama, he preempts the position of *vajrācārya*.[3]

If the Diamond Master is paired with the Chant Leader by facing him across the aisle, in many other contexts he has another partner, the ritual assistant, or Diamond Actor (*las kyi rdo rje*, *karmavajra*). This title has some of the same ambiguities as that of Diamond Master. On the one hand it may refer to someone assisting at a single given ritual. On the other, it may refer to someone who serves as assistant on a regular basis. Next to the Diamond Master, the Diamond Actor is the rituals' most active participant. It is he who hands the Diamond Master the appropriate ritual implement. It is he who holds the offerings up to the altar, and who removes them at the prescribed moment.

At Chiwong, the Diamond Actor is usually quite young, twelve years old or so. At Thubten Chöling, the Diamond Actor tends to be a few years older. If this pair of officiant and assistant form the core of the monastic ritual it is because they personify the basic pair of spiritual traditions everywhere, the master and the disciple. In some contexts, such as drawing the *maṇḍala*, the text refers to the pair specifically as such.

That we find the term here is no accident. This ritual recreates an archetypal moment in the tantric tradition—the master and disciple together creating the *maṇḍala* of initiation. This is the time and place where the tradition will be passed to the next generation, and in more than one sense, the world will be changed.

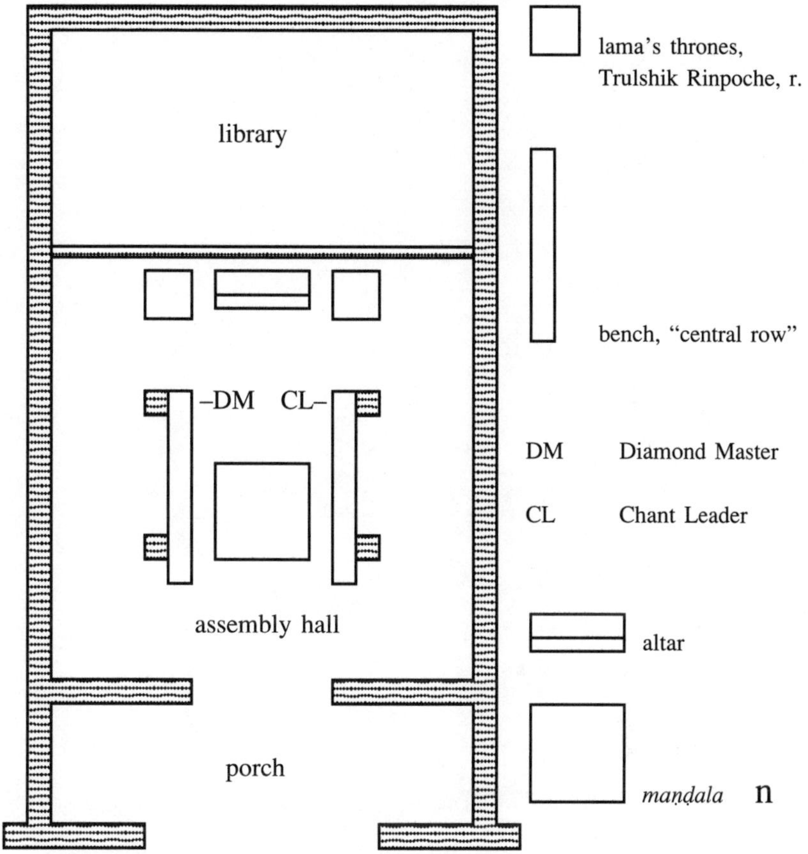

Chiwong Assembly Hall[a]
(not to scale)
showing seat placement

[a]Plan based on John Sanday Consultants International 1982: Dwg. 11C/14.

Part Two

The Days

8

The Days

Although Mani Rimdu actually starts weeks earlier, the villagers of Solu-Khumbu only know its public days of empowerment and dance. Some, if they have been laggard in leaving, may have witnessed the Burnt Offering that is performed on the day following the dance. Western writers, too, usually count Mani Rimdu as three or four days long. This suggests, in fact, that they have based their work on interviews with villagers, or on one another.[1]

For the monks who perform Mani Rimdu, however, the festival is at least a two week affair. In the lunar calendar of Tibet, the last day of each month, the thirtieth, is the dark of the moon and the fifteenth, the full moon. Traditionally, they say that Mani Rimdu begins on the dark of the moon, what Tibetans call the "full sky," the last day of the preceding month.

Since the festival at Chiwong is normally held in the tenth month, the first day is officially the thirtieth day of the ninth Tibetan month (T9/30). Thami holds the festival in the fourth month, as did Rongphu just across the Nangpala Pass in Tibet.[2] Thus, the first day of Mani Rimdu at Thami is the "full sky" day of the third month.

At Tengpoche, although Mani Rimdu originally had the same dates as Chiwong, in recent years the festival has been performed a month earlier. Thus, the festival there begins either on the dark of the moon of the eighth month or the first day of the ninth month. Tengpoche Rinpoche gives several reasons for the change: the coldness of the weather in the tenth month, water shortages, and the difficulty of coming for both locals and foreigners at that time. He adds that the H.M.G. office in charge of the guest house at the monastery has requested that they make the change, doubtless an important factor. It should be noted that Tengpoche is directly on the tourist route, and that for the past two decades, tourists have formed the majority of festival goers there. Since the ninth month is high season, tourist dollars were undoubtedly a factor in making the change.[3]

At Chiwong most years, the festival actually begins a few days after the official date. This is possible because several of the first days are devoted to the manufacture of ritual objects. The process, in and of itself, is relatively free of ritual constraint and can be expanded or contracted liberally.

Other parts of the schedule are also subject to alteration. At Chiwong in 1980, for example, the last two days of the festival were compressed into a single back breaking day to allow Trulshik Rinpoche, to return to his home monastery early. Subject, like the calendar itself, to pressures astrological and otherwise, the schedule of an ideal Mani Rimdu is seldom if ever adhered to with total precision.[4] In the chart that follows, the first column numbers the days of an idealized Chiwong performance.

MANI RIMDU SCHEDULE

		Tibetan Calendar Dates						
		Chiwong					*Thami*	
Day	Primary Ritual	1980	1982	1983	1984	1986	1980	1983
0	Preparing the Effigy	—	—	—	30	—	—	—
1	Site Ritual	2	2	*30*	1	—	30	30
1	Reception Ritual	2	2	*30*	1	—	1	1
2–5	Making Maṇḍala	3–4	3–4	*1–5*	2–4	—	1–4	1–4
5	Making Tormas	4	4	4–5	5	—	4	4
5	Arranging Ornaments	4	4	5	5	—	4	4
6–12	Daily Rituals	5–14	5–14	6–14	6–14	—	5–9	5–9
13	Dance Rehearsal	14	14	14	14	15_1^*	9	9
14	Public Empowerment	15	15	15*	15*	15_2	10	11†
15	Masked Dance	16	16	16*	16*	16	11	12†
16	Burnt Offering	17	17	17*	17*	17	12	13†
17	Invitation to River	17	18	18*	18*	18	13	14†

(*) In 1983, the tenth Tibetan month had two eighth days, and in 1984, two twelfths. The chart above is *not* adjusted to reflect the numbering of a "normal" Tibetan month. Thus, the fifteenth day of the month is counted as the fourteenth and so on, as it was in the Tibetan calendars published that year. In 1986, there was no seventh, but both the fourteenth and the fifteenth were called the "fifteenth," so that the calendar returned to "normal" on that day. These two fifteenths are indicated by subscripts. Duplication of numerals indicates that two events occur on the same day, not that identically numbered days occurred in sequence.

(†) In 1983, the fourth month had no tenth. Once again, the dates have not been adjusted.

Italics indicate data provided by informants.

(—) A dash indicates that no data was available.

The recognized astrologers and numerologists who prepare the Tibetan calendar each year do considerable tinkering to maximize the auspicious days and avoid the unlucky ones. Examining the relationship between the ritual and the Tibetan calendar (for all its vagaries), several things become obvious. The first is that Mani Rimdu at Chiwong is longer than at Thami. At Chiwong, it typically lasts seventeen days, at Thami, fourteen. The second is that Chiwong seems to follow the official calendar, whereas Thami apparently ignores calendrical irregularities.

More significantly however, we notice that at Thami, the entire performance occurs during the waxing of the moon; whereas at Chiwong, the festival waxes and wanes with the moon, reaching its climax when the moon is full.

When Tibetans discuss rituals, they often divide them into four classes: pacifying, extending, magnetizing, and destroying.[5] The first two are positive acts, and are said to be most efficacious if performed with the waxing moon. The second, negative pair should be performed with the waning moon. As a by and large positive and constructive ritual, it is appropriate that Mani Rimdu be performed with the waxing moon. In the parabolic trajectory of the Chiwong Mani Rimdu, the most negative days, the undoing of the protective circle and the erasure of the sand *maṇḍala*, take place during the waning of the moon, on the day of the burnt offering. The other destructive ritual, preparing the effigy, which we will discuss in a moment, occurs at the last moment of the waning moon preceding Mani Rimdu. In a thirty-day lunar month, the last day of the waxing moon is the fifteenth, the first day of the waning moon, the sixteenth. Logically then, the ceremony that falls on the fifteenth, the empowerment, should be the climax of Mani Rimdu. In fact, the lamas who preside over Mani Rimdu consider it so, and the dances on the sixteenth, a celebration of that achievement. According to Trulshik Rinpoche, the most important thing is the practice (*sgrub pa*) that begins with the site ritual and ends with the ceremony called "taking the true achievement." The dance is less important. It is just a celebration (*dga' ston*) and a thanksgiving for the achievement (*sgrub pa'i gtang rag*). In his terms, the practice is fundamental (*rtsa ba*); the dance and the burnt offering are secondary (*yan lag*).[6]

Trulshik Rinpoche goes so far as to say that the dances are unnecessary. Recently, he has backed up that claim. The Mani Rimdu he has instituted at Thubten Chöling is similar to the Chiwong performance in every detail but one. It has no dances.[7] Ironically, the whole of Mani Rimdu has become known in the West exactly for what the lamas think is the least important part of it. The first book about Mani Rimdu, wrttten by an American mountaineer in 1969, was subtitled a "Sherpa Dance-Drama."

9

Day Zero: Exorcism

Paper *lingka* from Thubten Chöling Monastery (*enlarged detail*)

Late in the night before the first day, the ranking monk—at Chiwong this would normally be the resident Diamond Master—makes a pair of ritual implements essential to Mani Rimdu, indeed to Tibetan sacred dance.[1] This ceremony, done in private, is called "Activating the Lingka." The day of activating the *lingka* is not normally counted as part of Mani Rimdu, or even discussed. Indeed, it was not until I had studied Mani Rimdu for more than five years that I observed the rite or even heard it mentioned. Thus, I have called this day "Day Zero."

The classic work on the subject of the *lingka* is R. A. Stein's 1957 article, "The Liṅga of Lamaist Masked Dance and the Theory of Souls."[2] Mani Rimdu amply demonstrates Stein's thesis that the *lingka* is the central object of Tibetan masked dance. The *lingka* is more than that, however. It is a *leitmotiv* that runs throughout the whole of Mani Rimdu.

The *lingka* is the symbol of the enemy of religion—be it conceived as internal or external: as passions or as demons. *Lingka* or *liṅga* is a Sanskrit word, familiar to readers of the *Kāmasūtra* in its significance of "penis." There may be a certain psychological sense to a group of celibate monks taking a word that means "penis" and using to mean "enemy of religion." In the rituals under discussion, however, Tibetans take the word in its other meaning of "person, mark or sign."[3]

The *lingka* makes a pair with a better known Tibetan ritual implement, the *phurbu*, the magic dagger or nail. So interrelated are these two, that Trulshik Rinpoche says that they "have the same meaning." As emptiness implies relativity; darkness, light; *yin, yang;* the *lingka* implies the *phurbu*. The *lingka* is there to be stabbed by the dagger; the demon is there to be transformed by the exorcist; just as, in a sense, *saṁsāra* is there to be transformed into *nirvāṇa*. The lama, the exorcist, does not travel without his dagger. In Mani Rimdu, a *lingka* is assassinated three times each day.[4]

As with most Tibetan rituals, "Activating the Lingka" can be done with varying degrees of elaboration. If the ceremony is done the long way, it is said to take a full seven days, but it can be done in four sessions, or if necessary, even in a single session the night before the rites in which the *lingka* is used begin.[5] The latter is the custom at Chiwong.

Although several different types of *lingka* are used in Mani Rimdu, the "activating" ceremony is only performed for the two paper effigies. One will be buried in the courtyard during the "Site Rituals" on the following day. The other will be put under the sand *maṇḍala* and used in the ritual of "Suppressing the Gnomes" that is performed twice each day of the festival. The second *lingka* also figures in the "Liberation Dance" performed during the public part of the festival. This appearance and reappearance of the *lingka* in different guises, and in rituals of less or more elaboration and less or more theatricality, is one of the most fascinating features of Mani Rimdu.

One, or, at some monasteries, two other types of *lingka* are found in the masked dance. The first is the effigy that the skeleton-costumed Lords of the Cemetery abuse during the Liberation Dance. This *lingka* is a floppy, long-limbed cloth doll about two feet in length. It is a dirty grey in color, perhaps originally white. It is entirely featureless. Its hands have no fingers; its feet, no toes. Its face is smooth, without eyes or mouth, nose, or ears. It is bound with ropes. Unlike the other *lingkas*, it is not destroyed, but reused year after year.

The third type of *lingka* is fashioned from the sort of dough used to make offering cakes. This type appears in the sword dance at Thami and Tengpoche, but is not used at Chiwong. Like the paper *lingkas*, it is an anthropomorphic figure of a gnome in chains. At Thami, the figure is approximately six inches in length. Its face has rudimentary features, modelled of dough and applied to the surface. Its chains are represented by a simple strip of dough laced over one leg and under the other. It has a small round concave well in its chest, covered over by a round lid also made of dough.

On the day of the dance, the figure is hidden beneath the courtyard altar until it is needed. It is then placed on the ground of the courtyard, where the dancers dismember it with swords. The dough effigy at Thami is made casually during the course of the ritual fortnight, and seems to require no special ceremony to fit it for service. Similarly, the cloth effigy does not figure in the ceremonies on the dark of the moon.[6]

The paper effigies used in Mani Rimdu are three inch squares of hand-made paper, with the image of a gnome in chains block printed on it. The examples that I have seen were printed at Thubten Chöling, but given the small size and general utility of such an item, blocks probably exist at other monasteries in Solu-Khumbu as well. The Thubten Chöling block is so well-carved that, even printed on rough local paper, many fine details are visible.

The image of the gnome is printed diagonally on the paper, encased in a 1 11/16 x 2 1/8 inch rectangle. The gnome's hair stands on end and his forehead is wrinkled. Open-mouthed, his expression suggests fear and dismay. His hands are behind his back and his arms are chained at the elbow. He crouches, knees bowed. Naked, his penis hangs down close to the heavy chains about his ankles. The four syllables of the mantra "jaḥ hūṁ baṁ hoḥ" are on his right shoulder, left shoulder, right knee, and left knee, respectively. As the ritual indicates, the syllable "tri," his seed syllable is at his heart. It is surrounded by the mantra, "ya ma dam sri suṁbhani jaḥ jaḥ."

The ceremony which activates the paper effigies has several parts. The first part is "Washing the Lingka" with the five elements. The physical actions are done by a ritual assistant caled the Diamond Actor, while the officiating Diamond Master recites the liturgy and does the visualizations. There are five sets of actions. Each is accompanied by a specific mantra and repeated twenty-one times.

WASHING THE *LINGKA*

	Action	*Mantra*
1.	sky gesture	e wa shuddhi shuddhi
2.	throwing earth on it	lam ho shuddhi shuddhi
3.	sprinkling water	wam ho shuddhi shuddhi
4.	waving a torch[a]	ram ho shuddhi shuddhi
5.	fanning air with a fan	yam ho shuddhi shuddhi

[a] The torch may be either a burning piece of thorn wood (*tsher shing*) or a small oil soaked torch. SST

In the second part, the officiants break the gnome's joints. This is done to both *lingkas*. According to Sang Sang Tulku, this may be accomplished either by folding the paper on every joint: neck, arms, and so forth; or by pasting the *lingka* on a goat's shoulder bone. In the case of the gnome effigy, the folding method is used. As will be seen later, the second method is used in Mani-Rimdu for an effigy of the Lord of Death (Tib., gShin rje; Ssk., Yama) used in the ceremony of "Purifying the Door" in the Site Ritual of Day One.

The Chant Leader of Thubten Chöling describes the making of the *lingka*, as I have observed it at Chiwong:

> First, the paper is pleated on the edge into a pear shape, with the head at the point. Then, it is bound near the hands and then near the head. A long cord is left at the head to lead to the sand *maṇḍala*. It is also acceptable for it to go to the leg of the *maṇḍala* table. The *phurbu* work is easy manually, but for us, very difficult mentally. It is Rinpoche's work.

The first *lingka*, the one used in the Site Ritual on the following day, is singled out for special treatment in the next set of actions. It is wrapped in a black cloth and then tied with a black string.[7] The second *lingka*, which will go underneath the *maṇḍala* table, is only tied with a black string. The two effigies are placed in a black triangular iron box. This box represents the fathomless slippery-sided pit in which the rituals imprison them.

These physical preparations complete, the recitations begin. First the officiant assumes the identity of Lord of the Dance and transforms the world into his paradise.[8]

> In the Truth Realm's pure natural *maṇḍala*
> Are victorious Great Compassion's divine hosts.
> Their bodies are a field of bodies of the light of appearance,
> emptiness and bliss.

Their voices are empty sounds — the song of incantation, the sound of mantras.
Their minds' nature—the pure from the first, unchanging Truth Realm.
Single-minded admiration of you gods
So long served and summoned, makes your bodies clear.
When we urge your holy streams of consciousness with melodious voiced incantations,
Bestow natural empowerment and true achievement! [18b3]

Next, This is followed in turn by:

- The Golden Libation *(ser skyems)*
- Creating (i.e., visualizing) the lingka *(ling ka bskyed pa)*
- Attracting the Gnomes *(dam sri 'gug pa)*. This is done by unfurling the *yab tar* scarf twenty-one times.
- Casting mustard seeds

The first two of these items follow short texts that are used again and again throughout Mani Rimdu. The Golden Libation, a common offering used in a variety of contexts, employs a special set of equipment consisting of a ewer, a chalice, and a shallow bowl. The officiant fills the chalice with saffron-colored liquid from the ewer, and then pours it out, either into the bowl or directly onto the ground. Our Golden Libation takes its text from the *Knowledge Holders' Root Tantra* and customizes it for Lord of the Dance [9]

O Knowledge Bearers, holy main and lineage Lamas,
And Union of the Blissful, omnipresent peaceful and wrathful god,
And most of all, Lord of the Dance Great Compassion's divine assembly,
Take this Golden Libation, and create legions of magic yogic powers!

O Virtuous One, O brother Great God and Guardian Mother sister, and you others
With your obedient servants, slaves and emissaries,
Take this Golden Libation, and create legions of magic yogic powers!

O Mantra Bearer, protector of my family;
And Lord who dwells in this land, in this part of the world;
O God of Empowerment—this year, month, day, hour, minute—
Take this Golden Libation, and create legions of magic yogic powers!

In the tantric Mahāyāna ideology of Tibet, the magic powers that the officiant requests are to be used in the compassionate service of living beings. The highest magic power, the greatest trick of all, is enlightenment.

The next acts deal with the lingka itself. Visualizing the lingka follows a short work called *Gnomes / Spying Ghosts* (*Dam sri nyul len*). It is of a class of rituals so commonly committed to memory that finding a printed version can be difficult. This version is from a handwritten manuscript collected at Thubten Chöling.[10] The officant summons "tribe of spying demons, the ghosts who interrupt achievement and lead it astray" into a sacrificial pit, "broad and profoundly deep."[11] He locks the fingers of both hands in the hook gesture (*lcags kyu rgya*). Reciting the mantra "tri yaṁ jaḥ tri diamond hook jaḥ hūṁ baṁ hoḥ," he "hooks" the ghosts and draws them to the pit.

The *yab tar*, or "silk scarf" is a square of fabric resembling the cloths with which Tibetans wrap their books. It is ornamented on three of its corners with a short ribbon. The fourth corner is tied to a *vajra*. The officiant flings the *yab tar* out in front of him to unfurl it and then rolls it up again. He usually repeats this sequence three times.

The purpose of the *yab tar* is clear. It is to summon the being beckoned by the ritual. The gesture is interpreted variously. According to some, it is a simple beckoning. In the *Playful Ocean* for instance, "The multi-colored silk scarf with which we beckon flutters as it moves."[12] According to others, the scarf flicks dust from the deities' eyes.[13] The "silk scarves" I have seen are made of cotton. The most common variety of *yab tar* is black, in keeping with the ferocity of the beings which it will beckon, and about two feet square.

The mustard seeds are used in the final segment of the ritual of the Spying Ghosts. They are kept in a carved horn called a "mustard weapon" or "mustard sickle" (*yung zor*). In casting them at the effigy, the officiant imagines that the seeds are boulders that batter the "one imagined" into submission.[14] The mantra for the mustard seeds, "oṁ hrīḥ vajrakrotahayagriva hulu hulu hūṁ phaṭ," invokes the horse-headed god Hayagrīva, the fierce power that dwells at the heart of compassion.

After stoning the effigies, the officiant performs a protector ritual. In typical Tibetan fashion there are three alternatives. The longest of the three makes use of the entire *Playful Ocean*, Mindroling Monastery's full, one-hundred-fifty-page protector ritual which invokes nine separate protector deities, each with a voluminous entourage, plus, of course, the tenth cycle of deities dictated by Rongphu custom, the Long Life Goddesses connected with the high Himālaya. A more moderate alternative uses a much shorter text *The General Torma for the Sworn Ones* (*Dam can spyi gtor*), abridging that text even further to propitiate only the deities known as the "Four New Treasures" (*gter gsar bzhi*): Four Faced One (Zhal bzhi); Guardian of Mantra (sNgags srung ma); Great God (Lha chen); Cemetery Goddess (Dur lha). The shortest option consists of propitiating Great God alone.

Following the propitiation, the ceremony of "Activating the Lingka" concludes with the final rituals from the *Union of the Blissful Manual*.[15]

The *lingka* represents different things at different points of the ritual. During the daily "Suppressing the Gnomes," it represents a *nyul len*, a spying ghost or a *dam sri*, a gnome. The *nyul len* are spirits that sneak about monasteries and interfere with religious observances.[16] The *dam sri* are members of the large and varied *sri* class of demons, which includes such loathsome specimens of supernatural fauna as demons that specialize in eating children. According to Giuseppe Tucci, the *dam sri* are specifically demons of death who "seduce away" the life and breath "of man, so that he falls ill and dies."[17]

Lama Tharchin states that when someone breaks a major vow, it can give birth to *dam sri*. Since these gnomes creep around and disturb meditators, they are also called *nyul len*, "those who creep" or "Spying Ghosts." This is not to say, however, that the tradition considers the gnomes invoked and killed to be mere symbols for psychological forces. They are sentient beings. In a segment of the Site Ritual virtually identical to the Spying Ghost rite, the text specifically states that "the family of *yama* gnomes" that it draws into the lingka are "unrighteous sentient beings."[18]

In *Oracles and Demons of Tibet*, Nebesky-Wojkowitz spends some time discussing the *sri* in general and the *dam sri* in particular. In his estimation, the *sri* are a native Tibetan class of deities of considerable antiquity.[19] Nebesky-Wojkowitz gives several different, but equally complicated accounts of the *sri* and their many subdivisions.

Pema Garwangtsel (Padma gar dbang rtsal) gives a particularly elaborate history of the *sri*.[20] According to his mythological schema, there seem to be four generations of *sri*, the last of which were born from the "thirteen eggs of existence." These eggs figure in origin myths of several different classes of spirits.

> . . . in the so-called "*sri*-country of nine continents" (*Sri yul gling dgu*), in the castle of the *sri* which consists of piled up skulls, there came forth the first ancestors of the *sri*. They were the "sky *sri*" (*gnam sri*) *Gal* and *Gel*, and the "earth *sri*" (*sa sri*) Cha ma mtsho dgu. Then originated the so-called *Ya ma dam sri*— who took their origin from men who had broken their oath—and the female *Ma nges dgu shor*, who came into existence out of women who had adhered to heretic teachings. As the next came into existence the father of the *sri*, called *"gNam gyi bya nag gshog chags*," "the black bird of the sky with the broken wing," and their mother, whose name was *Sa yi byi gshog*, "the winged earth-rat." Out of the union of these two, the "thirteen eggs of existence" (*srid pa'l sgo lnga bcu gsum*) originated.[21]

As Padma gar dbang rtsal's account continues, a different type of *sri* hatches from each of these eggs. Each has a human body and the head of a different animal. Some types had a characteristic abode, such as the points of weapons; others were responsible for a special form of mischief, such as arranging "that a person absent from home might suffer while away some damage to its reputation." From one egg came beings " . . . which had human bodies but the heads of pigs. They chose the points where three valleys meet as their abode; to these the name *dam sri* was given."[22]

It will be noted that Padma gar dbang rtsal gives the name *dam sri* to creatures of two separate generations. The first are the *Ya ma dam sri*. They are of human origin, and mediate between the first cosmological sky and earth-born ancestors and the bird and rat parents of the egg-born *sri*. Examining the *lingka* used in Mani Rimdu once more, we find that it is identified in the inscription as a *Ya ma dam sri*. The *sri* it portrays has a human head. While Padma gar dbang rtsal does not specify what the *Ya ma dam sri* look like, a human head would be fitting, given their human origin.

Whatever their form, class, or origin, one thing is clear: the *sri* must be suppressed. According to Tucci, this was the work of a special class of Bon priest called the *dur gshen*, the Cemetery Butchers.[23] According to Toussaint, Padmasambhava subdued the *dam sri* at Zul phug, at So ha, and in Nepal.[24]

There are ways of averting the *sri* demons other than the type of ceremony used in Mani Rimdu. One involves calling upon Padmasambhava in his fierce demon subduing form of rDo rje gro lod "Diamond Sagging Belly."[25] "The most efficacious method" recalls the animal-head imagery seen in the origin myth of the *sri*. It is to

> . . . bury or set out the skulls of men and animals which have been filled with slips of paper inscribed with magic spells. The kinds of skulls, the spells, and the nature of the place to which the skulls should be brought vary according to which particular class of *sri* should be defeated.[26]

The specific method prescribed for the *dam sri* is to "bury the skulls of a lynx, jackal, dog, goat, or pig in the center of an uninhabited place."[27]

The effigy of the *sri* will be assassinated twice each day of Mani Rimdu, close to the end of both the morning and afternoon sessions. During the daily tantric feast, a different set of enemies is drawn into the *lingka*, one whose murder would not trouble even the most literal-minded Buddhist. These are "the enemies and obstructors, who are the five poisons of ignorance." These are fittingly liberated "into the realm of wisdom free from thought!" [UB 22b1]

Recalling the article by R. A. Stein with which we started this chapter, we might ask what the *lingka* represents in its most famous rôle, when it appears in the vortex of the masked dance to be killed by the black-hatted *mantri* magicians?

A logical place to look is in the rituals that Trulshik Rinpoche performs with the paper effigy as the magicians torment its cloth counterpart on the dance floor. Here, in the dance of liberation, we find both rituals performed. In the first, as in today's ritual, the effigy represents the malevolent *dam sri.* In the second, it represents the ultimate enemy of Buddhists, the "poisons of ignorance."

If there is no moral problem attached to killing ignorance, how killing a *lingka* that represents a life form "can be justified in line with Buddhist philosophy," is a question that even Stein prefers to "abstain from examining."[28] Trulshik Rinpoche, on the other hand, feels no such reticence. Looking you straight in the eye, he says "if I killed *you*, and sent your spirit (*rnam shes*) to paradise (*zhing khams*), you couldn't say that I had *hurt* you, could you?"

The assassination of the *lingka* can be examined from a number of vantage points, and Trulshik Rinpoche's candor itself relates to a complex of factors. One is the oft observed moral relativism of Mahāyāna Buddhist philosophy. In earlier Buddhist philosophy, the act was paramount. Earlier Buddhist philosophers, for example, maintained that a monk should not endanger his vow by rescuing a drowning woman. The Mahāyāna position counts motivation as more important than physical act, and thus asks such questions as, "Is it a sin to steal a weapon from a madman?" and concludes that it is not if the motivation is to help rather than to harm.

This moral problem is so thorny, that as the Thubten Chöling Chant Leader said above, dealing with the *lingka* "is Rinpoche's work." In a similar vein, Sang Sang Tulku cited the oft cited tantric proverb, that on the tantric path, like a snake trapped in a bamboo, there is no room to move side to side; you go either straight up or straight down—straight up to heaven or straight down to hell. Although the gnome is a demon (*bdud*), a sentient being (*sems can*), the young lama continued, if he is killed with *bodhicitta* and his spirit is sent to paradise, there is no fault.

This moral standard does not, of course, operate in a vacuum. It is immersed in a world view in which not only does the universe teem with unseen supernatural entities, but one in which magic works. Hence, first, entities such as the spying ghosts exist and paradise exists; second, an adept in magic can separate out a ghost's consciousness non-traumatically and lead it to paradise. In this world view, the assassination of the *lingka* is not just a moral question, it is a practical consideration as well. Does the officiant have the magical and spiritual power to do it?

This is the framework in which Trulshik Rinpoche makes his point. Discussing what at the time was a recent event, the assassination of Indira Gandhi (which he abhorred), he observed, "If you can raise someone from the dead, then it may be alright to kill him. If you can send his spirit (*rnam shes*) to paradise, then it may be alright to kill him. If you cannot, it is not."

Trulshik Rinpoche is considered to be the incarnation of dPal gyi rdo rje of Lhalung, Tibet's most famous political assassin. Assassination is obviously a subject to which he has given some thought.

The life of Guru Chos dbang (1212–1270) provides another example. Once the great Nyingma Treasure Master demonstrated his magical powers by killing a hare and conducting its spirit to paradise. Describing the event, his biographer concludes that since the guru had "only killed the body which had come about by force of its *karma* and the five poisons and transferred the awareness component of the dead being to the dynamic centre of being-as-such (*chos-nyid-kyi klong*) . . . he had brought transmigration to an end. This was the most marvellous deed of 'killing and rescuing' (*gsad-gso*) that had ever been done."[29]

If killing visible beings is a thorny issue, supernatural assassination, it seems, is a subject on which everyone in Tibetan societies can agree, irrespective of level of education or intellectual sophistication. The texts claim that it can and should be done, and such, too, is the popular belief. Thus, a villager calls on the lama to deal with the supernatural; a ritual expert like the Chant Leader of Thubten Chöling says that murder on the supernatural plane is the prerogative of the lama; and the lama himself, the consummate professional, defines the problem not just in terms of morality, but in terms of professional competence.

This function of the lama as guide for the spirits of the departed is, of course, part of his wider social function in the community. He is also the guide par excellence of the spirits of the dead. A related rôle, that of guide of the spirits of sacrificial victims is part of the shamanic heritage. The Ugrian shaman, for example, does not kill the sacrificial victim,

> he is concerned only with the mystical itinerary of the sacrificed animal. The reason is plain: the shaman knows the road and, in addition, he has the ability to control and escort a "soul," whether that of a man or of a sacrificial victim.[30]

For the lama, as for the shaman, the trades of guide for the spirits of the departed men and for the spirits of the victims of sacrifice are closely allied.

As for the primacy of the assassination of the *lingka* among a lama's duties, at Mani Rimdu no clearer evidence need be given than Trulshik Rinpoche's schedule on the day of the dance. The lama, usually absent for most of the dances, makes his appearance just before the Liberation Dance and his exit immediately after it.

Despite a radical difference in the motivation for using them, it seems obvious that there is a structural similarity between the rituals of the *lingka* and black magic, and between the *lingka* and other magical substitutes. Nebesky-Wojkowitz gives a fascinating account of a ritual in which Mahākāla is invoked to murder an enemy. Much of it will seem familiar to a student of more benign rituals. All of the words that I have italicized below are elements also found in one or another of the *lingka* rituals of Mani Rimdu.

> To perform the ceremony at which Mahākāla is to be requested to kill someone, the sorcerer must put on a *black ritual garment* and a *broad brimmed hat* of the same color. He then stands a small table covered with the hide of a tiger or a human skin under a canopy of human skins. On the table he places three stones, and on these a shallow metal bowl containing five little piles of black grains mixed with blood. A small *triangular* platform is erected in front of this table, bearing in its center *a drawing of the victim*. On this platform is placed *an iron basin* containing a torma. The torma consists of dark flour mixed with blood and charred remains from a funeral pyre. Round this offering-cake are set various foodstuffs beloved of the demonic gods—onions, garlic, human flesh and beakers of freshly brewed beer. Finally, the *iron pan must be enveloped in black silk* and fresh entrails.
>
> Various other magic aids are then placed around the triangular platform: for example, a *figure* modelled from earth on which the victim left his footprint. A skull-bowl filled with black and white *mustard seeds*. Powdered medicines and iron dust from a smithy is also effective. Not until all these preparations have been made does the sorcerer begin, at the astrologically propitious hour, with the reading of the appropriate *ritual books*. [31]

It should be no cause for astonishment, then, that the proper use of exorcism can slide into abuse. The Tibetan tradition warns of the twin pitfalls of becoming obsessed with the supernatural and of spiritual chicanery. The outspoken nineteenth-century lama, Patrul Rinpoche, a frequent critic of spiritual abuse, remarked in a slightly different context:

> People today who claim to be practitioners of Chö do not understand any of this, and persist in thinking of spirits as something outside themselves. They believe in demons, and keep on perceiving them all the time; in everything that happens they see some ghost or *gyalgong*. They have no peace of mind themselves, and are always bewildering others with their lies, delivered with much assertive blustering:
>
> "There's a ghost up there! And down there, too, a spirit! That's a ghost! That's a demon! That's a *tsen*! I can see it . . . Ha!—I've got it, I've killed it! Watch out, there's one lying in wait for you! I've chased it away! There—it looked back!"

"If you cut your belief in demons at the root from within," he remarks, "you will perceive everything as pure, and, as the saying goes: Demons change into Dharma protectors, and those protectors' faces change into the face of the nirmanakaya."[32]

The *phurbu* itself has long been of importance in Tibetan culture. It figures in myths relating to the creation of Tibet, in which Tibet itself is the body of a demoness nailed down with magic spikes.[33] The function of the lama as bearer of the *phurbu* may be related in part to the to the pre-Buddhist Tibetan shaman's role as wielder of the sacrificial knife.[34]

This is not to say that the *phurbu* is a Tibetan invention. A Dunhuang account has Padmasambhava himself bringing *phur bu* (Ssk. *kīla*) rituals to Tibet from the great monastery of Nālandā in India. We also find mention, albeit brief, of the deity Vajrakīla in the canon and in the *Guhyasamāja-tantra* (8th century), and at least some use of the *kīla* among present-day Newar *vajrācārya*.[35]

The history and origin of the myths and symbols that coalesce in the *lingka / phurbu* complex may never be disentangled. In the present case, suffice it to say that the assassination of the *lingka* is similar to a variety of sacrifices. The knife-bearing shaman kills the victim and the victim's essence is sent to the upper regions to feed the gods. In many cultures, this latter is accomplished by burning, and indeed the *lingka* is burned for this purpose during the Liberation Dance.

It should be noted that in eleventh-century Tibet, the "liberation" or ritual sacrifice of animals was widespread enough among Buddhists for Lha bla ma ye shes 'od to complain that "since the growth (of rites) of 'liberation' (killing), goats and sheep no longer have rest."[36]

In a Buddhist context, the well-being of all concerned should be taken into account, not just the supernatural guest and the host who wishes to further his own ends by feeding him. The *lingka* rituals of Mani Rimdu carry out this premise. Thus, we see two things. First, that no blood is spilled, even though the beings drawn into the *lingka* and killed are believed to be quite real. Second, that the well-being of the victim is assured.

To accomplish this, the victim is bifurcated. His consciousness, purified, is sent to paradise—the pure land of the Buddha. His body, burnt, is carried upward to feed the supernatural guests.[37] The guests now are enjoined to repay their hosts kindness by putting their supernatural talents at his disposal.

Here we see a Buddhist transformation of two of humankind's earliest and most pervasive religious practices, the sacrifice and the burnt offering. In the Buddhist model however, there is no victim. It is strictly a win-win situation.

Looking deeper into the seemingly fathomless pool of this primary, if not primal scene, we find yet another level of symbolism, a yogic one. This level is hidden in the shapes of the tools.[38]

As Stephan Beyer has noted, the black triangular box in which the *lingka* is placed "represents the *dharmôdaya,* the primordial and feminine 'source of all events,' that it may be liberated into the Dharma realm, 'where there is neither slayer or slain.'"[39]

Shown as a triangle, Trulshik Rinpoche explains that in three dimensions, the *dharmôdaya,* in Tibetan *chos byung* (the source of things), is a pyramid. There are two types: the upward pointing (male) triangle or pyramid of method; and the downward pointing (female) triangle or pyramid of wisdom. The union of method and wisdom is shown as a six-pointed star. It forms the most typical of tantric *yantra,* seen, among other places, on modern Nepali coins and in the center of the Lord of the Dance *maṇḍala*. The association of the union of method and wisdom and sexual union is familiar to all students of Tibetan art—it is the standard explanation of the union of tantric deities in Tibetan painting and sculpture. As already mentioned, the plane of the transmundane deities is pure. Seen on this pure level, sexual union is the union of method and wisdom.

Let us now turn to the *phurbu*. To see a dagger as a male sexual symbol is perhaps too easy, but here, where the shape of the blade is itself a sexual symbol—a pyramid—the argument becomes more compelling. If the placing of the *phurbu* in the triangular box is a sexual act, we should expect to see further correspondences in the symbolism. We do. The central act of the creation-process yoga is rebirth on the divine plane, rebirth as a god. The place where this occurs is the center of the *maṇḍala*. In the Lord of the Dance *maṇḍala*, as in many used by the Nyingma order, the center lies within the embrace of the male and female *dharmôdaya.*

In the *lingka* ritual, the one "imagined in the pit" is slain to be reborn in paradise. To do so, his consciousness is sucked up the hollow tube in the center of the dagger, in the process purified, and finally ejected upward to the happier land. From what little we know of perfection-process yoga, it is clear that an analogous movement takes place. In certain contexts, we find that the yogin, in a sexual union real or imagined, withdraws his semen back from the tip of his penis. In others, energy moves into and up through the central channel. In the yoga of transference (*'pho ba*), which can be used to "gain rebirth in the Highest Pure Land at the time of death," wind and mind are moved upward through the central passage and out through the top of the head.[40]

The word *lingka,* it will be remembered, has a dual meaning of penis and body. Physically, the *phurbu* has the same duality—its lower half is a pyramid and its upper half is a torso and head. On a symbolic level, it seems to reflect a movement of yogic energy between the two poles of the sexual center and the head. In function, the *phurbu* is a tube though which consciousness moves literally and figuratively upward: it enters as a demon and exits as a deity. When the triangular blade of the *phurbu* (male) is inserted into the triangular box (female) containing the *lingka,* the essence of the *lingka,* its "seed" (*sa bon*) the syllable "nrī" is drawn up the central channel of the *phurbu.*[41]

Conversely, a narrow tube such as that of the *phurbu* is often seen in a process of spiritual rebirth as the birth canal. When we remember that elsewhere to be spiritually reborn is to be unborn, the movement upwards through the tube begins to remind us of the *regressus ad uterum* common to initiatic cults.[42]

We will see this image of regression or reversal to "primordial purity" again. The *zor,* another triangularly shaped magic weapon, is used to "turn back the enemies and obstructions of ignorance and egoism" and to turn back "*saṁsāra* to the realm of *nirvāṇa.*"[43]

In the case of the *lingka* and *phurbu,* the victim killed and the weapon that kills him seem to be alternate images of the same reality: the body impure, the body purified; consciousness impure, consciousness purified; sexuality impure, sexuality purified. The divine yogic body kills the impure body and replaces it, demonic consciousness is killed and transformed into divine consciousness, mortal sexuality is destroyed to make way for the divine union of method and wisdom, bliss and emptiness.

If the *phurbu* is a transformed vision of the *lingka* itself, this accords perfectly with the tantric principle of transforming rather than abandoning passions. There is a deeper logic to this mirroring of the killer and the killed. In our context, reality is unborn and unchanging, whether it is experienced as hell or heaven, *saṁsāra* or *nirvāṇa* depends on how one has chosen to see it.

10

Day One: Site, Preparation, Drawing the *Maṇḍala*

As we have seen at Thami, and in theory if not always in practice at Chiwong, the first official day of Mani Rimdu is the thirtieth day of the month, the dark of the moon. On this day, the monks perform the two types of ceremony that typically begin a long Tibetan ritual complex.[1] These are the Site Ritual (*sa chog*) and the Preparation Ritual (*sta gon*). The Site Ritual insures the cooperation of the autochthonous deities. The Preparation installs the tutelary deity and his entourage in the *maṇḍala.*

Xylograph editions of the Site Ritual and Preparation Ritual used in Mani Rimdu may exist in Tibet, but I have never seen any in Solu-Khumbu. There, the texts used belong to the miscellany of manuscripts that an individual monk copies for himself. Since the two rituals are not performed by every monk, they are not in every monk's collection, but Diamond Masters, Chant Leaders, and monks who have previously held these positions usually will have them.

The Site Ritual and Preparation Ritual are also described in the various commentaries to the Lord of the Dance ritual, such as the *Accompanying Methods* (*Lhan thabs*) and the *Precious Lamp* (*Rin chen sgron me*). Indeed, referring only to the *Precious Lamp*, a monk expert in ritual practice could perform the ceremonies or without difficulty create his own Site and Preparation manuscripts.

The ellipsis is the favorite punctuation mark among editors of Tibetan ritual texts, much to the frustration of the Tibetologist who does not know by heart the several hundred pages of liturgy necessary to fill in the gaps, who, indeed, is innocent of prayers known to an eight-year-old monkling. The Site and Preparation manuscripts in my possession, from the collection of a former Chant Leader of Chiwong, differ from the *Precious Lamp* mainly in the selection of passages elided. It may very well be that such manuscripts find their ultimate source in more generalized commentaries, expanded where an individual monk / copyist needs a fuller version of a given text and contracted where he is sufficiently familiar with the passage to do without a detailed transcription.

The text that forms the basis of this chapter was specially prepared for me in just this way by Trulshik Rinpoche's secretary, Ngawang Lodro.[2] The theory behind the transcription was that all elisions be expanded to their full length, so that even an ignorant foreigner could follow the text. Ngawang Lodro apparently had some difficulty imagining the extent of a foreigner's ignorance. Despite my instructions, he left a few passages to the memory of the reader. These were supplied by Ngawang Tsundru, Chant Leader of Thubten Chöling, when we edited the text, as were some additional stage directions from the *Precious Lamp* and other commentaries.

At Chiwong, the Site and Preparation rituals take from three to five hours to complete, depending on how they are scheduled. They may start as early as eight in the morning, as in 1982, or as late as half past three in the afternoon, as in 1980.

THE SITE RITUAL

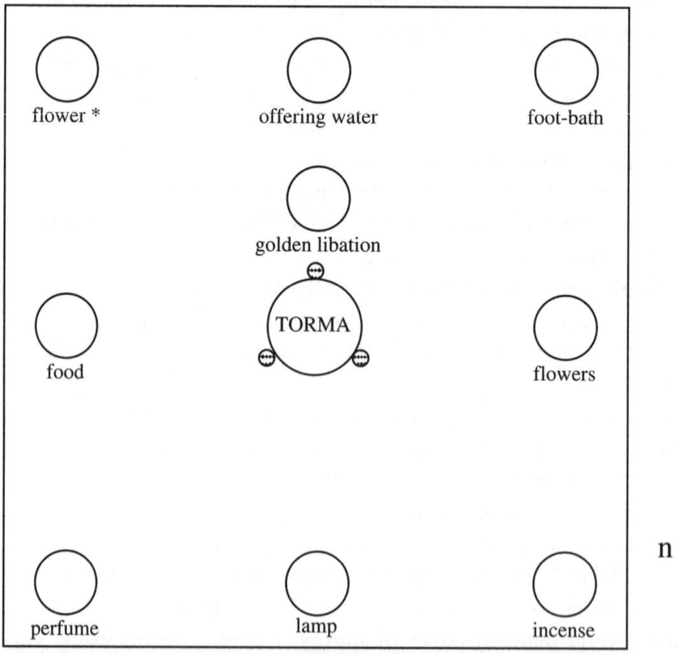

Arrangement of Offerings on the *Maṇḍala* Base for the Site Ritual[a]

[a] The sketch is based on the arrangement used at Chiwong in 1980 and in 1982. The letter n indicates the compass direction, not ritual direction of the *maṇḍala*.

The first step of the Site or Land Ritual is preparing offerings on the *maṇḍala* base for the Owner of the Land. These offerings are the familiar set of seven derived from Indian tradition: drinking water, footbath, flowers, incense, a lamp, perfume, and food; with the addition of eighth offering, the "flower on the edge" (**mtshams 'dzin me tog*), peculiar to offering arrangements on *maṇḍala* surfaces. The "flower on the edge" rounds out, or more accurately "squares out," the set of seven offerings. Traditionally, it is not numbered among them. A white torma for the Owner of the Land is placed on a tripod in the center of the table. Beneath the tripod is a small pile of grain. Behind it sits the "golden libation," an herbal elixir presented in a silver chalice, that will be offered along with the torma.

The ritual orientation of the *maṇḍala* does not necessarily correspond to the directions of the compass. Patterns of ritual activity indicate that at Chiwong, the eastern door of the *maṇḍala* lies to the geographical north. This is to be expected. At Chiwong, the lama's throne lies to the north, and as officiant he should face the *maṇḍala*'s eastern door.

This ambiguity becomes particularly confusing in the important northeast corner of the *maṇḍala*. The northeast is the fixed point from which circles of offerings begin. It is the direction in which a variety of important objects are placed: the "flower on the edge," the action flask, and the first ritual colors of sand. As can be seen in the preceding illustration, these objects are in the compass northwest, which is the ritual northeast in a *maṇḍala* whose eastern door lies to the compass north.[3]

This relativity of direction does not indicate slackness of execution. It is sanctioned by no less a bastion of orthodoxy than Tsongkhapa. The great progenitor of the Gelukpa order points out in *The Great Exposition of Secret Mantra* (*sNgags rim chen mo*) that although mother tantra *maṇḍalas* should start in the south and father tantra *maṇḍalas* in the east, since south and the other directions only exist relatively, any direction will do.

Before the Site Ritual begins, communal tea (*mang ja*) is taken.[4] The ritual is then introduced by that standby of Nyingma liturgy, the *Seven Syllable Prayer* addressed to Padmasambhava (*Tshig bdun gsol 'debs*).

On the northwest border of Orgyan-land
On a lotus stamen's stem,
Astounding supreme achievement was won.
You who as the Lotus-Born are renowned,
You who a vast entourage of Sky Walkers surround,
Come, we pray, inspire us
Who follow in your footsteps.

oṁ āḥ hūṁ vajraguru padmasiddhi hūṁ

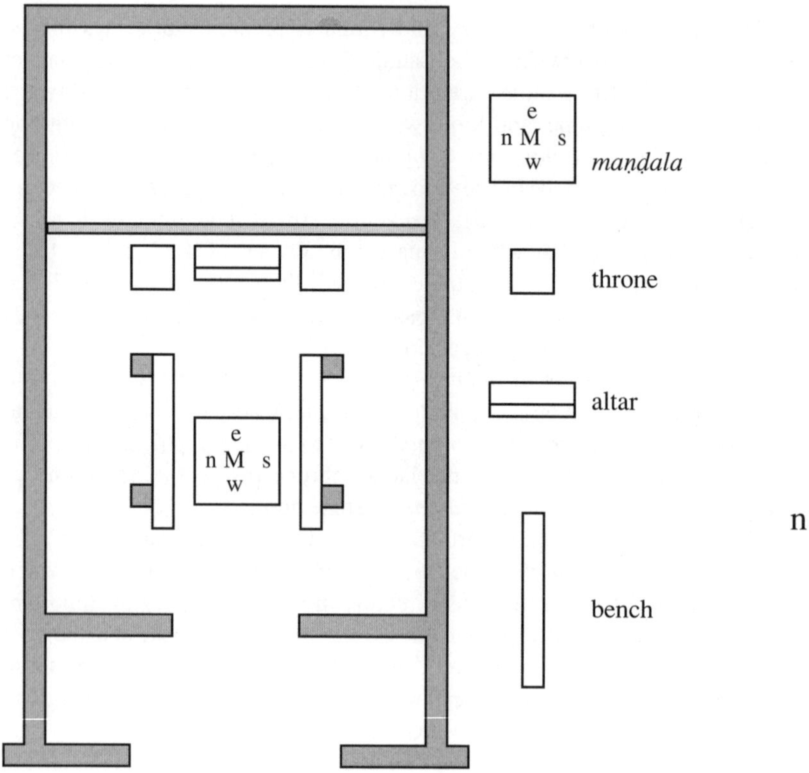

Chiwong Assembly Hall
showing compass directions and *maṇḍala* directions[a]

[a] Note that in the convention of Western cartography, north is up and south is down, but in the convention of Tibetan iconometry east is down and west is up. Sketches are marked to show which system they follow. The difference between ritual and compass directions is sufficiently confusing for informants, ethnographers, and even participants for it to seem on occasion that the orientation is reversed and that the ritual east actually faces south. See, for example, the "configuration of five" at the end of this chapter.

This is followed by two special prayers that introduce the *Union of the Blissful Manual* (*bDe kun las byang*), autobiographies in verse of gTer bdag gling pa 'gyur med rdo rje and his son, Ratnabīja. The monks then recite the first sections of *Manual* that center on the visualization of themselves as the deity, ending with the verses of praise dedicated to Lord of the Dance and his entourage (UB 20b4). The monks depart from the normal practice in only a few minor points.[5] They then skip to the conclusion of the *Manual*, which prepares the meditators to rise from their contemplation and reenter the conventional world. To do so, first they must dissolve the world of their visualizations step-by-step back into emptiness. From this void, reciting Lord of the Dance's mantra "oṁ āḥ hūṁ hrīḥ oṁ maṇi padme hūṁ," they "rise once more as the god," the god that they wish to become and that in a certain sense they already are.[6]

When this hour and a half of ritual is complete, a stick of incense is inserted in the back of the Site God's torma, and the offering lamp is lit. Now, the Site Ritual itself begins, following its own ritual texts.

The first step is to placate the Owner of the Land (S/P 1b1–2.1). In Tibetan belief, these autochthonous spirits are the true owners of the earth's surface. A Tibetan would no more undertake a ceremony without their permission than we would throw a party at a neighbor's house without asking first. The assembly blesses the offerings arranged on the table. Then, they invite the Owner of the Land, and present them to him.

> Hūṁ! Consider us, Classes of Owner[s] of the Land, God[s], Serpent[s] and [your] battalions!
> Take this truly blessed offering torma!
> We take this land in order to accomplish momentous deeds,
> Thus we offer what pleases you. [1b5]

Having fulfilled their purpose, the offerings, including the torma and the golden libation are cleared away.

Once the table is clear, the officiant and his assistant initiate a series of purificatory actions which begin with the *maṇḍala* base and expand until they seal off the entire sacred space.

The officiant circles the *maṇḍala*, sprinkling the surface with cow's urine. The assistant sweeps the *maṇḍala* table with his robe. The master touches the earth, and recites the mantra. He then mounts the surface of the *maṇḍala* and visualizes himself as Hayagrīva, the fierce horse-headed deity who lives within the heart of Lord of the Dance. He addresses any ghosts who may be lurking in the vicinity of the *maṇḍala* and demands that they leave posthaste. He threatens those who fail to do so with immediate pulverization. As if to give his threat credibility, he batters them with magical boulders in the guise of mustard seeds, and then assaults them with the fearsome Blazing Wheel Mantra (*Cakrajvalanovikanāma*).

The author of the Blazing Wheel Mantra, whose hidden text was discovered in the fourteenth century, is said to be µākyamuni Buddha himself. It is said that "Merely reciting this mantra, fierce entities will pant with fear, and [you] will be liberated from the gnomes who open the jaws of death."[7]

> oṁ dhuru dhuru cakra jaya jaya cakra hana hana cakra bhuru bhuru cakra bhramara bhramara cakra bedumani cakra jala jala cakra saṁbhavegana nayasara cakra sālaya sālayā cakra nāgaśaya nāgaśaya

cakra baṁ baṁ cakra hūṁ hūṁ phaṭ phaṭ samatagara cakra tibta cakra hūṁ phaṭ [161b1]

One person continues to recite this spell throughout the acts that follow.

Having dealt with the *maṇḍala* surface, the time has come to widen the circle of protection. The master, his assistant and the better part of the assembly move to the perimeter of the *maṇḍala* house. This is the path surrounding the assembly hall that the faithful use to circumambulate it. Here, the assembly will "Seal the Borders" (*tho sdom*), inviting the guardians of the four directions to protect the performance of the ritual and to eliminate interruptions.[8]

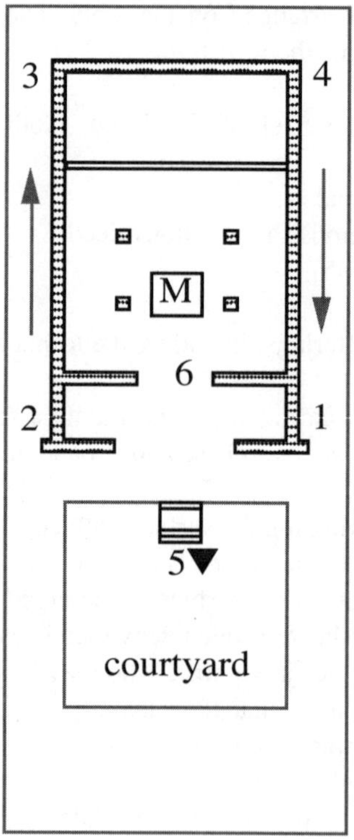

n

Chiwong Assembly Hall Complex
(not to scale)
M = *maṇḍala*
numbers indicate other
Site Ritual locations

To arrive at the site of the first offering, the southeast corner of the circumambulatory path, the assembly must make a nearly complete circuit of the assembly hall, bypassing the places where they will make offerings later in the sequence. At the southeast corner, a statue of *Yul 'khor srung*, Protector of the Realm, god of the eastern quarter is set in a niche in the wall (1). Starting with the east like the rising sun is a pattern of tantric ritual: it is through the eastern gate that the initiate enters the *maṇḍala*.[9]

At Chiwong, each corner of the monastery has a statue of one of the gods of the four directions. Protector of the Realm (Yul 'khor srung, Ssk. Dhṛitarāṣṭra) is the Great King of the East (1). Noble Son ('Phags skyes po, Ssk. Virūḍhaka) is the Great King of the South (2). Uneven Eye (Mig mi bzang, Ssk. Virūpakṣa) is the Great King of the West (3). The Great King of the North (4) is Son of Renown, Vaiśravaṇa, the best known of the four guardian kings.[10] Worshipped in other contexts as the god of wealth, he holds a jewel-spitting mongoose.

Below each statue is a niche which serves as an altar for the offerings that are about to be made. The simpler temples of Thami and Tengpoche have pedestals for the offerings, but no statues. As usual, it is the ritual / meditative realm that takes precedence. The art object, the physical reality so important to us, is merely an embellishment, an afterthought.

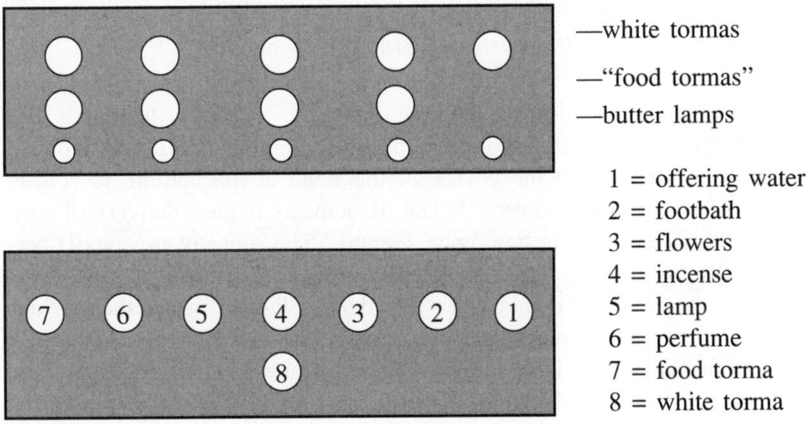

The Two Trays of Offerings Carried in the Sealing the Borders Ritual[11]

The monks nail a cylindrical multicolored pennant known as a "victory banner" (*rgyal mtshan*) in each direction. On a tray or shelf below the victory banner, they place a white torma of the king of the direction and a set of seven offerings for him. The guardian is invoked, worshipped, and asked to "fence out the Obstructors of the quarter" under his dominion.

Having secured the outer boundaries, the inner boundaries must be made safe. First, they bless the place where they will "suppress the gnomes," a small triangular pit (5) in the monastery's dance courtyard (*'chams rva*) near the steps leading to the porch and the chapel. Normally, the pit is covered with one of the flagstones that pave the courtyard. It is exposed only twice during Mani Rimdu: today and the day of the masked dance.

Pit in Courtyard for Effigy, Chiwong 1979

The first step in blessing the spot is to offer a golden libation.[12] The stated purpose of this offering is to induce the assembled gods, from Lord of the Dance at the top to the Owner of the Land at the bottom, to "create legions of magic yogic powers."[13] The participants request delivery of such powers "this year, month, day, hour, minute." The sense of urgency is pertinent. The assembly is about to embark on an archetypical magical act—exorcism, the slaying of demons. It is now that the *lingka,* created the previous night, first comes into play.

The power of truth is axiomatic in many cultures. In the life-story of the Buddha, we learn that the truth of his claim to enlightenment dispelled the hosts of the demon Māra. Now, when the gnomes are imagined "within the pit, broad and profoundly deep," the assembly musters all the truths of the Buddhist religion and concerts their power toward materializing "the unrighteous sentient beings, who are the family of *yama* gnomes" into the *lingka*, "this image . . . this symbolic substance."

> Hūṁ! In this great secret *maṇḍala*
> The obstructors who interrupt true achievement,
> The gnomes who transgress the word
> Are suppressed and afflicted.[14]

As on the night before, the power of the elements is evoked to suppress the gnomes. The cymbals begin to play, and are joined by the other musicians.[15] The pit is covered. Then, "the brothers in achievement cross their arms, right over left, and make contact by interlocking their little fingers."[16] They close upon the burial pit. Eyes closed, gently rocking side-to-side, they pray.

Horse Dance, Chiwong 1982

In a sense, this small set of rituals performed without witnesses encapsulates and prefigures the day of dance that for the public is the climax of the festival. The cycle begins with the Golden Libation, the offering made by the Black Hat Magicians who initiate the dancing. In the middle, the *lingka* is dispatched and buried in the courtyard. The cycle ends as we have just described—with the monks in a tight circle, fingers interlocked, dancing the "Horse Dance," the triumph of the god Hayagrīva who is the ferocious power of the god of compassion.

> Hūṁ! The Horse's great promise to behave—
> The great diamond dancing vow,
> The play of body, speech, mind, intelligence
> And action, the diamond dance—
> Makes the five poison passions' aggregates
> Thunder thundering into the five wisdoms!
> Makes the five bodies—spontaneously-born meteor—
> Evaporate into bliss!
> This is the glorious vow—
> To dissolve the three worlds in the objectless realm. (UB 37.5)

According to the long commentary (LIS 194.5 ff.), "by seeing the entire universe and all its inhabitants as the body of Excellent Horse Heruka, every action is accomplished."

Just as the first *lingka* is hidden in a triangular hole beneath the flagstones of the courtyard, the second *lingka* will be hidden in a black triangular iron box under the *maṇḍala* table inside the chapel. Twice each day of Mani Rimdu it will emerge to be slain.

Later each day, when the Horse Dance is recited, an assistant will seal an overturned offering plate by making a cross on it with the Diamond Master's *vajra.* According to the commentary (LIS 194.5 ff.), the plate is visualized as Mount Meru pressing down on the object imagined beneath it. Knowing this, we can appreciate the full weight, as it were, of the image of the *lingka* sealed beneath the stone in the courtyard.[17] In the iconography of the *maṇḍala*, the crossed *vajra* is the foundation of the universe—the base on which the *maṇḍala* rests. Even as the second *lingka* rests quiescent under the *maṇḍala* table, then, a symbolic event occurs—the weight of the universe presses down on it and on the untoward forces it represents.

Like parentheses within sets of parentheses, like gods within the hearts of gods, the imagery of the assassination of the *lingka* both permeates and embraces the festival. In the first instant, the ground is clearly laid: death and transcendence, but a death and transcendence whose imagery lacks any note of gothic morbidity. Rather, the participants—it is difficult to call them victims here—are instructed to evaporate into bliss, to thunder thundering into the five wisdoms.

Here, too, for the first time, the allotropes of Buddhist exorcism are laid out: the destruction of the gnomes, the destruction of the passions. One does not replace the other: the destruction of the gnomes is not a empty shell to be filled with a secret soteriological meaning. The gnomes are killed. As we have seen in the previous chapter, their murder is a moral issue. By its side, the act of destruction more familiar to students of Buddhism takes place—the destruction of the passions. With such complexity of liturgical diction, it is sometimes difficult to determine which parentheses are within which, which are next to which. When read enough times, however, the ritual can be parsed.

After the outdoor rituals comes a transitional ritual, a ritual at the threshold, Purifying the Door. The liturgy follows the pattern of the rituals of the four directions. Here, however, the deity invoked is Yama, the Black Slayer, the Lord of Death.[18] In the course of the ritual, a small image of the deity is affixed above the entrance to the assembly hall.

An image of the Lord of Death over the door is in no way unique to Mani Rimdu, nor is it a new idea. The Dukhang (*'dus khang*, assembly hall) at Alchi Monastery in Ladakh has a wall painting of the Inner Yamarāja above the door which dates to the eleventh century.[19]

Although sometimes numbered among the directional guardians, in a sense, the Lord of Death is not limited to any of the four directions.[20] Here, he is called upon to fulfill his promise not to let hostile forces past "the protective circle of the horizon" of the *maṇḍala*. According to Sang Sang Tulku, he is the gatekeeper who will not admit anyone who would disturb the rituals.

One of Yama's more common roles in Buddhist iconography is in "wheel of life" paintings, where he holds the outer circle of the wheel of *saṁsāra* in his jaws. All those trapped within the wheel are subject to death; none can elude his grasp. The present act mirrors and, as a mirror often does, inverts this function. Here, Yama's mastery of the limits of worldly existence forbids entrance rather than exit. Rather than being trapped, those within the circle of the *maṇḍala* will become free.

The Yama ritual makes use of an object not present in the rituals of the directional guardians: a second type of small paper image, called simply a *rten*, an "image" or "support." Of the same size as the effigy of the gnome, the image has the Lord of Death printed on it. He has one face with three eyes. As in the image over the door at Alchi and the one that embraces the Wheel of Life, the face is that of a *rākṣasa* demon not a bull. Like other fearsome deities, his hair stands on end and he is haloed with flames. He has two arms. His upraised right arm brandishes a club surmounted with a skull. His left hand, arm crooked, holds a lasso at his waist. He wears a tiger-skin skirt, but is naked from the waist up. His legs are extended in a striding posture.

The extraordinary thing about this image is not what is on it, but what it is on. It is pasted to a goat's shoulder bone. As mentioned earlier, this is a way of breaking a *lingka*'s bones equivalent to folding the paper on which it is printed. To understand why this is so, or to seek an alternative explanation, we must look a bit farther into the history of Asian religion.

The shoulder bone has been an oracular device of shamans throughout Asia for millennia. Scapulamancy, divination by examining the cracks that form when the bone is put in a fire, as Eliade remarked, is "common to all of Central Asia."[21] That cracks in bone are something to be read is reflected in the form of the earliest historical records we possess from China. They are inscribed on sheep shoulder bones.[22]

Sheep, or as in this case, goat bones seem to be the most common, although in some regions reindeer or even seal bones are used.[23] According to some sources, in certain periods, a human shoulder bone was employed.[24] Already known in Tibet in the royal period,[25] bone oracles have been used by the Buriat,[26] the Kalmyk, the Kirghiz, the Mongols,[27] and even by the Sherpas.[28]

Among the Bonpo of Tibet, it was, along with divination with colored threads and spirit possession, a major method of divination.[29] The literature on scapulamancy is nearly as vast as the subject itself.[30]

The function of the *scapula* in central Asian shamanism is not limited to divination, however. As Karjalainen reports, a Vasyugan-Ostyak shaman rows to the other world in his shaman's trunk using a shoulder bone as an oar.[31] For Eliade, *scapulæ* have a deep connection to the art of divination:

> Divination itself is a technique particularly adapted to actualizing the spiritual realities that are the basis of shamanism or to facilitating

> contact with them. Here again the animal's bone symbolizes the mystery of life in continual regeneration and hence includes in itself, if only virtually, everything that pertains to the past and future life.

When we examine Eliade's data, particularly the Vasyugan-Ostyak example, in the light of its use in Mani Rimdu, another interpretative structure seems to take shape. Like the colored thread and the central pole which we will see later, the shoulder bone can be seen as a link between realms—between the land of the living and the land of the dead, If divination is reading messages from that other world—the shaman's stock-in-trade—then the Bonpo's fire-cracked bone is as indicative of that passage as the oar with which the Vasyugan-Ostyak rows across the river that separates him from the spirit world.

As if to further our argument, Ferdinand D. Lessing, and later Samten G. Karmay, record a shoulder of sheep being used in a Tibetan rite to recall an errant soul. In that ritual, the meat of the "soul-leg" (*bla rkang*) is used to help restore the victim's soul and the bone examined to divine whether or not the ritual has taken effect.[32]

Another reason that the shoulder bone functions so well in these contexts has been elucidated by Michael Walter.[33] The sheep's shoulder is the same shape as Jambudvīpa, the southern continent of Indian cosmology, which represents the known world. Thus, here, just in Buddhist paintings of the Wheel of Life, an image of the Lord of Death is juxtaposed to an image of the world.

As we will see again later it is not just the shoulder bone of the goat or sheep that is a symbol of a change of planes, but its skull as well. In Tibet, the sheep skull represents the "sky-door" that leads to the upper realms.[34]

Taking all of this into account, it seems fitting that we find an image of Yama on a shoulder bone: an image of the Lord of Death on an image of the passage from the world of the living to the realm of the dead. It is also fitting that this is the ritual of the door, for it marks the passageway from the profane world to the world of the spirit. It is a liminal ritual in every sense of the word. Sang Sang Tulku's explanation, that Yama is here a gate-keeper, although different on one level, may relate to the same layer of symbolism.

The shoulder in its most common shamanic usage—divination—is by definition a cracked or broken bone, and as such, a simulacrum of breaking the *lingka*'s bones, a natural enough thing to want to do to the Lord of Death. In either case, the shoulder bone puts us in contact not so much with the mystery of life as with the Lord of Death. Given the continuity of symbolism, perhaps the flask-shaped bone with its small square of paper can be conceived according to one or more resemblance: old wine with a new label.

Having placed the image of Yama above the door, the monks reassemble in the chapel. Once more, they recite "Blazing Wheel."

Wooden Magic Dagger

The protective circle established by the Site Rituals is now further fortified with the energy of the ten spikes or "magic daggers." The term dagger (Tib. *phur bu;* Ssk. *kīla*) refers both to a set of deities and to a set of implements. The ten deities "have the body of a Wrathful One above and the blazing form of a spike below."[35] The Dagger Deities are visualized on the basis of ten wooden daggers.

The wooden daggers for the *maṇḍala* are simple in form. They lack the details that characterize the most elaborate examples of *phurbu.* The three-faced head of Hayagrīva surmounted by a neighing horse's head, the blade twined with snakes and disgorged from the gaping mouth of a *makara*, all are reduced to their simplest geometric equivalents.

In the visualized three-dimensional *maṇḍala*, the Dagger Deities occupy the ten directions: the east, south, west, north, northeast, northwest, southwest, southeast, above and below. Each of the wooden daggers is labeled with a strip of cloth naming its direction. When the wooden daggers are placed on the *maṇḍala* table, the dagger that represents the deity who occupies the zenith of the protective sphere is placed east of the eastern dagger, and is so marked. The dagger of the god who rests at the nadir of the protective sphere is marked "west of west."

At the beginning of the Site Ritual, the officiant mounted the *maṇḍala* table and in the person of Hayagrīva, threatened any lurking ghosts. Later, around the pit, the monks recited the "Horse Dance," the triumph of the Horse-Headed God. Now, the officiant visualizes himself as Hayagrīva and literally dances on the surface of the *maṇḍala.*

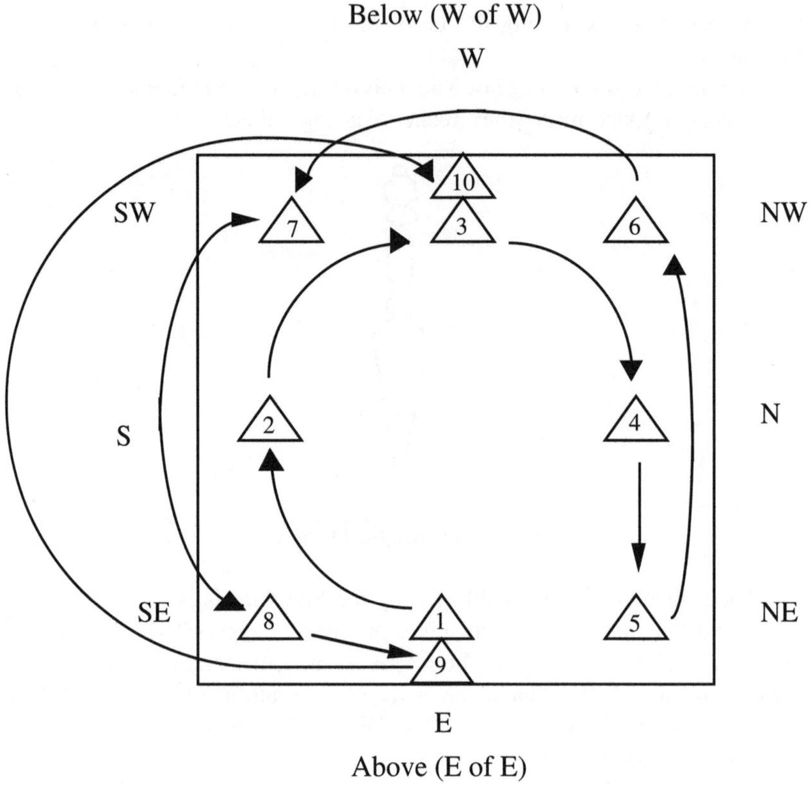

The Ten Spikes: Sequence of Placement (TCU)

This quiet little dance, often performed without a single witness, is one of Mani Rimdu's most awe-inspiring moments. Its movements are stylized and stately. Balanced on one foot, arms swaying to the slow and ponderous rhythm of the mantra that suppresses the ghosts, the dancer reminds one of Nāṭarāja, the Hindu Lord of the Dance. At the end of each series of movements, the recitation is punctuated by the sound of the master tapping the head of the magic nail with a wooden ritual hammer. As he nails down the ghosts, his assistant proffers a triangular base to hold the dagger upright. The master places the dagger in the base and the assistant places it in the appropriate direction at the edge of the *maṇḍala*. The daggers not only nail down enemies and obstructors so that they cannot move, but emit rays of light which become a protective sphere (*srung 'khor*) of fused *vajra* so dense that even air cannot enter.[36]

The bases in which the daggers stand are triangular, like the black iron box and the hole in the courtyard. The triangle is the prison of the *lingka*, the entity to be nailed down and suppressed. Here, the text specifies that these beings are "harmful ghosts" (*gnod byed 'byung po*).

It has been noted that both the god portrayed on the articulated form of magic daggers and the god evoked in the dagger dance are Hayagrīva. The reason for this is simple: the dagger itself *is* Hayagrīva.[37] The commentary calls this form of the Horse-Headed god Padmakīlaya, "Lotus Spike." The word lotus indicates his membership in the lotus family of Lord of the Dance.[38]

The Magic Dagger visualization is very complicated. To summarize the exegeses of Trulshik Rinpoche (TR), the Thubten Chöling Umze or Chant Leader (TCU) and the long commentary (LIS): the officiant imagines his fingers to be the five Tathāgatas and their consorts. At their point of union, the dagger is visualized as their "excellent son, Padmakīlaya" (LIS). This form of Hayagrīva has the body of the god from the waist up and a dagger from the waist down (TR). With the egos of these three visualizations firm, the officiant strikes the heart of the *lingka* (LIS). In the form of the letter "a," he absorbs the life-force (*tshe rlung*) of the Enemy / Obstructor (*dgra bgegs*) into his own life-force (TR). The *khru rlung* of the Enemy / Obstructor is sucked up into the dagger, where it is washed (*khru*) (TR). Then, its consciousness can go to the Akaniṣṭha heaven instead of to hell (TR). Its temporarily purified consciousness is sent to the Akaniṣṭha heaven, where it dissolves into the heart of Amitābha. Thence, it is liberated into the Truth Realm (LIS 190.1 ff.). The Diamond Master stabs the last feast, during the verse below, at the word "*khāhi*" in the mantra, the Diamond Actor brings it to the front of the *maṇḍala* (TCU).[39]

In the *Union of the Blissful Manual*, there are two major passages dedicated to Hayagrīva. The second of the two, the Horse Dance, was associated earlier with the dramatization of the triangular pit. Now, during the dramatization of the dagger, the last act of the Site Ritual, the monks recite the first passage. The *Manual* calls it "Defining the Borders." The commentary calls it the "Protective Circle."

> Hūṁ! I am the King of Wrath—the very soul of the speech of all the Blissful!
> From the great play of my mind,
> Which blazes with unbearable, awesome majesty,
> I project diamond weapons, blazing fire,
> As the upper and lower borders.
> Above, I spread a diamond tent.
> Below, I spread the diamond ground.
> I fill the border with a diamond fence.
> I project hosts of wrathful emanations,
> Weapons and blazing cones of firelight.
> The pavilion of the unvanquished protector
> Is built within the limits of the great *maṇḍala*.[40]

Amidst this high drama—and high drama it is—with its ringing poetry and stately dance—we must remember several other factors. Chiwong is a small monastery high in the forests of Nepal, far from the centers of Tibetan culture, of which many are now defunct. Mani-Rimdu is performed but once a year, and parts of it, particularly the rituals of the first and last days, are not repeated within a given year's cycle. The installation of the Magic Daggers is among the most complicated of these. The officiant, twirling clockwise and counterclockwise on a tabletop, is obliged to stop in the direction indicated by a small, limp cloth label dangling from the dagger in his grasp, a label reading, let us say, "east of east." His assistant, young, certainly inexperienced, a year gone since the last time, if any, that he has done this, must, in coordination with his twirling teacher, be at the right place at the right moment with the right dagger stand, receive the dagger, place it at the right place on the periphery of the *maṇḍala*, and then hand him the next in the unalterable sequence of an identical looking, but thankfully diminishing, dozen daggers. A degree of confusion is easily anticipated. Handled always with calm and often with grace, it nonetheless tends to deflate the dramatic tension of the scene.

Looking at the Site Rituals as a whole, we can chart a clear progression from small and local to more and more universal. Two-dimensional space is evoked with the god of the plane, the site, and is then defined by the four directions, each with its god. A larger sphere is evoked with the Lord of Death, the god of the limits of our world, whose jaws and claws—as seen in the well-known Tibetan wheel of life paintings—grasp the horizon. Space is further defined by gods of the ten directions, the ten Dagger Deities.

Later in the day, the surface of the *maṇḍala* is prepared and its lines ritually drawn along the same directional schema. If the Site Rituals seem to prefigure the drawing of the *maṇḍala*, it is because they are part of the same process. To define a sacred space is to make space itself sacred. The first step is to protect a territory where the fragile lineaments of this vision may be traced in peace.

THE PREPARATION

According to the commentaries, the Preparation Ritual *(sta gon),* [pronounced dawön] has two parts: the Gods' Preparation (*lha sta gon*) and the Flask Preparation (*bum pa sta gon*). The Gods' Preparation establishes the seats of the gods on the *maṇḍala*. The first stage in this process is to mark off each seat, the place that the symbol or syllable of god will occupy in the finished sand *maṇḍala*.

Each seat has not only a fixed position, but also a fixed size and shape. Lord of the Dance has the largest—a square in the center of the *maṇḍala*. The members of the entourage all have round seats. As we move outward, each group of deities is more peripheral to the *maṇḍala*, both literally and figuratively, and their seats diminish in size accordingly. The seating arrangement reveals other aspects of the *maṇḍala* not revealed in the sand painting that will replace it, such as the presence of Lord of the Dance's Consort, Secret Wisdom Mother; and of Horse-Headed One who resides in Lord of the Dance's heart.

The seats are drawn with "sweet-scented water mixed with the five ambrosias" and then covered with "flowers."[41] In Tibetan ritual, nurtured in that country's harsh climate, flowers are often replaced by grain. This gives Tibetan festivities an austere monochromatic cast: bowls of grain on the altar, grain flung in the air in celebration. One must see a Newar Vajrācārya, strewing a *maṇḍala* with the lush flowers of the Kathmandu Valley to picture of the original intention of the Indian texts.

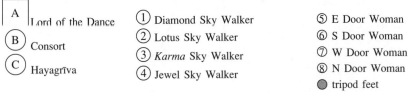

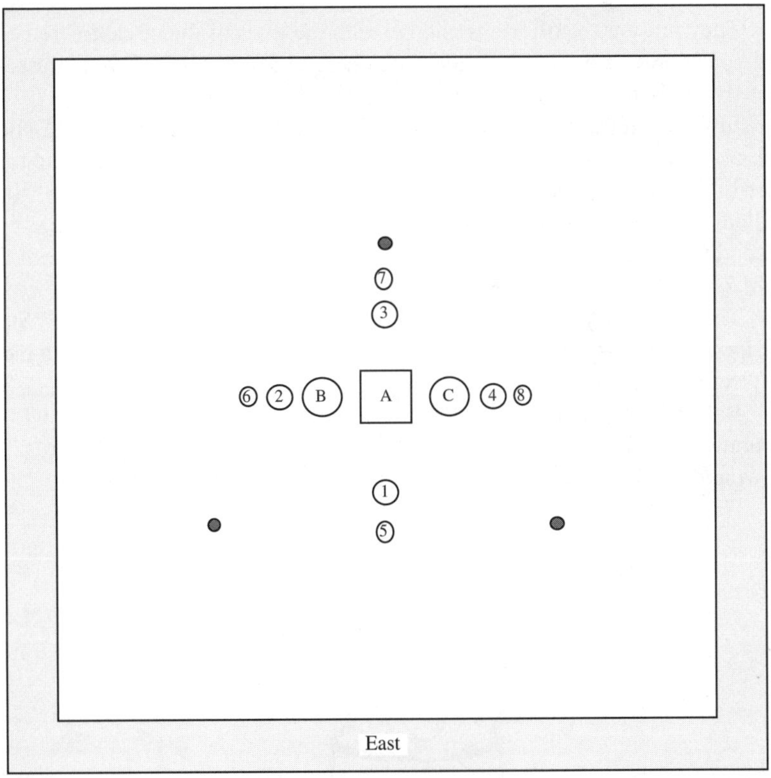

A Lord of the Dance
B Consort
C Hayagrīva

1 Diamond Sky Walker
2 Lotus Sky Walker
3 *Karma* Sky Walker
4 Jewel Sky Walker

5 E Door Woman
6 S Door Woman
7 W Door Woman
8 N Door Woman
● tripod feet

The Preparation Ritual: the Gods' Seats

Once the seats have been established, a multitude of offerings is arrayed on the *maṇḍala* surface. So great is their profusion that their pattern can be difficult to ascertain. Each quarter has a set of nine offerings: three each of incense, lamps, and food tormas. The whole is surrounded by the now familiar set of seven offerings plus one.

The monks make the assembled offerings ritually pure and then imagine that:

> The entire circle of the primordially existent Lord of the Dance Great Compassion's ocean of a *maṇḍala*, sits in the sky above the *maṇḍala* surface.[42]

They present the offerings and beseech the gods of the circle to "remember your vows of the past . . . and come here to this house." The text asserts that the gods then "rest pleasurably in their own places."[43]

In the center of the *maṇḍala*, over the square seat of Lord of the Dance, the monks have placed a group of objects that relate to the Flask Preparation. The flask itself is called the "victory flask," the *"rnam rgyal bum pa."* It is "filled with the essence of the thirty-five substances *(rdzas so lnga)*."[44] A second flask, the "action flask" *(las bum),* is set on the northeast corner of the *maṇḍala*.

The victory flask sits on a tripod called a *"mañji"* or *"manyinga."* Such a tripod is traditionally used to hold objects above a *maṇḍala*. The commentary refers to it as a throne.[45]

Balanced in the crook of the flask's spout is a *vajra* wrapped with a rainbow colored cord. The cord is called a *"gzungs thag,"* a (spell-cord).[46] It is wound of five different colors of thread and represents a rainbow.

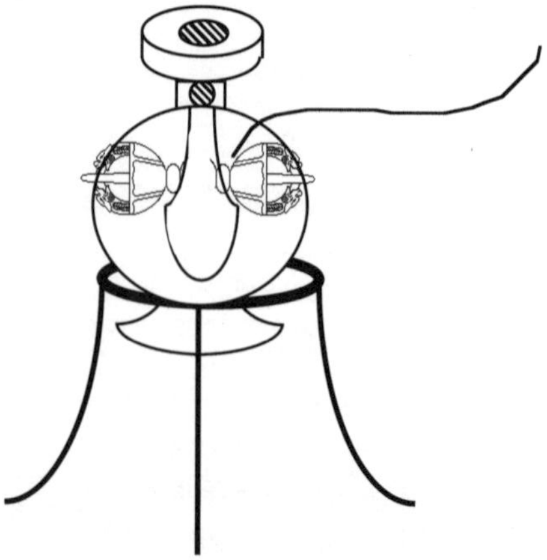

Victory flask on *mañji*, with *vajra* and cord

Like the shoulder bone, a cord representing the rainbow is a shamanic device of considerable distribution and antiquity. The *dmu*-rope by which the first kings of Tibet descended from the sky at birth (and into which they dissolved at death that they might re-ascend) was a rope of rainbow light.[47] In Buriat initiations, the rainbow cord is the shaman's road to "the realm of the spirits, the sky."[48] The Tungus of Manchuria use a cord of red silk or sinew for a similar purpose.[49]

We have already noted that Bonpo shamans use colored threads in divination. Nebesky-Wojkowitz describes the use of strings in Bonpo funerary rites, in which interestingly enough, an animal leg also appears.

> The Bonpo dispatches his soul to the other world in order to ascertain the fate which the soul of the deceased met and if necessary to free it from the power of malignant spirits. . . . Sometimes when carrying out such a rite, a string is tied with one end to one hand of the medium and with the other end to the severed leg of the sacrificed animal. The string should apparently serve as a kind of "path" through which the spirit enters the body of the medium.[50]

A fascination with rainbows, although typically Tibetan is in no way unique to Tibet. As Eliade observed,

> . . . a considerable number of peoples are known to see in it [the rainbow] the bridge connecting earth and sky, and especially the bridge of the gods. This is why its appearance after a storm is regarded as a sign of god's appeasement. It is always by way of the rainbow that mythical heroes reach the sky.[51]

Tibetan Buddhists have much symbology centered around the rainbow. One of the advanced states that are the goal of Nyingma practice, for example, is called the rainbow body.[52] The five colors of the rainbow are often said to symbolize the five families of Tathāgata. As if to prove Eliade's point, when the Dalai Lama first gave the Kālacakra initiation in the United States, a rainbow appeared and was greeted as a good omen.

Students of Tibetan painting will remember that one deity is often seen floating at the end of a rainbow that emerges from a more central deity's heart.[53] In a thangka, the deity at one end of the rainbow is projecting forth, manifesting, emanating the deity at the other. In fact, this is what will happen in the ritual that is about to commence. Each monk will visualize that he himself is Lord of the Dance, and that Lord of the Dance simultaneously floats above the *maṇḍala*. The rainbow of the ritual, like the rainbow of the thangka, is a symbol of the conduction of spiritual energy, a link between deities consubstantial in some sense. In the ritual, the monk will visualize that the mantra he recites, made of light, revolves in his heart. The light of the mantra swirls into the rainbow of the spell-cord, and flows into the heart of the deity floating at the center. This, in Tibetan ritual is the general function of the spell-cord. It transmits mantras from the practitioner to the object of his ritual performance.

As we have seen with the *lingka* and to a lesser extent with the spell-cord, the physical props used in ritual are stand-ins for objects that the ritualist / meditator visualizes. In a sense, it is particularly fitting to call them "props," not as an abbreviation for "properties" as in Western theater, but as an equivalent of the Tibetan word *rten*, a generic term for an image in its sense of being a support for something visualized.

Here then the flask is a support for the visualized flask that is manipulated on the more significant level of the ritual—the level to which visualization and imagination give access. Thus, we learn of the visualized flask that the meditator creates from the syllable *bhrūṁ*, that although "externally, it has the form of a flask, internally, is the wisdom palace, a realm of the clear, luminous, stainless five lights."[54] Within such a victory flask, sit Lord of the Dance and the deities of his entourage. Within the action flask, "the King of Wrath, Red Hayagrīva . . . blazes terrifying as the fires at the end of the world."[55]

In the flask preparation, the physical flasks are cleansed with water and mantras, to make them fit to be the basis of the visualization. Then, the rituals can proceed according to the *Manual*, up to the point where the mantras of Lord of the Dance and of Hayagrīva are transmitted to their respective flasks via the spell-cord. The spell-cord is unrolled from around the *vajra* and passed to the Diamond Master, the end with the *vajra* remaining on the victory flask. The assembly recites the mantras of Lord of the Dance and his entourage. Then, the cord and *vajra* are transferred to the action flask and Hayagrīva's mantra is recited. The rituals of the *Manual* continue until "the gods have melted into the substance of great bliss and become of one taste with the water in the flask."[56]

After the gods have been transubstantiated, the flasks are ready to be used in the ritual. They are removed from the table along with the offerings and the surface of the *maṇḍala* is wiped clean. The assembly disperses.

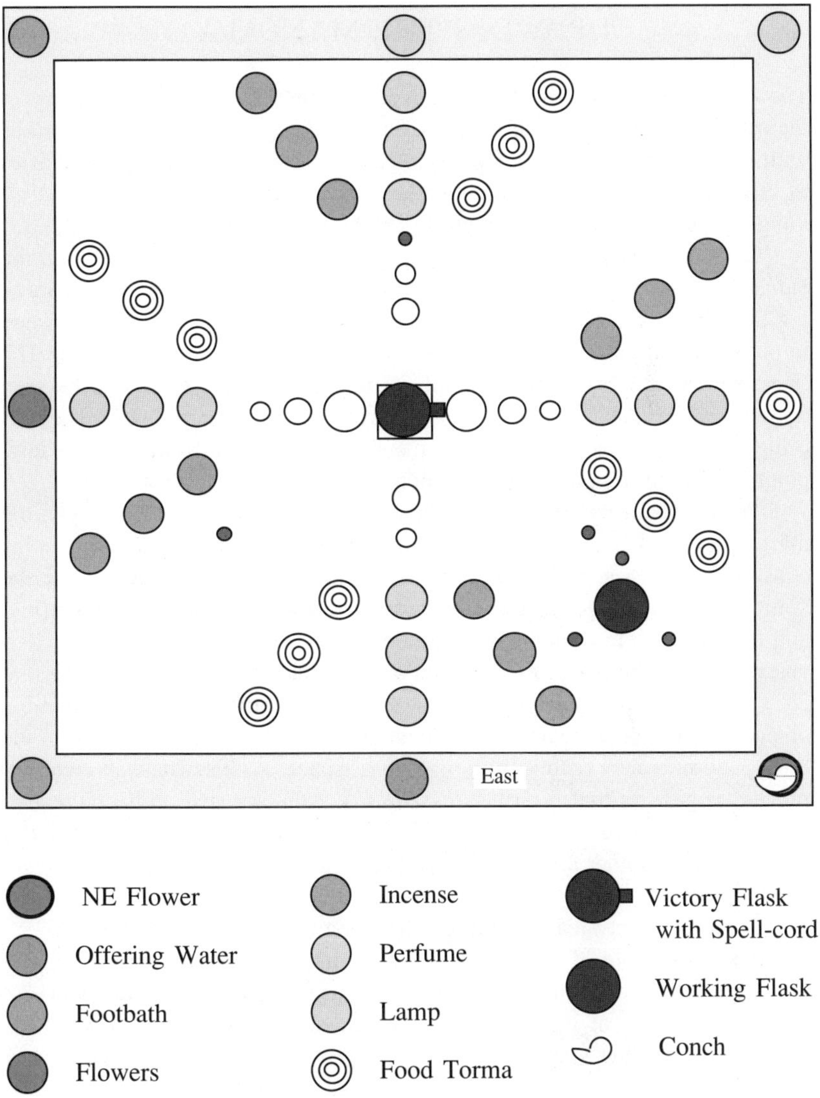

Schematic Diagram of the Preparation Ritual Offerings (Chiwong/TCU)

DRAWING THE MAṆḌALA

The site protected and the gods received into the *maṇḍala*, the geometry of the *maṇḍala* itself can be articulated. The first step is to cleanse the surface with the five products of the cow (*pañcagavya*), which the liturgy identifies as "five kinds of self-created ambrosia." The master circles the table, sprinkling the surface with this mixture using the middle fingers of both hands.[57]

Once the surface has been cleansed in this peculiarly Indic fashion, the *maṇḍala* may be drawn. There are two parts to drawing the *maṇḍala*, drawing the outline and coloring it in. The distinction, already hinted at, between is physical and ritual reality is nowhere clearer than at this moment. The lines, which from a ritual viewpoint do not yet exist, are clearly to be seen on the *maṇḍala* table where they were sketched many years past.[58] The coloring, which will take but a few moments to accomplish from a ritual viewpoint, will require many days of labor to make visible to profane eyes.

The rituals of the lines and of the colors are the work of two people: the master and an assistant, who are visualized as the god of the *maṇḍala* and his consort.[59] The assistant in this context is called either the "disciple" or the "line servant" (*thig gi g.yog*).[60] The tool used to draw a *maṇḍala* is a string, and the first step to drawing it is to prepare that string. As usual, the action takes place on two planes. The master and disciple place on the table the five colors of thread from which they will wind the string. Onto this humble object, they project a complex visualization in which the creative force of the lines patterns a new reality in the womb of space. As elsewhere in creation-process yoga, spiritual rebirth is cast in a vocabulary rich with procreative associations—one meaning of the word aspiration to enlightenment (*bodhicitta*) is semen; the mother's sky is the womb of the goddess.

> From the empty realm, from oṁ hūṁ trāṁ hrīḥ āḥ, line strings that have the nature of the five Tathāgata families come into existence. They enter my body. They melt into aspiration to enlightenment [and] become of one taste with the line string. They are projected into the Mother's sky.[61]

Picking up the threads, they wind them together to the rhythm of their breath. Then, they recite,

> Great bliss, Mother of Secrets,
> By drawing the diamond aspiration to enlightenment lines,
> Make all the billion worlds, all the paradises,
> Into the great natural *maṇḍala*.[62]

The master and disciple draw the lines of the *maṇḍala* in the air above the table, mimicking a carpenter with a chalk line. In changing places to draw each new line, they slowly circle the *maṇḍala* with a complicated backward-spinning motion, ducking under the string at points like dancers at a sorcerer's sock-hop. The master and disciple should imagine all the while "that in the sky above the *maṇḍala*, the real *maṇḍala* is clear in its splendor."[63]

Vajras in hand, they draw each of the "lines in the air" (*gnam thig*) by plucking the string and saying the mantra *bhrūṁ jñā*. Having drawn the images of the line, they invite the wisdom essence of the original, primordial lines (*ye thig gi ye shes pa*) to inhabit them.[64]

This is, of course, a pattern that we have seen before and will see again. An image of the item in question is created, either physically or mentally, and then the "original" item is invited to inhabit it. From the consecration of a statue to the initiation of a disciple, the principle of being able to magically invest your own creation with divine power is what makes tantric rituals possible. It is what makes a torma fit to offer and what "draws" the *maṇḍala* in a ritually meaningful sense. In many ways, it is the tantric ritual par excellence.

Drawing the lines is a complicated series of actions and, like the placement of the daggers, is done with a certain degree of trial and error and hesitancy. The text is not helpful here, as it uses a special vocabulary. The language would be difficult in any case because of the technical complexity of the process. It also seems specifically intended to conceal this magic technology from the uninitiated. As we will see, it occasionally conceals its meaning from legitimate practitioners. The commentary reads

> The two axes—east-west and north-south.
> The fire-wind and ghoul-power diagonals.
> Fire-power, wind-ghoul, east and west sides.
> Wind-power, fire-ghoul, north and south sides.[65]

It should be noted that the third and fourth lines of this stanza each seem to describe four sides, giving us an eight-sided square. To bring any clarity to the passage, we must first decipher it into "plain Tibetan."

> The two axes run from east to west (1) and north to south (2).
> The diagonals run from southeast-northwest (3) and from southwest-northeast (4).
> The east (5) and west (6) sides run
> from southeast to northeast and from northwest to southwest.
> The north (7) and south (8) sides run
> from northwest to northeast and from southeast to southwest.

The Chiwong Mani Rimdu of 1980 gives a good idea of the confusion to which such ciphers can lead. My notes for that year show the master and disciple taking twelve different positions. Adjusting the compass directions to *maṇḍala* directions, we can attempt to reconcile these to the text as follows.

	Master	Disciple	line	duplication?
1.	east	west	axis	
2.	west	east	axis	of 1
3.	southwest	northeast	diagonal	
4.	south	north	axis	
5.	southeast	northwest	diagonal	
6.	southwest	northeast	diagonal	of 3
7.	southeast	northwest	diagonal	
8.	southeast	northeast	E side	
9.	northwest	southwest	W side	
10.	northwest	northeast	N side	
11.	southeast	northwest	diagonal	of 7
12.	southeast	southwest	S side	

As we can see, four extra lines have appeared. They are the mysterious fire-power, wind-ghoul, wind-power and fire-ghoul sides transformed into the diagonals they resemble in name.[66]

At Thami in 1983, several details of the process could be observed which are not described in the commentaries. Nine lines were drawn, the first of which was possibly a symbolic "original line." The master wrapped his end of the string around a bell, the disciple his end around a *vajra*. For lines 2 and 3, logically the two axes, the master twisted his *vajra* in the middle of the string for a moment, and once again removed it, before saying the mantra and plucking the string as for the other lines.

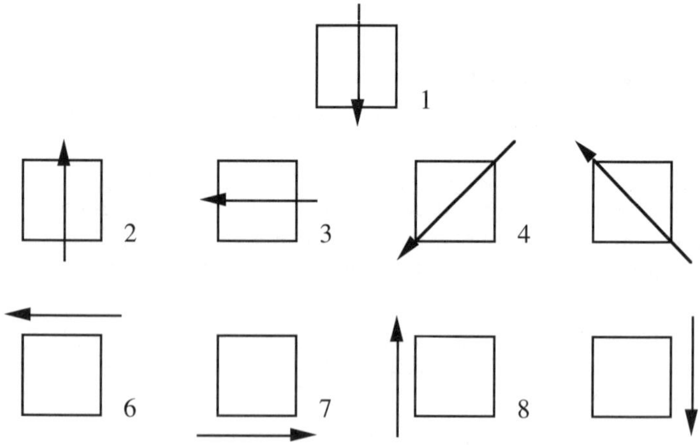

Master ——→ Disciple[67]

Drawing the Lines, Thami 1983

That the Master holds the bell and the disciple the *vajra* is somewhat puzzling. Generally speaking, the bell is the female symbol and the *vajra* the male, and in this ritual, the master is identified as the deity and the disciple as the consort. Seemingly then, the master should wield the *vajra* and the disciple hold the bell. Alternately, it may be that the bell-string-vajra is to be seen as a single unit wielded by the master with the assistance of the disciple, or even, although perhaps less likely, that the interchange of symbols reflects the intimate connection between the deities.

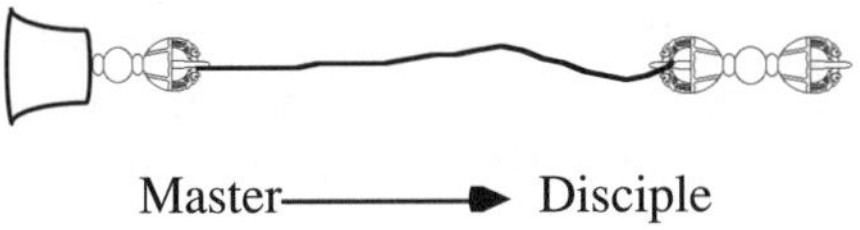

Bell and *Vajra*

Mani Rimdu has tens of thousands of similar details and to master every one is all but impossible. Small discrepancies are seen at every monastery and in no way diminish the monks achievement. Even an ethnographer with nothing to do but observe only discovered the discrepancies in the *maṇḍala* lines years later in cross-checking his notes.

Trivial as this example may be, it raises interesting issues of correctness *versus* error and tradition *versus* innovation in Tibetan culture. We discuss these issues at some length in the next chapter.

As in drawing the lines, the ritual coloring of the *maṇḍala* is a separate act from the physical coloring. The former is done in a few minutes on day one. The visible coloring process takes one or more monks working steadily several days to complete.

The colors are made by adding packaged Indian dye powder to wet sand. The mixture is then cooked dry and poured onto a piece of paper. Any clumps are broken up with the fingers. The colored sand is poured into a small bag for storage.[68] Each color is replenished as the supply runs low. I have observed the sand itself being manufactured at Chiwong by pulverizing quartz with a hammer; other Tibetan monasteries are also said to use quartz.[69] We will discuss the sand further when we reach the physical coloring of the *maṇḍala*.

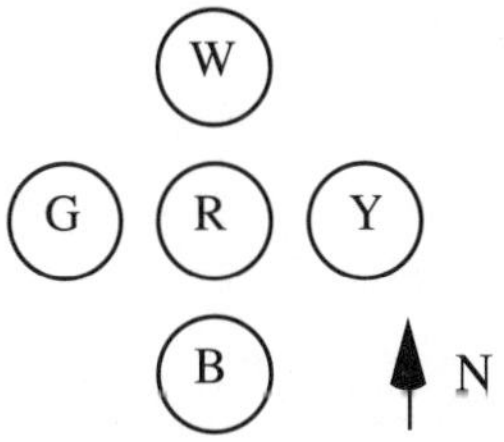

Configuration of Five: Chiwong, 1980

The sacks of color are brought out and poured into *ting*, the type of small bowl usually used for offerings. The *ting* are placed at the center of the *maṇḍala* in a pattern called the "configuration of five" (*lnga tshom*).

The Master draws the seed syllable appropriate to the color in the sand of each bowl. According to the ritual directions of the *maṇḍala*, the arrangement should be: in the center, *hrīḥ* in red; in the east, *hūṁ* in blue; in the west, *oṁ* in white; and in the north *āḥ*, in green.[70]

Following the commentary, the officiant takes a pinch of each color, mixes them in the palm of his hand, and then places the mixture in the northeast corner of the wall, covering the small pile with an upturned dish. At Chiwong in 1980, the master actually drew the northeast corner of the rainbow-colored *maṇḍala* wall and covered the drawing.

11

Days Two to Four: Making the Ritual Objects

The next several days have no ritual activity. Instead, the monks spend their time preparing the ritual objects that will be used during Mani Rimdu. These are the pills, the sand *maṇḍala*, and the many tormas necessary to the various supernatural entities that the festival evokes. Each of these activities is time consuming. With cooking, rolling, drying, and coloring, the pills take several days to make. The sand *maṇḍala* too is a matter of many man-days' labor. Creating the dozens of major tormas occupies most of the monks of Chiwong for a full day.

Making our usual distinction between mechanical and ritual processes, we will see that the physical creation of the pills is completed the next few days. The ritual creation of the pills is the ongoing business of Mani Rimdu; it will continue until the fourteenth day when they are distributed to the public. For the *maṇḍala*, the ratio is reversed. Ritually, the *maṇḍala* is complete in both line and color on the first day. For this reason, a prefabricated *maṇḍala* painted or drawn on cloth, paper or wood is an acceptable substitute. Physically, however, the process of fabricating the *maṇḍala* from sand grain-by-grain takes several man-days.

The tormas, each a complex three-dimensional sculpture, take a large group of monks the better part of a day to complete. Although the major tormas are physically present on their various altars throughout the festival, ritually, they only come to life for a few minutes each day.

The pills are a magical device, pure and simple. The beauty and careful crafting of the *maṇḍala* and the tormas rank them as works of art.

THE PILLS

Since *maṇi*-pills are the sine qua non of Mani Rimdu, we will discuss them first. At Chiwong, the pills are approximately 3–5 mm in diameter and have a slightly dull red finish. The *maṇi*-pills made at Thubten Chöling are slightly smaller, smoother, and more uniform. Their major ingredient is rice flour specially milled for the ritual using hand-operated mill stones. At Chiwong, this task usually falls to the older nuns.

To give the dough a consistency that will make it hold together as pills, the monks add a mucilaginous substance extracted by boiling from the root of a local plant called *hlere* in the Sherpa language.

The monks and nuns roll the dough into small balls and collect them on bronze plates. The still moist pills are poured into a cloth bag supported by two wooden handles. Over the next few days, each monk will take his turn with the bag, rolling the pills back and forth inside it to dry and smooth them. The dried pills are colored bright red with the extract of another edible root called *"ombulak,"* and then returned to the bag to smooth the coating.

Before the *hlere* is poured into the flour, minute quantities of two separate magic compounds are added. The first is powdered metal made of "five precious things," the *rin chen lnga.* A set for the manufacture of the *rin chen lnga* consists of a small metal bar with scraping bar chained to it. The bar is a sandwich of five metals: gold, silver, copper, brass, and iron, the last being the "bread" of the sandwich.[1]

The second magic compound is simply called *ril rdzas* (pill substance).[2] The *ril rdzas* used at Chiwong is compounded by Trulshik Rinpoche. When he was resident at Thami in 1959 and 1960, he prepared some for that monastery, but no longer knows if it is used there.

Trulshik Rinpoche compounds the pill substances from a variety of "blessings" (*byin brlab*). "Blessing" here refers to the hard dark-brown granular substance that lamas regularly give to those who seek audience with them. Each lama compounds his own blessings. They are also called "ambrosia" (*bdud rtsi*), or "ambrosial religious medicine" (*bdud rtsi chos sman*).

The word *bdud rtsi* itself translates the Sanskrit term *amṛta*, the divine "elixir of immortality" of Indian legend. It is an ambiguous term. In a Tantric context, there is much talk of five ambrosias: urine, excrement, semen, flesh, and blood.[3] From the Tibetan word, which etymologically translated would be "demon juice," we may infer that in Tibet the term possessed daemonic connotations from the outset.

In Tibet, the urine and excrement of great lamas is prized for its medicinal qualities. Reputedly the denizens of the village at the foot of the Potala once did a brisk trade in the Dalai Lama's excrement. It is quite possible that the ambrosia in the *ril rdzas* has similar ingredients. This would account for Trulshik Rinpoche's reticence and vagueness on the subject. However, we should note that even if *ril rdzas* was purely an herbal compound, it would likely be classified as part of a lama's secret knowledge.

Whatever their composition, the amount of *ril rdzas* added is minute. The pharmacological effect, if any, of either the pills or of *bdud rtsi* seems to be a subtle one. In any event, the "active ingredient" of the pills is not the *ril rdzas* but the mantras. Were it not, the public could come for the pills on the fourth day instead of after a further week or more of ritual.

Trulshik Rinpoche likens the process of making the pills to brewing beer. "The grain itself has no power to make you drunk, but after the work of brewing is done, it does."[4] Just as alcohol will have an effect regardless of one's belief system, the action of the pills does not depend on the faith of those who take them. The ritual text is equally clear on this subject. Once the divine light has entered the pills, "It can bring about the liberating experience of the four liberations of seeing, hearing, remembering, and touching."[5]

The pills are also said to have more modest spiritual effects. Through the ritual, each pill gains the power to generate faith in Avalokiteśvara equivalent to saying his mantra one thousand times.[6] According to Trulshik Rinpoche, the pills "have many benefits." For example, they also bestow worldly virtues such as long life and health.

While the pills are being made, a round, bronze mirror is prepared to cover them as they rest in their skull bowl atop the *maṇḍala*. The mirror used is a larger-sized version of the Tibetan magician's *me long*. It is covered with red colored butter. Two opposed equilateral triangles, forming a six-pointed star, the "origin of *dharmas*" are incised in the butter. The points of one of the triangles are decorated with swastikas, those of the other, with the equivalent "joyous swirl" (*dga' dkyil*) motif.

A four-petalled lotus is in the center of the star. In the hub of the lotus, a monk writes the mantras of the three central deities of the *maṇḍala:* Lord of the Dance, the Horse-Headed god Hayagrīva, and Lord of the Dance's consort. These are respectively: "oṁ āḥ hūṁ hrīḥ oṁ maṇi padme hūṁ," "oṁ hrīḥ vajrakrotahayagriva hulu hulu hūṁ phaṭ" and "oṁ dhumaghaye namaḥ svāhā."[7] The mantras of the four families of Sky Walkers as they appear in the "Empowerment of the Body" section of the *Manual* go clockwise around the lotus, one to a petal: "Vajra dhāka dhāki kara kāya . . .", Ratna dhāka dhāki nirica kāya . . .", Padma dhāka dhāki nihri kāya . . .", Karma dhāka dhāki saya kāya."[8] The mirror will not be employed until the monks "take the true achievement" of their efforts immediately before the public empowerment of the fourteenth day.

THE MANDALA

Maṇḍalas (Tib. *dkyil 'khor*) are a feature of many Tibetan rituals, particularly those involving empowerment.[9] One can look at a *maṇḍala* from many different viewpoints. On a very basic level, it is an architectural drawing, a two-dimensional rendering of a three-dimensional building and its grounds. The building is the palace of the god, the grounds are his paradise. The rendering is governed by fixed conventions. Certain features, the gates, for example, are shown in elevation, as if viewed from the outside at eye level. Other features are shown as a plan, viewed from above, such as the crossed-*vajras* that form the foundation of the palace. The juxtaposition of elevation and plan in a single drawing has some curious results. Beyond the deer and wheel motif that graces the portal roofs, we can see the edge of the *vajra* foundation, as if it were floating in air, or as if the walls of the *maṇḍala* had been blown out flat by a miraculous explosion that had toppled them outward but left them otherwise intact.

The visualization of the *maṇḍala* required by the ritual would be made easier with a three-dimensional model to refer to. Such models do exist, although there are none in Solu-Khumbu.[10]

The *maṇḍala* used in a ritual may be a ready-made drawing or painting on cloth, paper or wood, or it may be drawn for the occasion with pen and ink or with sand on the floor or other horizontal surface.

There are some differences in the conventions of sand *maṇḍalas* and *maṇḍalas* in other media. *Maṇḍalas* painted on cloth typically show the deities in bodily form in their respective places. Sand *maṇḍalas* (*rdul tshon dkyil 'khor; rajomaṇḍala*) represent the deities by their mantric seed syllables or by a characteristic hand implement.[11] Lord of the Dance, for example, is indicated by a *vajra*. The *vajra* here is doubly appropriate. It is the conventional way to represent the main deities and at the same time, the implement that Lord of the Dance holds in his first pair of hands. The Four Sorceresses are represented differently at different monasteries and on different occasions. At Chiwong in 1980, for example, they were shown by their syllables: "jaḥ hūṁ baṁ hoḥ." At Thami, they are represented by their hand implements: a sword (or better a hook), a lasso, a chain, and a bell.

The custom of drawing on the ground with colored powders is widespread on the Indian subcontinent. In many communities, women do floor paintings as a part of their household rituals. Certain South Indian communities are well-known for their Hindu religious floor paintings.

According to Tucci, originally, the *maṇḍala* was invariably made of colored powders (Ssk. *cūrṇa*). Solely an initiatic device, it was drawn for the occasion and erased when its purpose had been served. Later the *maṇḍala* became "confused with the *paṭa*," and began to be painted on cloth.[12]

The practice of making sand *maṇḍalas* was already a part of tantric Buddhism in India and is mentioned in the *Hevajra-tantra*. For materials, the tantra suggests several possibilities.

> . . . using the sacred writing-colours, or secondly powder made from the five gems, or else the grains of rice and so on. With these the *maṇḍala* should be made, in size three cubits plus three inches.[13]

The "five sacred writing-colours" are a grisly alternative to powdered gemstones. The tantra specifies them for a rainmaking ritual:

> Black colouring is obtained from charcoal of the cemetery, white from ground human bones, yellow from green lac, red from cemetery bricks, green from *caurya* leaves and ground human bones, and dark blue from ground human bones and cemetery charcoal.[14]

Chiwong employs neither of these picturesque recipes. The sand there is colored with packaged Indian dye powder purchased in the bazaar. As we have noted, at least sometimes the sand itself is pulverized quartz.[15]

Like all religious activity, drawing a *maṇḍala* gains merit for the one who does it. Je Tsongkhapa, the great fourteenth-century Tibetan scholar, religious reformer, and founder of the Gelugpa order, claimed that if you construct a *maṇḍala* of sand, the merit that you gain will be multiplied by the number of grains of sand.

The extra merit of making a sand *maṇḍala* is counterbalanced by the difficulty of the process. In 1978, when this research project began, Mani Rimdu was reputedly the only ritual performed in Nepal to use a sand *maṇḍala*. In pre-1959 Tibet, the practice was widespread, and, according to some reports, sand *maṇḍalas* are not uncommon in some of the refugee communities in India. In Nepal, sand *maṇḍalas* seem to be enjoying at least a minor renaissance. In the last few years, Thubten Chöling has taken to making them for two separate ritual cycles. Sand *maṇḍalas* are also made at Dingo Khyentse Rinpoche's monastery in Kathmandu.

Crude sand *maṇḍalas* and the larger blocks of color in finer specimens are made by taking a quantity of sand in the palm of the hand and slowly dribbling it out with the fingertips. For fine work, a tool is necessary. This tool is a small metal cone, usually between four and six inches in length. It is an inch to an inch and a half in diameter at its widest point, narrowing to a quarter of an inch or less at the business end of the tool. The longitudinal axis of the cone is ridged on one side.

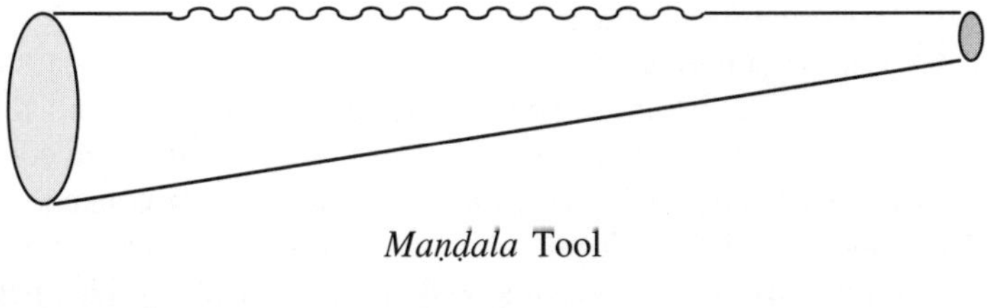

Maṇḍala Tool

The painter fills the tool with sand and then scrapes the striated edge with another metal object. At Chiwong a *vajra* is used for this purpose. The monks of Thami employ a less picturesque but equally effective butter knife. Scraped, the cone vibrates and sand trickles from its mouth. The flow of sand is determined in part by the size of the opening and roughness of the striations, but can be regulated by scraping with more or less vigor. A careful artist, using a finely made tool, can make lines a few grains of sand wide.

The sand painting may be done by a single monk or by as many as three or four. There is no set pattern as to who these may be. In Chiwong in 1979 and 1980, the head monk did the painting. After his decease, the job devolved to a succession of junior monks. At Thami the painting has been the job of the monastery's oboists, two young men with the multifaceted artistic talent that one encounters with regularity in Nepal's monasteries. Tengpoche, the largest of the three Sherpa monasteries that perform Mani Rimdu, is the home of a professional thangka painter. He is said to create the sand *maṇḍala* at that monastery.[16]

The sand *maṇḍala* always starts at the center and works its way out toward the edge. The work is done methodically and with logic. There is a tradition of how its various parts should be done and more experienced monks advise the less experienced in the fine points of the art. This does not rule out individual variations. The *maṇḍala* being symmetrical, one can sometimes observe two monks simultaneously creating the same motif in discernibly different styles.

The *maṇḍala* in each monastery differs in size, in color choice, and, naturally, in skill of execution. Like many aspects of monastery life, the skill shown in *maṇḍala* making is related to a monastery's size. The odds of finding a talented artist are twice as great when you have twenty men to choose from than when you have ten. Continuity is also an asset. All other things being equal, the more years of experience a given *maṇḍala* maker or *maṇḍala* making team has accumulated, the better the *maṇḍala*. Of course, all other things never are equal. As mentioned above, Tengpoche has the good fortune to have a professional painter. The monk who created the Chiwong *maṇḍala* in years past was renowned as a learned and kindly man. Painting, however, was not his calling, and the Chiwong *maṇḍala* has improved in the less experienced, but nimbler hands of his successors.

The monasteries' sand *maṇḍalas* differ, too, in color and in motif, although perhaps they should not, as the rules of iconography are strict and a *maṇḍala*'s proportions mathematically determined.

Such variation is not restricted to sand paintings, nor is it suggestive of a more casual attitude toward temporary media. The painted-wood Lord of the Dance *maṇḍalas* at Chiwong and Thubten Chöling also differ in color and detail. Different examples of a given *maṇḍala* in museum collections also vary. This should not be surprising: although iconographers have long since fixed the proportions of the Buddha's body in mathematical grids, there has never been a lack of variety in Buddha images.

During the ritual, the sand *maṇḍala* is housed in a wooden structure also called a *maṇḍala* (Tib. *dkyil 'khor*). The structure consists of a platform for the painting and a roof supported by four columns. Monasteries, even those which do not use sand paintings often possess such miniature houses, although those intended for drawings on cloth, paper, or wood can be considerably smaller.

The smaller structures often have a permanent place in the chapel, but those that house the Mani Rimdu *maṇḍala* are so large and cumbersome that they must be kept disassembled in storage during the rest of the year. At Chiwong, where the *maṇḍala* and its abode are particularly large and heavy, they must assemble the housing before the sand painting begins. At Thami, where the unencumbered *maṇḍala* is small and light enough to be rotated during the painting process, the housing is assembled after the *maṇḍala* is completed.

The housing is curtained to hide the *maṇḍala* from view during the ceremony. Indeed, supporting these curtains is a primary function of the structure as a whole. In full-scale initiations at Thubten Chöling, where the *maṇḍala* must be hidden during the first part of the ceremony and revealed in the latter part, curtains are often simply hung from four poles attached to the corners of the table on which the *maṇḍala* rests.

THE TORMAS

While the *maṇḍala* painters are busy inside the chapel, other monks begin making the tormas outside on the monastery porch.

For Tibetans, the word torma (*gtor ma*) identifies any of a variety of offering cakes sculpted from dough or grain and decorated with butter.[17] The substance traditionally used is the Tibetan staple, *tsampa*, roasted barley flour, although at Chiwong in 1982, corn meal was used for reasons of economy. One type of torma, the feast (*tshogs*) is usually made of rice, at least in Nepal where that grain is plentiful. Another, the true achievement torma, has butter and sugar mixed into the dough.

Butter is used on tormas in several different ways. "White tormas" are painted with plain melted butter. To make a red torma, *ombulak* root is cooked into the butter before it is applied.[18] Tormas painted with black-dyed butter are also used in Mani Rimdu.

Sculpted butter, plain or colored, is applied as surface decoration. At Chiwong, the butter is prepared by kneading it with a rolling pin on a corrugated stone. Once smooth and clean, the butter can be colored. Unlike red, which is made from an edible root, the other pigments are Indian dye powder and are quite inedible. While being worked into the various decorations, the butter is kept chilled in water. A kind of butter palette is sometimes used. This is a wooden box in which lumps of many different colors of butter are kept in the cool recesses of the monastery until needed.

The monks work the butter with their fingers to create the basic shapes: disks, dots, lunar crescents, flower petals, and so on. They model fine detail, such as the corolla of the flower in the "flower of the senses" torma, with a pointed stick. The most unique tool of the torma making process is the *mar dar*, the 'butter-wand'. This uniquely Tibetan device is a syringe made of metal or bamboo. It is used to extrude a thin spaghetti-like strand of butter, which is let drop into the cooling bucket and then rolled back up around the wand. These white strands are used to decorate the edges of the torma, and also for the filigree-like designs sometimes applied to their surface.

Different tormas have different purposes. Some represent a deity; others are magic weapons. The main torma in a ritual may pass through several layers of meaning. On a basic level, however, a torma is an offering for a deity. The Sanskrit word that the mantras for offering tormas employ is *bali*, the common term for an offering or sacrifice.

The sacrifice Tibetans identify as a torma is a cake, but the name may point to bloodier past. Although the etymology of the Tibetan word torma is not entirely clear, Ekvall's claim that it means "broken-up" is a cogent one.[19] Sacrifices were important in pre-Buddhist Tibetan religion, and in earlier times "torma" seems to have referred to the animals broken-up by sacrificial priests.[20] Dough figures used at Tibetan New Year represent the heads of sheep and goats—the proverbial "head on a platter" that we know of from our own heritage of animal sacrifice. Our texts speak of tormas "adorned with human blood," and many tormas are colored a very bloody red to signify this, albeit with root extracts.[21]

The "flower of the senses" (*dbang po'i me tog*) is an extremely common type of torma, used in Mani Rimdu as well as in many other rituals. A gruesome, if formal arrangement of human eyeballs, ears, a tongue, and so on—all crafted from dough and butter—it is set in a real skull. It is an offering which symbolizes the gift of the officiants' own sense organs. Fittingly, it has become an outlet for artistic creativity. Examples vary greatly in style and monks lavish care on each macabre detail: the pupils of the eyes, the lobes of the ear, or the flower that symbolizes the mind.

According to Helmut Hoffmann and Robert B. Ekvall, the torma's legendary origin in Tibet dates from Padmasambhava's prohibition of blood sacrifice, animal and human. Thus, it is a common belief that Padmasambhava personally taught the Bonpo to make "substitute effigies of their victims."[22] Similarly, in Nepal, where blood sacrifice is still common, refugee Tibetans are critical of the practice, sometimes claiming that it shows that non-Buddhist customs lack compassion.

The substitution of a cake for a corpse is quite logical in a Buddhist ritual context, but it is not certain that the substitution was a Tibetan innovation. Food in its infinite variety is a ritual offering worldwide. Indic rituals such as the *Vājapeya*, "the drink of strength" recorded in Brāhmanic literature, specifically mention offering cakes.[23] This ritual, which like the related horse sacrifice, the *Aśvamedha*, was a means by which "the magical power which pervaded the king at his consecration was restored and strengthened."[24] The *Vājapeya* employs a wheel-shaped offering cake representing the sun.[25] Considering the influence of royal ritual on later Buddhist practice—the empowerment, the signal Tantric ritual is both named for and modeled on the ancient Indian royal consecration—it is possible that the offering cake entered Buddhist praxis in India.

There is both anthropological and art historical evidence to support to this argument. Newar Buddhists also employ *bali* made of grain; the fifth-century Buddhist caves at Ajanta, India house an image of a man holding a dun-colored pear-shaped object that looks suspiciously like a modern feast torma.[26]

A score of different types of tormas and groups of tormas are used during Mani Rimdu. Some are iconic; some non-iconic. Some are linked to a specific ritual and/or a specific god. Others are a generic type that can be used in a number of different contexts. Some are offerings, pure and simple; others fulfill a complex set of functions. Certain tormas, for example, are given in worship, whereas others are objects of worship. Some are both. Although all are food in one sense or the other, only three of the types of tormas used in Mani Rimdu are intended to be eaten: the feast tormas, the achievement torma, and the "true achievement."[27]

Each torma must be transformed by the meditative imagination before it is fit for use. These meditations are given in the liturgy with which the torma is associated. William Stablein explains one such transformation in his comparison of Newar and Tibetan ritual practice.

> Because the main deity and his consort are outwardly projected to couple within the food and produce the *bodhicitta* and ensuing ambrosia, the process is known as *baliyoga*, i.e., the union within the offerings which generally occurs near the end of the *samādhipūja*.[28]

The most elaborate tormas are kept for the length of the festival, simpler ones are thrown out after a single use. Even those tormas that endure the entire festival by Tibetan standards are short-lived. According to Trulshik Rinpoche tormas can be divided into three categories according to their longevity. The most durable, are the permanent tormas, *rtag gtor*. Although fashioned of *tsampa* and butter like the tormas of Mani Rimdu, the *rtag gtor* were kept "forever" like statues, a feat impossible outside of the arid, frigid, microbe-free monastery interiors of Tibet proper. Next in longevity are the *rten gtor* (durable tormas). Even in the atmosphere of Solu-Khumbu, relatively septic by Tibetan standards, a "durable torma" can be kept for one to five years. The bulk of tormas are session tormas, *thun gtor*. They are made for a given ritual and then disposed of. All the tormas of Mani Rimdu are *thun gtor*.

If we were to count all the tormas made for Mani Rimdu, they would number in the hundreds. In this chapter, we will discuss some of the principal examples. Others will be handled as they occur in the ritual.

TORMAS USED IN MANI RIMDU

type	*Generic/Specific (G/S)*	*kept? (Y/N)*	*days used*	*forms known*
achievement torma (*sgrub gtor*)	S	Y	general	2
offering torma (*mchod gtor*)	G	Y	general	1
Sky Walker torma (*mkha' 'gro bral gtor*)	S	Y	general	1
Protector tormas	S	Y	general	3[a]
Followers tormas (*rjes 'brang*)	S	Y	general	1
propitiation tormas (*bskang gtor*)	G	Y	general	2
food torma #2 (*zhal zas*)	G	Y	general	2
food torma #1 (*zhal zas*)	G	N	general	1
fierce food (*drag po'i zhal zas*)	G	Y	general	2
flower of the senses (*dbang po'i me tog*)	G	Y	general	
feast (*tshogs*)	G	Y	general	
lama's feast (*bla tshogs*)	G	N	general	1
obstructor tormas (*bgegs gtor*)	G	N	general	1
three-Part torma (*cha gsum*)	S	N	general	1
Steadfast Women's torma (*brtan gtor*)	S	N	general	1
contract torma (*chad tho*)	S	N	general	1
gift tormas (*'bul gtor*)	S	N	general	4
torma balls (*gtor ril*)	G	N	13, 15	1
white tormas/red tormas (*dkar dmar gtor*)	S	N	13, 15	1
magic weapon tormas (*zor*)	G	N	13, 15	1
true achievement torma (*dngos grub*)	S	Y	14/16[b]	1
Serpent Spirit (*klu*) offering torma	[c]	N	17	1

[a] At Thami, the elaborate form was used in 1980 and the intermediate form in 1983. Chiwong invariably uses the simple form. The intermediate form is also said to be the type of torma employed at Tengpoche. Interview with Tengpoche Rinpoche Ngawang Tenzing, 5/26/83.

[b] At Tengpoche, the True Achievement Torma is used on the sixteenth day, immediately after the destruction of the sand *maṇḍala*.

[c] At Chiwong and at Thami a generic torma is used. At Tengpoche, they use a special *klu* torma. According to Trulshik Rinpoche, the Chiwong practice is correct.

THE MAIN TORMA

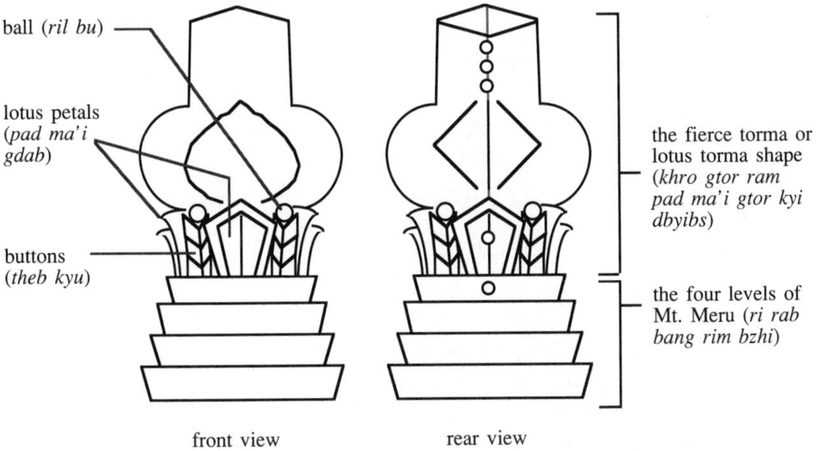

The Main Torma at Chiwong

The main torma of Mani Rimdu is called "the achievement torma of the main god" (*lha gtso bo'i sgrub gtor*), or more fully, "the torma which is the substance that serves as a basis for achieving the god" (*lha sgrub pa'i rten rdzas kyi gtor ma*). Red in color, it is also known as "the red glorious torma" (*dpal gtor dmar po*).

The torma represents a god sitting atop the world mountain, surrounded by his entourage. The body of the torma stands for the body of the god. The stick that runs vertically through its center is called the torma's spine, literally its "tree of life."[29] The four steps that form the base are the four levels of Mount Meru. Smaller elements represent the lesser deities that surround Lord of the Dance, his "minions." The four lotus petals (*pad ma'i gdab bzhi*), one on each of the four sides, represent the four Sky Walkers. The four balls at the corners represent the Four Sorceresses. The four sets of three "buttons" beneath them represent the assembled gods of the entourage.[30]

Although in its detail the main torma of Mani Rimdu is specific to Lord of the Dance, in its basic form it is the same as the tormas of other gods. This shape is called "the fierce torma or lotus torma shape" (*khro gtor ram pad ma'i gtor kyi dbyibs*). The "elaborate" torma for Zhal bzhi 'the Four-Faced One', for example, has the same basic shape. It differs, however, in having black steps and no leaves, buttons or balls. It is surrounded on the lowest step and at its base by an entourage of small tormas.

The "face" (*zhal*) of the torma is decorated with "flowers"—flat disks of white or red butter. The red disk is decorated at the center with a small white dot. The white disks are decorated with a small set of concentric circles, made by piling up ever smaller dots of various shades of red. The corners of each step of the world mountain has a tiny board carrying a flame decorated with a series of dots graduated in size and shade.

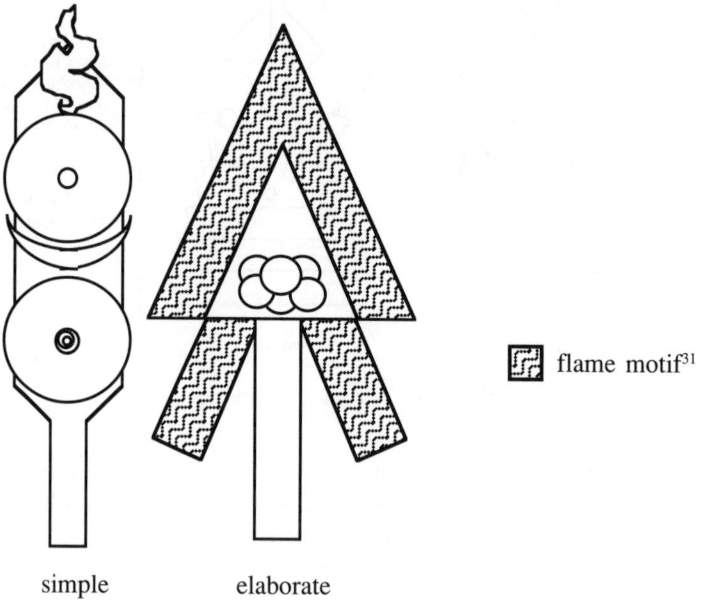

gtor sgrom

A thin flat board called a *gtor sgrom* surmounts the torma. This board has further decorations of butter. In their simpler form, the decorations consist of further disks—a white one below and a red one above, with a white crescent moon between them. Surmounting the disks is a white flame.

Elaborate *gtor sgrom* may be either made anew of butter each time or made for reuse, in which case they are painted on a thin sheet of wood or metal.

The *gtor sgrom* used in Solu-Khumbu are of a distinctive shape said to be peculiar to the Nyingma sect.[32] The outer edge of these *gtor sgrom* are decorated with a multicolored band of flames. An inner triangular area contains a lotus throne surmounted by a symbol particular to the god in question. In the case of the main torma at Thami, the Sanskrit syllable "hrī" is employed. In the case of a torma for the God of the Planets, the symbol would be a bow and arrow or a crocodile victory banner (*chu srin rgyal mtshan*). For Guardian of Mantra, the symbol would be the mummy-club that ferocious goddess brandishes.[33]

An achievement torma is only necessary in the extended worship of the deity. In the brief worship of Lord of the Dance that is done regularly at Thubten Chöling, only an offering torma is used.

When asked to comment on the rationale behind the specific shape of the achievement torma, Trulshik Rinpoche says that it is "like the cross in Christianity. It is the symbol of the god. He likes it."

Tormas vary somewhat in form from monastery to monastery. At Thami, the steps of the torma are higher and the "body" smaller. The decorations that halo the torma are more elaborate. At Chiwong the protrusion on the back of the torma is angular as in the illustration. At Thami, it is more rounded. The small balls are not found at Thami. In the Thubten Chöling version, deemed correct by Trulshik Rinpoche and Chant Leader Ngawang Tsundru, the steps are even smaller in proportion to the body of the torma than they are at Chiwong. Although variations in peripheral decoration and so on are considered to be legitimate; others, such as changes of proportion are deemed incorrect.

Decorated Achievement Torma
Based on a sketch made at Thubten Chöling

Most tormas are made from memory. There are manuscripts that describe how to make tormas, and when they are available, monks may rely on them for more elaborate and less commonly used examples. The work consulted at Thami is the elaborately illustrated Rongphu guide to ritual implements.[34] This fascinating work of indigenous ethnography is based on research done at Mindroling monastery. The use of it was abandoned at Rongphu when later research revealed that it had many inaccuracies. Trulshik Rinpoche considers the work to be obsolete and classifies tormas made from it as "old Rongphu style." Indeed, the tormas of Thami differ in proportion and in detail from those made at Thubten Chöling, which follows the purer Mindroling style based on the findings of a second research expedition. At Thami, the *Ritual Guide* also provides the model for the protector tormas.

At Chiwong, a short un-illustrated manuscript is used. It presumably is accurate. However, making a torma from a written recipe is laborious indeed. Once the monks of Chiwong discovered that I had sketches of previous years' tormas, they began to borrow my notebooks. Thus, future accounts of the Mani Rimdu lineage may include one rather bemused member who spoke Tibetan with an American accent.

The meaning of the main torma is different at different moments in the ritual. In the Nyingma tradition, a torma such as this, or rather, our perception of a torma such as this passes through three phases.[35] At first, during the rituals of the Lord of the Dance *Manual*, it is perceived as something to be offered (*mchod rdzas du shes pa*). Then, during the public empowerment, it is perceived as the god (*lha ru shes pa*). After the empowerment, it is perceived as the very substance of true achievement, of *siddhi* (*dngos grub du shes pa* or *dngos grub kyi rdzas su shes pa*).

These various states are reflected in the liturgy.

In the section of the *Manual* called "Offering the Torma," we read:

> In the pure torma dish of the Truth Realm
> All things desired in a torma are heaped in a heap.
> I pray you receive this ambrosia of the vow,
> Excellent amidst uncorrupted blissful offerings! [16b1]

The empowerment ritual used on Day Fifteen states that during the "Actual Empowerment":

> The torma vessel becomes a great self-emergent spontaneously built paradise. The torma substances sit in it in the form of the gods of the circle of Union of the Blissful, Lord of the Dance, Great Compassion's *maṇḍala*.

Sang Sang Tulku notes that during the Medicine and Rakta Offerings, a daily part of the *Manual* rituals, the torma is thought of as the god. Thus, the medicine and *rakta* are first offered to the torma, and then to the lamas and gods of the *maṇḍala* mentioned in the Medicine Offering verses.[36]

The torma reaches its third level of significance after the empowerment on Day Fifteen. To quote the text, "The torma substance, into which the gods, as light, have melted, is given as true achievement." At this point, the text goes on to direct the disciples to eat the torma, and indeed, according to Trulshik Rinpoche, a little piece of the main torma is eaten when such a ritual is done for a small group. With hundreds participating in its public empowerment, the custom is not followed at Mani Rimdu, as it would demolish the torma.

Through most of the Mani Rimdu, the main torma stays on the shelf at the edge of the *maṇḍala.*

For the Lord of the Dance rituals at Thubten Chöling, an offering torma (*mchod gtor*) is made instead of the elaborate achievement torma. This simple torma is of a generic shape, similar to the offering torma for the Serpent Spirits (*klu*) used on the last day of Mani Rimdu. However, the Lord of the Dance offering torma is red in color as befits that deity, instead of white as for the *klu.*[37] According to Chant Leader Ngawang Tsundru, since Mani Rimdu uses an achievement torma no offering torma is necessary.

THE PROTECTOR TORMAS

After the main torma, next in importance and care of manufacture are the tormas of the Great Protectors (*mgon chen gyi gtor ma*). The Protector tormas are food offerings to the gods known as the Sworn Protectors of Religion worshipped in the *Playful Ocean of True Achievement*, the second of Mani Rimdu's two major ritual texts. During Mani Rimdu, the Protector tormas are kept in a glass-doored case at the north end of the chapel.

Since there are ten Sworn Protectors in all, each with his own entourage, the Protector tormas are quite complex. Whereas the main torma of Lord of the Dance is made from memory, the monks often consult a manuscript for the Protector tormas.

As with many things Tibetan, tormas may be made in any of three ways—simply, elaborately, or somewhere in between. At Chiwong the simple pattern is followed. At Tengpoche, the medium type is preferred.[38] At Thami, either the medium or elaborate type is used, depending on how much time the monks feel they can relegate to the task that year. The elaborate tormas are quite elaborate. The torma for Planet, for example, is covered with the eyes that cover that god's body.

Even so-called simple tormas may be quite elaborate. Planet's does not have his eyes, but the god's writhing snake tail is represented by a coil of dough that spirals down the body of the torma. The god Mahādeva, who is shown in an ithyphallic form in the iconography of Mani Rimdu, is given an appropriately phallic torma. Its form is obviously related to the *lingam* which represents Mahādeva in Hindu culture, but is more anatomically detailed.

The rest of the simple protector tormas fall into a few groups. One group is white and round, that is to say in the shape of a truncated cone, rounded at the top. The rest are red and of one of two forms: triangular (*zur gsum*) or "shouldered" (*dpung ro*).[39] A "triangular" torma is a tall triangular pyramid with a flattened top. The shape of a "shouldered" torma is suggested by its name. It has two shallow depressions on its face.

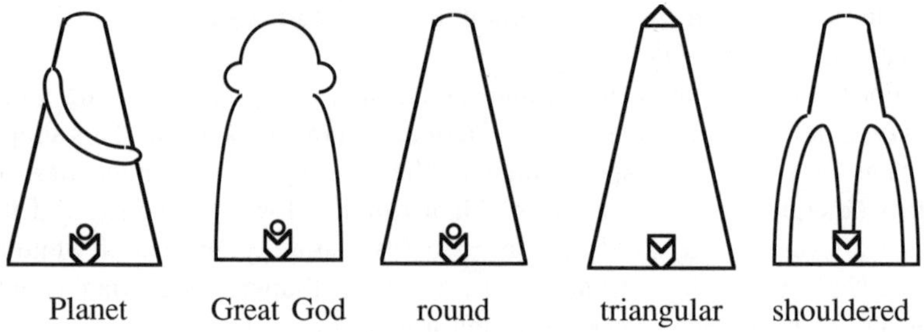

"Simple" Torma Shapes

PROTECTOR TORMAS[a]

deity (left to right)	*color*	*shape*	*#*[b]	*ball*	*banner*
1. Planet	red	snake	4	Y	black
2. Four-Faced One	red	shouldered	?	N	red
3. Neuter	red	shouldered	?	N	red
4. Four-Handed One	red	shouldered	?	N	red
5. Virtuous One	red	shouldered	5	N	black
6. Guardian of Mantra	red	triangular	4	N	black
7. Great God (Mahādeva)	red	phallic	4	Y	red
8. Son of Renown	red	shouldered	4	Y	red
9. Cemetery Goddess	red	triangular	4	N	black
10. Long Life Woman	white	round	4	Y	white

[a] This chart is based on sketches made at Chiwong in 1980 and 1983.
[b] # = number of front row entourage tormas.

It will be noticed from the chart, that if we remove deities like µiva and Rāhula, whose bodily eccentricities suggest their unusual form, the tormas fall into two types neatly according to sex: shoulders for the male deities and triangles, the archetypical symbol of the female sex organ, for the goddesses. Long Life Woman is truly the odd-woman out. Her torma is peacefully white and round—this gentle goddess of the pristine Himalayan peaks lacks any hint of the sexuality and danger suggested by the blood-red vagina-shaped tormas of the terrifying Guardian of Mantra and Cemetery Goddess.

Each of the tormas has a row of smaller tormas in front of it and other smaller tormas to the side and rear. Those in the front row are the same shape as their master; the others may differ. As with the main tormas, unusual shapes are reserved for unusual deities. Thus, a small snake-wound (*sbrul 'khril*) torma is found behind the tormas of Mantra Guardian and Four Handed One—Planet (gZa') being in those gods' entourages as well as being worshipped in his own right. In Planet's own torma, we find another four snake-wound tormas to his right, with the four in front giving a total of eight, corresponding to the eight major gods of his retinue. The bodily form of these gods, the liturgy reminds us, "are like their chief."[40]

The side and back tormas are of varying sizes. Not all of them correspond in shape to the major torma with which they are associated. Among the larger of the side and back tormas, a twisted shape and a miniature version of the shouldered shape are most common. Each of the principal tormas and their front row companions has a small cup-shaped "button" before it. In some cases, this cup is empty. In others, it contains a small ball.

With all these tormas and sub-tormas, naturally there is confusion. That of rDo rje legs pa (Good Diamond) is a case in point. This deity, in addition to being a protector of the "Followers" class in his own right, appears in the entourages of Four-Handed One (PO f 11.6) and of Mantra Guardian (PO f 19.5). In 1983, however, his torma perplexingly replaced one of the small snake-shaped tormas in Planet's entourage, although the former god is not mentioned in the *sādhana* of the latter. In 1980, his small but distinctive torma (see in the next section on the *Followers*) lurked in the background of Great God, another deity with whom he has no connection. Similarly in 1983, the order of the tormas was changed, and both years that I recorded the ritual at Thami, there was a different number of Followers tormas from the prescribed fifteen.[41]

Paradoxically, the intermediate form of the torma, which as mentioned above is used at Tengpoche and sometimes at Thami, is the simplest. In their intermediate form, the tormas of all the deities are identical in shape—a small, nearly rectangular rhomboid placed atop a larger one and flush with it in front. Perhaps to make up for this unaccountable uniformity, the intermediate tormas are often the most meticulously crafted.

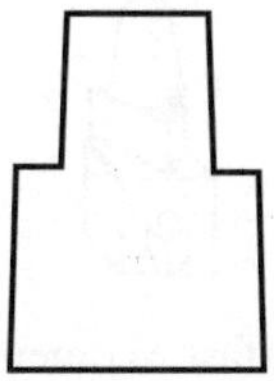

"Intermediate" Torma Shape

THE FOLLOWERS

The next major group of tormas is for the Followers (*rjes 'brang*), those deities who follow the main Protectors. These tormas are considerably smaller than the Protectors—approximately six inches tall exclusive of decorations. They are also much simpler, inasmuch as they lack subsidiary entourage tormas. Each Followers torma is decorated with two white disks of butter with a small pink and a tiny red dot in the center. Most of the Followers tormas are red and triangular. A few are distinctively shaped. King Pehar has a "six-shouldered" (*shog drug*) torma. Good Diamond has a torma with tusk-like forms protruding from the cup in front of it.[42]

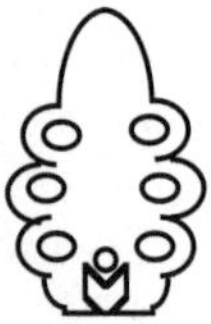

The "Six-Shouldered" Torma of King Pehar

Serpent's torma is white and like those of the minor Planets, wound with a snake (*sbrul 'khril*). Both God of the Plain and the Owners of the Land (*gzhi bdag*) have round (*zlum po*) white tormas.[43] The white torma for Medicine Ladies is called *ka zlum ldir can*, after its round bulging shape.

The *ka zlum ldir can* Torma Shape

Demon's (bDud) torma is appropriately black and comes to a droopy hooked point (*rtse gug*) on top. The Steadfast Women have an unusual three-tiered torma. The bottom is a cube. This is surmounted by a triangular wedge, which in turn is capped by a rounded cone. The Steadfast Women's torma is red.

The Steadfast Women's Torma

FOLLOWERS TORMAS

	deity (left to right)	#[c]	*color*	*shape*	*ball?*
1.	Treasure Master	PO	red	triangle	N
2.	Stern One	9	red	triangle	N
3.	King [Pehar]	8	red	six-shouldered	Y
4.	Furious Haughty One[a]	7	red	triangle	N
5.	Good Diamond	6	red	triangle	[b]
6.	Dagger Guardians	3	red	triangle	N
7.	Governors of the Haughty	2	red	triangle	N
8.	Lion Face	1	red	triangle	N
9.	Steadfast Women	4	red	cube/triangle/cone	Y
10.	Medicine Ladies	5	white	*ka zlum ldir can*	Y
11.	Demon	10	black	hooked point	Y
12.	Stern One	10	red	triangle	N
13.	Serpent	10	white	snake-wound	Y
14.	God of the Plain	11	white	round	Y
15.	Owners of the Land	PO	white	round	Y

[a] One informant in discussing the tormas, maintained that the *khro gtum dregs pa* were also called *sha med*, "the Fleshless One[s]." This, however, is the name of one of the twelve Steadfast Women.

[b] My 1985 sketch shows #5 not even having a cup. My 1980 sketch shows #5, 6, 7 and 8 lacking cups. In my 1982 sketch, all the tormas have cups. In an alternate form, Good Diamond's torma has a cup with two half-crescent shaped prongs emerging from it.

[c] # = number of deity in the *Followers* ritual text, if any. PO = the Treasure Master and the Owners of the Land are worshipped in the part of *Playful Ocean* into which the worship of the other Followers is inserted, section 2.4, f 38b2 ff.

OTHER PROTECTOR TORMAS

Two other kinds of tormas are associated with the protector ritual, the propitiation torma (*bskang gtor*) and the gift tormas (*'bul gtor*). Each of these has a special relation to a specific part of the *Playful Ocean*.

The propitiation torma is associated with the "Propitiation Process." At Thami, a row of ten identical red tormas is made near the rear edge of a board.[44] Each has a "button" in front of it and is decorated with four white disks of butter and a simple *gtor sgrom*. At the front edge of the board, is a low, wavy-edged proscenium, red with a white border, representing the Himālayas. The space between the two serves as a trough for various "propitiation substances," as if the meditators had filled the vast Tibetan plateau with their offerings.

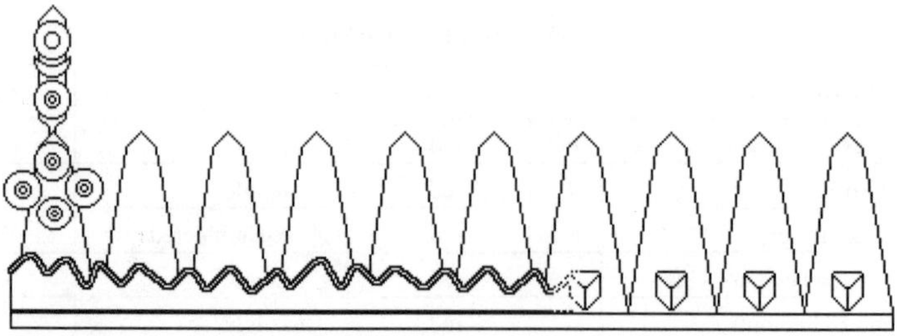

The Propitiation Torma at Thami Monastery (cut-away view)

Only one propitiation torma is made for each Mani Rimdu; a new gift torma is made each day. The gift torma consists of two rows of small tormas. In the center of the first row is a "shouldered" torma somewhat larger than the rest, the "torma for the Sworn Ones in general" (*dam can spyi gtor*).[45] Flanking it left and right, are tormas for the Land Owner (*gzhi bdag*) and Treasure Masters (*gter bdag*) who are worshipped each day just before the Followers ritual.[46] The Treasure Masters have a triangular red torma with a "button" in front of it. That of the Land Owners is white and "round" with a button and a ball. The proportions of the various parts of the gift torma are fixed. According to TCU, the "shoulders" of the *dam can* torma should be two thirds of its height. The surrounding tormas should be slightly more than half the height of the shoulders. On the back of the *dam can* there are two vertical rows of nine buttons, each surmounted by a ball.[47] As these deities are worshipped each day, the front row does not vary.

According to Trulshik Rinpoche, the gift tormas have the same function as the larger protector tormas kept for the length of the festival. Both are food, but whereas the protector tormas are as extensive as a "royal banquet," the gift tormas are like a short snack.[48]

The rituals for the Protectors and their Followers are not done in their entirety each day. The deities are broken down into four groups and rotated according to a fixed schedule.[49] The rear row of the gift torma reflects this, and has tormas for gods of that day's schedule. Each gift torma is a smaller version of the main torma of that god. Thus, for example, on Day Fourteen of the 1983 Chiwong Mani Rimdu, a type-four day, the rear row had, left to right: a shouldered torma for Four-faced One, a triangular torma for Mantra Guardian, a phallic torma for Great God, and a triangular torma for the Cemetery Goddess. Sometimes the gift torma shows variations that are difficult to account for. Day eight of the same year, for example, a type two day, had the expected tormas for Four-Handed One, Great God, and Cemetery Goddess, but instead of a torma for Son of Renown, had the red torma of Good Diamond and the white torma of the Medicine Ladies, the only deities among the Followers to be worshipped every day.

Thubten Chöling follows the Mindroling system and takes the gift tormas to the Protector room (*mgon khang*) for a few minutes before disposing of them outside of the monastery. Chiwong and Thami, however, follow the Rongphu system and take the gift tormas directly outdoors.[50]

The nature of the tormas offered is described in the section of the *Playful Ocean* called "Feeding [them] the Tormas." Having invoked the power of the truth to aid in the transformation, the assembly prays:

> . . . may the enemies of the teaching and of beings in general,
> In particular, the past enemies who attack us Knowledge Bearers and our patrons and entourages,
> The future enemies who think about us,
> The present enemies who hate us, the embodied who point us out as enemies
> And the host of disembodied harmful obstructors—all of them, no matter where they live, where they run within the three existences,
> In an instant, in a moment, be drawn into this, the basis of our imaginings! [53.2]

After making this astonishing offering of "the flesh and blood of enemies and obstructors and the rest of the nine desirable things," pleasing to the ferocious nature of the gods to whom it is offered, and reciting the appropriate mantras, the assembly explains the bargain they are making in prayer:[51]

> If [I] give this in thanks for the good deeds you have done before
> And that you might bestow in the future, the desired true achievement
> Of the four unflagging activities,
> Receive it with great pleasure, and delighting in it,
> Enhance all the benefit and pleasure of the teaching and beings,
> Particularly [for] us disciples and masters and our entourages!
> Elevate us with oceans of health and unchanging life and fame and wealth!
> And pacify all the unrighteous demon enemy's strife!
> Achieve a wish-fulfilling ocean of multitudinous deeds!
> Hoist the standard of universal victory!
> Guard and defend until enlightenment! [53b4]

THE SKY WALKER TORMA

Throughout the festival, a torma sits in a place of honor on the ritual east (at Chiwong south) ledge of the *maṇḍala* enclosure facing the door. It is the *mkha' 'gro bral gtor* given to the *ḍākiṇīs* during the *Sky Walker Torma*

Offering. The name *bral gtor* refers to the torma's shape, whose flat front is much like a triangular torma, but whose back has the conical form of a "round" torma. It is approximately ten inches in height and rests in a copper bowl fashioned to look like a human skull. The ritual is unique to Mani Rimdu. When Thubten Chöling performs Lord of the Dance rituals separately, they replace it with a Sky Walker ritual using an entirely different torma.[52]

12

Day Five: Arranging the Ornaments

Once the tormas and the *maṇḍala* are complete, usually sometime in the afternoon of the fifth day, the rituals resume with "Arranging the Ornaments" (*rgyan 'god*). The monks carry symbolic implements and ritual devices around the *maṇḍala* in procession, and then arrange them on the *maṇḍala* surface and around the periphery of the structure that houses it. The procession, performed in ceremonial dress to musical accompaniment, has a feeling of pomp. The liturgy recited during the ritual gives the symbolism of the key objects.

Now, the configuration of ritual implements in the center of the *maṇḍala* reaches its final form, a variation of the arrangement used during the Preparation Ritual. A tripod forms the base, balanced on which is a skull bowl full of *maṇi*-pills. A red cloth covers the skull. On the cloth, rests the magic mirror painted with the "origin of things" and mantras. As before, the *vajra* wrapped with the rainbow-colored spell-cord surmounts the edifice.[1]

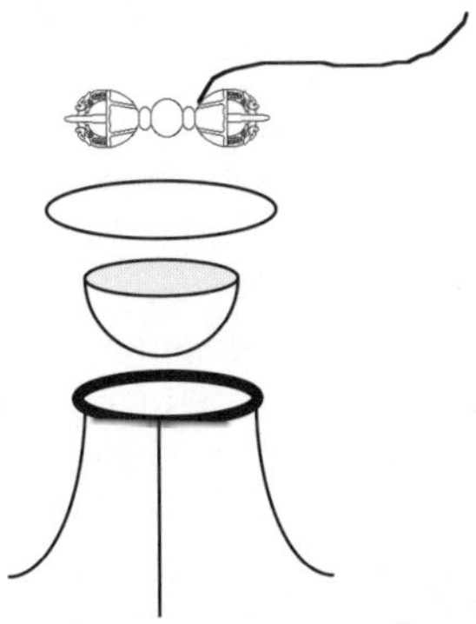

Implements in Center of *Maṇḍala*

This structure is appropriate to the center of the *maṇḍala*, as it is the center of Mani Rimdu. Some of its constituents have already been discussed.[2] Others are new to us, and deserve discussion in detail.

The skull is particularly interesting. Skulls are a common enough symbol of the philosophic contemplation of the transience of life and magical dominion over the world of the dead. At Chiwong, the skull in which the pills are placed is said to be that of a soldier who died in armed conflict. Such embellishments are common in the Tibetan tradition, a sign, as if another were needed, that we are operating in the realm of magic power.

Lamas sometimes advance another explanation of the skull. Here, the value of the skull lies in the fact that it is a "natural vessel," a vessel not made by human hands.[3] This image calls up the natural, unelaborated state of pure awareness, the state back to which tantric practice should lead. In Buddhist parlance, the word "vessel" often denotes the world. One might say that the skull vessel suggests the world in its pristine, original divine state, unsullied by sordid conceptual thought. Since the addition of the pill element, the actual *maṇi ril sgrub*, to the ritual was a Rongphu innovation, there is no mention of either the pills or the skull that contains them in the Mindroling commentaries.

The tripod minimizes the destruction of the sand painting by the objects placed on it. Although smaller and more ornate, it is quite similar to the tripods Tibetans use for cooking. Indeed, the configuration of flask and tripod suggests a cooking process—it resembles nothing so much as a device for heating tea.

In tantric ritual, skulls also have a connotation of a cooking vessel. The traditional tripod stand upon which a skull bowl, real or simulated, rests suggests the cooking process. It is a triangular configuration, the shape that symbolizes fire. Sometimes, it takes the form of three miniature skulls, arranged as hearth stones. Sometimes it is a triangular box, often redundantly patterned with flames. Many times, it is a combination of all these motives—a flame-patterned triangular box with a skull at each corner. As usual in Tibetan art, these details correspond to the visualization prescribed by ritual.[4]

The imagery of cooking should not be surprising. Heat and warmth are common symbols of spiritual attainment. A short lineage is said to have kept its warmth (*drod*), because it has not dissipated its heat over too many generations. The grace bestowed by an empowerment also can be measured in terms of its heat.[5] A well-known Tibetan yoga is that of psychic heat (*gtum mo*). Cooking is, after all, a transformation.

The remaining objects are directly mentioned in the "Arrangement" liturgy. Each is called upon to fulfill its symbolic function:

> Wisdom sword, cut the net of illusion!
> Wisdom arrow, pierce ignorance, the three poisons!
> Dagger of Action, subdue the battalions of obstructive demons!
> We beg you to stay as ornaments to the great *maṇḍala*! [7b2]

Excellent umbrella of love, protect *saṁsāra* from the heat of longing!
Victory banner of religion, give victory over obstructive demons!
Flag of Wisdom, perfect the doctrines of enlightenment!
We offer you as ornaments to beautify the Conqueror's *maṇḍala*! [7b4]

Arghaṁ, flowers, incense, butter-lamps,
And perfume, food, music, and other offerings actually assembled,
Plus the mentally emanated offerings of Samantabhadra,
We give in worship of the gods of the *maṇḍala*! [7b6][6]

Although the commentary mentions a procession of but four *mchod g.yog* (offering servants), according to TCU if there are enough participants, the procession should consist of fourteen:

1. the Diamond Master with incense
2. conch player
3. conch player
4. oboe player
5. oboe player
6. flask
7. skull bowl full of achievement pills (*sgrub ril*) covered by the magic mirror
8. four skulls[7]
9. four arrows
10. ten daggers
11. four victory banners
12. four pennants (*'phan*)
13. the *nyer spyod* offerings
14. the achievement torma (*sgrub gtor*).

In practice, the procession varies from the "ideal" and even from year to year. In 1983 at Chiwong, for example, the procession had eleven members.

1. oboe player
2. oboe player
3. incense
4. cymbals
5. Diamond Master with bell and *vajra*
6. daggers
7. mirror and pills plus four swords
8. four arrows
9. twelve daggers
10. *nyer spyod* offerings
11. victory banners and pennants

The participants circumambulate the *maṇḍala* three times, playing their instruments. They then stand in front of the structure to recite the liturgy. As the manuscript directs, the verses are interspersed with musical interludes.[8] At the end of the recitation, the participants unceremoniously arrange the ornaments in their respective places. In 1982, they were placed in the following order: first the tripod, skull, cloth, and mirror; then the daggers and offerings on the surface of the *maṇḍala;* finally the victory banners, pennants, and so on; the *vajra* and mantra cord; the achievement torma; and the offerings around the *maṇḍala*'s periphery. The entire process took about thirty minutes.

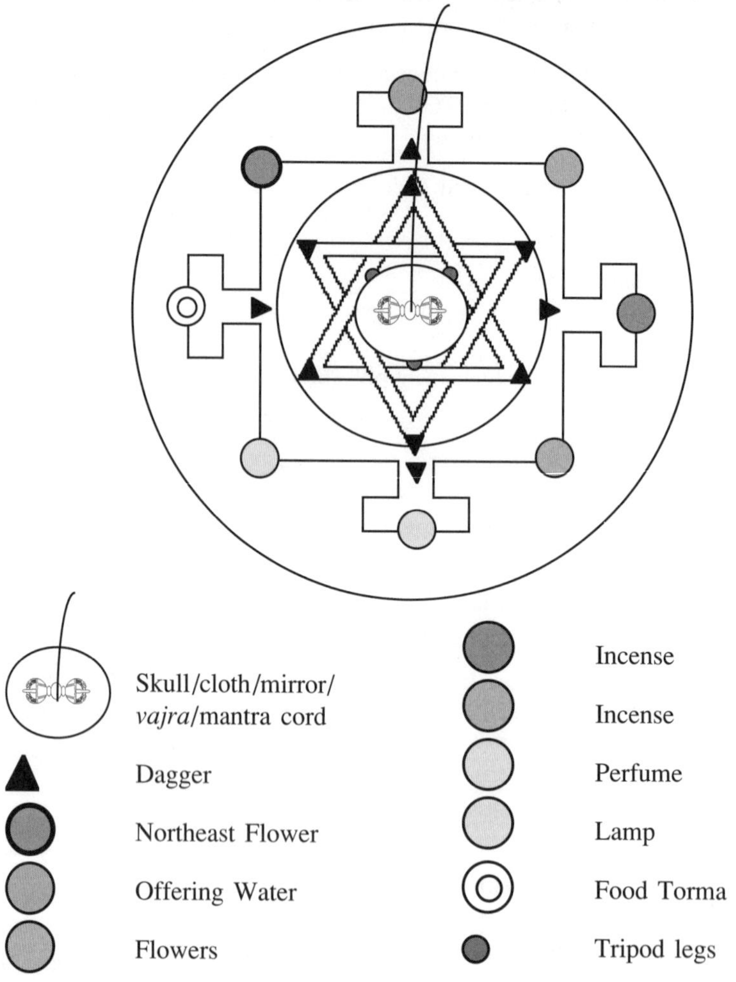

Arrangement of Offerings and Daggers on *Maṇḍala*, 1980[a] *(not to scale)*

[a] With the superstructure of the *maṇḍala* enclosure and the curtains in place, it is difficult to position objects with total precision on the easily marred sand painting. As the sketch indicates, the actual position of some of these objects at Chiwong in 1982 was slightly irregular. The orientation of the daggers was even more difficult to determine and may not be precisely as shown in the sketch.

The tripod is placed in the center of the *maṇḍala*. In the sand around it, the *nyer spyod* offerings form one circle and the twelve daggers another.

The external ornaments are placed as follows: ribbons (*cod pan*) hang from the roof corners; an arrow is on each of the four pillars; the four pennants and the four swords are to the left and right of the four gateways. The offerings are placed in small bowls on the shelf below the gateway on each side: the peaceful offerings to the left and wrathful offerings, in mirror image, to the right. An extra bowl of flowers separates the two sets. Thus, from left to right there are: two waters; flowers, incense, lamp, "perfume," food torma, flowers, fierce food torma, water, lamp, incense, flower of the senses, two waters.

The north and south sides of the torma (ritual east and west) are special. To the compass north, either in the gateway itself or on a small table placed below the gateway, is the achievement torma of Lord of the Dance, flanked by miniature skull bowls containing "medicine" and *rakta*. To the left is the contract torma, to the right, the Steadfast Women's torma. The Sky Walkers torma is on the south side facing the chapel door, flanked by medicine and *rakta*.

The arrows have ribbons of different colors: red, white, green, and yellow. They are said to correspond to the colors of the directional guardians: on the northwest corner, white; on the northeast corner, yellow, on the southwest corner, red; and on the southeast corner, green.[9]

13

Days Six to Twelve: The Practice

It is said that a story should have a beginning, a middle, and an end. For Tibetans, a ritual should have preparatory practices, the ritual itself, and a concluding ceremony. If we look at Mani Rimdu in this way, we might call the first five days preparatory rituals and the next seven, the actual practice.[1] Informally, these seven are simply called the *sgrub pa*, the practice.

The rituals that take place during this period are more or less the same each day. As we have seen, the pattern varies in the major and minor protectors worshipped. Some variation in the daily prayers which begin and end each day's practice is also normal.

Although the entire festival occupies three weeks and the daily practice is done all day every day, in a certain very narrow way the actual Mani Rimdu is a single quatrain inserted into the text of the Lord of the Dance *Manual*. This quatrain, composed by Ngawang Tenzin Norbu of Rongphu Monastery, dissolves the transformative power of the deity into the pills the monks have prepared. It is this act that transforms the ordinary Mindroling Monastery meditations on Lord of the Dance into a "pill practice." All the rest can be seen as a three-week elaboration of this central minute.

For many parts of the ritual, several alternate texts can be found, each with a different level of elaboration. There is a logic to the choices made between the alternatives. One guiding principle seems to be a sense of the degree of elaboration appropriate to the occasion as a whole. A certain level of elaboration in one area implies a commensurate level in others. Since Mani Rimdu is a major festival, it is appropriate that Ngawang Tenzin Norbu's quatrain be embedded in the full Lord of the Dance ritual, as opposed to a shorter text such as five-folio long *Heart of the Profound Path*.

The ritual of the personal deity should be accompanied by a protector ritual. According to the Mindroling tradition expressed in the commentary called the *Precious Lamp*, the closest thing that the monks of Solu-Khumbu have to a commentary on Mani Rimdu itself, the Protector ritual of choice is the *Guardians of the Word*. This relatively short text concentrates on Mahādeva, the Protector most closely associated with Lord of the Dance. A major festival, however, demands more. Thus, the full Mindroling protector ritual, the *Playful Ocean*, is substituted. In the Mindroling tradition, the *Playful Ocean* implies the use of a separate ritual for the minor protectors. Thus, the *Followers* ritual is brought into the picture.

At Rongphu, a tenth deity was worshipped at the same level of elaboration as the nine gods of the *Playful Ocean*. This was Long Life Woman, a goddess associated with neighboring mountain peaks. Hence, the *Long Life Woman* ritual is found in Mani Rimdu as well.

With all this, it would be inappropriate to ignore the local protectors of Rongphu and those associated with the other monasteries where Mani Rimdu is performed. At Chiwong, Shar lung, the protector of Rongphu is worshipped alongside Tashi Palchen (bKra shis dpal chen), the protector of Mount Numbur and other local gods.[2] At Tengpoche, Shar lung and distant Tashi Palchen are ignored, and a half-dozen others worshipped in their stead—Jo mo glang ma, Goddess of Everest and local protector (*gnas srung*) of Rongphu; Zur ra rva skyes, protector of the hidden valley of Kembalung in Khumbu; the Tibetan epic hero Gesar of Ling; Drag shul dbang po; and Khum bu yul lha, the local god of Khumbu who lives on the mountain we call "Khumbila."[3]

A variety of other auxiliary rituals, mostly of the Mindroling tradition enter at this point. The *Three-Part Torma* is an example. This ceremony, a commonly performed ritual for the Guardians of the Directions (*phyogs skyong*), the Ghosts (*'byung po*), and the Obstructors (*bgegs*) comes from the Mindroling *Religious Practice* collection.[4]

A liturgical banquet of such richness and complexity becomes difficult to define or even to comprehend. Certain rituals are always performed, yet are said to be "unnecessary." Others are deemed to be necessary, but may not be performed. Occasionally, an extraneous ritual commissioned by a particular patron or dictated by a specific circumstance interposes itself into the sequence of events. With so much activity, it is sometimes difficult even for a participant to say with precision whether a given ritual has been performed or not.

Even where the rituals are constant, there are subtle variations of performance. On any given day, some rituals and parts of rituals are recited in that hypnotically slow cadence that only those familiar with Tibetan chant know, others, at a tempo rapid enough to do an American tobacco auctioneer proud. Many are recited at a speed between these extremes. Certain rituals, for example, daily prayers, are always set at high speed. Others, such as parts of the visualization, offerings and self-empowerment of Lord of the Dance *Manual*, will vary from one day to the next. In this way, each passage gets its contemplative due, although, presumably, an experienced meditator can achieve the necessary visualizations even when reciting at breakneck pace.

The music also differs from day-to-day. The orchestra at Chiwong during Mani Rimdu is typical of small monastic assemblies. It normally consists of a pair of cymbals, a pair of conches, a pair of oboes, a pair of thigh-bone trumpets (in this case made of copper), and a large pole-drum. At Chiwong, only one drum is used; in Tibet, as many as twenty to thirty were employed.[5] The orchestra plays set interludes. Many of these are indicated in stage directions included in the ritual text. Sometimes the text gives the required selection a name, such as a "longing melody" or "fierce sounding music."[6] More often, simply the word "music" is used.

This word is somewhat ambiguous, however. *Rol mo*, from the verb *rol*, to play or to enjoy, in addition to denoting music in general, is also a common name for the large-domed cymbals of the monastic orchestra. These are otherwise called *sbub 'chal*, as opposed to the smaller-domed, higher pitched *sil gnyan* cymbals.[7] Passages marked *rol mo* are sometimes played with cymbals alone, sometimes by the full orchestra.

Musical interludes are also performed where none is indicated in the stage directions. An example being the doubling of musical interludes in parts of the "General Invitation for the Defenders of Religion." Indicated in the text or not, a given passage may be alternately included or excluded as the degree of elaboration changes from day-to-day.[8]

The instrumentation changes in a similar manner. During the protector rituals, for example, the orchestra uses the long telescopic trumpets known as *dung chen* only on alternate days.[9]

Certain instruments are played whenever their name appears in the text. Thus, when Planet Demon is invited, the thigh-bone and the whistle are sounded as the text races past their names:

> Human thigh trumpet—*di ri ri!*
> Thousand-eyed conflagration—*'u ru ru!*
> Tune played on a whistle—*kyu ru ru!*[10]

As in Indian classical music, instrumental passages are sung for teaching purposes. An experienced chant leader (*dbu mdzad*) can sing and mime all of a ritual's musical passages. The Thubten Chöling Chant Leader, for example, sings certain cymbal passages using the syllables "pram" and "pi-pa-ram." These syllables are also found in written form.[11]

THE FIRST SESSION

At a Tibetan monastery, the day begins with the sound of a gong. After a few minutes, a pair of novices climbs the stairway that leads to a special gable in the courtyard roof. Soon, the smooth reverberation of a conch and a rollicking prayer read in childish voices echo throughout the monastic compound.[12] Within twenty to thirty minutes, the monks are in their seats and have begun their prayers.

During Mani Rimdu, the day's rituals are performed in two sessions. The first session typically begins between 5:00 A.M. and 7:00 A.M., and takes about three hours to complete, including breaks. The session begins with the daily prayers common to a variety of monastic rituals. At the monasteries that perform Mani Rimdu, these prayers are drawn for the most part from the Mindroling *Religious Practice* collection.

Next, two preliminary prayers are performed that specifically relate to the Lord of the Dance ritual: the "Biographical Prayer" of the Great Treasure Master gTer bdag gling pa and an "Abridged Chronicle in Verse of the Unsuccessful Actions of the Life" of his son Ratnabija. These pæans of praise to the founding fathers of the Mindroling tradition are included in the Thubten Chöling edition of the Lord of the Dance ritual.

After this, the monks embark on Lord of the Dance *Manual* itself.

The *Manual* is forty-one folios long and its organization is a typical of tantric meditation texts. Following a short description of the preparation of the ritual equipment, the text is divided into three sections: the Preliminaries (f. 3.4 ff.), the Actual Practice (f. 9.2 ff.), and the Concluding Sequence (f. 20b5 ff.). Only the first two are performed in the morning session.

The preliminary practices begin with a set of five rituals common to all tantric worship: Going for Refuge, Generating the Aspiration to Enlightenment, Diamond Mind (Vajrasattva) Meditation, an Offering *Maṇḍala*, and Guru Yoga.

Occasionally, these generic rites are modified to the specific context. The refuge, for example, reads—

> Namo! Until all beings, including myself are enlightened,
> I go for refuge to the Sky Walkers,
> The lama, Buddha, Holy Religion,
> The Best of Congregations and the god of the *maṇḍala*—
> Union of the Blissful. [3b4]

In recent years, a number of fine works have been published on preliminary practice.[13] It is pointless to dwell on them here, except to note that they lay the psychological foundation believed necessary for the successful completion of tantric ritual practice.

The General Preliminaries are followed by a series of five Special Preliminaries (f. 6b4 ff.). In the first two, Expelling Demons, and Defining the Borders, the meditator visualizes him/herself as Hayagrīva in order to expel obstructive forces and to create a sphere of protection, a sacred space into which they cannot return.

I am the King of Wrath—the very soul of the speech of all the Blissful!
From the great play of my mind,
Which blazes with unbearable, awesome majesty,
I project diamond weapons, blazing fire, [7b1]

As the upper and lower borders.
Above, I spread a diamond tent.
Below, I spread the diamond ground.
I fill the border with a diamond fence. [7b3]

Confession, Showering Blessings, and Blessing the Things to be Offered round out the Special Preliminaries.

Showering Blessings is an act that occurs with several different degrees of elaboration, even within Mani Rimdu. The present form is the most basic—

Hūṁ! From the Truth Realm of unchanging bliss,
O host of gods of the ocean of Conquerors,
Regard me lovingly, with unflagging compassion,
And bestow empowerment, blessing and true achievement.
Manifest your battalions of magic powers (*mthu*)[14]
And quickly show your marks and signs. [8.5]

Blessing the Things to be Offered infuses the material offerings used with their ideal counterparts. This is done both for the outer and inner offerings. It is clear from the text that this is not so much a question of modifying an external substance as it is modifying one's own view. Thus, the sequence begins—

I come into focus as the god. From my heart
I project *raṁ yaṁ khaṁ*. Fire, wind and water
Burn and toss and wash the impure grasping of things as discrete entities.[15] [8b2]

Similarly, it is revealed that the Medicine (*amṛta*) and Rakta, a pair of offerings that, among other things, symbolizes the semen and menstrual blood of spiritual rebirth, are in actuality the five wisdoms and non-attachment.

The Actual Practice (f. 9.2 ff.) begins with the Meditation on the *Maṇḍala* of the Residence and the Residents. This is where the monks first create their visualization of Lord of the Dance's paradise, his palace, his body, and his entourage.

The ritual weaves meditative and philosophical terminology into an evocative description of the creation *ex nihilo* of this new world—

> Oṁ. *saṁsāra*, *nirvāṇa*—all things are originally
> Unfeigned, free from elaboration—suchness,
> Self-emergent wisdom, the all-encompassing realm,
> The truth Body, whose nature never changes. [9.3]
>
> Āḥ. From the sky, like a rainbow,
> From the heart of emptiness, the creative power of illusion rises
> As compassion for the six kinds of beings everywhere—
> The natural unceasing Enjoyment Body cloud—[9.4]
>
> Hūṁ. Emptiness and great compassion
> Unified—the blissful diamond mind.
> Meditate that from the limpidly lustrous letter *hrīḥ*—
> The great drop of semen that causes the incarnated body—[9.4]
>
> The whole circle of the *maṇḍala*
> Is gradually elaborated. [9.5]

The *maṇḍala* palace and its inhabitants are described in the loving detail necessary to visualize them.

The syllable *hrīḥ* appears in the sky above the *maṇḍala*, and descends to the throne—"It becomes a red *utpala* flower marked with a *hrīḥ*" [9b4]. The syllable suffuses the universe with light, a light that invites all the myriad Buddhas who dwell in the ten directions of space. They melt into the syllable that has thus invited them. In an instant, it becomes at once the meditator and the god, Lord of the Dance—

> A red body, the color of rubies.
> One face, four hands, blazing light.
> A captivating smile of pleasing anger. [10.1]

Lord of the Dance and his consort, in turn, propagate their entourage in a passage that highlights that procreative imagery that abounds in creation stage yoga, projecting "a cloud wheel of *bodhicitta* (semen) letters . . . to the homes of the gods of the entourage" that produce them "from their individual seeds" [10b3].

Each figure of this vision must then be consecrated by the syllables *oṁ āḥ hūṁ*, to bless his or her body, speech and mind. Then, the Wisdom Circle, the actual deities (as opposed to their visualized shells) can be Invited.

Hūṁ! Arise! Arise! Mighty gods of the ten forces!
Do not miss the chance! You, who by the power of compassion
Have the interests of all sentient beings at heart! Noble Avalokiteśvara!
I beg you to come with every one of your entourage!
Head of the family, Protector Boundless Light! I beg you to come
From your blissful paradise whose nature is Truth's Body!
Blissful Great Compassion! I beg you to come
From Mount Potala, that spontaneous magic apparition!
Great glorious King Hayagrīva! I beg you to come
From the half-moon *maṇḍala* of fierce [and] powerful play!
Secret Wisdom Sky Walker! I beg you to come
From the Orgyan Incarnation's fortress in the western quarter!
Sky Walkers! Heroes of the four families! I beg you to come
From your residence in the twenty-four cemeteries!
Obedient Sorceresses! I beg you to come
From the fortress of the strict word and vow! [12.1]

Once present, the deities are Entreated to Stay, Saluted with respect and presented with a series of Offerings: Outer Offerings to the five senses and so on, Inner Offerings of Medicine (i.e., *amṛta*), Tormas, and Rakta, and Secret Offerings of Union, Freedom, and Suchness. The Actual Practice ends with Praise and the Recitation of the mantras of Lord of the Dance and his entourage.

In the morning session, the *Manual* is performed straight through to this point—the section entitled "Doing the Recitation" (f 18.5ff.).

To set the stage for the recitation, its "object" must be "clarified." This entails summoning the profoundest insights of creation stage practice. If we take seriously the tantras claim to be an "effect vehicle," that is, a practice that seeks to meditatively recreate the experience of Buddhahood rather than simply amass its causes, then a ritual text such as the Lord of the Dance *Manual* would be a sensible place to look for a vision of what the mentality and activity of a Buddha might be. The *Manual*, as does many a tantric text, does indeed present such a vision. Moreover, it presents it at precisely the juncture one might expect it—during the central act of creation stage yoga: mantra recitation.[16]

As we have seen before, a general pattern of tantric ritual is for the meditator to first create a visualization discursively described by the text and then to recite a mantra which actualizes the imagined scenario.

"This," the *Manual* tells us, "clarifies the object of the recitation—

In the hearts of the assembled gods, on a lotus, sun
And moon pedestal, there is a [syllable] *hrīḥ*, its end
Encircled by very fine mantras.[17]
Radiating light, it worships the Buddhas of the ten directions.

[They] steep me in grace and in true achievement.
I purify obstruction, complete accumulation, and obtain the four empowerments.
It strikes sentient beings in the three worlds and the six migrations,
And cleanses their karma, passion, sin and obstruction.
The world outside becomes a divine palace.
Its inhabitants are perfected as the gods of the circle.
Sounds that resound: the mantra's own sound.
The mind's memories and thoughts: the Body of Truth." [18.5]

In mantra practice, we should note, action consists of radiation of light from the heart. The first set of actions establishes a reciprocal relation with the Buddhas that inhabit the ten directions of the cosmos, linking the practitioner to them in a web of exchanged light. The second set of actions fulfills the *bodhisattva* vow by cleaning all sentient beings of fault and establishing what is the logical result *bodhisattva* practice as well as its ultimate goal, the transformation of the world into the paradise of a Buddha.

The visualization begins with definable actions: things are worshipped (*mchod*), dissolve (*thim*), are cleansed (*sbyangs*) and become transformed (*gyur*). As the final act progresses, verbs fall away: "Sounds that resound: the mantra's own sound./ The mind's memories and thoughts: the Body of Truth" (*sgra grags sngags kyi rang sgra ste/ sems kyi dran rtog chos sku'i ngang*). What began as a transformation, is, in the end, a fait accompli, echoing the Mahāyāna dictum that between *saṁsāra* and *nirvāṇa*, there is not a hair's breadth of difference.

Mantra practice, in a sense, limns a portrait of a Buddha and of Buddha activity. The portrait is prescriptive rather than descriptive; it aims not so much at defining a Buddha as at creating one. There are, however, parallels with the more familiar descriptive portraits. A Buddha, a *sūtra* tells us, does not act in a sequential premeditated way, but rather directly and spontaneously. His action is without intention or volition (*cetanā, abhisaṁskāra*), effort (*yatna, ābhoga*) or deliberation (*vikalpa*).[18] In the words of the *Mahāyānasūtrālaṅkāra*, a Buddha does not bring beings to spiritual maturity, "living beings advance to maturity without volitional action [on the Buddha's part]."[19]

Although nothing within the purview of normal human activity could conform perfectly to this standard, the curiously quiescent activity that we see in mantra recitation does at the very least resonate with the canonical descriptions. After all, what could be closer to spontaneous effortless action than the works of a radiant heart. Nor is it impossible, given its simplicity, to imagine such activity evolving, becoming with practice even more spontaneous, less deliberate. The *Mantrayāna* tradition, by definition, puts mantra recitation forward as the royal road to Buddhahood. Its direct, imaginative engagement of the human heart may form part of the foundation for this claim.

Since the "actual Mani Rimdu"—the practice that involves the pills—is a special kind of mantra recitation, it is here that it is inserted.

The light of my heart is wound with the spell-cord.
It incites the hearts of the god[s] produced in front. Beams of light
Dissolve *saṁsāra* and *nirvāṇa* into all-pervasive clear light.
It dissolves into me and the achievement substance. It can liberate
The experience of the four liberations of seeing, hearing, remembering and touching.

Trulshik Rinpoche explains "the four liberations" as "having seen the pills, you are liberated. Having heard about the pills, you are liberated . . . ," and so on. For the pill incantation, a long spell-cord is passed down each of the two rows of monks, and a third to Trulshik Rinpoche. The cords each have a vajra at the end. They lead over the rafters to the main cord that goes down to the pills in the center of the *maṇḍala*. Since these are *maṇi*-pills, only the *maṇi*—Avalokiteśvara's mantra—is recited at this point.

The recitation from the *Manual* ends with a ebullient passage of devotional verse, one of the many small masterpieces of liturgical art that forms a part of Mani Rimdu.

Oṁ. It is good! It is good! Teacher, you
Stop karma and passion;
Lead suffering to bliss;
Awaken the Truth Realm;
Purify body, speech and mind
With the melodious sound of bliss!
From the home of bliss—the path of bliss!
The unexcelled fruit of bliss!
Emaho! Great body of bliss!
Emaho! Great secret mantra of bliss!
Emaho! Awakening worlds of bliss!
Emaho! Living in the home of bliss!
Emaho! Bliss incorruptible!
I salute forever
The wholly blissful in nature! [20.6]

The morning session concludes with an assortment of short practices. The first is the *Spying Ghosts*, a ritual assassination of the *lingka* similar to those of the first days. The second is the *Shower of Blessings.* This text, also composed by Ngawang Tenzin Norbu especially for use in Mani Rimdu, expands on the same theme we saw above in the *Manual,* calling down the blessings of the cosmic principles, deities, and lamas associated with the festival. Next, the assembly produces the "*maṇi*-sound" by repeating Lord of the Dance's mantra, "oṁ āḥ hūṁ hrīḥ oṁ maṇi padme hūṁ." Session One ends with a group of concluding prayers drawn, like those that began the session, from the *Religious Practice* collection.

THE SECOND SESSION

The second session typically begins between 2:00 P.M. and 3:00 P.M., and lasts approximately four hours. Since the preliminary practices from the *Manual* were completed in the first session, they are not repeated. Following a short prayer, the second session leads off with "The Actual Practice."[20]

The rituals continue through the mantra recitations, and then embark on the *Manual's* Concluding Sequence.[21] This includes the ritual of the tantric feast, one of the most common and most typical of tantric rituals; and a self-administered empowerment, in which the monks revivify the initiation that they have received from the lama.

In all, the Concluding Sequence (f. 20b5 ff.) has four parts: [Dedicating the Guardians' Tormas], the Feast Offering, the Empowerment and the Conclusion.

Feast offerings *(gaṇacakra)* (f. 20b6 ff.), as a genre, originated among the groups of yogis who congregated in the cemeteries of ancient India. The Tibetan word *tshogs*, which I translate as "feast," signifies an assemblage both of persons and of foodstuffs. The Lord of the Dance feast is similar to that of any number of tantric deities. It consists of Arrangement and Blessing, Inviting the Guests to the Feast, Offering, Confession, Liberation, Enjoying the Feast, and Discarding the Leftovers. Elements of the feast are dramatized in Tibetan sacred dance, and we will discuss them further when we treat the Mani Rimdu dances.

Another sine qua non of tantric practice is empowerment. Without empowerment one cannot fully engage in the rituals of Mani Rimdu. Empowerment (f. 22b5 ff.) in this context is self-administered, and presupposes a regular empowerment by a qualified lama. A place to insert an empowerment for others is provided immediately following the self-empowerment. Thus, a lama may the easily adopt the ritual to that purpose.

The self-empowerment has two major divisions: the so-called entrance to the empowerment and the actual empowerment. These, in turn, have numerous subdivisions.[22] It is during the Entrance that the monks visualize that they enter the *maṇḍala*.

The Actual Empowerments consist of the three-part Flask Empowerment and the three-part Highest Unelaborated Empowerment.[23] After this, in theory, new disciples may enter and receive empowerment (34.5), although I have never seen this happen in Mani Rimdu.

Inasmuch as empowerment is at the heart of creation stage yoga, the thrust of the self-administered empowerment is clear. As the yogi declares:

> From now on, do everything saying,
> "I am Avalokiteśvara." [25.3]

Like an empowerment given by a lama, the self-administration has many stages. We will touch on a few key points here.

Having prepared oneself, one must open the four doors of the *maṇḍala*. The doors, it will be remembered are the abodes of the Sorceresses, the animal-headed goddesses who incarnate immeasurable compassion, love, joy, and equanimity. The door one actually enters is the eastern door, home of "The Diamond Sorceress who summons/ With the iron hook of immeasurable compassion."[24]

Tantra in general and empowerment in particular are always said to be secret. Before crossing the threshold, the initiate promises to keep the secrets of having entered the *maṇḍala* and of Avalokiteśvara having entered one's heart. Following this is one of the most extraordinary events—and passages of prose—of the ritual. The actual deities, the wisdom beings come to inhabit the simulacrum of the deity that the initiate has created—his vision of himself as Lord of the Dance.

> The red letter *hrīḥ* in the heart of this body of mine that has become that of the Lord of the Dance Great Compassion, burns like a butter-lamp. Its shining light stimulates the gods of the *maṇḍala* to project countless forms from their minds—bodies and syllables, symbols which blaze in a mass of beams of light, which come helter-skelter like rain and snow, like a blizzard. They enter through [my] pores and fill [my] body completely to the brim. Bliss blazes unbearably. [25.5]

At this point, the pungent incense known as *gu gul* is burned. This scent is always a signal of an extraordinary event, but the text calls for even more extraordinary scents to be mixed with it—balls of dried menstrual blood, cat droppings, and the five ambrosias—excrement, urine, semen, flesh, and blood. Despite the textual injunction, these are not employed at Chiwong.

Trulshik Rinpoche explains that these scents are used to summon the deity because he enjoys them. Much has been written elsewhere about such tantric paraphernalia, and without adding to the general debate, I would like to suggest that here they are symbols of chaos, evidence of the crack in the worlds that occurs if a man becomes a god. In another sense, they are ciphers of a greater truth in which distinctions between the sublime and the foul are irrelevant. As the *Manual* itself says elsewhere,

Hoḥ! If you question and examine all things,
Nature is not to be found.
Brahmin, untouchable, dog and pig
Enjoy the self same nature.
A ho mahāsukhaṁ—E ma 'o! Bliss! [34b2]

At the beginning of other-oriented (as opposed to self-administered) empowerments, initiates are given strips of red cloth, blindfolds, to tie across their faces. In Mani Rimdu the blindfolds are represented by a *mudrā* rather than by a cloth, but the meaning is the same. As they are removed, the assembly chants—

O mighty Avalokiteśvara, endeavor
To open your eyes today!
Open them and see everything!
Unsurpassable diamond eyes! [26.1]

These blindfolds are interesting from a number of viewpoints. For one thing they represent a thread that runs not just through tantric ritual but through the greater culture of Asia.

Tibetan *thangka* painters paint the eyes of the central deity last and follow it on the full moon by an "opening the eyes" ceremony.[25] Newar Buddhist sculptors, tantrics like the Tibetans, use a similar ritual to open the eyes of their statues and wood carvings and imbue them with the divine presence.[26] In Japanese popular culture, we find statues of Daruma (Bodhidharma) traditionally sold with the pupil of one eye left unpainted.[27]

The blindfold is also an article of shaman's gear. A Samoyed shaman carries a kerchief "with which to blindfold his eyes so that he can enter the spirit world by his own inner light."[28] Contemporary shamans among the Magar of Nepal have a similar custom. During the ritual "birth" of a shaman, the initiate is blindfolded and the blindfold pierced with a needle to "open up the passage of sight." The shamans believe that if the candidate is a true one, he will be able to see with the blindfold on and thus to dance properly atop the tree of life.[29] As we have seen, like the hub of the *maṇḍala*, the shaman's tree of life is in the center of the universe.

When the Lord of the Dance initiate, that "great hero of the mind" removes his blindfold, enjoined to "look well." He then declares,

I see the whole *maṇḍala* of Union of the Blissful Lord of the Dance Great Compassion, the residence and its residents, just as if it were right before my eyes. [26.4]

The rest of the empowerment follows suit. The initiate is empowered by the instruments of the five families of Tathāgatas.

THE FIVE BUDDHA FAMILIES

Direction	*Center*	*East*	*South*	*West*	*North*
Color	White	Blue	Yellow	Red	Green
Family	Tathāgata Tathāgata	Diamond Vajra	Jewel Ratna	Lotus Padma	Action Karma
Family Symbol	wheel	vajra	jewel	lotus	sword
Family Head	Illuminator Vairocana	Imperturbable Akṣobhya	Jewel-Born Ratnasaṁbhava	Boundless Light Amitābha	Infallible Success Amoghasiddhi
Buddha Gesture	Preaching	Earth-witness	Giving	Meditation	Fear-not
Type of Wisdom	Truth Realm	Mirror-Like	Equanimitous	Discriminating	Active
Type of Evil	Stupidity	Anger	Pride/ Egocentricity	Desire	Envy
Aggregate	Form	Consciousness	Feelings	Perception	Miscellaneous
Instrument of Empowerment	Name	Flask	Crown	Vajra	Bell

This sequence makes the explicit correspondences between the five families, the five types of wisdom and the five poisons that we noted in chapter 2. The chart above summarizes the symbolic equations as they are given in the Lord of the Dance *Manual.*

During the Bell Empowerment, for example, the initiate makes this request—

> Hūṁ! Empowerment by the wisdom (*shes rab*) Truth Realm bell
> Has the identity of active wisdom.[30]
> Empower me into the karma family
> In order to completely purify envy! [28.5]

Immediately following these "Five Ordinary Empowerments of Awareness," the initiate is empowered to become a Diamond Master, a perfect Tantric teacher. The instrument of empowerment is the tantric adept's basic set of tools: the vajra and bell, identified as the deity in union with his consort. This unification of polar forces, of masculine and feminine, the text implies, bestows the flexibility and sensitivity required of a spiritual master—

> Hūṁ! Great vajra and great bell—
> Pair who are the holy bliss Pledge Being
> In union with the Wisdom Goddess—
> Whatever training methods you use on anyone,
> They are psychologically appropriate to him.
> You give the power to rise
> To the exalted rank of Diamond Master. [29.6]

The successful completion of the Master's empowerment is celebrated by a passage which highlights in poetic fashion the creativity of a Diamond Master—

> Hūṁ! Blow for your disciples, O fortunate one,
> The auspicious conch of religious teaching
> In harmony with their varied inclinations,
> Easing them home in enlightened state![31] [29b4]

During the Empowerments of Body, the lama flashes a miniature painting (*tsakali*) of each god of the *maṇḍala* before the initiates.

The Speech Empowerment employs a rosary and a *tsakali* inscribed with the mantras of the divine assembly. The initiate visualizes that

> The gods assembled in my heart become a *maṇḍala* of syllables (*gsung yi ge*). Rosaries of mantras come from the heart of the *maṇḍala* and enter via the pathway of my throat. They melt into the circle of letters in my heart. [31b6]

In so doing,

> The power of the sixty aspects of melodious speech,
> Gives the empowerment which fully proclaims
> Religion's eighty-four thousand doors
> Adapted to the minds of the unimaginable number that are to be tamed. [32.2]

For the mind empowerment, the lama displays the "master's mirror," a small bronze disk, as the text exhorts the initiate to cleave to his or her realization of the absolute.[32]

> Hūṁ! All things are like a reflection in a mirror,
> The unelaborated, empty, clear, infinite realm.
> The playful creativity of self-arising wisdom
> Is unimpeded, like the play
> Of a magician at a magic show.
> Stay in the realm of unelaborated original purity! [32b1]

The foregoing rituals are classed as flask empowerments, common to all four classes of the tantra.[33] The three last empowerments belong to the *anuttarayogatantra* alone—the Secret Empowerment, the Discrimination Woman's Wisdom Empowerment, and the Fourth Empowerment. Each empowerment in succession is more subtle. Each takes place in a different *maṇḍala*, cleanses a specific mental defilement, empowers the disciple for a special type of meditation, and serves as a harbinger of one of the four bodies of the Buddha. In the Fourth Empowerment, for example, the disciple is told that—

> Thus, in the absolute aspiration to enlightenment *maṇḍala*, one obtains the fourth empowerment. The stains are cleansed from innate wisdom. One is empowered for the path of meditation on the Great Fulfillment. One is granted the fortune of obtaining the fruit of the Actuality Body.[34] [33b5]

Finally, all dissolves into the emptiness that is the nature of the mind.

> Hoḥ! The mind itself is rootless.
> From the beginning it is unborn, insubstantial.
> There is neither meditation nor meditator.
> Everything from the beginning is pure,
> And rises as great innate wisdom's play.
> Therefore, all substances' lack of substance
> Is the reality of all the Buddhas. [33b4]

THE THREE ASPECTS OF THE HIGHEST UNELABORATED EMPOWERMENT

Empowerment	*Maṇḍala*	*Stain cleansed*	*Path Empowered*	*Fruit*	*Instrument*
Secret Empowerment	Conventional aspiration to enlightenment	Speech	Veins and winds	Enjoyment Body	Seminal Drop of aspiration to enlightenment
The Wisdom [Woman's] Innate Wisdom Empowerment	*Bhaga*	Mind	Meditation on the Seminal Drop	Truth Body	The Awareness Woman
Fourth Empowerment	Absolute aspiration to enlightenment	Innate wisdom	Great Perfection	Actuality Body	[The realm of just-this-ness]

After the empowerment comes a welter of interpolated material. The series starts with the *Three-Part Torma* ritual. Following this comes the first of the Protector rituals, "The General Invitation of the Defenders of Religion" from the *Guardians of the Word*, a ritual summary in which all the Sworn Protectors and their Followers receive their due. Such a summary is necessary whenever the *Playful Ocean* is not performed in full.

This is the case in Mani Rimdu. As we have seen, the ceremony alternates daily between four sets of four or five deities drawn from the ten Great Protectors worshipped at Rongphu: the nine protectors of the *Playful Ocean* plus Long-Life Woman. The Followers rituals have their own rotation schedule.[35]

The "General Invitation" summons and then exhorts the entire terrifying assemblage—

> . . . guardians who defend holy religion along with your entourages, your armies of attendants and messengers—take this enormous torma given in worship and guard the Buddha's teaching! Praise the grandeur of the [Three] Jewels! Defend the rule of the Virtuous Community and religion! Cure the ills of the three worlds! Increase sentient beings' benefit and pleasure! Be a friend who helps Yogis! Complete the Mantra Holders' work! Subdue the enemy of anger! Vanquish harmful Obstructors! In particular, pacify all outer, inner and secret opposing conditions; increase and expand conducive conditions—the panoply of good we wish for; and act to bring success to each and every highest and ordinary true achievement, for all those who participate in this vow! [6.1]

After this, the participants perform the *Playful Ocean* straight through for the deities of the day, first doing "Ceremonies" (*phrin las*) that invoke the chosen protectors, then continuing with the offerings and praises for those gods.[36] Parts of the first section of the *Playful Ocean* are redundant in the context of a larger performance and are skipped. The monks omit the "Yoga of Self," for example, as they have already visualized themselves as a god during the Lord of the Dance rituals.

After the Praise section, which lauds each deity in the fullness of his or her gruesome grandeur, the worship of the day's Followers is inserted. The Followers are a collection of autochthonous Tibetan deities that have been subsumed into the Buddhist pantheon. Following the Followers, rituals are performed for the specific local deity or deities worshipped at the monastery in question, such as Tashi Palchen at Chiwong or Zur ra rva skyes at Tengpoche.[37]

The *Playful Ocean* rituals resume with the Torma Offerings for two other types of *genii loci,* the Treasure Owners and the Land Owners, and continue through the Confession.

In the midst of this, one of the most important phases of the process occurs—the actual propitiation of the Protectors. The word Propitiation (*bskang gso*), we have seen, is not only the commonly used cover term for Protector rituals, but part of the working vocabulary of ordinary Sherpa villagers.

Propitiation also is the *locus classicus* for much of the imagery found in that unique form of Tibetan painting, *rgyan tshogs*, (assembled offerings), which shows all the offerings pleasing to a Protector, including his clothes and ornaments, which, unoccupied, mysteriously stand in the air as if the unseen god were wearing them. If, then, one wishes to understand the herds of black animals that crowd such canvases, one need go no farther than the *Playful Ocean*'s Propitiation of the Four-Handed Mahākāla we cited in the Introduction.[38]

> The black horse, bedecked with ornaments, gambols like the wind.
> The shaggy bull yak is as majestic as a thunderhead.
> The demon sheep has a white rump and a curling iron horn.
> The black bear-like dog trots following tracks of blood.
> The black bird with the thunder-iron beak swoops and soars.
> Birds and beasts of prey pounce on the life of enemies and obstructors,
> And other support substances crowd every paradise.
> By these, Wisdom Protector and entourage, be propitiated! [42b1]

Propitiation is followed by confession.[39] The confession is specifically addressed to the Protectors and specifically refers to infractions of tantric vows. For example—

> Having agreed to meditate the four-session yoga,
> Contrite, [I] confess to being diverted to ordinary activities.
> Having agreed to incite the minds of the Blissful,
> Contrite, I confess to gossiping about ordinary pastimes. [49.4]

Another interpolation, Ngawang Tenzin Norbu's miniature Protector ritual, the *Unelaborated*, falls between the latter two confessions. A two-folio distillation of the *Playful Ocean* and *Followers*' seventy folia, the *Unelaborated* is a good example of the category of rituals that an expert Chant Leader may deem unnecessary, yet seemingly is always performed.

After this brief interpolation, the *Playful Ocean* continues through its concluding rituals: Thanksgiving, Praise, Confessing Fault, Staying Firm, Request to Go (*omitted in Mani Rimdu*), Dedicatory Prayer, and Auspicious Speech.

The monks then return once more to the Lord of the Dance *Manual*, beginning with the sections entitled "Enjoying the Feast" (f. 34.6) and "Throwing Out the Remains" (f. 35.1), where the feast is actually shared by the assembly and a small portion of leftover food collected as a further offering to the protectors associated with Lord of the Dance.

> Hūṁ! Among Great Compassion's circle of attendants,
> You who possess a vow to defend the teaching—
> The hosts of Ladies, Sky Walkers,
> Ging [and] Langka, and Sorcerers, Slow-Walkers and Malefactor/
> Benefactors.[40]

You are fearsome in form; you have ornaments of violence.
You judge [our] quality; you gauge the warmth [of our practice].
You follow vows;[41] you circulate among the cemeteries.
Together with your individual incarnations and messengers,

Please eat these glorious leftovers!
And act in accord with your vows! [35.4]

The assembly then continues with the Lord of the Dance Follow-up or Conclusion (f. 35b2 ff.). This begins with a cycle of rituals that make use of a small, obelisk-shaped offering called the "Contract Torma." The cycle begins with an Entreaty, followed by "Proclaiming the Contract Torma" and "Inciting it to be a Weapon."

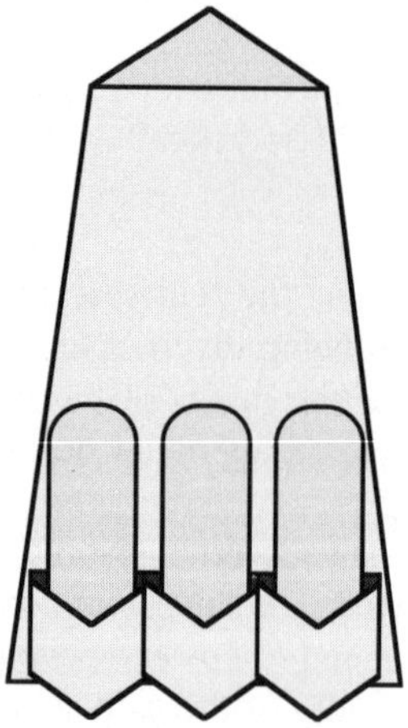

Contract Torma

The contract recalls Padmasambhava's encounter with the autochthonous spirits of Tibet.

Hūṁ! All you accomplished Knowledge Bearers,
Guardians Sworn to an Oath!
Come to this torma, this holy thing,
And fulfill your promises! [36.4]

The Master Padmasambhava
Called you great and haughty gods of Tibet
To account as lackeys, as messengers.
Having been sworn to an oath,

I urge you to the stringent vows enjoined upon you!
Complete your appointed task! [36.5]

O Knowledge Bearers following Orgyan [Padmasambhava],
And patrons who support the teachings,
Reach the zenith, the highest high,
And protect your children the lowly low! [36b1]

In this four-horned kingdom of Tibet,
Protect us from vicious invaders!
Pacify all disease, darkness, disturbance and strife!
Make our harvests good, our cattle healthy—make things pleasant! [36b2]

Turning the Contract Torma into a weapon demonstrates once more how thoroughly Buddhistic even the most magic-laden moments of Tibetan ritual are. Here, the torma, which is literally the stele that commemorates Padmasambhava's contract with the gods of Tibet (much as the stelæ of the ancient Tibetan kings proclaimed their edicts and treaties), is turned into an instrument of spiritual transformation of the world—

Hūṁ! Turn back the enemies and obstructions of ignorance and egoism
Compassed by appearing and existing!
O magic torma weapon of the play of wisdom,
Turn the vessel of the world into a divine palace!
Sentient beings, born and transient, to Buddhahood!
Suffering to the realm of bliss!
Saṁsāra to the realm of *nirvāṇa*!
Turn the five poisonous passions into the five wisdoms!
The five father aggregates into the five mother elements!
Saṁsāra to the element of *nirvāṇa*!
Everything into primordial purity! [36b4]

The torma celebrating Padmasambhava's contract with the indigenous spirits is followed by the Steadfast Woman Protectors (*brtan ma*), a brief offering to the mountain-goddesses he encountered as he entered Tibet, and the prayer to Hayagrīva known as the Horse's Dance (f. 37.5; see Day One).

Immediately following the Horse's Dance, the *Spying Ghosts* ritual is repeated. We have seen this prayer before in the Site Rituals where it followed the burial of the ghosts in the courtyard. Given the intimate connection between Hayagrīva and the magic dagger that the officiant uses to dispatch the ghosts, both are fitting junctures to invoke him.

The Horse Dance also reenacts the burial of the *lingka*. By making a cross with the master's *vajra*, the assistant symbolically creates the foundation of the universe (which is visualized as a vajra-cross) and presses down on the *lingka* with the weight of Mount Meru, with the full weight of the world.

Another interpolation follows, *The Completely Agreeable Sky Walker Torma Offering*. This is an short invocation of the five families of *ḍākiṇī* and other *ḍākiṇī* associated with Lord of the Dance. A special Sky Walker torma is made for this offering at the beginning of the festival. It rests on the edge of the *maṇḍala* enclosure nearest the chapel door

The Follow-up section of the *Manual* begins with Taking the True Achievement (37b2) and continues with variations on the same themes that we have just seen in the *Playful Ocean*—Thanksgiving, Praise, Confessing your Failings, Prayer to Remain Firm, Request to Go, Retraction, a Dedicatory Prayer, and the Auspicious Recitation.

The Retraction deserves special mention. It is here that the meditative vision conjured out of emptiness is returned to it. The *maṇḍala* residence dissolves into the gods who dwell within it. They, in turn, dissolve into Lord of the Dance, who dissolves into Hayagrīva, who dissolves into the syllable *hrīḥ* in his heart. The *hrīḥ* itself then dissolves upward, finally disappearing into the arch of the vowel *i* that surmounts it and from there flickering out into emptiness.

The customs observed during this part of Mani Rimdu follow the *Manual* with few exceptions. The section called "Taking the True Achievement" is performed only on the last day, the day of empowerment. As Mani Rimdu uses a sand *maṇḍala*, the normal prayer to Remain Firm (*brtan bzhugs*) and Request to Go (*gshegs gsol*) are omitted. Instead, a passage of the *Playful Ocean* is specially modified for the occasion.

> Consider me, all Buddhas and Bodhisattvas who dwell in the ten directions!
> Conquerors! Until all the living beings that exist, who are as vast as the sky, achieve the state of non-abiding *nirvāṇa*, do not go to *nirvāṇa* [yourselves]! Stay firm!
> We pray you stay firm in this sand *maṇḍala* until we perform the ritual that asks you to go.
> Having stayed firm, we also pray you grant every supreme and common true achievement to us and to all sentient beings.

Finally, the monks recite a prayer written by Ngawang Tenzin Norbu, *The Valley of Benefit and Pleasure* (*sMon lam phan bde'i ljong*); the "Auspicious Recitation" (39b2) and "Shower of Blessings" from the *Manual;* and produce the "*maṇi*-sound"—again they recite Lord of the Dance's mantra "oṁ āḥ hūṁ hrīḥ oṁ maṇi padme hūṁ."[42]

Auspicious Recitations (*bkra shis*) [pronounced "tashi"] involve throwing grain, *tsampa*, or flowers in the air and are performed in public by the throngs that gather during Tibetan New Year. The Auspicious Recitation from the Lord of the Dance *Manual* is a short version of that common Tibetan ritual.

Oṁ! May it come! The boon of the highest blessing—
The good fortune of the Lama, the head of the hundred families!
May it come! The rain of true achievement—the good fortune
Of the heavenly host of the peaceful and wrathful tutelaries!
May it come! The good fortune of the Sky Walkers—
The heroes whose actions succeed without fail!
May it come! All the success ever imagined!
The good fortune of the highest virtue and goodness! [39b2]

The second session ends with concluding prayers from *Religious Practice*. Several of them are traditionally associated with Mani Rimdu.[43] The rest are drawn from the common stock of closing prayers performed at the monastery.

14

The Public Days

The thirteenth day is the first of Mani Rimdu's three public days. These days are marked by large outdoor events easily accessible to and often designed for a mass audience. Since this is the case, many villagers think of the festival as consisting only of these days. Even residents of nearby villages usually are unaware of the earlier and later parts of the ritual. Foreigners who have written about Mani Rimdu, presumably relying on such informants, have spread this impression to the outside world.

Many of these days' events take place in the monastery's dance courtyard (*'chams ra*). This includes not only formal occasions of dance and empowerment, but much of the audience's informal eating, drinking, and merrymaking. On the path leading to the courtyard, hawkers sell oranges, peanuts, and apples. At all three monasteries, there used to be a tradition of neighboring villagers feeding all comers to the public festival. As late as 1983, this custom partially survived at Thami, where *chang* and snacks of fruit and pastries were provided to local people on the day of the dance. Previously all in attendance were served, but in 1983, foreign tourists, an ever-increasing presence at Mani Rimdu, were served food but not *chang*. This is doubtless due to the lack of manners that Sherpas perceive in foreigners: a Sherpa needs to have refreshments forced on him in an elaborate interchange of refusal and insistence; a foreigner will summon a donor to him like a waitress.

A major reason Sherpas and Tibetans give for attending the Chiwong Mani Rimdu is to see Trulshik Rinpoche and to receive his blessings. This, of course, is done *en masse* on the day of empowerment. For many participants a hurried contact as part of a rapidly moving queue is not enough. Thus, throughout the public days a constant stream seeks audience with the lama.

They dress for the occasion in their richest attire. The amalgam of Western and Nepali dress that most Sherpas nowadays prefer often gives way to traditional costume. The long robe of rare Chinese brocade or local wool, the women's finest blouse or in some cases, her family's wedding vest, emerge from a rarely opened trunk. Even the incurably modern put on their cleanest expedition parka or NATO jacket. Outside the monastery, they rinse their mouths before approaching the lama.

When the lama is on stage, they, too, are on stage. They load his table with ceremonial scarves and with elaborately arranged offerings—pastries piled like the logs of a cabin; a broad tray of grain dotted with coins.

According to Buddhist belief, the magnitude of a gift depends on the donor's attitude, not on its material worth. A mind fixed purely on giving, myth tells us, makes the most of even the humblest offering. In their most elaborate form, the offerings made on the dais are ritually transformed into a *maṇḍala*—a world of offerings.[1] This is done with recitations and through passing a set of symbolic objects from donor to lama. These objects represent both the universe that is offered and the three jewels—the Buddha, teaching and spiritual community who are the recipients of the offering. Ideally, the ritual is accompanied by a corresponding visualization. The patrons of this elaborate ceremonial are usually, although not exclusively, the wealthy, high-status members of the lay community. Occasionally, a less prominent person gives such an offering, perhaps in part as a demonstration of upward mobility. The offerings, discreetly hidden in envelopes, are presumably large.

When Trulshik Rinpoche is in his private chamber above the chapel, the audiences continue. Here, they are more intimate and individualized but no less ritualized. Lay audience seekers usually come as a family group. Both nuclear and extended families can be seen. Professional *religieux* often come with a contingent from their monastery or nunnery.

The audiences are similar to those Trulshik Rinpoche grants at Thubten Chöling. The group prostrates on the ground three times in the traditional manner and then it makes its presentations and requests. A medicament, an amulet or a prayer may be needed. A baby or an invalid may need a new name. Advice or prophecy may be sought. In the end, Trulshik Rinpoche gives them what they want (or at least an explanation of why he cannot) and they are sent away, each with a blessing, a protective cord, and perhaps a packet of "ambrosial spiritual medicine."

Sometimes a party delivers a wholesale lot of offerings and requests from Tibet or a distant part of Solu-Khumbu. Each individual's donation and request is tallied. The lama's staff assembles the order and provides a receipt for each donation, no matter how small.

15

Day Thirteen: Dance Rehearsal

The thirteenth day of Mani Rimdu is the day of the dance rehearsal. Sherpas call this day by several names: *cham-gyu, cham-gyi,* or *cham-chong*. Of these terms, the latter corresponds to the Tibetan phrase *'chams sbyong* (also pronounced *cham-chong*) 'dance practice' or 'dance training'. The most prevalent term found in Western writings, *tsam-ki-bulu* (or *cham-ki-bulu*) "showing of the dance," seems somewhat less frequently used by Sherpas than the other terms.[1] Presumably it is equivalent to the Tibetan *'chams rgyugs 'bul,* the term Ngawang Tsundru, Chant Leader of Thubten Chöling, prefers as a description of the events of the thirteenth day. According to him, *rgyugs 'bul* means "showing for inspection, as a student shows a teacher his work for correction." The phrase *Cham-gyu* or *cham-gyi* may also be a variation on the Tibetan term *'chams rgyugs 'bul.* On its own, it could be taken to mean a "quick dance" or a "dance run-through."[2]

According to informants, the theoretical justification of the Day Thirteen dances is indeed to present them to the lama for his inspection and approval.[3] Although with hundreds of spectators pouring into the monastery every hour, how a lama could cancel even a hopelessly faulty performance is purely a matter of conjecture. To my knowledge, this dreadful scenario has never taken place.

Starting on the thirteenth day, the routine of the past weeks is broken. The normal rotation of protector deities is abandoned and both the *Playful Ocean* and the *Followers* are performed in full. The monks begin before dawn to allow time for the dance. If there is not time to complete the ritual marathon before the dance, the monks will complete it that evening following the dance.[4] This allows for some flexibility in the starting time of the day's rituals.

When the ceremonies in the assembly hall are finished, the monks assemble on the porch facing the courtyard, and perform the *Mountain Incense Offering* (*Ri bo bsangs mchod*). The *Mountain Incense Offering* is a common Tibetan ceremony. It is often performed by itself, or, as here, in combination with other rituals. In this Buddhist adaptation of an ancient indigenous ritual, incense is offered to two sets of "guests."[5] The "upper guests" are the assembly of gods. The "lower guests" are those to whom one owes a karmic debt by virtue of having mistreated them in previous lifetimes. According to Tibetan belief, the demons that afflict one in this life are the spirits of those one has injured in the past reborn. In paying back such debts, the *Mountain Incense Offering* deals with karmic situations that would shorten one's life, either by direct karmic retribution or by revenge of an individual karmic creditor—if such a distinction can be made.[6]

In the elaborate version of the *Mountain Incense Offering* used at Chiwong Mani Rimdu several other ceremonies are appended to the basic ritual—"The Praise of the War God" (*dGra lha'i dpang bstod*) from *The Diamond Heart of Pure Appearance* (*Dag snang rdo rje snying po*); and "Attracting Fortune" (*g.Yang 'gugs*) composed by Lha btsun nam mkha' jigs med, author of the *Mountain Incense Offering*. Both, like the *bsangs* itself, are examples of extremely old types of Tibetan ritual.[7] A special "Auspicious Omens" (*bkra shis*) and "Dedicatory Prayer" (*bsngo ba smon lam*) are also included in the collection. Protector rituals from other sources, in the form of the *Unelaborated* and/or extracts from the *Playful Ocean* are inserted before "Attracting Fortune."[8]

At Chiwong, in addition to the specified incense, two groups of tormas and a golden libation are offered. The first group is a gift torma for the *Mountain Incense Offering*. It is similar in appearance to the gift torma for the Sworn Ones (*dam can 'bul gtor*).[9]

The second group is usually just called "the six white and [six] red tormas" (*dkar gtor dmar gtor drug*), although I have also heard it referred to as the "offering torma for the *Mountain Incense Offering*."[10] A dozen small tormas are arranged in a row on a board, six round white ones to the left and six red triangular ones to the right. Each white torma has a "button and ball" in front of it; each red one, an empty button. The tormas are placed together with the libation cup on a stemmed metal platter. According to Trulshik Rinpoche, the white and red tormas are sometimes said to be offerings to the twelve Steadfast Women (*brtan ma*). In his opinion however, they are an offering to the Lama, Tutelary, Sky Walkers and Protectors in general, the white tormas being dedicated to the vegetarians among them, and the red to the meat eaters.[11]

According to Sang Sang Tulku, the tormas and the golden libation are connected with the interpolated Protector Rituals. This is consistent with the general timing of their exit. The red and white tormas and golden libation are removed first. At this point, the assembly can be heard to recite the mantras of the protectors, "Oṁ Mahākāla. . . ." A few minutes later, the gift torma is removed.[12]

Trulshik Rinpoche specifies that the beribboned arrow on the courtyard altar is connected to "Attracting Fortune," and indeed, near the end of the *Mountain Incense Offering* sequence, the arrow is removed from the altar and given to the lama.[13] Holding it by its point, the lama rotates the arrow in a clockwise arc, the movement inscribing an invisible inverted cone. Such a movement seems to be common usage with the beribboned arrow. Indeed, in Mongolian the *mda' dar* is called *dalalgha,* which comes from the verb "to rotate or gyrate."[14]

At the same time, beer (*chang*) and parched barley flour (*tsampa*) are held up to the altar as directed in the text. An assistant then replaces the arrow on the altar.[15] The text also specifies the offering of a goat. This leads one to suspect that the goat's shoulder bone on the altar also is connected to the "Attracting Fortune." We will speak of this again shortly.

I have not included a translation of the *Mountain Incense Offering*. Although a scholarly study of this complex work is yet to be done, translations do exist.[16]

"Attracting Fortune" is even rarer and is as yet untranslated.[17] For the time being, I will summarize some of its key points, as it refers to many items of indigenous Tibetan and northern Asian origin found on the dance altar. These will be discussed more fully at the end of this chapter.

"Attracting Fortune" is an offering of a sacred goat (*g.yang ra*). In this context, goats and sheep seem to be interchangeable. Rolf Alfred Stein has published a fragment of an early *g.yang 'gug,* obsessed with sheep and wool: "The material of the good-fortune bag is wool. The father was the sky sheep Reddish-white, the mother the earth sheep Reddish. These two united and had sons. Of five were sweet smelling lambs."[18]

The beneficiary of the offering is an assemblage of indigenous gods of the Tibetan highlands, lowlands, and middle lands. These include, respectively: the Five Malefactor/Benefactor Brothers; the Ocean Medicine Spirits and the Steadfast Ones; and the Seven Siblings—Demons, Stern Ones and Blazing Ones. Last on the list and apparently taking pride of place, is the important indigenous deity Good Diamond (rDo rje legs pa). In addition to the goat, Attracting Fortune mentions offerings of "sacred beer, an auspicious beribboned arrow, and flour and butter."

Interestingly enough, the leg of a sheep figures in another Tibetan ritual of attracting or calling, the "Calling the Soul" (*bla 'gugs*). In that context, a leg of mutton called the "soul-leg" (*bla rkang*) is among the items needed first to rescue a victim of demonic soul-snatching, and then to judge if the effort was a success. The ritual also uses an effigy of a sheep itself. This effigy is called the "soul-sheep" (*bla lug*) and is used to divine if the errant soul has or has not returned. As Lessing has observed, "The Tibetans and other peoples assume a mysterious relation between the soul and the sheep and lamb."[19]

In the words of Tucci, the sheep is of "cosmogonic significance" in early Tibetan myth.[20] It is involved with the origins of the Earth, and of milk and barley. Several myths link it to the invention of prophecy. In one myth, the first divination thread (*ju thig*), a key tool of Bonpo prophesy and the "receptacle for the soul of the world," originates from the shoulder of the "Divine Sheep with the Great Wool."[21] The other device central to the *g.yang 'gug*, the magic arrow, is of evil origins. Through the intervention of the primal sheep, it comes into the possession of the forces of good.[22]

In early Tibetan ritual, the smoke of the *bsangs* was said to force open the door in the sky, and give access to the heavens. The head of the ram also sometimes represented the "sky-door."[23]

Like the rite of "cutting-off" (*gcod*) and the *Mountain Incense Offering* itself, "Attracting Fortune" is a perfect example of Tibetan Tantric ritual, in that it unifies, even homologizes indigenous Tibetan and northern Asian elements with yogic physiology and Buddhist soteriology, mythology, and metaphysics. The goat is identified as the "sacred goat of the rainbow body, the diamond truth body," and is asked to "Grant the true achievement of the great rainbow body transference!" After the goat is further infused with blessings, it and the other gifts—the arrow, beer, and so on—are offered to the assembled deities, who are asked in return to bestow a typical list of magic and spiritual attainments, similar to those we have seen in the *Playful Ocean* and elsewhere.

The "Auspicious Omens" ritual done after the dance—or considered as the last part of the dance—also belongs to the *Mountain Incense Offering*. It, too, is an elaborate example of its type, in which parched barley flour and barley beer are offered.[24]

The requisites of the ritual are displayed on the courtyard altar. Thus, in 1983, the altar held the following:

- Upper shelf, (l, r): a bowl of *tsampa;* ambrosia in a miniature skull-shaped cup; the gift torma for the *Mountain Incense Offering; rakta* in a miniature skull cup; a bowl of *chang*.[25]
- Upper shelf, rear: the beribboned arrow, upright.
  Lower shelf, front row: the white and red tormas.[26]
- Lower shelf, back row (l, r): the "seven offerings"—water, footbath, flowers, incense, lamp, and food (torma).

Luther G. Jerstad, paraphrasing von Fürer-Haimendorf, reported that the "dance of showing" is "complete with music, chants, and ritual articles, but minus the masks, costumes, and audience."[27]

This is somewhat inexact. There is an audience, although not nearly in the numbers of the day of the masked performance, varying in number from dozens to hundreds, depending on the monastery and the year. There are also costumes of a sort—not the elaborate brocades of two days hence, but the formal set of a monks regalia, including the vestigial water bottle that the *vinaya* regulations permitted mendicant monks to carry in the heat of the Indian sun.[28]

As to chants and ritual articles: true, the *Mountain Incense Offering* remains the same as on the day of the masked dance. The other liturgy which accompanies the masked dance, however, is totally absent. This is no trifling distinction. Indeed, it is the absence of rituals more than the absence of masks that marks this *'chams* as a rehearsal rather than an actual performance.

The individual dances and the part the liturgy plays in them will be discussed in detail later. For now we will restrict our discussion to the ways in which the Day Thirteen dances differ from those of Day Fifteen.

The absence of liturgy itself affects the performance of the dance. On Day Fifteen, the dancers stand stock still in the courtyard as the monks on the dais recite lengthy passages of text. Without these chants, they pause but momentarily. The two comic sequences that are a much loved part of the masked dance, the Long-Life Man and the Seer, are omitted on Day Thirteen. Without the liturgy and the comedy, the dances are considerably shorter. At Chiwong in 1983, the dance rehearsal took two hours and twenty minutes. The masked dances were eight hours *longer*. Correcting for the comic sequences, about four hours and twenty minutes in 1983,[29] we see that the liturgy adds some three and a half hours to the performance. Thus, although unnoticed by previous observers, the liturgy performed in the midst of the dance actually consumes more time than does the dance itself.

In its broad outlines, each act of the dance is similar to the others. A row of monks sits on the porch of the courtyard to chant the liturgy and serve as the orchestra for the dance. Behind them, a makeshift curtain separates the stage—the front of the porch—from the wings. From within the chapel beyond, now transformed into a dressing room, a thigh-bone trumpet sounds.[30] It is answered by a musician on the dais. The curtain parts and the dancers enter. They descend, typically by pairs, to the courtyard floor. They dance, moving around the courtyard in a clockwise direction. They pause in the cardinal and/or intermediate directions and execute repetitive series of steps. They march forward and back, make small circles and twirl in place. Their hands move; many of the motions are identifiable as one or another of the *mudrās* typical of Indian influenced ritual and dance. As the act draws to a close, the dancers line up in two rows at the far end of the courtyard and exit, once again by pairs.

Without elaborate costumes and masks, the dances become difficult to distinguish one from another. Occasionally a telltale idiosyncrasy provides an easy identification, at least for the frequent Mani Rimdu-goer. Two pairs of dancers, one with cymbals, one with drums must be the Ging. Dancers with swords belong to the Sword Dance. A lone dancer can only be Dorje Drolö. Even without their skeleton costumes, the Lords of the Cemetery can be identified by their jangling, loose-boned, capering dance.

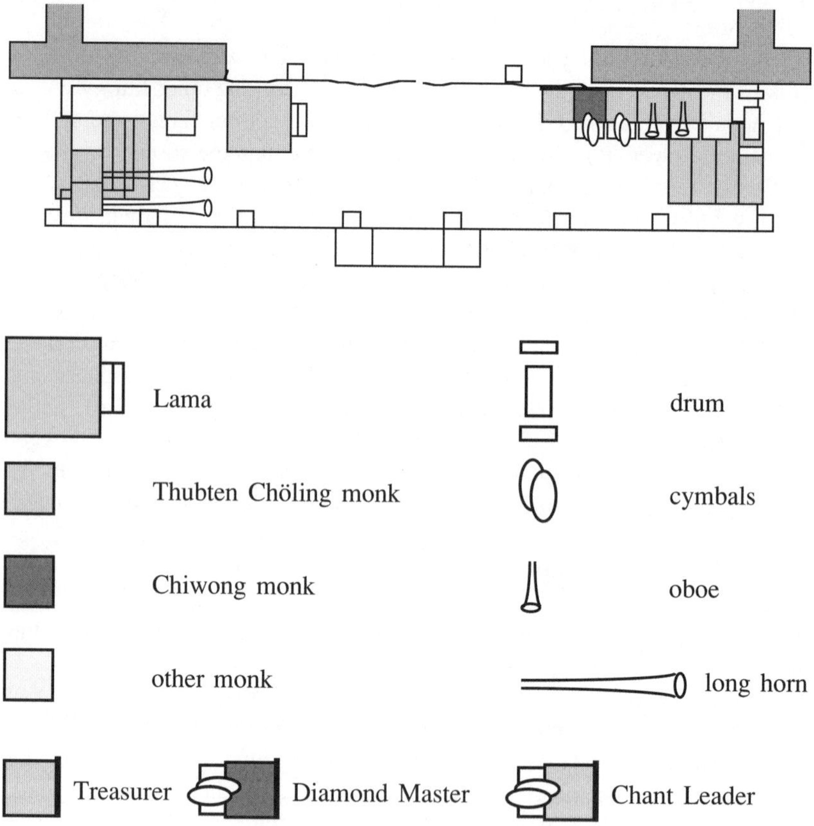

Seating Arrangement on Dais for Dance Rehearsal: Chiwong, 1982

The props used in the masked dance may or may not be present. The sword dancers have their swords and Dorje Drolö his *vajra* and dagger; but the Protectors lack the identifying implements they will carry.[31]

The position of a given dance relative to the others also identifies it, as do, although with less precision, the number of participants. For the most part subtler qualities differentiate the dances. To the expert ear, the music changes; and to the practiced eye, there are variations in sequence of movements, *mudrās* and individual steps. For identifying most of the dances, an ethnographer armed with notes of previous years' performances has a distinct advantage over an ordinary spectator, Sherpa or foreign.

After the last dance, the "Auspicious Omens" from the *Mountain Incense Offering* is recited. *Tsampa* and *chang* from the altar are distributed to the monks on the dais. The monks throw the *tsampa* in the air, some saying aloud as they do so the traditional "tashi delek phunsum tsok"—"Auspicious omens, pleasure and goodness! May virtue accumulate!" Then, each at his own pace, they pass behind the curtains, and retire to the interior of the chapel.

Before we leave the dance rehearsal, we should discuss a few of the implications or at least associations of some of objects we have seen that relate more to the common religious heritage of central Asia, the "shamanic" heritage if you will, and less to the Buddhist tradition.

The most obvious of these are the arrow and the shoulder bone. Lessing, Nebesky-Wojkowitz, and others have discussed the beribboned arrow at length.[32] According to Nebesky-Wojkowitz, its original use was a divinatory device of Bonpo shamans, although Buddhists, particularly those of the Nyingma sect, make use of a great variety of them.[33] Beribboned arrows are known to every Tibetan, as they are used in the wedding ceremony.

The arrow is a common enough implement in classic Siberian shamanism as well, and the connection between their use among Tibetans and Siberian shamans has been made some thirty years since.[34] The arrow plays a part in shaman's séances.[35] Magar shaman of West Nepal, for example, use miniature bows and arrows to shoot back the poisoned arrows that malignant spirits and witches have shot into their patient.[36] According to Eliade:

> The arrow embodies a two-fold magico-religious significance; on the one hand, it is an exemplary image of speed, of "flight"; on the other, it is the magical weapon par excellence (the arrow kills at a distance). Used in purification ceremonies or ceremonies to eject demons, the arrow "kills" as well as "drives away" and "expels" evil spirits.[37]

As we have seen in the earlier days of Mani Rimdu and will see tomorrow, the flight to another plane and the "slaying of demons" have elements in common.

Another use of the arrow by Tibetans, Chukchi and others, is as a pipe "to suck the illness out of the body of a patient."[38] The change of planes effected by means of being sucked through a pipe, is a theme we have seen and will see again elsewhere, in the use of the magic dagger and in the eating habits of the gods.

The goat's shoulder bone is another object with strong shamanic associations. Some were mentioned on the first day of Mani Rimdu, when we first encountered a shoulder bone, others, were mentioned concerning the ritual of

"Attracting Fortune." As we have seen, the shoulder bone is a device associated, one way or another, with a passage between planes, an oar with which the shaman may row to the other world.[39] This theme, like the flight of the arrow, fits in the context of the symbols that cluster in the center of the dance courtyard.

At Chiwong, on the day of the dance, the altar is set up against the central pole of the awning that shades the dancers. Thami, lacking Chiwong's elaborate dance theater (*'chams rva*), lacks a full awning. There, the altar is set against a flagpole placed in the center of the dance area. Both poles are newly erected. At Chiwong, the tent pole replaces the usual flag pole. At Thami, a new flag pole replaces the previous year's.[40]

A visitor to one or the other monastery might be misled by the flags or the awning. A visitor to both, readily sees that it is the pole itself that is important. Indeed, the erection of the pole in the center of the circular dance area is a common feature of Tibetan sacred dance. According to Nebesky-Wojkowitz:

> These flagpoles are called *phya dar* (also *cha dar*). They are the ensigns of the highest ranking divinities represented in the *'chams.* The cloth of the flags should correspond to the ritual color of those gods, goddesses, or groups of deities appearing in the *'chams.* Accordingly, in the case of many *dharmapālas,* the flag is black or dark blue. On it are printed magic spells invoking the protector of the creed in whose honor the ensign has been set up.[41]

The pole, of course, is an important religious symbol in Siberian shamanism: it is the route to the other world. In Nepal, Magar shamans climb a pole during their initiations.[42] Indeed, in many cultures trees or poles serve as the link between two planes; between earth and the heavens. The pole, the mountain, and similar symbols may all well be, as Eliade has noted, variations of "the symbolism of the 'center.' "[43] In Bon mythology, for example, the instrument of passage is often a rope, by which one escapes "to the heavens and a very real bliss."[44] The placement of the shoulder bone and the beribboned arrow only reinforces the pole's already strong shamanic associations.

The rupture of planes that occurs as the shaman climbs the tree is similar to the rupture of planes that occurs when the initiate enters the center of the god's *maṇḍala.* In the dance, the pole is in the center of the stage on which the gods dance. The dances, for the most part are symmetrical, and the gods arranged around the center as if in a *maṇḍala.* In some Tibetan monastic dances, the dancers actually move within circles outlined on the courtyard in chalk.[45] The symbolism is also linked on another level: a *maṇḍala* is a vision of a god's home in paradise. Mani Rimdu and many other Tibetan sacred dances are often said to be based on yogis' visions of the paradises and the gods' movements in them.[46]

An altar is placed against the world-tree to hold the various items used in the ceremonies and in the dance. An altar is another kind of intermediary between the planes of the human and the divine. It is where the offerings are placed that make the voyage between the two realms. It is fitting that the altar, the receptacle of the offerings, be plugged into the wire that, so to speak, conducts power between the two planes.[47]

The tent-pole and altar recall a basic level of symbolism in Tibetan culture to which many Tibetan rituals can be related: the symbolism of the nomads tent and the Tibetan house. In the tent, the hearth is in the center, the smoke hole, the door to the upper levels of the world, above it. The central pole of the tent lies next to the hearth. By climbing a notched pole, one reaches the upper storeys of the house; by climbing the *dmu*-pole one ascends to the upper storeys of the universe. The name of the flagpole, *phya dar,* itself relates to this belief. The *phya*, like the *dmu* were gods of ancient Tibet, just as the *mu-bya* were the ancient Qiang gods of the sky. Thus, the rope or ladder of the *phya* is the same as that of the *dmu*.[48]

An image of the soul in flight, the arrow that we saw earlier relates to the same set of symbols. As Stein has observed,

> In handbooks known as "Opening the door to the sky" (*nam-mkha' sgo-byed*) . . . the "soul" consisting of light, is seen going off into the distance through the "roof hole" of the sky like a flying arrow.[49]

Another symbolic complex of considerable antiquity is the mountain at the center of the world and the tree that grows upon it. Inside the monastery, in the torma, the symbols of the tree and the *maṇḍala* coalesce with each other and with the symbol of the world-mountain. The torma is placed in front of the *maṇḍala* and alternates with it as the outward location of the deity. In shamanic cosmology, the world-tree grows atop the world-mountain.[50] Just as the world-mountain is in the center of the world, a god dwells at the center of his *maṇḍala,* the diagram of his paradise, his world. The four steps at the base of the main torma are the steps of the world-mountain, and the stick within the body of the torma, the life-tree.[51] At various points in Mani Rimdu, the torma is considered the body of the god. The spine is the life-tree of a man's body; the "life-tree" of a torma is the backbone that holds it up. The main pole of a thread-cross (*mdos*) is also called its "life-tree," and the foundation on which it is erected, "*ri rab lhun-po,* the world-mountain."[52] The *Śricakrasaṁvaratantra* explicitly homologizes the spine of the divine body to the axis of Mount Meru. In his 1919 edition of the tantra, Dawa-samdup notes that "in Sanskrit the spine is called Merudanda, *i.e.*, Meru axis."[53]

Western students of Buddhism and other Indic religions have sometimes tried to make a distinction between religions which seek salvation upwards in heaven ("Western Religions") and religions that seek salvation within

("Eastern Religions"). This sometimes leads to a sensation of conflict when approaching Tibetan data. Having created this neat duality, it is annoying to find data that doesn't fit. If salvation is within, why do Tibetans worship gods that are outside? If the real enemy is within, the real demons in the mind, how is it possible for Buddhists to routinely "kill" external demonic forces? We can use the life-tree/torma/*maṇḍala* complex as a window (or perhaps more a propos, as a smoke-hole) to look through to a point in the history of religions when upwards or inwards may not have been so much a clash of opposing theologies as a modality of symbols. It is fitting that in Mani Rimdu the *maṇḍala* should be next to the life-tree imbedded in the torma. It is also fitting that the monks dance around the central tree in the way that the gods of their visualizations are arranged around the *maṇḍala*.

In a Buddhist philosophical context, the duality of outside and inside blurs. In a Nyingma meditational context, one may generate the tutelary god upwards (in the sky or in front) and inwards at the same time.

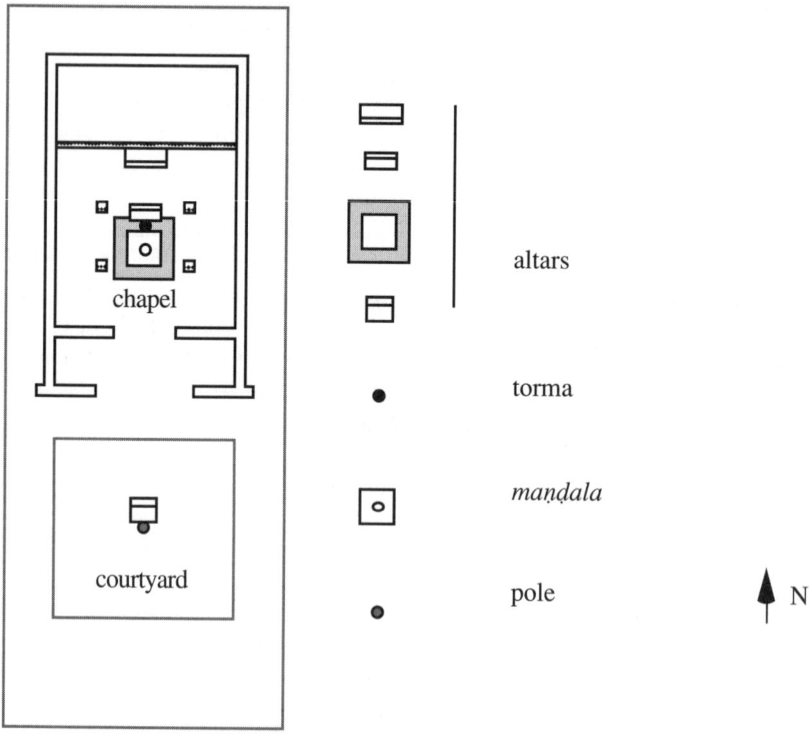

Monastery: Showing Orientation of Objects *(not to scale)*

16

Day Fourteen: Empowerment

Just as butter is not churned from sand,
Without empowerment there is no siddhi.

Mahāmudrā-tilaka tantra[1]

The fourteenth day is the day of public empowerment. According to many of those who attend Mani Rimdu, including Trulshik Rinpoche, the empowerment is the most important of its public events.

Empowerment is the sine qua non of the tantric experience. It ritually transforms the disciple into his chosen deity. In creation-stage yoga, the disciple will meditate that he or she is that god. Without empowerment, as the *Mahāmudrā-tilaka tantra* suggests, such meditation is fruitless.

Generally, the empowerment is said to be modeled on the royal consecration of ancient India. The Sanskrit name for both ceremonies is *abhiṣeka*, indicating the "sprinkling" that baptizes a prince and turns him into a king. In India, according to that venerable expert A. L. Basham, "the king was evidently the fellow of the gods, if not a god himself"; the *Śatapatha Brāhmaṇa* identifies the king with both Prajāpati and Viṣṇu.[2]

By no means everyone who attends that uniquely Tibetan celebration, the mass empowerment, has an intention of practicing creation-process yoga. Despite the growing popularity of his cult, it is doubtful if many of those who come to Mani Rimdu meditate on the god Union of the Blissful/Lord of the Dance/Great Compassion. There is even some doubt that the initiation bestowed at Mani Rimdu is sufficient to empower one to practice deity yoga. Be that as it may, the empowerment is stated to have a direct effect on those who receive it. The *Torma Empowerment* text read on Mani Rimdu's fourteenth day enumerates some of the signs of successful empowerment.[3]

> The first sign of grace
> By virtue of such an empowerment
> Is that, unasked for, aspiration and respect are born in one's stream of consciousness.
> The second sign of grace
> Is that whatever you turn your imagination to is firm and clear.
> The third sign of grace
> Is that understanding of self-emergent wisdom rises.

The empowerment is also said to have more concrete benefits, and ones that demand less of its recipients, among them long life and health.

Previous authors have identified the public empowerment of Mani Rimdu as a "life empowerment" (*tshe dbang*). True, the Mani Rimdu empowerment shares several features with that common ritual. "Liquor of life" (*tshe chang*) and the centimeter wide balls of sweetened *tsampa* known as "life pills" (*tshe ril*) are distributed to the public at both ceremonies. The fame of the life empowerment further confuses the issue. Many foreigners—and Sherpas—know of no similar public ceremony and routinely misidentify the Mani Rimdu empowerment as a *tshe dbang*.[4]

In one of my first interviews with Trulshik Rinpoche, I asked him about the "life empowerment" that I had read was a part of Mani Rimdu. He answered with more than a little exasperation in his voice, "Why does everyone call it that! It is not a life empowerment!"

The name of the principal manuscript used makes this clear. It is *The Utterance which is the Essence of Ambrosia: The Annotated Torma Empowerment of Great Compassion Union of the Blissful*. As Trulshik Rinpoche went on to explain, the Mani Rimdu empowerment is a torma empowerment rather than a life empowerment. Even were the text and the lama not so insistent, we might suspect that we were not dealing with a life empowerment here simply because the deity of Mani Rimdu is Avalokiteśvara, and not one of those more frequently associated with life empowerments, such as Amitāyus.

In *The Cult of Tārā*, Stephan Beyer describes a torma empowerment as an addition to a larger empowerment ceremony. In it:

> . . . the Master (to use an informant's metaphor) "introduces" the deity to the recipient; here the deity is generated in a torma, the Master prays the deity's favor for his disciple, and the deity is absorbed by contact into the recipient's body, now rendered a fit vessel to contain this power throughout the preceding ritual of permission. . . . Thus the power to contemplate the deity is transmitted through the primary magical means of the Master's visualization and recitation in the ritual of permission, and to this there may be added

the further magical device of the torma, in its second and third aspects—as an evocation and as a substance of magical attainment.[5]

According to Trulshik Rinpoche, there are three types of empowerment that might be used, an elaborate flask empowerment (*spros bcas bum pa'i dbang*), the three forms of unelaborated supreme empowerment (*spros med mchog dbang rnam gsum*), and the essentially meaningful torma empowerment (*snying po don gyi gtor dbang*). Only the last of these is employed here.[6] We will discuss the Union of the Blissful *Torma Empowerment* in a moment.

To accommodate the very full schedule of the fourteenth day, the rituals in the chapel start exceedingly early. In 1980, the morning gong rang at five A.M.

Shortly before the indoor ceremonies, a singular event occurs.[7] Those loitering at the threshold are given notice that they must either go in or out. The door is closed and fastened from the inside. It is time for the ritual known as the "Taking the True Achievement" (*dngos grub blang ba*).

At first glance, this seems to be (finally) one of the secret rituals with which everyone insists Tibetan Buddhism is rife. Perhaps it is, but when questioned about the closed door policy, Trulshik Rinpoche suggests simply that here it is not a matter so much of excluding people per se as it is that only those who have done the ritual have any "achievement" to "take."

That no one is ejected from the chapel bears this out. Typically the room is filled by a score or two of visiting monks and nuns, a few pious laymen, and an occasional stray swept in at the crucial moment.

The ceremony for "Taking the True Achievement" is taken directly from the Lord of the Dance *Manual.*

> Oṁ! From the Truth Realm's excellent fortress—
> From the maṇḍala of apparitions that tame beings—
> O victorious, accomplished, noble Avalokiteśvara
> And entourage, pray consider us!
> We have entered this *maṇḍala*.
> We have sought refuge in you.
> When we reverently pray to you and the Protectors,
> Consider us with a Protector's compassion!
> Bestow upon us immediately,
> Blessings of body, speech and mind;
> And all the highest and ordinary true achievements
> From the fine flask of your victorious mind!
> In order to liberate many beings,
> I pray you bestow upon us
> True achievements of the four types of action—
> Purifying, extending, magnetizing, and fierce!
>
> Oṁ āḥ hūṁ sarvasiddhi phala hūṁ [37b2]

This prayer is only recited on Day Fourteen. Coming between the interpolated Sky Walker torma offering and the prayer of thanksgiving, it is counted as part of "The Conclusion" of the *Manual.*

The liturgy here may be unique, but the actions that accompany it parallel events that transpire later during the public empowerment. Structurally, if not liturgically, "Taking the True Achievement" is a "private empowerment." All the empowerment substances are assembled, carried by a troop of monks wearing their yellow ceremonial hats.

The liturgy is read and the achievement mantras recited. The band strikes up and the procession forms, carrying the *maṇi*-pills, flask, mirror, life pills, life liquor, and the main torma on its wooden base.[8] Each monk in turn offers the ritual device he bears to Trulshik Rinpoche and to the hierarchy of participant monks. Finally, the spectators sitting on the periphery of the chapel are served.

There is a specific procedure for each item. The pills are placed in your right hand, the liquor in your left. A smear of colored butter is wiped from the mirror and a deft vertical stripe painted on your proffered throat. Finally, the torma bearer approaches and places the weighty object, the substance of *siddhi*, upon your head. Venerable clerics are approached gingerly. Ethnographers and other youngsters often receive the *siddhi* with a playful and resounding clunk on the head.

Since the torma has been the body of the god, one might suspect that it would be consumed as a sacrament. According to Trulshik Rinpoche, this is indeed the custom when the empowerment is given to a small group. With so many in attendance at Mani Rimdu, it is impractical. As Trulshik Rinpoche points out, it would destroy the torma.

Instead, another torma is employed for this purpose. This small sweetened torma is called the "substance of true achievement" (*dngos grub kyi rdzas*), or more simply "true achievement" (*dngos grub*; Ssk., *siddhi*).[9]

According to Trulshik Rinpoche, three substances used in the empowerment have the meaning of true achievement: the torma, the life pills, and the life liquor. They are not, however, to be found in any of the Mani Rimdu texts, but originate in the traditions of Rongphu Monastery.[10]

In shape, the bottom of the true achievement torma is much like that of a round torma. The top, with four spade-shaped faces, has a unique design. During the ceremony, it rests, along with the life pills, the skull bowl of liquor and related items on a table to the north of the *maṇḍala*. It is consumed at a later point.

The True Achievement Torma

After the procession, the sacred substances are placed on the table north of the *maṇḍala*. There is a short prayer, the doors are opened, and the visitors leave.[11]

Unlike the other days of Mani Rimdu, Day Fourteen has only one session of ritual instead of two.[12] The day begins in a normal fashion, adjusted, of course, to take into account the changed circumstance—the pill recitation, the core of Mani Rimdu, has been completed. The content of the day-to-day ritual has already been discussed in some detail.[13] The following lists summarize the special way in which these rituals are ordered on Day Fourteen. Some of the other activities unique to the day of Empowerment will be discussed later in this chapter.

1. Preliminary Practices (*sngon 'gro*) from going for refuge to blessing the offerings (*Manual* [UB] 2b1 ff.)
2. Actual Practice (*dngos gzhi*) from meditating on the *maṇḍala* to reciting the mantras of Lord of the Dance and his entourage. (UB 3.4 ff.) Since no more mantras are to be sent to the pills and flasks, the spell cords are removed after the recitation of the mantras.
3. Spying Ghosts.
4. Shower of Blessings
5. Feast, Self-Application of the Empowerment, etc., as usual until the interpolated Sky Walker Torma Offering (*Thun mtshams mka' 'gro gtor 'bul*).
6. Sky Walker Torma Offering. Today is the last day that the Sky Walker ritual is performed. Thus, the Sky Walker torma is taken out immediately after the offering is read. According to the custom of Chiwong, the torma is taken out with a fanfare played on the oboe, and removed to the roof gable.[14]

After this, the special regimen begins.

1. Obstructor Torma (*bgegs gtor*). This ritual is the first of the Special Preliminaries performed each day. In it, the practitioners assume the guise of Hayagrīva, and alternately bribe and threaten Obstructive forces. (UB 6b4).
2. Defining the Borders (*mtshams gcod*). Continuing to visualize themselves as Hayagrīva, the meditators imagine that they build a protective diamond pavilion around the *maṇḍala*. (UB 7b1).
3. Showering Blessings (*byin 'bebs*) (UB 8.5). The assembly exhorts the divine host to "Manifest your battalions of magic powers/And quickly show your marks and signs." Confession (*bshags pa*) omitted today.
4. Recitation Exhortation (*'dzab skul*) (UB 18b3).

5. Recitation. Accomplishment mantra "oṁ āḥ hūṁ sarvasiddhi phala hūṁ" is added as an appendix every time each mantra is said. Gathering Blessings (*byin sdus*) (UB 19.5), however, is not used.
6. Medicine (i.e., ambrosia; Ssk., *amṛta*) Offering (*sman mchod*) (UB 15b4).
7. Torma Offering (*gtor ma*) (UB 16b1).
8. The Offering of Rakta, ceremonial "blood" (UB 16b2–b3)
9. Confession (*bshags pa*) (UB 7b6–8.3)
10. Taking the True Achievement (*dngos sgrub blang*) (UB 37b1)
11. Procession of monks carrying: i. flask, ii. pills in skull + mirror, iii. life pills, iv. life beer, v. achievement torma.
12. The monks replace the above items on the *maṇḍala* table. [recitation of Avalokiteśvara mantra (*maṇi sgra*)][15]
13. Offering (*mchod*) (UB 38.1)
14. Praise (*bstod pa*) (UB 38.2)
15. The Hundred Syllable Mantra, i.e., the purificatory meditation on Vajrasattva.
16. Confessing your Failings (*nongs bshags*) (UB 38.3)
17. Prayer to Remain Firm (*brtan bzhugs*) (PO 54b3, emended.
18. Retraction (*bsdus rim*) (UB 38b2)
19. Dedicatory Prayer (*bsngo smon*).
20. Auspicious Omens (*bkra shis*).
21. Two selections from the Mindroling *Religious Practice* anthology: (a) The *mTsho rgyal* Prayer (*mTsho rgyal smon lam*) (RP 178.3 ff.), and (b) "The Three Jewels' . . . " Prayer ("*dKon mchog gsum kyi* . . .") (RP 183.1–183.4)

An hour or two later, the horn and oboe players ascend the roof to play the duets that signal the beginning of main events during the latter part of the festival.

Another hour passes as the stage is prepared. The lama's throne is moved and rearranged. Seats are set out for the descendants of Chiwong's founder. These broad chairs, handsome pieces of Sherpa household furniture, directly face the lama's throne at distance of no more than a few feet. Nothing could more strongly reinforce the family's special status as patrons of the monastery.

In recent years, one prominent local has provided a homemade public address system with determined generosity. This modern enhancement transforms the afternoon's prayers and religious discourses, which were formerly simply inaudible, into an incomprehensible din.

The crowd begins to gather. Soon, a procession forms in the courtyard to greet Trulshik Rinpoche. Visitors, often children, man the long-poled ceremonial flags, forming a line with the monastery orchestra. The orchestra plays a stately fanfare to welcome the lama. With hours to go before the climax of the ceremony, several hundred people already have gathered.[16] More will trickle in as the day goes on.

From the stairwell that leads down from the lama's quarters to the porch, a pair of oboes sounds. Wearing his flame-shaped scarlet mitre, the lama descends to the stage accompanied by a formal cortège of monks. One twirls a large parasol above the lama's head. Another walks backward before him, cleansing his path with a sheaf of burning incense sticks. The lama ascends his throne, sitting motionless for five minutes or more until the fanfare is concluded, as groups of nuns make prostrations in the courtyard below.

One member of the procession that greets the lama wears the mask of the Long-Life Man and, as the lama takes his seat, presents him with a ceremonial scarf. The Long-Life Man, a beaming figure with a long white beard and the smooth round face of an infant, will play a comic role in the dances tomorrow. In the context of a procession, however, he reverts to his generic function of a harbinger of longevity. In Tibet, as in China and Japan, the Long-Life Man is one of a group of such symbols—the pine tree and the deer being others. Across Asia, they are a frequent motif in every medium of art; they can be found in paintings, frescos, porcelain, woodwork, and even carpets.

The *Torma Empowerment* text states, if the empowerment is given "in connection with the basic empowerment," that is to say the "self-application" from the *Manual* completed that morning, "a separate accomplishment service is unnecessary."[17] Many of the rituals which would accompany a free-standing initiation can be omitted.

Be that as it may, the lama must still complete nearly half an hour of preliminary prayers and religious discourse before beginning the main ceremony. The text leaves the content of this address up to the officiant, specifying only an "appropriate religious discourse." The teaching is a general one, beginning with impermanence and death and leading up to the desirability of seeking empowerments.[18]

Around this time, lay people begin to make their formal offerings. A representative of the main line of the founder's descendants presents a *maṇḍala*, using the objects we have already seen symbolizing the offering and its recipients.

Before the actual empowerment begins, a representative of the monastery reads a long list of donors and their contributions. "Tenzin Sherpa of village A, 20 rupees; Tsering Lama of village B, 30 rupees," and so on. Such recitations are invariably part of elaborate Sherpa rituals from individually sponsored ceremonies to public festivals. They advertise a Sherpa's sponsorship of his religion: both his desire to give and his ability to do so. Although Buddhist ethicists sometime stress the special virtue of secret generosity, here the principle is clearly that no good deed should go unnoticed. In their small and intimate way, these proclamations are similar to the announcements of corporate and foundation sponsors on American public television.

This done, the actual empowerment begins. Small additions are made to the published text, for example, the oral transmission of a few additional mantras, such as that of Padmasambhava or of µākyamuni.[19]

An empowerment ritual is a participatory drama and takes the form of call and response. The lama prompts the initiates at each turn, asking questions or requesting them to repeat passages after him. "Imagine something like this," he instructs them, "this very place on earth, purified, becomes the great *maṇḍala* of omnipresent wisdom." "Repeat after me," he commands, 'O Diamond Master, pray consider me!' " At Mani Rimdu, however, few can hear the lama's commands and even fewer are sufficiently acquainted with the ritual to comply with them. Those that can and do are mostly confined to the small crowd of monks and patrons seated for the ceremony on the dais.

Following the ceremony, it is the time for an event the public has eagerly anticipated—the distribution of the empowerment substances. The band strikes up a fanfare and the faithful crush up to the dais. In a good year they may be eight hundred or more. In an off year, such as 1983, when Trulshik Rinpoche was ill and Sang Sang Tulku, the younger and less revered incarnation of Trulshik Rinpoche's father officiated in his stead, there were about 250 present.

The crowd is high-spirited, even pushy. Guards, usually monks from other monasteries or young, pious villagers, help control the crowd. The combination and alternation of attitudes with which a well-brought-up Sherpa youth tries to dissuade a man old enough to be his grandfather from vaulting over the ledge of the dais into the thick of the crowd provide an interesting spectacle. Firmness is tempered by gentleness; resolution dissolves in respect for age. Tentativeness reigns. Though those in the midst of the crowd are often as helpless as tempest-tossed flotsam and must ride the ebb and flow of the human sea, miraculously, no one loses his temper. Even the threats of the guards are imitations of mock threats. The message is "I'm supposed to try to stop you from coming up here, so please don't," or "I'm supposed be firm now, so please pretend that I'm serious." Confrontation, such as there is, turns into a joke or a shrug.

In some recent years, Nepali police officers have been present at Chiwong—the district capital is just down the hill at Saleri. These officers are non-Sherpas and their approach, while hardly tough as nails, lacks the charming air of unreality that marks the Sherpas' efforts to police themselves.

One practical innovation in crowd control of recent years, employed by both the official and the unofficial police, has been to restrict access to the stage by blocking off all but a single entrance to the east and a single exit to the west, and periodically barring the stairs until the crowd on the dais thins to tolerable proportions.

It takes about an hour for everyone to go through the receiving line and obtain all the blessings. Since this is a torma empowerment, the main blessing is bestowed by the torma itself. To this end, the torma rests on the table to Trulshik Rinpoche's right (west). As in procession that followed the "taking the true achievement" ritual that morning, the empowerment is received by contact between a person's head and the piece of wood that supports the torma.

The torma rests on Trulshik Rinpoche's table, which a pious Sherpa will anyway touch with his head in respect. Thus, it is difficult to say what proportion of the supplicants are actually aware of the torma's role in the proceedings. After they pass the torma, Trulshik Rinpoche gives them his hand-blessing (*phyag dbang*), usually by tapping them with the beribboned arrow. When asked about the significance of the arrow here, Trulshik Rinpoche replies that it is convenient for the purpose. Indeed, it is just the right length to allow him to tap those who pass with ease. Lamas often use the nearest item of even the most remote spiritual connotation to bestow a hand-blessing. Sometimes, when pressed, they grab a somewhat incongruous object. No one seems to mind, however. Whatever the object, it is a conduit for the blessings that flow from the person of the lama himself.[20]

The location of the actual empowerment substances, the pills and so on, and of the line of monks who serve them differs from year to year. Usually they stand to the west of the lama's throne, although some years they are to its east. The supplicants jostle by, receiving each blessing in turn. Some eat the pills immediately, some save them for later, some split their options. Occasionally, someone asks the pill-server for a double dose on behalf of a person unable to attend.

In a festive mood, the villagers retire to eat, drink and be merry at the tea shop/beer-hall/restaurant/hotels in the quadrangle below the monastery.

17

Day Fifteen: Masked Dance

Day Fifteen occasions the most widely known part of Mani Rimdu, the Masked Dance. Like most other days, however, a great deal of time actually is devoted to ritual. The sequence of rituals differs from that of previous days. The pills and the flask water have fulfilled their purpose in the empowerment and no longer need ritual attention. The entire ceremony is done in one session. As in the rehearsal of Day Thirteen, all the Great Protectors and all the Followers are worshipped. The first part of the rituals is completed inside the monastic assembly hall. To accommodate the full cycle of protectors, the monks begin very early. In 1983, the first long horn sounded at 4:30 A.M. and the session ended by nine. The second part follows a break of several hours. It is performed on the courtyard porch, which, as usual on days of public ceremony, serves as a dais. At Rongphu, where the *'chams* was held on the fifteenth day of the fourth month, the entire process began much earlier and the dances were underway at dawn.[1]

The rituals may be summarized as follows:[2]

Indoor:

1. Preliminaries
2. Actual Practice (minus outer offerings).[3] In Recitation—flask practice and pill practice are not done. Ritual skips to "Offering and Praise" of Lord of the Dance and his entourage (20.2). The monks also skip three other segments: the Shower of Blessings, Self-Application, and Three-Part Torma.
3. On a typical day of Mani Rimdu, the monks worship only a fraction of the full complement of Protectors. To give each his or her daily

due, the monks add the "Invitation for the Protectors in General" (5.2). Since today the entire Propitiation (*Playful Ocean + Followers*) is performed, the General Invitation (5.2) is not necessary. The "Recitation" (ff. 5.1, 5.3–5.9), however, is done.[4]

Outdoor:

4. *Mountain Incense Offering*, including "Auspicious Omens."
5. The dances.

Today's dances are usually referred to simply as *'chams*, although to distinguish them from the dances of Day Thirteen, the term *'bag 'chams*, 'masked dance' may be used.

For the most part, each deity has its own mask, although some are recycled to serve for several deities. The protector masks first seen in Dance Seven, for example, also are used to portray an entirely different set of deities in Dance Twelve—the Liberation Ging. Masks of more important figures, such as Dorje Drolö (Dance Three) and the Great Protectors (Dance Seven) tend to be larger than those of lesser figures.

Certain dancers wear distinctive headgear in lieu of a mask. The Magicians who appear at various times during the day and the drum dancers of Dance Four don broad-brimmed papier-mâché hats. The Sky Walkers wear the crowns and wigs of the five families of Tathāgatas.

Most of the costumes fall into a few main types, distinguished according to the position the character occupies within the spiritual hierarchy.[5]

The basic costume of upper-echelon figures consists of a long, triangular-sleeved robe (*phod ka*) constructed of strips of various colors of silk brocade. To this is added a diamond-shaped bib or tippet of silk appliqué, worn over the head like a poncho.[6] A similar bib is a part of the "five families" regalia worn during the burnt offering and certain stages of the empowerment rituals. To this are added various details. Some dancers wear bone-ornaments (*ru rgyan*), others, an apron bearing the face of a fierce deity.[7]

Higher echelon figures are always shod. Their boots (*lham*) are usually the special white-sided variety reserved for dance, although sometimes the ordinary maroon woolen boots of a monk are seen.[8]

The dress of lower-echelon figures exhibits more variation. Padmasambhava's messengers, the Ging, wear a sort of multicolored motley. The Lords of the Cemetery (Dance Six) dress like skeletons. Other minor figures wear the outfits of the Black Men who accompany the local deity of dance eight, even though the performers, as in Dance Twelve, may represent entirely different supernatural entities. Lower-echelon characters dance barefoot.

Each of the various comic figures, the Long-Life Man, and the Seer and his companions, has his own characteristic dress.

In discussing the dances of Day Thirteen, we observed that more than a mere absence of masks differentiated them from the dances of Day Fifteen.

It was in fact, the absence of rituals that marked them as a rehearsal rather than the "real thing". The chart that follows lists the dances and the rituals associated with them.

The demarcation of the various dances is somewhat arbitrary and different informants count them differently. For each source that refers to the Liberation Dance as a unit, for example, there is another that lists the Lords of the Cemetery and the Black Hat Magicians separately. A list posted on the chapel wall at Thami, for instance, divides the action into sixteen or seventeen parts:

> Magicians/Ging/Dorje Drolö/Drum Dance/Long-Life Man/Lords of the Cemetery/Liberation Dance/Great Protectors/Black Men/Sharlung/Sky Walker/Seer/Remainder Sword Dance/Magic Weapon Dance/Ensemble/Auspicious Omens//[9]

Each dance and the rituals associated with it will be discussed at length in the succeeding pages. It should be noted from the outset that accounts of the rituals used in a given dance vary somewhat from informant to informant, and even among different interviews with a single informant. Further, because of the logistics involved, it is difficult to confirm or deny these accounts by observation. To complicate matters further, ritual practice varies from monastery to monastery and perhaps even at a given monastery from year to year.

DANCE AND ITS RITUALS[a]

Dance/	*Approximate Duration*	*Ritual*	*Source*
0. Music Dance [Overture]	40"	none	
—	30"	*Mountain Incense Offering*	own
1. Golden Libation [8 Black Hat Magicians]	14"	Golden Libation	*Knowledge Bearers' Root Tantra*
2. Ging [2 drums + 2 cymbals]	18"	1. *Seven-syllable Prayer* 2. "*gnas mchog 'di ru . . .*"	*Le'u bdun ma*
3. Diamond Sagging Belly [solo]	14"	1. *Seven-syllable Prayer* 2. "*gnas mchog 'di ru...*" [The Feast Offering:] 3. Blessing the Feast 4. Inviting the Guests 5. The First Course 6. Confessing to the Guests	 UB 20b6 UB 21.4 UB 21b4 UB 22.3
4. Drum Dance [6 Magicians = 4 drums + 2 cymbals]	23"	*Seven-syllable Prayer*	
5. Long-Life Man	1'45"	Pantomime/Comedy	—

continued on next page

DANCE AND ITS RITUALS[a] *(continued)*

Dance/ Approximate Duration			*Ritual*	*Source*
6. Liberation Dance	23"			
—Two Lords of the Cemetery			—	—
—Two Magicians			(1) Mindroling Gnomes	
			(2) Liberation of Last Feast	UB 22.4-b2
			(3) "*nyon mongs bdag lta'i . . .*"	
	segment #			
7. The Four Great Protectors	33"			
		1	(Blessing Propitiation Substances)	PO 40b1
		2–5	—Propitiation	
			—Confession	49.2–50.6
			—Requesting Action	51.1–b6
		6	—Feeding the Torma	53.3–54.3
		7	—	—
			—Final Rituals[b]	PO 54.4
8. Sharlung [+ Black Men]	15"		Requesting Action	*Sharlung*
9. Sky Walkers	20"		*Song of the Queen of Spring*	[c]
10. The Seer	3'19"		1. own 2. before sword trick, Showering Blessings & Iron Hook gesture 3. Horse Dance	UB 37.5
11. The Remains [2 Black Men]	06"		The Remains of the Feast	UB 35.4–b1
Exit Trulshik Rinpoche				
12. Sword Dance [Liberation Ging]	15"		1. Entreaty	UB 35b3
			(2. Torma to Defenders of Religion in General)	(PO 53.2)[d]
Interlude			(3. Concluding Rituals)	(PO 54.4)[e]
13. Sickle Dance [2 magicians + 2 Black Men] (no dancing)	08"		1. Proclaiming Contract	UB 36.3
			2. (Torma a Weapon)	UB 36b4
			3. Steadfast Women	UB 37.1
14. Ensemble [6 black hats + 2 Black Men]	15"		1. "*rigs 'dzin rtsa brgyud . . .*" *cf.*	PO 53.2
			2. Horse Dance	UB 37.4
			3. Concluding Rituals	UB 38.2
			4. Auspicious Signs	UB

[a] The identification of texts in this chart is drawn from the accounts various informants. It was checked with the Diamond Master and monks of Chiwong, 12/2/84. Material in parentheses is from one informant only, or otherwise in question. Timings are from Chiwong performances.

[b] According to TCU 1982, 1983, the protector rituals conclude in Dance Seven, and the final rituals from the *Playful Ocean* come after the protector dancers exit. Trulshik Rinpoche in a separate interview, assigns a further protector ritual to Dance Twelve, and places the final rituals after that dance. See below in chart and notes.

[c] Pha bong kha's *Bla ma'i mchod pa*, up to 1b2 ". . . ARALI HO."

[d] There is some confusion about exactly what rituals are used here. See note 209, in the discussion of Dance Twelve.

[e] Trulshik Rinpoche interview, 11/27/83. See preceding note d.

If we take a moment to analyze this chart, we see that the bulk of the rituals fall into three main groups. Although the state of our knowledge of other *'chams* is sketchy at best, it is evident that these groups are present elsewhere, albeit in different combinations. The way the three ritual complexes are interwoven in Mani Rimdu makes it difficult to separate them. In one case, for example, two halves of what in other traditions is a single sequence are isolated from each other by several extraneous dances. In one case—Dance Twelve—because of a change of liturgy, a dance that elsewhere has a strong relationship to one group of rituals is now associated with another. In some cases, an individual dance performs more than one function.

The first of the three groups of rituals is the tantric feast and the homologous ritual of suppressing the spying ghosts. This ritual type is by far the most pervasive. In one way or another it is related to no less than six separate dances—three, six, eight, eleven, twelve, and fourteen.

The first sequence of feast rituals occurs in Dance Three. The feast is blessed, the guests—the gods of the *maṇḍala*, represented here by Dorje Drolö—invited, and the feast torma offered to them.[10] The second act, Dance Six, sees the liberation of both the last of the feast and the gnomes. During Dance Eight, the feast is offered to the lama. The dance of the remains (11) deals with the remains of the feast. Although the liturgy of the feast is now complete, the action of Dance Six—liberation of the effigy—continues in the twelfth dance. The fourteenth dance contains the "Horse Dance" ritual which suppresses the forces attacked in the liberation dance.

The second major ritual complex, that of the protector deities is represented by the seventh and eighth dance. In Dance Seven the Great Protectors of the *Playful Ocean* are propitiated; in Dance Eight, the local protector. Although as we have just seen, the twelfth dance belongs in a sense to the feast complex, according to some accounts, at Mani Rimdu a torma is offered to the protectors at this time. The protector rituals are brought to an end in the interlude between Dance Twelve and Thirteen.

Some places in Tibet, the third ritual complex, throwing the torma, was a separate festival. In Mani Rimdu it figures in Dance Thirteen and Fourteen. In Dance Thirteen, Padmasambhava's contract with the "great and haughty gods of Tibet" is proclaimed and the torma changed into a magic weapon that will return "*saṁsāra* to the realm of *nirvāṇa!*" As in the daily rituals, the "Horse Dance" usually follows the contract. Here, it not only carries on the theme of suppression, but the theme of the world reverting to paradise. Thus, Dance Fourteen continues the sequence of the feast and furthers the theme introduced by throwing the torma. The twelfth dance contains the entreaty to the gods of the *maṇḍala* that precedes the magic weapon sequence in the *Manual* and can be considered an introduction to it.

As we have already observed, the dances mirror the structure of the site ritual performed on the first day of Mani Rimdu. They begin with a Golden

Libation (Dance One), have the suppression of the *lingka* at their center (Six, Twelve), and end with the Horse Dance (Fourteen).

OVERTURE—THE MUSIC DANCE

A dance more in name than in deed, the Music Dance (*rol 'chams*) serves as an overture to the other dances. According to Trulshik Rinpoche, the Music Dance originated at Mindroling.[11] But for a few ceremonial touches, the monks who perform it wear monastic dress.

A full orchestra complete with long horns assembles in the courtyard. The overture begins. After a few minutes, the sound of the orchestra is amplified by music from within the chapel. A multitude unseen of cymbals sound, crashing like waves. Drum beats and syncopated metallic clangs punctuate the orchestration. The rhythm is unusual and compelling; the effect startling and electric.

The curtains behind the dais part and a monk steps onto the porch. He wears the sickle-shaped yellow hat of a pandit, and plays a pair of cymbals joined with a long white ceremonial scarf (*kha btags*) draped around his back. He descends to the stair landing that is midway between the dais and the courtyard floor. Here, he halts, and without missing a beat, continues to play in unison with the cymbals inside.

Two minutes later, others begin to emerge. Like the first, each wears a ceremonial hat and has a sash across his shoulders. The sash may be a *kha btags*, a red sash, or, in the case of senior monks, yellow robes that mark strict adherence to the *vinaya*, the Buddha's rules for the monastic order.[12] The monks form a line that stretches from the backstage area through the curtain to the dais. The first monk descends to the courtyard floor and stands northeast of the central altar. The second monk replaces him on the stair landing. The first monk turns to face him. As they play, they watch each other's hands closely. Their duet is still in unison with their companions.

Every two minutes the process repeats. As each monk quits the landing, he is replaced by another from the line on the dais. The monks displaced from the position northeast of the altar form an diagonal arc southeast of it. As each new monk joins, his companions move to their left, enlarging the arc and forcing it clockwise.

When the eighth and final cymbalist descends to the courtyard, the oboe players exit.[13] The cymbalists, now in two rows (one east and one west of the

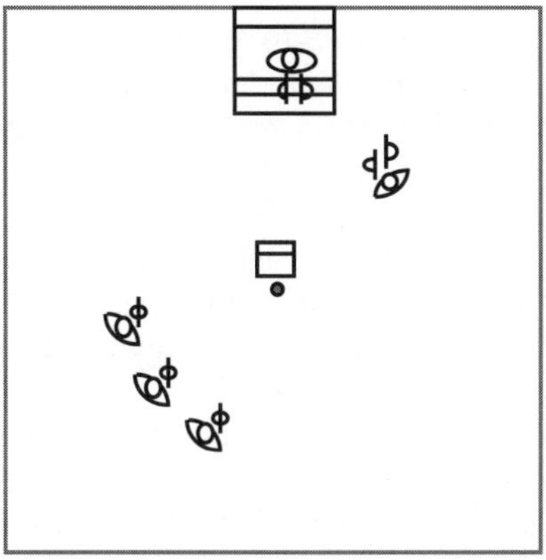

The Overture, with First Five of Eight Cymbal Players Present
(*not to scale*)

altar), face each other to play a octet. After a few minutes, the cymbalists begin to dance, playing continuously as they execute their steps. The dancing stops, but the two rows continue playing to each other for several minutes. Finally, they reform their arc and, playing softly, exit the courtyard.

Immediately following their exit, as during the rehearsal two days earlier, the monks seated on the dais begin the *Mountain Incense Offering*. According to Trulshik Rinpoche, a "noble yak" and "noble steed" are offered to propitiate the defenders of religion in connection with the *Mountain Incense Offering*. At Rongphu, this occurred at about six in the morning. This offering is also apparently made at Chiwong, at least in some years.[14]

The *Mountain Incense Offering* is rooted in archaic Tibetan religious practice. The offering of a richly decorated horse and yak may be a bloodless survival of pre-Buddhist animal sacrifices.[15]

DANCE ONE—THE GOLDEN LIBATION

The first actual dance is sometimes called the "black hat" dance (*zhva nag*) or the *sngags pa*, the dance of the "tantric magicians."[16] In Tibet, Magician, or literally "Tantric," has become a hereditary profession. Here, the name refers to the costume and presumably the character—of the dancer with the traditional black hat, coat with wide triangular sleeves (*phod ka*), and so on.[17]

According to Trulshik Rinpoche, the dance is properly called the "Golden Libation," after the ritual that it enacts.[18] Many different golden libations are known to Tibetan Buddhist practice. In Mani Rimdu, it is an offering to the gods of Lord of the Dance's *maṇḍala*.[19] The text used is the same one employed during the site rituals to bless the "the site where the gnomes will be suppressed."[20]

Thigh-bone trumpets sound inside the chapel and are answered by the musicians on the dais outside. Eight black-hat dancers emerge, each with a *vajra* in his right hand.[21] In their left hands, the dancers hold a silver chalice—at Chiwong actually a large butter lamp—for offering the libation.[22]

The magicians dance and then stop and stand in a circle. An attendant passes among them and places a torma ball and some liquor in their chalices. As the offerings are distributed, the monks on the dais recite the liturgy to a soft accompaniment on the cymbal.[23] The long horns and drums join in and the music and dance resume. With a sidelong sweep of the arm, the dancers toss the offerings in the air. The sequence is done three times in all.

The dance itself has a complex choreography.[24] In one characteristic movement, the performers have their arms outstretched at the sides. This is likely the gesture the *'chams yig* calls "stretched out like the wings of a vulture" (*lag pa rgod gshog ltar brgyangs pa*).[25] After the offering sequences are complete, the long horns join in once more. The dancers form two rows and exit by pairs.[26] The dance lasts approximately fourteen minutes.

Black hat dances are a feature of many *'chams* traditions. Some of the examples recorded in the literature also involve a golden libation. One is the dance witnessed by G. A. Combe in a Nyingma monastery in eastern Tibet in the 1920s. Performed on the tenth day of the seventh month in honor of Padmasambhava, the dance Combe described is virtually identical to the one practiced in Solu-Khumbu today.[27] The Fifth Dalai Lama's *'chams yig* also calls for mantra bearers (*sngags 'chang*) to perform a golden libation.[28]

The black hat dance, of course, is famous for another reason. In the year 846, while performing it, the *sngags pa* Lhalung Pelki Dorje assassinated King Langdarma. This story is so well known, that even today performances of the black hat dance recall Pelki Dorje to the Tibetan mind. Strictly speaking, however, the dance does not commemorate that occasion, as some authors have claimed.[29] As Stein rightly points out, if the Black Hat Dance with its attendant (and structurally similar) ceremony of killing the *lingka* (see Dance Six) was the occasion of assassination of Langdarma, we must presume that it antedates the assassination.[30]

The magician's dance is considered a very serious business. According to one expert, the lead Black Hat Dancer should do a week retreat before performing it.[31]

DANCE TWO—THE GING

The literary and oral traditions both record an abundant variety of spirits styled Ging.[32] Although the term *ging* or *'gying* or *gying* originally may have referred to a class of Bon deities, it can also be used as an epithet of *dharmapālas*, heroes (*dpa' bo*), messengers (*pho nya*), and even the Lords of the Cemetery.[33]

In Mani Rimdu, two types of Ging are mentioned. One, Liberation Ging (*sgrol ging*), are gods of high rank. We will meet them later in the Sword Dance. The Ging of Dance Two are somewhat less lofty beings—heralds that come from Padmasambhava's paradise, the Copper-Colored Glorious Mountain (Zangs mdog dpal ri), to announce his arrival.[34] The prayer chosen to introduce their dance (and the dance of Dorje Drolö that follows) is an obvious one. It is the *Seven-syllable Prayer*, the standard invocation of Padmasambhava, and perhaps the best-known piece of Nyingma liturgy.[35]

> On the northwest border of Orgyan-land
> On a lotus stamen's stem,
> Astounding supreme achievement was won.
> You who as the Lotus-Born are renowned,
> You who a vast entourage of Sky Walkers surround,
> Come, we pray, inspire us
> Who follow in your footsteps.
> Oṁ āḥ hūṁ vajraguru padmasiddhi hūṁ

To this is appended another stanza, a type of *byin 'bebs* (shower of blessings) often known simply by its first line, "*gnas mchog 'di ru . . .*":

> Bless this place so excellent;
> Grant us excellent achievers the four empowerments!
> Remove all obstructions and misleading interruptions!
> Bestow enlightenment and magic power![36]

Two of the Ging are male and play cymbals; two female, and play drums.[37] One cymbal player's mask is white and the other's green. The drummers' are red and yellow.[38] Each mask has a diadem of a single skull, a pair of triangular pennants at the temples and a pair of rainbow colored fans at the ears.[39] The expression on their faces is said to be slightly wrathful.

By nature, the Ging are frolicsome and funny. They hop, wiggle, and leap; they make the audience smile and laugh. In one of their characteristic movements they dance toward each other in pairs, turning back-to-back when they meet, rotate in that position 180°, and part, now heading in the direction opposite from the way they came (see position 3, in sketch 34).

The Ging bound in so cheerfully, playing their small drums and cymbals, grinning and wagging their brightly colored heads, that one can easily imagine another traditional function of Padmasambhava's messengers—a yogi's alarm clock. Contemporary scholar Khetsun Sangpo Rinpoche might be describing the drum beating Ging when he advises:

> As soon as you awaken in the morning, imagine that Padma Sambhava with his retinue of Bodhisattvas appear vividly before you, ringing bells and beating small drums. Their music dispels all drowsiness, rousing you into complete wakefulness.[40]

Like other sets of four, the Ging are sometimes credited with performing the four actions. This correlation may be somewhat arbitrary, however. Although four Ging appear in Solu-Khumbu; at Rongphu, there were eight.[41] At the monastery visited by Combe in the 1920s, either four or eight drum-playing Ging appeared. As in Mani Rimdu, they corresponded to the directions and were identified as denizens of Padmasambhava paradise. Eight Ging participated in the Lhasa New Year's festival. Two types of Ging: the '*ging* of the sky' (*nam ging*) and the '*ging* of the earth' (*sa ging*) are reported in dances at Hemis. In other parts of Tibet, dances with sixteen Ging were also known.[42]

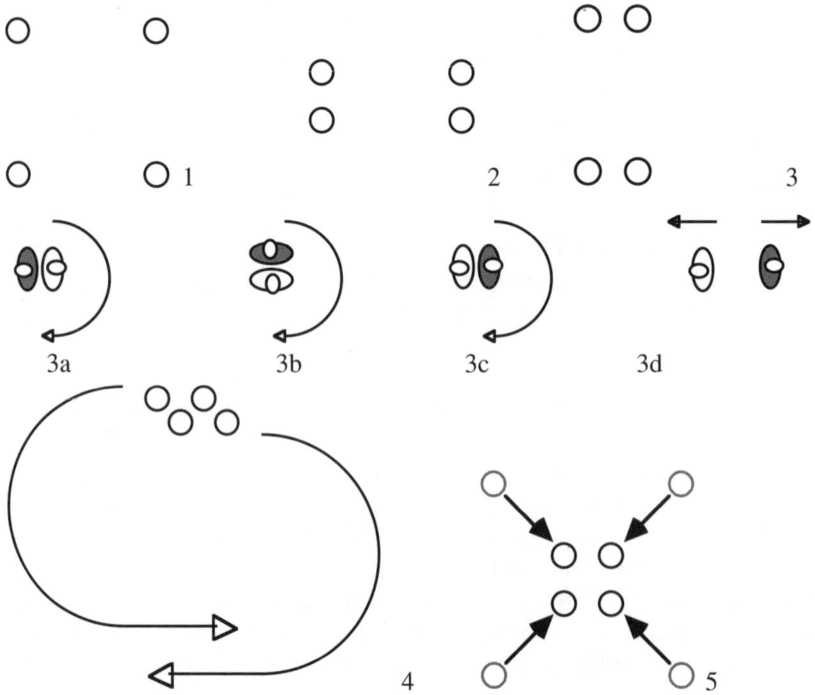

Some Characteristic Movements of the Ging

DANCE THREE—DORJE DROLÖ

As it was for his heralds the Ging, the *Seven-Syllable Prayer* is used to summon Dorje Drolö (rDo rje gro lod). Dorje Drolö, whose picturesque name means Diamond Sagging Belly, is a fierce manifestation of Padmasambhava. Various forms of Padmasambhava are a common feature of Tibetan sacred dance; often all eight of his major emanations are portrayed.[43] Dorje Drolö is the form the saint took to vanquish the demons of Tibet.[44]

The mask of Dorje Drolö conforms to the general iconography of that figure. It is large and dark brown. Its eyes bulge and its fangs protrude. Its hair is made of yak-tail. Its eyebrows and beard are raised golden swirls. It has a crown of five skulls and large earrings decorated with a wheel.[45] In addition to his mask, Dorje Drolö wears a *phod ka* and a bib appliquéd with a large crossed *vajra.*

The "reason for the necessity" of the dance is the offering of the first and second feasts to Padmasambhava.[46] The offering of feasts in the dance of Dorje Drolö is said to be a Rongphu tradition, not found in other monasteries in Tibet.[47]

The musicians on the dais begin the act with a flourish on the thigh-bone trumpet. The cymbals and long horns join in, and within the chapel, a pair of oboes. The lama begins to ring his bell. The eccentric, compelling rhythm of the metal clanger rings out from behind the curtain.

Three ceremonial figures enter the courtyard to honor Dorje Drolö in the same way that later they will honor the lama's entrance. The oboists are first to enter, followed by a monk holding a smoldering sheaf of incense or the wand that represents one. He enters respectfully, walking backwards and preceding the one he honors. The three figures descend to the courtyard floor and take their positions, the oboists to the west of the staircase, the incense bearer to the west. Each wears a yellow ceremonial hat.

Dorje Drolö enters on their heels. In his right hand he bears a tasseled *vajra*, his left brandishes his magic dagger. An assistant brings out a chair, carpet, and table and places them one yard to the southwest of the "center-stage" altar.[48] A large feast torma is also brought out and placed on the altar's lower shelf. Dorje Drolö makes a clockwise circuit of the courtyard. He stops in each of the cardinal points to dance, turning and stabbing in all directions before continuing on his way. Two-thirds through his act, he reaches the chair and sits down. The monks on the dais begin their liturgy. Above the noise of the crowd, one can catch the seed syllables that bless the feast.

> Hūṁ! I project from my mind *raṁ yaṁ khaṁ.*
> They burn, cast out and wash away all wrong and fault.
> In the natural bliss guardian *kāpala*,
> These holy substances—the five meats, the five ambrosias
> Melt into desirable uncorrupted ambrosia,
> Swirl in the essence of all true achievement. [UB 21.2]

An assistant goes to the courtyard altar and cuts the feast torma. He brings the first serving—top of the torma—to Dorje Drolö on a platter. In the daily ritual, this part is reserved for the lama. The assistant then brings a spoon of sacramental liquor from a skull-bowl or glass on the altar. Dorje Drolö takes the liquor in his hand and drinks beneath his mask.

The liturgy that accompanies the offering of the top of the torma is "Inviting the Guests."

Hūṁ! Victorious Accomplished Protector, treasure of compassion!
Chief, together with your entourage,
Come here from the pure nature fortress!
Partake of the proffered feast!

Your headdress, your top-knot flutter, flap!
Ribbons! Ribands! Pu ru ru!
Jewels! Bone ornaments! Tra la la!
Sweet sounding music! Di ri ri!

Singing! Dancing! Zigging! Zagging!
Hundred thousand circle host! Sha ra ra!
Come here! Partake of the proffered feast!
Bless this dwelling place!

Put some juice in these feast tormas!
Bestow upon us yogis, us supreme achievers assembled here,
The highest and ordinary true achievements!
Guru dheva dhākini samaya jaḥ jaḥ e āralli hrī hrīḥ [UB 21.5]

The assistant brings a second portion of the feast torma. Dorje Drolö motions at it with his magic dagger, gesturing as if to stab it.

At first, this seems illogical. Stabbing the torma belongs to the last part of the feast, the liberation ritual, related to the dance of the same name which will be performed later in the day. Trulshik Rinpoche, however, dispels the seeming contradiction. Dorje Drolö's gesture does not indicate stabbing, he says, but eating. A more conventional demonstration of that act, like putting food in one's mouth, he adds, would be difficult while wearing Dorje Drolö's enormous mask. The use of the magic dagger takes on additional significance when we consider that the dagger is a symbol of the divine metabolism that purifies what passes through it, digesting obstreperous spirits and converting them into gods of the pure lands. The act of eating here and the acts of Dance Six and Eight have a certain similarity. When a yogi eats a feast, he feeds the gods that dwell in his body. When he stabs it, it is eaten by his dagger. When he burns the equivalent *lingka*, he feeds the gods of paradise.[49]

Dorje Drolö's act of eating echoes the liturgy recited on the dais.

Hoḥ! The five great meats of the Buddha vow—
The essence of the five blameless ambrosias—
Things to really eat and chew—
That have color, aroma and flavor—
This feast offering which commingles everything—
This unexcelled yogic offering—
Enjoy it in joy, O maṇḍala god host!
Pray take it in the realm of bliss! [21b5]

Gaṇacakrapūja khāhi.[50]

The feast eaten, Dorje Drolö rises. An assistant removes the table, chair, and carpet. Dorje Drolö dances northward to the stair, stabbing in the air as he advances. The oboists rejoin the ensemble. When the dancer reaches the landing, he circles once to face the crowd and exits. His performance takes some fifteen minutes.

Of the many beings portrayed in the dances, Dorje Drolö is the highest. He is not a protector, but rather the archetype of the subduer of protectors—Padmasambhava. Padmasambhava is a character well known to the audience. He is the hero of myth, the role model of yogis, and perhaps the most worshipped figure of the Nyingma Order. Although in one sense a figure of history and myth, for the Nyingma the Precious Guru is much more. As a personal deity, he is intimately involved in the reconfiguration of meditators' personal identity.

The role of Dorje Drolö is one of Mani Rimdu's "meatier" parts. A solo, the dance requires much of its performer. The character has a distinct and dynamic persona—the fierce demon-slaying form of the divine hero/saint. It is a role full of subtext—the character's very presence implies scenarios well known to the audience even if they are unseen on stage. Dorje Drolö is generally reserved for the most talented dancers. As performing art, it is the best Mani Rimdu has to offer.

DANCE FOUR—THE DRUM DANCE

Thigh-bone trumpets sound inside the monastery and are echoed from the dais. The long horn begins a solo. It is soon joined by instruments inside the chapel—cymbals and, more faintly, drums. The dancers enter dressed in black-hat costumes. Two play cymbals; two, medium-sized drums; two, small drums.[51] They stand for a moment in a circle inside the door, playing their instruments.[52] Then, they descend by pairs to the courtyard, a small drum and cymbal roll providing a fanfare for each pair. As the first two reach the courtyard, the long horn stops playing. The dancers continue their steps. Moving by pairs, they stand and face the center, circle the courtyard clockwise, turn to and fro; and then stand in place playing softly.

According to Trulshik Rinpoche, the drum dance is "just a dance."[53] This it not to say that it is devoid of liturgy. At certain points, as the dancers stand in place, the monks on the dais can be seen praying.[54] According to participants, the liturgy is once again the *Seven-Syllable Prayer* dedicated to Padmasambhava. About twenty minutes from the first pair's entrance, the musicians on the dais join in once more. The dancers line up and exit as they entered, by pairs.

Although it is the drums (*rnga*) that undoubtedly give the drum dance its name (*rnga 'chams*) [pronounced "nga cham"], it should be noted that many Sherpa monks pronounce the name "ngak cham" and spell it *sngags 'chams* or even *ngag chams*.[55] Thus, an alternate, if less correct, title for this segment would be the "mantra dance."

At Tengpoche, rather than the black hats of tantric magicians, the dancers wear golden-colored hats (*gser thebs*) of a similar shape. Such hats are worn by protectors such as Pehar and Good Diamond (rDo rje legs pa). Their use in Mani Rimdu was an innovation of Tengpoche Rinpoche, adapted from a dance at Samye which honors Guru Rinpoche's subduing of the autochthonous gods of Tibet's first monastery.[56]

Drum dances are known in other traditions of *'chams*. In Bhutan, the drum dance is said to be connected with the worship of Padmasambhava.[57] In the dance of Vajrakīla, black-hatted drum dancers are accompanied by a dancer wearing the mask of that deity.[58]

Magician Playing Cymbals, Drum Dance, Chiwong

DANCE FIVE—THE LONG-LIFE MAN

In Solu-Khumbu layman and monk alike identify the principal figure of Mani Rimdu's fifth dance as Long-Life Man. Some Western authors, however, identify this figure as Hva Shang. Hva Shang or Ho Shang Mahāyāna was the well-known Ch'an Buddhist monk who debated the Indian Pandit Kamalaśīla at Samye c.779. Tibetans assert his defeat marked the end of Chinese influence on their religion.[59] Given the unanimity of local opinion, the idea that Hva Shang appears in Mani Rimdu is without doubt mistaken. Secondary sources do place him in a wide range of other monastic dances, however, and this is most likely the source of the error. To exacerbate the confusion, the appearance—and antics—of various Hva Shang closely resemble those of Mani Rimdu's Long-Life Man. Typically, he is

> a dancer wearing a huge, bald-headed mask showing a fat, smiling face with Chinese features. The attire of this figure consists of a crown of colorful brocade, a jacket in Chinese fashion, high boots, and a long rosary worn around the neck.[60]

In Mani Rimdu, the face of the mask is broad and pale but not conspicuously "Chinese." Its countenance is youthful, almost infantile; its expression is radiant. Unlike Hva Shang, Long-Life Man does not sport a crown. The jacket covers an absurd plenitude of brocade robes, one layer hiding the other. The jacket and outer robe are yellow, a color traditionally reserved for those with religious vows. His rosary is accompanied by a stout brass-bound staff.

As at Mani Rimdu, Hva Shang often is joined by a pair of assistants or servants who make him the butt of their jokes. In an account given by Lessing, they "drag him on the scene in an undignified manner," much as they do at Mani Rimdu.[61] In Solu-Khumbu, these assistants wear ordinary clothes, or if they have been serving as such, the fringed hats of monastery proctors.

The Long-Life Man act at Chiwong can be broken down into several distinct scenes.[62] The first is his entrance. Long-Life Man appears to no fanfare. He simply walks out on the dais and to the stairs. Once there, however, he must descend to the courtyard floor, a challenge for such an old, old man. To achieve this, he enlists his assistants. As elsewhere, they are usually young men or boys.[63] One or both of them are the proctors who keep the crowds from infringing on the playing area, and so have already been seen by the audience.[64]

Long-Life Man is too fat, too feeble, and, most of all, too arrogant to walk down a flight of stairs unassisted. His descent, like every part of the act of the Long-Life Man is a comedy of errors. Several methods are tried. Most of these attempts end with the Long-Life Man on the ground. Using their hats, whips, or similar items, his assistants help to brush the dust from his voluminous robes, battering him about the groin as they do so. In this sequence, Long-Life Man's wealth and pride become a decided disadvantage to him. He possesses no less than eight layers of silk robes. As each is revealed, the absurd iteration elicits laughter from the crowd. The laughter quickens as Long-Life Man demands that his servants clean each garment in turn, giving them eight full chances to abuse his person.

Finally, Long-Life Man decides to yoke his servants with his rosary and ride them down the steps like horses. Nearly every year, this ends with the three of them in a mangled heap. Once in a great while, they succeed in this absurd task. To the amazement and delight of the crowd—and doubtless the actors themselves—Long-Life Man descends the stairs on his curious steed to ride in triumph at least part way around the courtyard floor.

The second scene is the mock presentation of a ceremonial scarf (*kha btags*). The presentation of *kha btags* marks formal greeting and leave-taking among Tibetans and Sherpas. For Tibetans it was once an indispensable part of meeting any individual of markedly higher status, although at present, in Solu-Khumbu at least, it is mostly used for greeting lamas. As we shall see in a moment, a major function of the Long-Life Man is to present a *kha btags* in earnest. It is fitting then, that the first scene after his elaborate entrance should be a parody of his serious function.

The Long-Life Man wanders the courtyard looking for a suitable candidate to honor. He bends his neck to "squint" up at the balcony. Finding no one worthy, he swivels his wrist in the Nepali gesture of "nothing doing."[65] Occasionally, he threatens to present the scarf to a member of the audience who invariably cringes and wriggles under his attentions.[66] Finally, having found no one on whom to bestow it, he puts his *kha btags* away.

The mock *kha btags* presentation parodies both an important cultural ritual and the social hierarchy it reaffirms, but does not undercut them. In the end, it is not that the process of bestowing honor is found lacking, just that for the moment no fit—or willing—recipient has been found. In a humorous way, the scene reaffirms a perception shared by actor and audience, that the one worthy of honor is not among them: it is the lama alone.

In the third scene, the servants help Long-Life Man lay a carpet on the floor. A Tibetan carpet measures one yard by two. Even with a yak-hair blanket beneath it as a pad, it is normally no problem to lay. In the hands of our "three stooges," it becomes a major undertaking. However the carpet is arranged, it is not right. It is lumpy. It is wrinkled. It is arranged in an outrageous manner, humped up the way a monk arranges his heavy winter cassock so that it will sit empty in his seat. Some parts of the act are improvisation. One year, one servant used the carpet as a lap rug while the other wore the blanket as a shawl.[67]

Finally, the carpet is arranged properly. Upon further consideration, however, Long-Life Man determines that it is not quite in the right spot, and his servants must move it again. They cringe as Long-Life Man cuffs them roundly for their incompetence. If abused, they give as good as they get. One servant dusts the carpet with his hat, dealing Long-Life Man a stout blow to the face in the process. When the carpet is finally placed, the servants invariably lie on it themselves.

The fourth scene is the prostration lesson. By now, the carpet is finally in its proper place, oriented north-south on the west side of the courtyard. Now we discover its purpose. The carpet now lies in front of the lama's throne. It is there so that the threesome can prostrate to him.

The long prostration is a ritualized demonstration of respect and obeisance for Sherpas and Tibetans. It is the common formal salutation made to high lamas, monastery altars, and sacred shrines. The prostration begins with the palms pressed together at the heart. The hands are then placed first on top of the head, then at the throat, and finally at the chest. The devotee then goes down on his knees, places his palms on the ground and stretches out flat. After a final salute of his pressed palms, he returns to an upright position.

Although the smallest Sherpa or Tibetan child knows how to do this, in their outlandish ignorance (or monumental perversity) the assistants do not. They put their hands in the wrong place and at the wrong angle. They stand facing in the wrong direction. They fall down. They get distracted and wander away.

Through all this, the Long-Life Man is the tireless, if irascible teacher. Again and again, he bends their bodies to the proper position. He does not

Long Life Man's Prostration Lesson, Chiwong 1979

allow them to make a salutation from the groin instead of from the heart. When they wander, he drags them back. When they fail to rise, he lifts them to their feet. When they are out of synch, he shoves them into unison. Under his implacable tutelage, they finally succeed in achieving at least a semblance of a prostration.[68]

Like the mock-offering of the *kha btags*, the theme of the prostration lesson is honoring the lama. The Long-Life Man may be vain and proud, his assistants may be ignorant and foolish, but in the end the *act* of honoring the lama is itself honored. Like the *kha btags* sequence, it does not question social hierarchy but ultimately affirms it.

The fifth is the water-torma offering. Like the preceding scene, it is a lesson in a widespread Himalayan Buddhist practice: an offering to the *yi dvags*, hungry ghosts that wander among us unseen. Before this is done, however, the seat must be moved from the northwest quadrant to the northeast. Then, a small Tibetan folding table is brought out, and the torma offering kit. This consists of a pot with a spout, a pan, a small plate, and a folding tripod to hold the plate above the pan. Also included are a miniature cymbal to call the ghosts, and a crystal rosary. When in storage, everything but the pan, which is too broad, is kept wedged inside the offering pot.

To begin the offering, this paraphernalia must be carefully unpacked. The tripod must be assembled—a Chinese puzzle-like affair that is a challenge even to the deft of touch. The pot must be filled with water, and the water offered to the spirits (rather than poured on the crowd).[69]

All this is achieved with complications best left to the imagination. One routine observed at Thami deserves special mention. When the Long-Life Man rings to call the spirits, he looks up at the sky with expectation, as if waiting to see them descend in the flesh. He repeats the action, again to no avail. Then he rings his cymbal in every direction. No possible hiding place is spared, including his own posterior and his assistants ears. At this point, he rises to threaten the audience with a dousing from the water pot.

The earlier scenes are affirmations of the real and unwavering personal bond between laymen and the lama, traditionally the basis of Buddhist society. The torma offering is a more equivocal statement. The lama may possess intangible spiritual qualities but he is a person one can see and touch. The various disembodied entities with which the Himalayas are crowded are another matter. Tibetans and Sherpas universally acknowledge they exist, but spiritual etiquette (at least among lamas) dictates that no one admit to seeing them personally, except in the most exceptional circumstances. To do so may be considered tantamount to bragging of spiritual prowess, one of the graver forms of spiritual pride. On the other hand, it is also acknowledged that if contact with supernatural entities is sought for the wrong reason, in the wrong way, or by the wrong person, they can fail to appear or worse. From a Tibetan viewpoint the Long-Life Man's failure to perceive the hungry ghosts likely would be due to his own lack of yogic prowess rather than to the nonexistence of the supernatural. Nonetheless, the torma offering is hardly the unflinching affirmation of supernaturalism that the *kha btags* presentations or the prostration lesson are of the socioreligious contract.

The sixth act is the genuine *kha btags* presentation. As we saw on Day Fourteen, a primary function of the Long-Life Man is as a symbol of long life itself and the wish that those he salutes live long. Indeed, speaking of the purpose of the various dances, Trulshik Rinpoche specifies that the Long-Life Man sequence is "like a welcoming ceremony."[70]

At Chiwong, Trulshik Rinpoche traditionally makes his entrance during the final scene of the Long-Life Man act. When he enters, Long-Life Man interrupts his performance, often midroutine, and reverts to his iconic function. Draping a *kha btags* across his arms in the prescribed manner, he approaches the dais and makes obeisance. He spreads his *kha btags* across Trulshik Rinpoche's table. The lama hands it to an assistant who puts it around the Long-Life Man's neck.[71]

Sometimes, particularly if his act has gone longer than usual, the Long-Life Man will abruptly break off his performance at this point, and the dances resume with the sixth segment.[72] In any event, the final act Long-Life Man performs before his exit is the presentation of a *kha btags* to the lama.

Accounts confirm that similar figures perform this function elsewhere. In a Buriat monastery visited by Labbé, a "Hva Shang" presents ceremonial scarves.[73] "According to the schedule of the dance" witnessed by G. A. Combe, the old man and his two companions "should be the first to greet the *Gu ru mtshan brgyad*"—the eight manifestations of Padmasambhava.[74] The Khachine Khan of Buriat *'chams* presents scarves to the major deities as they enter the courtyard.[75]

Long Life Man in general and the *kha btags* presentation in particular also present an occasion to affirm the social contract between the monastery and its founding family. During Long-Life Man's performance, the family, seated in their private section of the balcony, is served lavish dishes of food. In 1994, when it came to the *kha btags* presentation, Long-Life Man first used his scarf to salute the head of Chiwong's male line, then the monks on the dais, and only then, Trulshik Rinpoche's still empty throne. At that point, the monastery presented elaborate displays of food to its patron. Immediately after Trulshik Rinpoche's entrance, the ranking female of the line completed the symmetry, presenting food to the lama—in 1994, a rare and costly foreign delicacy: a large heart-shaped box of valentine candy upended to resemble a torma. She was followed by the leading woman of the Tamang tribe, the second most important Buddhist ethnic group of Solu and devoted patrons of Mani Rimdu and Trulshik Rinpoche.

The ironic antiphony between the activity on the balcony where real big shots are treated to a stream of obsequious service and the shenanigans of the masked and obviously over-fed "big shot" below (and his obsequious servants) is perhaps intentional. But if there is social criticism here, it is tempered by the fact that the display on the balcony is real; that on the stage is clowning. As always in Mani Rimdu, the social order is reaffirmed.

Bearded elders similar to the Long-Life Man can be found in Chinese dance. It is quite possible that the name the Mani Rimdu tradition gives this figure, "Long-Life Man," corresponds to his original function. The name "Hva Shang," in so far as it occurs in other *'chams* traditions, may refer to a Chinese origin of the figure, be it real or imagined.

Although according to some accounts, the historical figure Hva Shang Mahāyāna appears in certain *'chams*, such a precise identification is even more doubtful than the general one.[76] We should note, first, that the word *hva shang,* or *ho shang* in Chinese is a generic term for Buddhist monk, and second, that Hva Shang Mahāyāna is the only "Hva Shang" most Tibetans know. Thus, a misidentification at this point could as easily be indigenous as be the product of a Western observer's speculation.

Inasmuch as Long-Life Man appears in art in Tibet and across Asia with an identical appearance and function to the figure in Mani Rimdu, if we wish to advance a candidate for the *ur-form* of the figure we find in dance, Long-Life Man would be a good choice. As for the character in Mani Rimdu there is no doubt. He is never called "Hva Shang" in Solu-Khumbu. In light of this, one wonders how many other "Hva Shang" in the spotty literature on Tibetan dance were similarly extrapolated from secondary sources and how many were based on ethnographic research.

The enormous popularity of the Long-Life Man ensures maximum attendance for the crucial act that follows it—the Liberation Dance.

DANCE SIX—THE LIBERATION DANCE

The Liberation Dance contains what by all accounts is the central act of Tibetan sacred dance—the liberation of the effigy known as the *lingka*. It is an act that occurs in most, if not all major *'chams* performances.[77] The themes of demon-slaying and ritual sacrifice—for "liberation" is a peculiar Buddhist form of those universal religious acts—is also central to *'chams* cousin, Newar *carya* dance.[78]

The action begins with a one-minute *pas de deux* by the Lords of the Cemetery. In an alternate schema used in Solu-Khumbu, the Liberation Dance is sometimes described as two separate dances: the *pas de deux* of the Lords of the Cemetery (*dur bdag gnyis*) and the Magicians' *pas de deux* (*sngags pa gnyis*).[79]

The Lords of the Cemetery, or better, the Lord and Lady of the Cemetery—for one is male and one is female—are stock figures of Tibetan art and of Tibetan dance. In paintings and sculpture they are shown as two skeletons dancing with arms and/or legs intertwined. Although there are several sorts of skeleton deities in the Tibetan pantheon, the Lord and Lady of the Cemetery can be distinguished by their crowns of five small skulls and by the fan-shaped ornaments behind their ears.[80]

Whatever their grisly associations in our minds, in Tibetan art and in dance the Lords of the Cemetery are joyous, even comic figures. Contemporary lama and Tibetologist Namkhai Norbu explains the phenomenon in this way:

> The dancing, grinning skeletons . . . express a dynamic vision of death and transformation, unchanging inner essence transcending the constant mutations of externals. Meditation on the impermanence of all phenomena should lead to a joyful freedom from attachment, and not a morbid pessimism.[81]

In the Nyingma and Sakya sects, Lords of the Cemetery are said to be "among the more important Worldly Guardians, *'jigs rten pa'i srung ma.*"[82] According to Trulshik Rinpoche, they are the emissaries (*pho nya*) of the Magicians, much as the Ging are the emissaries of Padmasambhava. Other sources identify them as emissaries of Yama, the Lord of Death.[83] As we will see later, in addition to its iconographic logic, this fits with their role in dances at other monasteries.

The Lords of the Cemetery enter and begin their bony jangling dance. Their movements are so close to the way they are represented in art that they seem to be a painting come to life. The dancers carry sticks with a small flat spade or spoon-shaped end to represent the mummy-club that is their weapon.[84] Like the other servants and emissaries—the Ging and the Black Men—the Lords of the Cemetery dance barefoot.

Following their frolicsome duet, the skeletons (*ru rang*) stand for a moment facing each other. It is then that the two black-hatted Magicians enter.[85]

The Magicians wear special black and brocade costumes. Each carries a magic dagger in his left hand and a *vajra* in his right. They join the Lords of the Cemetery in a stately dance, with the Magicians in the center of the line and the skeletons to their left and right. They begin to circle the courtyard. The motions of the four are similar at first. Later, each pair adopts its own set of movements.

The dancers move to the south end of the courtyard. As the monks on the dais begin to recite, the dancers stand—still facing each other—their hands twisted into the *mudrā* known as the hook gesture (*lcags kyu rgya*). Like the *mudrā*, the liturgy is taken from the Spying Ghosts ritual. The first section of the text is recited once:

E yaṁ raṁ jvala raṁ
Within the pit, broad and profoundly deep,
From [the letter] *tri*, comes the tribe of spying demons,
The ghosts who interrupt achievement and lead it astray.
The bodies they all assume are exhausted.[86]

An assistant uncovers the burial-pit near the stairs in the courtyard floor. The dancers continue to stand as the officiants recite the second passage.

Namo! Homage to the Three Jewels!
Homage to the Three Jewels!
Homage to talk of truly pure reality!
Homage to undeceiving talk of the subject of cause and effect!
And especially, blessed by the true word of the divine host of the
Union of the Blissful/Lord of the Dance/Great Compassion *maṇḍala*, and by the great truth—
May all the ghosts who interrupt realization and lead it astray—the family of spying demons—come to be in this image, in this symbolic substance!

Tri yaṁ jaḥ tri vajra āṁkuśaja jaḥ hūṁ baṁ hoḥ

There is music; with a flick of his wrist, the lama flings out his black scarf; the skeletons break into motion and dance helter-skelter away. The magicians hold fast, never breaking the *mudrā* that summons the spirits to the spot.

The skeletons return and the dancers resume their tableau. Again, there is the liturgy, the music, the scarf, and the skeletons skittering away.[87] The act is repeated three times.[88] The third time, all four dancers dance together.

The black hats dance and exit. Now alone, the skeletons dance mid-courtyard to the altar, and as the music continues, unwrap the *lingka* that has been kept for them underneath the altar. A floppy, featureless doll of graying white cloth, the effigy is bound in the middle of a long and stout rope.[89] The skeletons take either end and circle the courtyard, abusing the doll with their clubs in rhythm with their dance. They fling the cloth figure down in front of the steps, near to the triangular pit in which the paper effigy was buried on the first day. They dance a moment longer and exit. According to one expert, the hallmark of Lord of the Cemetery dancers in Tibet was their exit, in which they would vault from the courtyard floor to the monastery porch in a single bound.[90] The performance in Solu-Khumbu, though bouncy, is not nearly this athletic; and the skeletons leave the courtyard in a more conventional fashion.

The music continues, but the focus of attention now shifts to the dais. The lama rolls his magic dagger between his palms and stabs the "last feast." The ritual of liberation is carried out according to the directions in the Union of the Blissful *Manual*. In the case of the Vajrakīla dances done elsewhere in Tibet, the corresponding part of that ritual would be used.[91]

Hūṁ! Excellent Horse (Hayagrīva), projecting hosts of messengers
From his mind, puts those poisoned with ignorance
Into the pit of unliberated action,
So that they are exhausted and without a refuge. [22.5]

Hūṁ! May the fiercely cruel blood drinker's weapon
Sharp and hard—the tool of wisdom—
Liberate the enemies and obstructors,
who are the five poisons of ignorance,
Into the realm of wisdom free from thought! [22b1]

Oṁ padmakrota sarvaduṣṭam vajrakīlaya sarvaśatrūṁ māraya *rbad*

The lama then sprinkles the feast with ambrosia, using the lid of the small skull cup. An assistant rushes the liberated feast to the courtyard altar.[92]

The liturgy continues. Then, to the sound of music, the lama takes a pair of iron tongs and removes the paper *lingka* from the black iron box in which it has been kept. On a plate on his table, there is a triangular pyre made of small sticks. As the crucial moment draws near, an assistant sets it aflame.

Hūṁ! This thing that has been liberated into the selfless realm,
The five passions and view of the self
which are its aggregates and body,
This desirable thing, this great diamond pledge,
Partake of it pray, to liberate the world! [22b3]

Mahāmāṁsa rakta keṁniriti guhyasamaya kharaṁ khāhi

Having recited the "burnt offering" which feeds the body of the passions to the gods of the *maṇḍala*, the lama places the effigy into the flames, triangle into triangle.[93] To cleanse the black triangular box, he waves it over the fire. After waiting a minute for the flames to die down, the assistant takes the still-burning pyre to the triangular burial-pit near the stair.[94]

Ten minutes pass with neither ritual nor fanfare. Finally, the assistant places the ashes of the *lingka* into the burial pit. There they join the remains of the other paper effigy that was made on the dark of the moon and buried on the first day of ritual. The assistant places the heavy flagstone over the pit, sealing it for another year.

Whether or not the Black Hat dance commemorates the assassination of Langdarma (see Dance One), the structural similarities between that event and the liberation dance are striking. Each is a magical act in which a Tantric Magician (*sngags pa*) kills an incarnation of evil (an evil bull incarnated as a king, an evil spirit incarnated in the *lingka*) with a magic weapon. In each case, the weapon (an arrow, a *phur bu*) has tube-like properties appropriate to the metabolic model of transcendence. In each case, the magician breaks the flow of the victim's karma and propels his consciousness to paradise.

The metabolic metaphor works two ways. In one sense, the tube of the arrow or dagger digests its victim, extracting the sublime essence from his coarse matter. Given the upward direction of the spirit through the tube, however, we might also see it as peristalsis in reverse: what begins as spiritual offal is turned back into life-giving spirit.

DANCE SEVEN—THE GREAT PROTECTORS

There is a strong connection between the cult of the protector deities and Tibetan religious dance and many *'chams* include dances of one or more protectors.[95] In a certain sense, despite our earlier caveat, dance is itself a ritual; at the very least, it is an offering to the protector gods. As the propitiation ritual itself puts it,

> Brilliant displays stretch to the horizon;
> Ritual dance, and music and dance with hand gestures, are carefully, brilliantly done.
> The ingredients of a scapegoat and the world of a thread cross appear, and are not mixed up.
> May this mass of all things inanimate and animate propitiate you![96]

As one who has followed the progress of the festival for the past two weeks would expect, the deities of the Mani Rimdu protector dance come from the Mindroling protector ritual that has been used throughout Mani Rimdu—*The Playful Ocean of True Achievement*.[97] The deities of the Mindroling cycle, nine in number, are supplemented by one from the Rongphu tradition—Long Life Woman. At present, the full ten are not danced anywhere. The selection of those that are varies from monastery to monastery.

At Chiwong and, formerly, at Thami four deities are represented. At Tengpoche (and at Thami from 1983 on) eight are portrayed. The tradition at Rongphu was originally eight. The groupings of four or of eight are the same at each monastery that employs them (see chart below). In 1958 and 1959—

the last years before the Chinese Army came to Rongphu and the Mani Rimdu tradition ended in Tibet—the full ten were danced there.[98]

When a lesser number of dancers is used, it is usually attributed to lack of personnel. No doubt capital for the extravagant costumes and masks also is a factor. To change the number of dancers as Thami did in 1983, first a monastery must gain permission from the proper authorities, in this case, Trulshik Rinpoche. Then they must assemble the necessary masks and costumes. It is evident that some desire to "keep up with the Joneses" was involved in the innovations of 1983 at Thami. For years, the nearby larger and more famous monastery at Tengpoche had presented an eight protector dance.

When the dance is restricted to four deities the logic behind their choice is easy to ascertain, at least in part. One of the four is a form of Mahākāla, the archetypical protector; another is Mahādeva, the specific protector associated with Lord of the Dance. Although the last of the four, Mantra Guardian and Cemetery Grandmother, are both considered forms of Devī, each is a unique and important goddess in her own right. When greater numbers of dancers are available, the strategy seems to be to add the more unique deities and ignore one or more of the redundant Mahākālas.[99]

In the interlude before the Great Protectors enter, the "Blessing of the Propitiation Substances" from the *Playful Ocean* is performed to prepare the offerings. While the Protectors are on stage, the monks perform the Propitiation (*bskang ba*), Confession (*bshags pa*), and Entrusting the Deeds (*phrin las bcol ba*) for each god.[100]

THE PROTECTOR DANCE AT DIFFERENT MONASTERIES

	deity	*Rongphu*	*Chiwong*	*Thami*[a]	*Thami*[b]	*Teng*[c]
1	Virtuous One †[d]	—	—	—	—	—
2	Four-Handed One †*					
3	Neuter †		—	—		
4	Four-Faced One	—	—	—	—	—
5	Mantra Guardian †*					
6	Great God †					
7	Planet Demon †*		—	—		
8	Son of Renown †		—	—		
9	Cemetery *Mamo* †					
10	Long Life Woman †		—	—		

[a] Thami[a], before 1983.
[b] Thami[b], 1983 and onward.
[c] According to Tengpoche Rinpoche, 5/29/83 interview; confirmed by observation, Tengpoche, 11/17/86.
[d] Illustrated in Khempo Sangyay Tenzin, et al. 1975 (*Kailash* III: 4) (†) or in Beyer 1973: 49 ff. (*). The iconography of the deity illustrated may not correspond in every detail to form specified in the *Playful Ocean*.

PROTECTOR DANCE MASKS AND PROPS[a]

			hand implements	
	deity	*color*	*right hand*	*left hand*
1	**Four-Handed One**	**blue**	**skull**	**"knife"/chopper[b]**
2	Neuter	blue	spear	heart
3	**Mantra Guardian**	**brown**	**mannequin**	**heart/"rat" club[c]**
4	**Great God**	**red**	**hook**	**snare**
5	Planet Demon	brown	sword	bow
6	Son of Renown	red	lance/victory banner	mongoose
7	**Cemetery *Mamo***	**brown**	**mirror**	**heart**
8	Long Life Woman	white	*vajra*	life flask

[a] Based on performances at Thami 5/23/83 and Tengpoche 11/17/86. Where two items separated by a slash (/) are shown, the former was at Thami, the latter at Tengpoche. The initial identifications were made by Thami Rinpoche in 1983, and the order of the deities in the chart is his. In the dance of 1983, Son of Renown preceded Planet Demon. Otherwise, the order of the chart is the order in which the dancers entered the courtyard that year. The masks and implements used at Chiwong (N°s 1, 3, 4, and 7, indicated by bold type) are identical unless otherwise noted.

[b] Chiwong 1980: skull and a sword. Four-Handed One, who, of course, has four arms holds all of these items. The *Playful Ocean*, "His first two hands, holding a chopper marked with the enemy's heart above a skull of blood, embrace his consort. His lower two [hands] brandish a flaming sword and a *khaṭvāṅga*." [10b1]

[c] Chiwong 1980: a hammer-like implement with a half-*vajra* on one side, a *makara* head on the other, and surmounted by a half-*vajra* finial. It is difficult to tell what these "rat" or "*makara*" clubs could represent. The *Playful Ocean* mentions neither: "With her right hand, she raises a human cudgel (*zhing gi dbyug*) above her head. In her left, she [holds] the enemy's heart [from which] iron wolves scatter, swooping like falcons." [18b2] Trulshik Rinpoche's *thang ka* agrees with the *sādhana* in every respect, down to showing an iron wolf leaping from the enemy's heart.

Like Dorje Drolö, the Great Protectors are significant figures, and like him they are greeted with full pomp. The oboe duet, the clanging percussion and the incense wand herald their entrance.

At Chiwong, the dance has eight movements.[101]

The dancers enter in the order they will retain throughout most of the dance: Four-Handed One, Mantra Guardian, Great God and Cemetery Goddess.[102] They dance to the courtyard and array themselves in the four corners, clockwise from the northwest. They dance first east to west and then west to east, returning to their places.[103] As the dancers stand in place, the monks on the dais begin the first of the required selections from the *Playful Ocean*—Blessing the Propitiation Substances.

> From the empty realm [comes] [the syllable] *bhrūṁ*. From it [comes] an unimaginable realm of fierce cemetery residences. In it, is the

> entire panoply of outer, inner and secret offerings, displays, sympathetic substances, support substances, propitiation substances and so forth—the nine necessary types of desirable goods which pacify existence. They are enriched with the nine goodnesses. They are adorned with the nine beauties. Their nature is innate wisdom, illusion. They rise [to perception] as every form of pleasure. They fill the realm of the sky.[104] [40b6]

The chant continues. The cymbals and drums on the dais begin to mark a slow cadence, and the Protectors start to dance, still in place. After half a minute, there is a loud cymbal passage and the chanting stops. The gods dance, bending their knees, their weapons making gestures of attack.

The second movement begins with a rapid chant. The text is the Propitiation of the Four-Handed Protector.[105] At the words, "Although from the Truth Realm, you display the body of a glorious blood drinker . . .", the gods start to dance, the cymbals growing louder over the last part of the chant.[106]

> Although from the Truth Realm, you display the body of a glorious Blood Drinker,
> Originally, you are pure. We propitiate you
> With progress on the paths of creation and fulfillment,
> Such as the yoga that recognizes that you are indivisible from our own minds!
>
> Rejoice in non-dual bliss!
> Bestow each and every true achievement,
> And spread all the Sage's teaching far and wide,
> Especially, the Diamond Vehicle! [43.3]

The cymbals grow yet louder and the liturgy stops, but the dance continues.

The third movement is the Propitiation of the Guardian of Mantra.[107] The chant is very fast now; the cymbals and drums soft. The dancers stand still, facing each other as the monks on the dais catalogue the substances that will please the fearsome goddess.

> The skull castle shimmering in fury—the cemetery residence,
> The garments of glory, ornaments and necklaces,
> And a varied wealth of riches, displays, and so forth,
> By the desirables, the nine necessities be propitiated.[108] [45.6]

As before, the drums and cymbals grow louder, as to the slow chanting which propitiates the last members of Guardian of the Mantra's entourage, "Butcher Black Murderess" and her companions, the gods begin to dance.[109]

Once more, the cymbals and drums play loudly when the chanting stops. The gods dance in place.

The fourth movement begins like the third with a chant in quick-tempo. The chorus of Great God's Propitiation is heard—"be propitiated . . . be propitiated."[110] The chant slows and the gods dance, starting just at the point that the propitiation moves from the mundane to the transcendent, from the material to the ethereal.

> May the character of awareness, pure from the beginning mind itself,
> [And] that which appears from its energy, arises without impediment—the magic illusion [which is the god's body]
> Arising spontaneously and liberated spontaneously—the realm of just-the-way-things are,[111]
> Propitiate the Great God brother and sister! [47.2]

Arms down, elbows bent, the dancers wave their forearms back and forth in time. The music grows louder and the chant ends. The Protectors spin and march back and forth from east to west.

The fifth movement, the Propitiation of Cemetery Grandmother begins with a very fast chant.[112] The second passage again begins with a slow dance accompanied softly on the cymbals and drum. As in the previous segments, the dancing starts when the chant reaches its climax.

> Since we worship and serve you, Field Defending Grandmother,
> In a Sūtra-Tantra Religious Island of accomplished Knowledge Bearers such as this,
> Do not waver from acting as a refuge
> From plagues such as smallpox,
> And unsympathetic, contrary conditions, the forces of harm;
> And completely purify sympathetic conditions, [and] quickly achieve the goal we have in mind! [48b6][113]

The music grows louder and the dance continues. After half a minute, the dancers begin a clockwise circle, backtracking sometimes as they move around the courtyard. The movement ends with them standing still once more, but the circle has rotated 180° so that the Four-Handed One is now in the southeast.

The sixth movement is dedicated to "Requesting Action" from the Protectors.[114]

> In the ten directions, spread the Conqueror's teaching,
> The basis from which all the virtues of existence and peace spring!
> And thus make the adherents to the teaching grow like the waxing moon—

They nourish it by explaining the transmissions and achieving understanding. [52.4]

Pacify all difficulties for beings [whose numbers are] vast as the sky,
And nourish them with an ocean of the wealth of the ten virtues,
And increase all the good in the vessel of the world and its inhabitants,
And elevate it with the glory of the golden age! [52.5]

Particularly for us yogis and our followers, do the [four] deeds—
Pacify all discordant decline, [both] internal and external,
Such as disease, malignancy and obstructors,[115] and interruption!
Achieve total victory in the war against the demonic legions!

Increase and extend life, merit, greatness
Enjoyment, strength, and hearing, thinking and meditating!
Bring the beings of the three levels, and all their
Virtues and glory *under your power*! [52b1]

With unbearably *fierce* actions, liberate
Into the Realm of Wisdom
The enemies and obstructors whose minds are wild and topsy-turvy,
Along with the forces of darkness, the demon battalions! [52b2]

O mind itself, original guardian of the teaching, unadulterated
By the smell of hope or fear—free from extremes,[116] reveal true bliss!
And with four kinds of action glorify
The ocean of true achievement which fulfills beings hopes! [52b3]

The movement is structured like the previous one, except that in the final dance, the gods execute a series of kicks and short steps to the east and west. They spin, then stop when the music stops.

According to the Chant Leader of Thubten Chöling, the seventh movement is Feeding the Torma.[117] The unaccompanied liturgy invokes the power of the truth and uses it to sweep the enemies of religion into the torma.

And depending on the magic power of these great truths, may the enemies of the teaching and of beings in general,
In particular, the past enemies who attack us Knowledge Bearers and our patrons and entourages,
The future enemies who think about us, [53.2]

The present enemies who hate us, the embodied who point us out as enemies,

And the host of disembodied harmful obstructors—all of them, no matter where they live, where they run within the three existences,
In an instant, in a moment, be drawn into this, the basis of our imaginings! [53b1]

Then, after a short musical interlude for the cymbals, drum and long horns, the monks recite the mantras that feed the tormas to the Protectors, as they do so, placing their finger-tips together and pulling them apart. The mantras give way to a rapidly recited verse; then, to a piece of music for full orchestra—thigh-bone trumpet, long horn, cymbals, drum, and oboes. The gods resume their dance, spinning in place. They line up with Four-Handed One and Mantra Guardian to the northwest and northeast, and Great God and Cemetery Grandmother to the southwest and southeast.

The assistant removes the Protector torma from the altar. Having prostrated on the steps, he brings a plate of feast and the skull beer from courtyard altar to Trulshik Rinpoche. Trulshik Rinpoche puts sacramental beer on his wrist and licks it off. The Protectors dance up the stairs and exit by pairs.[118]

The orchestral accompaniment continues after their departure, the percussion becoming muted, then louder again. The final note is a long trailing groan from the long horn.

Although the courtyard is now empty, the dance of the Protectors continues into its eighth and final movement. This segment is dedicated to the closing prayers of the *Playful Ocean*.[119] The lama accompanies the musicians on his *ḍamaru*. The music stops and the monks recite at a rapid tempo, placing their palms together their hands in the *añjali* gesture and making the other necessary *mudrās*. The chant becomes rhythmic as the cymbals and drums begin a soft accompaniment. Finally, the monks chant the "Auspicious Omens" that end the *Playful Ocean*.

Come, good fortune of the root and lineage lamas!
Protector[s] of the circle of the infinite *maṇḍala* ocean!
The unchanging, thrice secret bliss diamond mind![120]
Wish-granting tree that grants beings supreme benefit and pleasure!

Come, good fortune of the hosts of tutelary deities,
Countless Form Body clouds in the Truth Body sky,
Who having risen, playful with a hundred peaceful and wrathful aspects,
Hurl down the rain of the nine-fold desirable true achievement! [55.5]

Come, good fortune of glorious blazing Mahākāla,
Who brings the black ones to an end, root, branch and tribe

With a dazzling brilliance that is hard to bear—
The dance of Glorious Heruka's compassionate play! [55b1]

Come, good fortune of the ocean-like host of Sworn Ones,
The Conqueror's attendants, the unbearably furious ones
Who annihilate the demon army, who defend the supreme achievement
like a son,
Who guard the teaching with the four forms of action!

The dance of the Protectors concludes with an orchestral arrangement for long horns, oboes, *ḍamaru*, bells, cymbals, and drums.

At monasteries outside of Solu-Khumbu, some protector dances seem to portray a lone deity and his entourage.[121] Others feature groups of eight to ten protectors, such as the eight (or nine) *drag gshed* of gSang chen rdo rje Monastery in the Pedong Valley of Bhutan.[122] Although these dances have features in common with Mani Rimdu's dance of the Great Protectors, without knowledge of their liturgical bases it is difficult to say whether the deities they portray correspond in any way to those of Mani Rimdu.

The Dance of the Great Protectors, in fact, is an ideal illustration of the difficulty of studying *'chams*—or any other Tibetan ritual activity—without access to its liturgy, and the history of scholarship on the subject provides the perfect cautionary tale. In the late 1960s, Luther Jerstad witnessed a dance with eight protectors at Tengpoche.[123] He also found a list of eight protectors in Antoinette Gordon's *Iconography of Tibetan Lamaism.*[124] Putting two and two—or eight and eight—together, he concluded that Gordon's list described the deities in Mani Rimdu. Unfortunately, the list was irrelevant. Thus, Jerstad's identifications of the deities in this dance are all incorrect, except for one, Mahākāla, which is merely imprecise.

To make matters worse, Jerstad often avoided his own field data in favor of Gordon's iconographic descriptions. Thus, we read that the red-masked gShin rje gshed, who only appears in the Mani Rimdu of Jerstad's imagination, holds a skull bowl and a "*gri-gug*, a tantric knife, shaped like a small hatchet."[125] In fact, neither of the red-masked figures of Mani Rimdu holds implements even resembling these. Jerstad himself noted at least one of the discrepancies between what he had seen and what he had read. When he sought an explanation for it, he put the blame on the monks. He did, however, charitably allow that "this probably owes to lack of properties, and not to deficiency of knowledge of his proper form."[126]

Seven years later, the great alpinist and mountaineering authority Mario Fantin followed in Jerstad's footsteps and reproduced all of his errors in a large format picture book.[127]

To add to the confusion, a later publication indicates that Gordon's group of eight deities—the *drag gshed brgyad*—may actually figure in unrelated dance festivals at other sites. After Jerstad and Fantin, however, one reads such accounts with a skeptical eye.[128]

DANCE EIGHT—SHARLUNG MAHĀ-UPĀSAKA AND THE BLACK MEN

At Chiwong and Thami, as at Rongphu, the eighth dance represents Shar lung dge bsnyen chen po, the local god of the latter Monastery. Although the term *upāsaka* in Sanskrit is quintessentially Buddhist, describing the vows of a lay cleric, in Tibet the term *dge bsnyen* is also applied to various local deities, including the twenty-one *dge bsnyen*, "an ancient group of Mountain gods," who, Nebesky-Wojkowitz explains, "are named after the mountains and valleys which are supposed to be their residence."[129]

As was the case with the Lords of the Cemetery and the Magicians, the dances of the Black Men and of Sharlung *dge bsnyen chen po* are often counted as separate dances. According to Trulshik Rinpoche, much as the Lords of the Cemetery are the emissaries (*pho nya*) who precede the Magicians, and the Ging the heralds of Padmasambhava, the Black Men are the servants of Sharlung. The Black Men carry swords and wear black clothes of a unique design: a baggy blouse and trousers, each with wide tight-fitting cuffs. Each wears an appliquéd bib (*stod le*) and a small black or brown mask.[130] Like the other servants in the Mani Rimdu *'chams*, they are barefoot.[131]

The music that marks the entrance of the Black Men is unlike the other compositions played at Mani Rimdu. The long-horn passages have weirdly abrupt crescendos and diminuendos, perhaps a survival of pre-Buddhist liturgy. They dance until the music stops, then exit.

The strange groaning fanfare resumes as Sharlung enters. Sharlung carries a banner-draped spear in his right hand and a whip in his left. His brown mask is surmounted by a cylindrical banner flanked by triangular pennants. His entrance is unusual, in that he walks backwards to and down the stairs. He wends his way around the courtyard, dancing until he reaches the south. Then, the long horn stops playing, and Sharlung dances in his place to the cymbals and drums. A monk brings out a chair. As Dorje Drolö before him, Sharlung sits.

The Black Men enter for second time, dancing wildly to a fast passage for long horns and percussion. This time they carry white ropes or *kha btags*.[132] As they dance together, they make knotting gestures. Trulshik Rinpoche explains that the ropes are their black lassos (*zhags pa nag po*). "At Rongphu, they were long and black and thrown at the ground, to mimic lassoing an animal. At Chiwong, they do not know this and do it in the air with *kha btags*." At Thami, the Rongphu tradition of black ropes is preserved.[133]

The Black Men position themselves at the southeast and southwest. The three dance together in the south. Then the chair is removed and they all exit.

The ritual action, the "reason for the necessity" of the dance of Sharlung is to feed a feast offering to the Lama. Earlier, the feast was offered to the gods. Now it is a pledge substance (*dam tshig gi rdzas*) offered to the body god (*lus lha*).[134]

The liturgy used in the dance of Sharlung is an excerpt from *The Fulfillment of the Practitioner's Hopes: A Cloud of Offerings for the Guardian of the Oral Tradition of rDza rong phu Hermitage, Shar lung Upāsaka.*[135] The section excerpted is entitled "Putting him to Work." It highlights both Sharlung's duty as body god of the lama of Rongphu and his obligations to the community at large.

> Hūṁ! Such is the work with which you are charged—
> To guard the Buddha's teaching strictly!
> To praise the Conqueror's grandeur greatly!
> To make flourish the Lama's life and body!
> To remove discord and create harmony
> By practicing the doctrines that establish the definite meaning!
> Magically grant us yogis' every wish,
> And extend each enjoyment we desire!
> Above all, be a support at our backs, an unwavering legion of powers!
> We practice holy religion properly
> In this great place!
> Help us practice holy religion!

A local protector is by definition parochial. When a festival like Mani Rimdu is transplanted, such deities are likely to be supplemented or replaced by gods of more immediate interest. In the daily liturgy of the local protectors, we saw the former occur when bKra shis dpal chen, the god of Solu's Mount Numbur was added to the roster of deities. At Tengpoche, we see an example of the latter.

Dance eight is the dance of the local protector (*gnas srung*), and Tengpoche Rinpoche, a lama of an independent cast of mind. He has replaced the god of Rongphu with one more close at hand, Zur ra rva skyes, who is worshipped as the protector of Khembalung—a hidden valley nearby in Khumbu.[136]

Trulshik Rinpoche's description of his supernatural neighbor is both personal and picturesque.

> Zur ra rva skyes is a little bit like a demon (*bdud*). He is the younger brother of the Cemetery Goddess (Dur khrod lha mo = Dur khrod ma mo)—her only brother. He kills people. Since he has been got

at by many lamas, he's become a little better, though. He is the god of Khembalung, a site sacred (*gnas*) to Padmasambhava.[137]

Like Shar lung, Zur ra is worshipped during the dance with a short prayer. Although the character and the liturgy are different, according to Tengpoche Rinpoche, the dance is the same.[138]

The ultimate origin of Zur ra rva skyes is unknown. A similar name appears in the Tibetan epic: Senglong Ragyey (Seng blon ra skyes), Gesar's father.[139] However, beyond their names, a relationship between the two figures is as yet to be discovered.

DANCE NINE—THE SKY WALKERS

Dances both of male and female Sky Walkers are known in Tibet. Although the present example features Sky Walking Women, it partakes of elements of each kind of dance. As in some *ḍāka* dances, the participants play the *ḍamaru*. As in some *ḍākiṇī* dances, each wears the five-lobed *pañcatathāgata* headdress rather than a mask.[140]

As is typical in monasteries, the Mani Rimdu Sky Walkers are portrayed by young boys, often the youngest of the monastery's novices. They are five in number, referring to the five Tathāgata families into which Sky Walkers are commonly grouped.[141] According to Trulshik Rinpoche, the Sky Walker dance is a celebration (*dga' ston*) of the enjoyment the feast.[142]

The thigh trumpets sound and the music begins—a trio for long horns, cymbals and drums.[143] The Sky Walkers enter the courtyard. Each carries a *ḍamaru* in her right hand and a bell in her left. As the Sky Walkers dance around the central altar, the oboists begin to play. Within a minute of their entrance, the dancers have lined up in front of and facing the dais. Each stands holding her *ḍamaru* near her head and her bell at her waist. The dancers hold the bell with elbow bent and the wrist curiously turned inward so that the back of the hand rests on the hip and the bell is upside down. The monks on the dais recite the Sky Walker prayer.

The prayer, an excerpt from "The Song of the Queen of Spring" (*dPyid gyi rgyal mo*), is not used elsewhere in Mani Rimdu. It celebrates the union of bDe mchog (Saṁvara). and his consort and contains numerous references to sexual yoga.[144] Despite the Nyingma's reputation for being perhaps a bit more free-spoken on this subject than the other orders, the prayer is Gelugpa in origin and comes from Pha bong kha's *Lama Worship* (*Bla ma'i mchod pa*). Trulshik Rinpoche sometimes refers to the Sky Walker dance itself as a Gelugpa dance.

Ḍākiṇī Dancer, Thami 1983

If you want to sing the Song of the Queen of Spring—

Hūṁ! I pray
To every Tathāgata,
And to all the Heroes and Yoginīs,
Sky Walkers and Sky Walking Women!

In bliss Joyous Heruka,
Maddened with bliss, comes to the Mother,
And enjoys [her] according to ritual,
Entering into innately blissful union.

A la la! La la hoḥ! A i āḥ! Arali ho!
Stainless hosts of Sky Walkers!
Look on me with love! Do every deed!

Hūṁ! I pray
To every Tathāgata,
And to all the Heroes and Yoginīs,
Sky Walkers and Sky Walking Women!

Bliss has much moved my mind,
So, my body moving much in dance
Plays in the lotus of the *mudrā*. Make this bliss
An offering to the hosts of Yoginīs!

A la la! La la hoḥ! A i āḥ! Arali ho!

The prayer takes but a minute to read. Then, to a soft accompaniment of cymbals and drums, the Sky Walkers begin their elegant and gentle dance.

A minute later, they face the dais once more and the monks begin to pray.

Their final dance is somewhat different. At first, the dancers move forward and backward a short distance, perhaps a foot. Then, they circle the altar playing their *ḍamaru*. Their playing stops as they wait to make their exit, but each resumes as he leaves the stage.

DANCE TEN—THE SEER

The Sherpas call the star of tenth act the "Tolden" (Tib., rTogs ldan), the Seer. Like the Sky Walker dance, the Seer is a celebration of the enjoyment the feast. However, Trulshik Rinpoche explains, whereas the former was serious celebration, the latter is comic.[145]

At Rongphu, the act is said to have been a rather short affair—no more than two hours long. The Seer simply explains a little Buddhist doctrine and then leaves.[146] In Solu-Khumbu, the Seer is by far the longest act of Mani Rimdu—often enduring a staggering four-and-one-half hours. It is also the most beloved. The day of the dance is a long one. Now and again, members of the audience take a break at the tea shops. During most of the day, these shops do a thriving business; during the Seer, they are often deserted.[147] In 1994, a thousand people jammed the monastery to see the Tolden.

Much of the present-day Seer's performance is devoted to clowning. One highly placed Tibetan monastic informant voiced mild disapproval of this custom, finding it inexplicable except for the fact that, in his words, "Sherpas like a lot of 'ha ha.'" In general though, Tibetans enjoy the Seer's antics every bit as much as the Sherpas, and monks laugh as loudly as laymen. Most years, the monks can be seen crowding the dais—their place of privilege—craning around the pillars to catch a better view.

The name rTogs ldan, "Seer," means "he who has penetrating insight." According to Ngawang Yonten, who has played the part for many years at Chiwong, the Seer lives up to his name. He is a Buddhist yogi capable of doing in truth all the things he acts out in the dance, such as balancing on the point of a sword without being impaled.

The Seer wears the red and white striped shawl of a Buddhist yogi. The rest of his costume is in keeping with his character: bone earrings, a top-knot, and a yellow vest or shirt. He carries the thigh-bone trumpet and large double-headed *ḍamaru* drum (*gcod ḍam*) which mark the chöpa (*gcod pa*), the practitioner of the yoga of cutting-off. gCod is a fearsome rite steeped in the shamanic traditions of an earlier age. The meditator imagines that he cuts up his body and offers it to all flesh-eating demonic forces in want of food. The Seer's script specifies that he perform the rite, which he does, circling the courtyard and singing in the plaintive voice typical of *gcod* song. During one performance of Mani Rimdu, I heard the Seer shout, "I am a Kagyü yogi!"[148] According to some sources, the Seer represents a specific historical figure, and the dance portrays his life and demonstrates his powers.[149]

The Seer's half-mask has the dark complexion, large nose, and protruding eyes of a caricature Indian. The half-mask leaves his mouth relatively free, and indeed he is the only character in Mani Rimdu that speaks. Much of what he says is found in manuscript form, although some dialog may be transmitted orally, without reference to a printed page. Some of this memorized but unwritten material belongs to the *'dre dkar* tradition—a school of itinerant satirical performance. For Stein, the *'dre dkar*, or "white demon," actor exemplifies that uniquely Tibetan personality: "ambiguous figures whose character is at once sacred and hilarious."[150] The same could be easily said of our Seer, and to an extent, of the other comic figure of Mani Rimdu, the Long-Life Man.

The script used for much of the Seer's dialog at Chiwong is a ragtag miscellany of papers, obviously in many hands and possibly of several generations. The text begins with a description of the Seer's entrance and then goes into his rather lengthy sermon. The selection below gives all of his entrance and a little of the sermon—just enough to give its flavor.[151]

The Seer's Schedule
At the beginning, when coming from inside the Assembly Hall, come out saying,
Maṇi ho, Padme hrīḥ
[Then, go for refuge][152]
Then, make yourself known.[153]
Then, [recite]—
The three roots, collected . . .[154]
Also, then explain religion.[155]
Then, teach about impermanence.[156]
[Then, the ten non-virtues, etc.][157]
Then, offer incense to the gods.[158]
Also do a song and dance.[159]
[Also, then, there is the 'dre dkar *dance.]*[160]
Then, the Bro brdung.[161]
Then, do an empowerment.[162]
Then, do the "Attracting Fortune"[163]*—*

ris gu 'khu yo 'khu yo!
smug pa 'khu yo 'khu yo![164]
On this residence, today
Luck and fortune, *'khu yo!*
'khu yo, fortune, *'khu 'khu yo!*

Then, offer a Long Life Prayer.
Then, do the Auspicious Omens.[165]
The Long Life Prayer *is done after the "Truths"*[166]*—*

Oṁ svasti! By the intrinsic power of
The three supreme undeceiving truths of the Lama,
And the truth of the Tutelary and Sky Walkers,
And the truth of the Sages (*ṛṣi*) and Knowledge Bearers—
Here and now, may I achieve the results of my wishes![167]

Ānanda, the sublime son of the Fourth Guide,
The incarnations that in succession come, [each] a new dance [of]
The sublime one named Ngawang Losang Donag,[168]

That their lives remain firm for a hundred æons,
I offer with respect this long life prayer![169]

The Lama's body is a diamond body,
Brilliantly shining, forever everywhere—
Inconceivable, perfect in its qualities—
I offer with respect this long life prayer to the Lama's body!

The Lama's voice is the song of Brahmā.
It resounds like the unstoppable lion's roar.
I offer with respect . . .
To the Lama's speech, which vanquishes the non-believer's perverted views!

The Lama's mind is like the sky—
The blissful, clear, unimpeded realm of the sky!
I offer with respect . . .
To the Lama's mind!

The unchanging body! The Lama's body!
The unimpeded speech! The Lama's speech!
The unmistaken mind! The Lama's mind!
I offer . . . this long life prayer to the Lama's body, speech and mind.

Especially, all the holy, highly born who uphold
The Sugar Cane Man's precious teaching,[170]
Those who uphold the teaching in broad Jambu-land,[171]
That their lives remain firm for a hundred æons . . .

The noble clergy who cleave to the Conqueror's teaching,
Beautified by the jeweled ornaments of the three learnings, the transmissions and understanding,
Those who strive to hold others dearer than themselves,
That their lives...

Especially, the kind patrons of the teaching who bear the lineage
Of the Sovereign Nyima Wözer,[172]
Those who, in general, bear the lineage
Of he who was named Lama Sangyay of the Nyang clan,
I offer with respect . . .

Especially, to work for the pleasure, happiness and glory
Of every form of being born in broad Jambu-land,

And to pacify all disease, darkness, strife, dispute and trouble,
And then to spread the Buddha's teaching, with respect, I offer a long-life prayer!

Namo Guru! I bow to Ngawang Norbu's feet!
The root of all religious [teachings]
Is twofold—Philosophy (*mtshan nyid*), the cause vehicle;
And Mantra, the effect vehicle.
In the cause [vehicle], Philosophy, there are the ten perfections, and so on;
And in the effect [vehicle], Mantra, there are the nine successive vehicles, and so on.
Action Tantra, Behavior Tantra, Yoga, [and] Unexcelled [Yoga] Tantra
Are the four classes of tantra.

The first, *Philosophy* (*mtshan nyid*), has two parts:
The Branches of What is to be Explained,
And *What is Actually to be Explained.*

The first among these is the door
—the method of relying on a spiritual friend.
Also, there is the thing to be abandoned—a perverted spiritual friend;
And the thing to be taken up—the method of relying on a spiritual friend, and so on.
If this has not been done already,[173]
The Great Orgyan said—
"Not checking a lama is like drinking poison.
Not checking a disciple is like jumping off a cliff."
The method of relying on a virtuous friend—since that's over with—

Part two has three parts—*The Way a Master Explains Religion*, *The Way a Disciple Listens*, and *How Master and Disciple Explain and Listen to Religion Respectively.*[174]

Among these, there is also the way the Master, the Buddha, explained religion; the way the Arhats explained religion; the way the masters, the *paṇḍita*s explained religion—and so on. There are many of them.
However, if you summarize them—

Part Two—*The Way Disciples Listen*, has two parts: *Motivation* and *Behavior*. This also has two parts: *The Vast Concept* of the

Bodhisattva's Motivation, and *The Vast Method* of the Motivation of the Secret Mantra.

Regarding the first, *The Vast Concept*—
you must cast aside thoughts of this life.
The all-pervading sky is pervaded by beings,

And among all those beings, who are pervaded by suffering, there is not a one who has not been your father and mother. When they were your parents, their kindness was great. They gave you the first taste of food, covered you up with the very best of clothes—put simply, they had extreme loving kindness.

In order to liberate all those who have acted with such kindness from the ocean of *saṁsāra*, and to get them liberation and the precious state of enlightenment, right now, having heard the holy and profound, I must have the sound motivation which considers that [I should] practice it.

A monk of Khumbu interviewed by anthropologist Vincanne Adams sums up the Seer's message:

When you are born, you must die. Everyone gets sick, but this [process] shows one the physical body. It will get sick, disease and die. The main idea is that you must meditate. Otherwise, you are wasting your time. Tolden says that the lama, shaman, doctor—none can save your life. They will care for the sick people, but we are all mortal—*jiktenpa* (*'jig rten pa*)—destructible bodies. At the time of death, nobody can save you. Not even your relatives can help you then. You must leave your body behind. Then you must walk by yourself.[175]

The Seer's speech is a linguistic hodgepodge. One moment he will banter with the CDO in Nepali. The next, he will speak Sherpa, or quite passable central Tibetan dialect. Religious discourses, like the one above are in a more classical Tibetan.

There is hardly the space here to describe four-and-one-half hours of comedy. Many elements of the Seer's performance, such as the *'dre dkar* tradition are yet to be explored by Western scholarship. The Seer himself could easily be the subject of an entire book. Before we leave him however, it would be good to describe one of his more significant acts in some detail.

The sword trick is a major feature of the Seer's yearly performance. In preparation, the actor strips off his upper garments and takes up a large sword. He prays over the weapon, dances in a circle and sings. Halting near the edge of the courtyard, he places the sword upright, bracing the handle against the flagstone floor. He bends over, placing his weight on the sword point and balancing from the waist. The crowd begins to throw money.

The Seer circles the courtyard further and stops at another spot to repeat his balancing act. A second flurry of coins clatters to the ground.

Once more, the Seer moves on and for a third time bends over his sword. This time he puts on the pressure and the sword bends. Money hails.

The liturgy the Seer recites during his trick is real. It is one of the "Showering Blessings" rituals used in Mani Rimdu. The *mudrā* he makes is likewise genuine—the iron hook gesture that is used to summon supernatural entities/forces into our realm. The sword, however is fake. Dull-pointed and made of flexible steel, it is easily bent when braced in the heavy folds of cloth around the waist of the Seer's costume.[176]

The actor who plays the Seer discusses this piece of stagecraft openly and without any reticence. To at least some of the members of the audience, however, his act is no trick. For them, it is only the power of the mantra that protects the Seer from certain death. For one Sherpa informant, a young, successful English-speaking businessman, the sword trick was a sign of the very efficacy of his religion. Were he to think it was fake, he said, he would lose faith in his own culture. Others less subject to the pressure of foreign ideas might have a less drastic reaction.

As the Seer leaves the courtyard, he shouts "Farewell, good-bye, I'll come back tomorrow or the next day."[177] It will be a year before the audience sees the Seer again. Many members of that audience will be the same as this year and year before. No matter how often they have seen him and how many times they have heard his jokes, they will await him eagerly. An old joke is an old friend and he who brings one is always welcome.

The figure of the Seer has features in common with characters of other *'chams*. Like the Mongolian *cagan öbö*, the "White Old Man," he alone among the dancers is allowed to speak.[178] Like both the *cagan öbö* and the *atsara* of other traditions, he collects money from the spectators.

The *atsara*—their name is presumably from the Sanskrit *ācārya*—are worth a few more words. Like the Seer, their masks are dark brown or black, often bearded and have a large nose. Their hair is long or in a top-knot. According to all accounts the *atsara* represent the Indian yogis they indeed resemble—figures designed to "ridicule the priesthood of Hinduism."[179]

There is evidently some relation between the Seer and the *atsara*, but of what it consists we may only speculate. As we have shown above, the Mani Rimdu Seer is no figure of ridicule, nor is he considered to be a Hindu. It may be that here we see the mask and costume of a comic stock Hindu given a new name and put to a new use. It should not be forgotten that the long-haired yogis of ancient India (or of modern Tibet) were not all Hindus. It may well be that at least some of the *atsara* of other traditions like the Seer are

Buddhist yogis, and for all the laughter they provoke, figures of reverence rather than ridicule.

Throughout much of his act, the Seer is accompanied by the figures of an old man and woman, and their child, the rag doll effigy of the liberation dance. The old man and woman also have analogues elsewhere. In eastern Tibet, for example, we find a nomadic yak-herd and his wife leading a cow, the man armed with a sling and his wife, carrying a milk pail.[180]

The old couple that appear with the "Ha Shang" at Choni have some interesting parallels to our own. The couple at Mani Rimdu carry a doll, and to some extent abuse it. At Choni, "after the *liṅga* had been cut up," the old couple "hurled pieces of the dough effigy among the spectators."[181]

The sword trick also has analogues outside the realm of sacred dance. Similar demonstrations are in the repertoire of several Tibetan oracles. Candidates for the oracle of Nechung must twist a heavy sword into a spiral.[182] In his memoirs, Nebesky-Wojkowitz describes a performance by an oracle of the god Dorje Shugden:

> A servant pressed a short sword into the oracle priest's right hand. The seer placed the point against his hip, where a strong leather strap showed under his brightly colored apron, and pushed on the handle until the blade doubled up.[183]

Such a twisted sword is called a "knotted thunderbolt" and is valued as a defense against the supernatural. Hung next to the door, it can prevent malignant spirits from entering.[184]

DANCE ELEVEN—THE REMAINDER

The eleventh dance concerns the remainder of food on the feast plate, the "*juṭho*," to use the Indian and Nepali term,[185] the leftovers from the offerings to the gods of the *maṇḍala* and the gods of the body. The figures of the remainder dance wear the costumes of the two Black Men, the relatively lowly supernatural entities that were seen earlier serving the local god. The Chant Leader of Thubten Chöling firmly states, however, that they are not the two Black Men, identifying them instead simply as the "Remainders" (*lhag ma*).[186]

As the name implies, the ritual used here is the Remainder of the Feast:

> Hūṁ! Among Great Compassion's circle of attendants,
> You who possess a vow to defend the teaching—
> The hosts of Ladies, Sky Walkers,
> Ging [and] Langka, and Sorcerers, Slow-Walkers (*shugs 'gro*) and
> Malefactor/Benefactors.

> You are fearsome in form; you have ornaments of violence.
> You judge [our] quality; you gauge the warmth [of our practice].
> You follow vows; you circulate among the cemeteries.
> Together with your individual incarnations and messengers,
>
> Please eat these glorious left-overs!
> And act in accord with your vows!
>
> Oṁ ucchiṣṭa baliṁta khāhi[187]

The commentary further refines the list of the guests to be invited to offering or the remainders.

> The twenty eight *Īśvarī*, the thirty-two Sky Walkers, the eighteen great Ging, the three types of *langka*.[188] Further, the seven Grandmothers, the four Sisters, the eight Blazing Women, the three-hundred sixty Messengers, and so on. And those of the race of Sorceresses, *shugs 'gro*, and Malefactor/Benefactors.[189]

Taking these passages into consideration, it would seem that the "Remainders" costume represents a status in the supernatural hierarchy rather than an absolute identity. As Tengpoche Rinpoche puts it, these beings are "servants who are not supposed to feast with the other deities."[190]

The dance is simple and short.[191] Two black-clad dancers enter, one wearing a green mask, the other a red one. They race around the courtyard and proceed to the southeast and southwest corners. A monk gives each a plate of leftover feast from the central altar.[192] The remainder ritual is recited, the music begins, the "Remainders" dance briefly and exit.[193]

The Vajrakīla *'chams yig* describes a dance of the remains, but its movements seem to have little to do with ours.[194]

DANCE TWELVE—THE SWORD DANCE

The characters of the Sword Dance are the Liberation Ging (*sgrol ging*), although in Solu-Khumbu their masks are borrowed from the Protector Dance.[195] According to Trulshik Rinpoche, if we think of the Great Protectors as "Ministers of War" in the armies of righteousness, "then the Liberation Ging are like colonels (*steng dpon*)." Each sword dancer carries a sword in his right hand and a scabbard in his left.[196] The Sword Dance at Chiwong is a simple affair. At Thami, as we will see in a moment, it is rather more complex.

At Chiwong, the dancers enter one by one. Each jumps from the bottom step to the courtyard floor and goes to the northeast corner, where he dances while the others wait on the stairs. After a half minute or so, he relinquishes his corner and moves one place clockwise around the circle. Once all the dancers are the courtyard, they dance until the music stops, then stand, each in his own corner, as a passage of liturgy is read. In all there are three recitations, alternating with sequences of dance.[197] At a certain point, the assistant removes a pair of tormas.[198] The Liberation Ging resume their dance, stabbing and slashing in the air with their swords. They exit by pairs.

The Sword Dance is sometimes called the Liberation Dance (*bsgral 'chams*), the name normally given to Dance Six.[199] As this alternate title implies, at some monasteries at least, the Sword Dance is a continuation of that dance. Dance Six, it will be remembered, contains attacks on three separate effigies. Skeleton dancers abused a cloth *lingka*, and the lama stabbed a dough effigy (the last of the feast) and a burned a paper *lingka*.

At Thami and Tengpoche,[200] as before them at Rongphu,[201] the sword dance features a *lingka* made of dough which the dancers cut up with swords. At Chiwong, however, a dough effigy is not used. At Thami, the effigy is perhaps six inches long. To all appearances it is made from the same sort of barley flour dough as a torma. It is painted red.[202]

The figure has a rudimentary face—ears, eyes, and nose, but no mouth. It has no hands, or at least no details of a hand articulated. Its left arm is at its side; its right arm is bent at the elbow, with the hand end pointing to the chest. As in paper effigies, the *lingka's* legs should be bent outward at the knee,[203] and are bound by a strip of dough representing iron chains (*lcags sgrog*). The chest of the dough effigy has a deep cavity in it, with a raised lip and a lid. This cavity serves as a receptacle for blood or a blood substitute.[204] The Vajrakīla *'chams yig* identifies the *lingka* as "an image of the enemies and obstructors,"[205] and specifies that it should be: ". . . complete with brain, heart, bowels etc., just like a real corpse, of great and terrifying splendor."[206]

At Thami, the dough *lingka* is kept under the altar in a triangular black wooden box until it is needed. After a passage of liturgy and a musical interlude, the box is removed. The music resumes and the dancers close on the box. They cut up the *lingka*, pick up the dismembered pieces with the tips of their swords and continue their dance. The music stops and there is liturgy on the dais. An assistant wearing a yellow ceremonial hat approaches the courtyard altar, and sprinkles a gift torma (*'bul gtor*) of the protector type with ambrosia and ceremonial blood (*rakta*).[207] He places a piece of the cut up effigy next to the torma and carries it out. The Liberation Ging resume their dance and then exit by pairs.[208]

According to Trulshik Rinpoche, the Sword Dance contains two rituals, "Urging the Contract" from the Lord of the Dance *Manual*, and "Giving the Torma to the Defenders of Religion." Although this identification has its problems, there is much to argue in its favor.[209] If in the earlier "Liberation Dance," the corpse of the enemy was fed to the gods of the *maṇḍala*, here it is fed directly to the protectors. The liturgy of the "Feeding" itself offers "the flesh and blood of enemies and obstructors" to the protectors in thanks for the boons they have already granted and in expectation of those yet to come.[210]

Trulshik Rinpoche describes the Sword dancers as killers of the enemy; they stab the *lingka* with their swords. Nowadays, he adds, they rush through the prayer instead of doing it to the rhythm of the dance.[211]

The dismemberment of a dough *lingka* is a common feature of Tibetan sacred dance. Many times it follows close on the heels of the other effigy related dances. Different dancers dispatch the effigy in different traditions. It is common for either Yama—the Lord of Death—or the stag-headed creature who sometimes is counted among his minions to do the cutting. In some traditions, skeleton dancers, also often considered subalterns of Yama, tear the *lingka* to pieces.[212]

The chart that follows this section compares the key features of the two sorts of "liberation dance" as they are performed at various parts of the Himalayas.

Other types of sword dances are known in Tibet, but it is difficult to see their immediate relation to the present type. One is an athletic/military event performed by warriors or dancers costumed in the flagged helmets and other paraphernalia of Tibetan warriors of old.[213] Another, called the "noble offering" or "glorious gift" (*dpal 'bul*) is performed by the Nechung oracle while possessed by Pehar.[214]

LIBERATION DANCES COMPARED

carrying	*daggers/stabbing*	*swords/cutting*	*place*	*source*
skeletons[a]	black hat/lama	*sgrol ging*	Solu-Khumbu	Kohn
"attendants"	black hat (rite)	stag[b]	E. Tibet	Combe
"a lama"	?	Yama	Hemis	—
—	black hat, 8 *drag gshed*	black hat	'Gye mur	Pott
skeletons[c]	black hat	black hat?	Potala	[d]
skeletons	—	stag	Choni (Co ni)	Rock
Yama	Yama (rite)	stag	Mi nyag	Stein
atsaras	—	Yama	Kumbum	Tafel
skeletons	Yama	stag	Mongolia	Lessing
lamas		Yama ("killing")	Inner Mongolia	Haslund-Chr.
skeletons	—	—	Thimpu	Davis

[a] In Mani Rimdu, the skeletons bear a *lingka* of cloth suspended from a rope. The dough effigy, where used, is not brought out theatrically, but is kept out of sight beneath the courtyard altar until needed.

[b] It should be noted that after the *lingka* is cut up, the previous dancers, seemingly Vajrakīla and his entourage and/or the black-hat dancers, return. Then, "Each member of this group was given a piece of the dough effigy, which he held a while, throwing it eventually into one of the four main directions." Nebesky-Wojkowitz, *Tibetan Religious Dances*, 1976: 19.

[c] The skeletons "wheel around" the *lingka*. It is unclear how it gets on stage. Nebesky-Wojkowitz, Ibid., 1976: 44.

[d] From various sources, see Nebesky-Wojkowitz, Ibid., 1976: 43, n. 84. For other references, see my note on the Liberation Dance in note 77.

DANCE THIRTEEN—THE MAGIC WEAPON DANCE

Like the Overture, the Magic Weapon Dance originated at Mindroling. The dance takes its name from the magic weapon the dancers employ. The magic weapon here is a torma. Its name, *zor*, is related to the Tibetan word for sickle. There are many different kinds of *zor*, and rituals to make use of them. In Mani Rimdu, the *zor* is a red four inch tall pyramid of dough with three sides edged with a white motif of flames.

The *zor* is a form of the contract torma used each day in the Lord of the Dance rituals. In this ritual, the torma begins as a representation of the contract between Padmasambhava and the "great and haughty gods of Tibet," and ends as a magic weapon that rights the spiritually topsy-turvy condition of the world. The ritual content of the dance is the same as in the daily ritual—Giving the Contact Torma.[215] Only the form of the torma changes. In the daily ritual, the contract torma form is used, in the dance, the magic weapon. As in the daily ritual, after the Magic Weapon Dance, a torma is offered to the Steadfast Women. This offering however, is not acted out by the dancers.

The first figures to enter the courtyard are two Magicians. They dance at the north end and then circle the courtyard making a *mudrā*. The *mudrā* consists of touching the backs of the hands together, fingers bent in, knuckles touching, then flinging the hands outward.[216] There are two such sequences, separated by pauses in the music and movement.

During one of the pauses, a monk hands them a magic weapon torma. The dancers stand with hands on hips as the liturgy is recited on the dais:[217]

> Hūṁ! Turn back the enemies and obstructions of ignorance and egoism
> Compassed by appearing and existing!
> O magic torma weapon of the play of wisdom,
> Turn the vessel of the world into a divine palace!
> Sentient beings, born and transient, to Buddhahood!
> Suffering to the realm of bliss!
> Saṁsāra to the realm of nirvāṇa!
> Turn the five poisonous passions into the five wisdoms!
> The five father aggregates into the five mother elements!
> Saṁsāra to the element of nirvāṇa!
> Everything into primordial purity! [UB 36b4]

The music resumes and the magicians carry out in a literal way what the stage directions in the *Manual* have urged them to do each day. They take the torma from the altar and "hurl it as a weapon."[218]

Another pair of dancers enters wearing the costumes of the Black Men. The Counting Book (*'Chams gyi tho dge*) calls these figures messengers (*pho nya*). The Magicians dance with them, first at the north side of the courtyard. The dancers move a quarter circle clockwise around the courtyard, and then a quarter circle counterclockwise. This sequence is repeated twice.

The dancers line up by pairs, the Magicians to the north and the Black Men to the south. As the Magicians dance, the Black Men stand still. The Magicians exit, and then in turn the Black Men dance out.

The Magic Weapon Dance is a cousin to another of the most common Tibetan dances—and major rituals—the *gtor rgyab*.[219] This ceremony typically employs several magic weapons and other tormas and culminates in their cremation. *Zor 'chams* as such are also known at other monasteries. In Bhutan, they are counted as one of the major forms of *'chams*.[220]

Thanks to the commentary, we have precise instructions on the view that should be taken during the magic weapon ritual:

> Transform the Guardians' tormas into the torma weapon of the play of wisdom (*ye shes*), then, with an attitude of understanding the non-duality of saṁsāra and nirvāṇa, hurl it on top of the dualism that is characterized by the view of self.[221]

With perfect Buddhist orthodoxy, the *zor* is a weapon turned inward against the enemy within the mind—the false view of self that separates sentient beings from Buddhahood.

DANCE FOURTEEN—THE ENSEMBLE

At Chiwong, the Ensemble (*'chams sna*) consists of six Magicians and two dancers in the costumes of the "Black Men."[222] At Thami, four dancers wearing protector masks are also present. According to Tengpoche Rinpoche, if there are enough dancers, all of the characters should reappear at this time. If there are not, half will suffice.[223] At Rongphu, there were twenty-two dancers.[224]

The purpose of the Ensemble is the ritual known in the *Manual* as the "Horse Dance" and the hook *mudrā* that goes along with it. The rite invokes Hayagrīva, the spirit of the magic dagger, the suppressor of obstructive forces. As we saw during the site rituals on Day One, the "Horse Dance" is an exultant celebration around the grave-like prison of the *lingka*—the triangular pit.

The dancers enter one at a time, the Magicians in the lead. Once they are all present, the music stops and they stand as the liturgy is recited.[225]

The music resumes and the monks make their *mudrā* and dance. They reenact the ceremony of the first day, but now in the splendid costumes of the dance. They form a circle in the center of the courtyard, and with arms crossed and hands in the hook gesture, lock one to another by their little fingers. They close on the central pole and then disperse outward. After a few moments of dancing, they form two lines and exit by pairs.

Trulshik Rinpoche explains that the Enemies and Obstructors have been stabbed and burned, and now must be suppressed. When (if ever) they generate the *bodhicitta*, the aspiration to enlightenment for the sake of all sentient beings, they will be allowed to emerge from their prison.

As we have seen before, the Horse Dance invokes the foundation of the *maṇḍala* of the universe and presses down on the "those that have been imagined" with the weight of the world mountain. In the Site Ritual, the dancers surround the burial pit. Now, the focal point of the Horse Dance is the central pole, a few yards away. The mythological geography, however is identical. The central pole is the spine of the world, the spine of the world mountain which the Horse Dance places over the pit. The Ensemble realigns the universe and returns order to the world.

In one way, this order is conceived in quite ancient terms. The baleful spirits, the "spying" or wandering ghosts are put back in the underworld where they belong, with nothing less than the entire world mountain to prevent their escape. The hierarchy of the universe is restored.

It is not just the weight of the world, however, that seals the enemy in, but the very principal of an orderly universe. The crossed *vajra* (and the circle of dance) also evoke tantric cosmology—the *maṇḍala*—the world put back into the divine order that is its birthright. In the divine world of the *maṇḍala*, demons and passions—the objects to be suppressed—the allotropes of "those who are imagined," are totally transformed. In the ordered world of the *maṇḍala* all beings are divine; all thought forms, primordial wisdom.

FIFTEEN—THE AUSPICIOUS OMENS

If the Music Dance is the overture to the Mani Rimdu *'chams*, the Auspicious Omens is its coda. Like the Music Dance, it figures in the traditional lists of dances; like the Music Dance, it is not really a dance in the full sense of the word.

The Auspicious Omens is a recitation of the short "Auspicious Omens" normally recited toward the end of each day's session:

> Oṁ! May it come! The boon of the highest blessing—
> The good fortune of the Lama, the head of the hundred families!
> May it come! The rain of true achievement—the good fortune
> Of the heavenly host of the peaceful and wrathful tutelaries!
> May it come! The good fortune of the Sky Walkers—
> The heroes whose actions succeed without fail!

May it come! All the success ever imagined!
The good fortune of the highest virtue and goodness![226]

As in the daily version of the auspicious recitation, the monks wear their ceremonial hats for the occasion. The orchestra plays and an assistant distributes spoonsful of offering liquid from a glass on the altar and pinches of *tsampa*. The *tsampa* is thrown in the air as part of the ceremony. When *tsampa* is thrown out of doors, it is said to represent erasing the tracks of the "black ones," the forces of evil, from the ground.[227]

When the prayers draw to a close, the monks pack up and leave without any further ceremony. It is now ten o'clock at night and most of the spectators, who have been trickling out during the past several dances, are already gone.

After the dances are over, it is the custom at Thami and Tengpoche for the villagers to gather in the monastery courtyard. There they form a large circle and do Sherpa folk dances to the accompaniment of their own voices. That evening, the monastery is buying the beer and monks navigate the circle of dancers with a large bucket of *chang*. They ply their wares with the good humored insistence that is the hallmark of Sherpa and Tibetan hospitality. Even were it to be given as one, "no" would not be taken for an answer. The merriment lasts far into night.

At Chiwong, at least in the 1980s, this custom did not prevail. Instead, the public retired to the tea shops at the edge of the monastery compound. There the songs and dances are more likely to be Nepali—or of late, disco—than Sherpa, but the spirits of the celebrants are equally high.

EXTRACURRICULAR ACTIVITIES

Since the evening of the twelfth day, hostelers and tea shop concessionaires have set up shop on the monastery grounds. At Thami, as was the case previously at Chiwong, these entrepreneurs must content themselves with tents and tarpaulins for shelter. Since 1980, there has been a large permanent structure at Chiwong to accommodate them, consisting of a dozen or so partially open wooden stalls built around a central courtyard.

As a rule, each stall is occupied by the same tenant year after year. Most of these concessionaires come from nearby villages. Many are professional tea shop owners, local men of prominence, or have family contacts to the monastery. One, for example, is from a branch of the family that built Chiwong. Another is related to one of the monastery's novices. Some of the tenants belong to more than one category.

The tea shops are a gathering place throughout the festival. People come for a break in the dances, to drink tea, a glass of *chang*, or to eat noodle soup (*tukpa*) or dumplings (*mo mo*), two foods that Sherpas rarely eat at home, but are a special treat at festivals and bazaars. Each night, but especially the night of the masked dance, people will gather here to sing and dance.

One of Mani Rimdu's myriad functions is as a place for young men and women to meet. A tea shop may become the home of a dance party where, under the watchful eye of elder kinswomen, young men and women can display their bravado and grace through dance. As is traditional, men dance with men and women with women, although in a show of brave modernity, a mixed couple may take to the floor, to a farrago of giggling.

For some in Solu-Khumbu, drinking to excess is part of the pleasure of a large public gathering. Despite its religious purpose, Mani Rimdu is no exception. If we compare the drunkenness at Mani Rimdu to the drunkenness of a bazaar, where the ground may be littered with unconscious men at the close of the business day, it is relatively mild.

Occasionally, after a night of drinking, a shouting match will break out in the tea shop courtyard, or more rarely, a fight. Onlookers invariably intercede to separate and mollify the combatants, who are nearly always young males. Often no real resolution is reached, and the quarrel may flare up again later in the evening or the next day. As with the drunkenness to which it is related, fewer conflicts seem to arise at Mani Rimdu than at a typical bazaar.

It has already been noted that Trulshik Rinpoche considers the dances of Mani Rimdu to be relatively unimportant.[228] To many people in Solu-Khumbu, however, they are the reason for attending the festival. They watch the dances with amazement, amusement or boredom. Sometimes they do not watch them at all. Many members of a Mani Rimdu audience claim to receive a spiritual value, either directly or indirectly from the dances. Some feel they are beneficial simply because they are a religious event. Others, feel that they are educational, that they prepare one for death by introducing one to the appearance and manner of the beings one will meet in the intermediate state. This is not just true of Mani Rimdu. It was noted by researchers as early as Bleichsteiner in 1937.

> But, [the dances] also have a practical interest for the spectators. . . . Demoniacal protective divinities especially surge through the bardo, among the terrible visions. One of the goals of cultural dances consists in making them known to believers, to familiarize them with their physiognomy, so that, in the intermediate state they do not lose heart when faced by their saviors.[229]

18

Day Sixteen: Burnt Offering, Releasing the Borders, Erasing the Sand

By early morning on the sixteenth day, the greater part of the spectators have left Chiwong. The monks who perform the ritual, of course, and the family of the monastery's founder remain. A few of the concessionaires who have serviced the festival may not be quite ready to depart and there are always stragglers.

After the hullabaloo of the last few days, the courtyard, strangely empty, echoes to every footfall. The monks, exhausted from their marathon performance, seem pensive. A calm atmosphere prevails.

The majority of the day's ceremonies are performed with few if any spectators present. As usual, there are rituals for Lord of the Dance and for the Protectors of Religion. The day's main events though are the Burnt Offering, Releasing the Borders and Erasing the Sand Maṇḍala.

The version of the daily ritual done in the chapel follows the general pattern of the other days: the preliminary and actual practices from the *Manual*, the Protector rituals, the feast and so on. Since the pills and even the flasks have been left behind, the recitations that infuse them with divine power are not done. The self-administered empowerment of other days is also skipped and the schedule of Protectors curtailed.[1]

The sixteenth day is characterized by continual shiftings of venue, and one way to divide the action is by where it takes place. Some rituals are indoors in the chapel. Others, outdoors in the courtyard or on the path that circumambulates the chapel. Before we describe the days events, it is useful to gain an overview.[2]

I Outdoor—courtyard:

1. Site Ritual for Burnt Offering *maṇḍala*. (BO 3.3–3b6)
   Making the Burnt Offering sand *maṇḍala*.

II Indoor—chapel (daily rituals):

2a. The Lord of the Dance *Manual* is performed as usual from the two introductory Prayers up to the Confession (f. 8.3). At this point a number of minor elisions are made:
— General Confession (*spyi bshags*) is skipped
— In the Shower of Blessings (f 8.4) only one measure of music is needed instead of the usual three. It is unnecessary to use the beckoning scarf (*yab dar).*
— Outer Offering (f 12b5–15.5) not needed.
— Flask Recitation *(bum 'dzab)* (f 19b3–20.2) not needed.
— No Pill Recitation.
3. Protector rituals of three major deities from the *Playful Ocean*, two of the Followers, and two sets of local deities are done: Four-faced One, Great God, Cemetery Grandmother; Medicine Ladies and Good Diamond; and the *Abridged Prayer*[3] and Tashi Palchen. The progression of these rituals is as follows:
— *Playful Ocean* from the beginning, Blessing the Offerings (*mchod rdzas byin gyis rlobs pa*) and the General Invitation from the *Guardians of the Word*,[4] up to and including:
— The Recitation *(bzlas pa)*
2b. The monks then return to the Lord of the Dance *Manual* to perform the Feast (*tshogs*) and selected rituals associated with it:
— Blessing the Propitiation Substances (*skong rdzas byin rlabs*)
— Propitiation of Four-Faced One, Great God, and Cemetery Grandmother. During this time Enjoying the Feast (*tshogs la rol*) is recited.
— Confessions (*bshags pa*): Great God's; the Confession from Scripture (*gzhung gi bshags pa*).
— Request to Act (*phrin las gsol ba*): Four-Faced One's; Great God's; and the Request from Scripture (*gzhung gi phrin las*, i.e. the *phrin las gsol ba dngos*).
— Feeding the Torma (*gtor ma stob*). Gift Torma (*'bul gtor*)[5] and Followers Torma (*rjes 'brang*) are removed from chapel.[6]
— *Playful Ocean* Follow-up Rituals (*rjes chog*)
4. *Three-Part Torma* (*cha gsum*).[7]
2c. *Union of the Blissful Manual*, continued, including:
— Remains of the Feast (*tshogs gyi lhag ma*)

— Exhortation (*bskul ba*)
— Contract Torma (*chad tho*)
— Steadfast Women Torma (*brTan ma*)
— Horse Dance (*rta bro*)

III Outdoor—courtyard:

5. Burnt Offering ritual itself (BO 4.3–8.2)

IV Indoor—chapel (daily rituals, continued):

2d. Conclusion (*rjes kyi bya ba*) of the Lord of the Dance *Manual*, continued:
— The Offering and Praise (*mchod bstod*) beginning "Oṁ! The assortment of offerings enjoyed by Samantabhadra . . ."[8]
— Confessing Fault (*nongs bshags*) (UB 38.3)
— Hundred Syllable mantra of Vajrasattva (*yig brgya*) (3X)
— The Recitation for Remaining Firm (*brtan bzhugs kyi dzab*, i.e. the emended *gshegs gsol*)[9]
— Retraction Sequence (*bsdu rim*)
— Rising as the God (*lhar ldang*)
— The *maṇi*-sound, i.e., a final recitation of the Lord of the Dance mantra

V Outdoor—circumambulatory path:

6. Releasing the Borders (*mtha' sgrol*)
7. Clearing the Door (*sgo byang*)

VI Indoor—*maṇḍala:*

8. Gathering the Magic Daggers (*phur bu bsdu*)
9. Erasing the Sand (*rdul tshon bsubs*)
10. Lord of the Dance Dedicatory Prayer (UB 34b6)
11. Lord of the Dance Auspicious Omens (UB 39b2)

BURNT OFFERING

The Burnt Offering or *homavidhi* is among the oldest rites in South Asia for which we have literary evidence. Found in the Veda, it is a basic ritual of orthodox Hinduism. It is also performed by Newar *Vajrācārya*, and is likely to have long been a feature of Buddhist tantracism.[10] The Tibetan Burnt Offering has been described in some detail by Lessing, Beyer and others. We will concentrate here on the form it takes in Mani Rimdu.[11]

Like the other rituals of Mani Rimdu, the Burnt Offering centers around the deity Union of the Blissful / Lord of the Dance / Great Compassion. The offering has is own text, *The Profound Path Union of the Blissful Burnt Offering Rite*, entitled *"Quickly Achieving the Desired Goal"* (BO).

The text offers five alternative rituals. They correspond to the usual four actions (*las bzhi*) of tantric ritual with the addition of a "Supreme Burnt Offering" (*mchog gi sbyin sreg*). Among these, the Mani Rimdu ceremony is a peaceful or pacifying Burnt Offering.

According to the ritual text, the peaceful Burnt Offering has numerous benefits:

> In general, it is for all sentient beings in the three worlds. Pacification is done principally from the point of view of human beings; the harmful and the sinful, the poor, those who have wrong views, the arrogant, and so on, down to the spirits of disease, and so on. [BO 2b4]

The text states that a peaceful offering should occur on "the first day of the waxing moon."[12] The way that the festival is scheduled at Chiwong this requirement is fulfilled. Thami's ritual cycle is shorter and the ceremony falls a few days short, on the twelfth day of the Tibetan month. As this is the date that the *Precious Lamp* suggests for a Burnt Offering, it is possible that Thami derived its custom from that text. Once accepted, this assumption leads us to the conclusion that Thami's abbreviated schedule as a whole may be a result of an attempt to reconcile the festival with the requirement of the commentary.[13]

As usual for a major ritual undertaking, the text specifies that a Site Ritual first be performed. The officiant, assuming the awe-inspiring form of Hayagrīva, apologizes to the inhabitants of the land about to be used. For this purpose, a small white torma (*dkar gtor*) is prepared and set on a tripod. The torma is blessed with a sprinkling of flask water and the recitation of the horse mantra dedicated to Lord of the Dance's fierce manifestation, Hayagrīva.[14]

The actual request for the land is as follows,

> Hūṁ! Forgive us, O legions of lords of the soil, of gods and of serpents and your generals!
> Take the offering torma we have blessed and dedicated!
> We take this land, that we may do fearful deeds.
> We please you with what delights you—please give it to us! [3b2]

A stick of incense is put in the back of the torma. The horse mantra is recited,[15] followed by, "Oṁ āḥ hūṁ hana hana krota hūṁ phaṭ." Then, *vajra* in hand, the officiant touches the ground to seal the bargain.[16] The torma is removed and the ritual concludes. The entire proceeding takes but three minutes.

Sometime in the spacious and loosely structured morning, work on a sand *maṇḍala* for the Burnt Offering will begin. The first step is to construct the hearth on which it will be drawn. For this purpose, earth is piled on the courtyard floor. Using planks as a mold and rope or stones as buttresses, the earth is pressed into a square about eight inches high and a foot and a half on a side, or as the text says "one cubit (*khru*) across and half a cubit high."[17] Before the ceremony begins, this frame will be removed.

The principal Mani Rimdu *maṇḍala* inside the chapel is on a wooden table which has the outline of the *maṇḍala* drawn permanently, if faintly, on it. The much smaller and simpler geometry of the Burnt Offering *maṇḍala* must be laid out afresh every year with compasses and measuring strings.

The text indicates specific proportions for the *maṇḍala*, and these are followed although the measurements are taken in a loose and approximate way. This casual approach extends to the sand painting itself. Lines are drawn quickly and broadly, and areas colored loosely. At Thubten Chöling, there is a one-page manuscript that illustrates all four varieties of sand *maṇḍala* for the Lord of the Dance Burnt Offering. Chiwong does not possess a copy, and, drawn from memory, the *maṇḍala* there varies considerably from year to year. The *Precious Lamp* also describes the *maṇḍala* in some detail, although it lacks illustrations.

Sometime during the day, the canopy is removed from the courtyard and a miscellany of other preparations for the special ceremony set under way. Among these are seating arrangements for the participants. The lama's throne is erected on the west side of the courtyard. It is adorned for the occasion with a drawing of the seven seas and seven mountains marked with the syllable "baṁ."[18] Tables for the offerings are placed nearby. Along the south end of the courtyard, benches and tables are set out for the monks.

On the east side, facing the lama across the hearth, the monastery honors the family of its founder with a bank of comfortable seats. Offering seats at the hearth is an important feature of Sherpa etiquette, and seating arrangements a way of reaffirming status within the community.[19] Throughout the festival special seating has been arranged for the family of the patron. On the day of empowerment, they are on the dais before the lama's throne. During the dance, they are front row center in the balcony with a private kitchen nearby so that they can provide themselves with tea and snacks.[20]

In the present arrangement, the lama is as always, both literally and figuratively on top of the heap. From there on, however, the status flow is ambiguous and arguably intentionally so. In Sherpa seating arrangements, status usually flows clockwise. The host is seated closest to the fire, the highest status guest to his left and so on down the line. This corresponds to a general Tibetan practice of positioning: to honor someone (or something), you place it to your right,[21] hence such customs as the clockwise circumambulation of *stūpas* and other sacred spots.

In the seating arrangement observed in the 1980s, the elements of the status pattern were separated and diffused. The first important factor, propinquity to the highest status person (the lama) was ceded to the monks. The second, clockwise orientation to him, was granted to the patrons. Or, looked at in a different way, the patrons stared across the fire at the lama, coequal horizontally but appropriately lower in elevation. By 1993, the positions had changed somewhat. The lama and monks retained their places. The patron's family now sat facing the monks. This position corresponds to the second and marginally lower status row of monks found inside the temple, making them, in effect, somewhat junior monks, an interesting turn, given their family name: Lama.

If the flow of the hierarchy is ambiguous, its presence is certainly not. Woe betide the Sherpa who in error sits in the patron's rank. He will be removed, politely to be sure, but firmly; the forces of religion and society united against him.[22] Sitting in the patron's seats when they are unoccupied, however, is not taboo as is sitting in the lama's throne.

The metaphor of seating is one more reminder of the strong relationship between the monastery and the family of its founder. During the public festival, a portrait of Sangyay Lama has always been placed in the courtyard rafters on an equal level with those of the royal family of Nepal. The Lama clan has traditionally perceived Chiwong as a "private monastery" belonging to their family. This perception is not universally shared, although it has been willingly or grudgingly ceded to one extent or another by a wider circle.[23] The descendants of the founder continue to be important patrons of Chiwong, and at the monastery it is certainly felt that respect and honor are due to them.

As preparations for the Burnt Offering continue, a pyre of split wood is built on top of the *maṇḍala*. The wood is arranged in neat layers, the ends of one stick resting crosswise on two below it, somewhat in the manner of a log cabin. At Thami, where firewood is scarce, yak dung is used instead. For the peaceful Burnt Offering used at Mani Rimdu, the pyre should be circular in shape, although most years it more resembles a six-pointed star. The triangle and star, in theory, are reserved for the fierce Burnt Offering

The monks ready the offerings to be burned. Branches of "milk-wood" (*'o ma shing*, *yam shing;* Ssk. *samidh*), a special wood with a smooth bark are cut in a special way—in twelve finger-width lengths with the ends cut "in the four directions" so that they resemble a radish rose.[24] A pair of fire-tormas (*me gtor*) are made. Grain, biscuits, *kuśa*-grass, strips of cloth and other offerings are put in bowls. A pot of ghee is warmed.

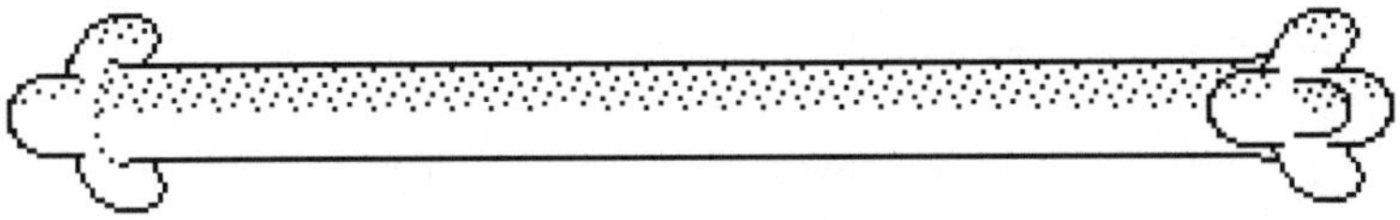

Stick with Ends Cut in the Four Directions

In simpler Burnt Offering ceremonies, the lama sits directly before the fire and consigns the offerings to the flames with his own hands. In such ceremonies, a fire wall is built between the lama's throne and the hearth.[25] In the Mani Rimdu ritual, the lama sits at a distance from the hearth and an assistant—the text calls him a fire-servant (*me g.yog*)—conveys the offerings from the lama to the fire.

The indoor rituals start sometime in late morning or early afternoon and last about one-and-one-half hours. After a short break, the monks assemble outside for the actual Burnt Offering.

The offering begins with a prayer. Then, the officiating lama puts on the "five families" crown and the associated regalia.[26]

The monks visualize the hearth in its pure form—

> Out of the empty realm, there appears before me a peaceful hearth space, the nature of moon [and] water [and] crystal, white and round of edge, radiant with white light. [4b4]

The hearth is sprinkled with holy water from the flask, and lit using a fire starter in the shape of a small butter lamp made of dough.

The ritual proceeds according to the text. The first deity worshipped Agni, the Vedic god of fire. Like other forms of Agni, he rides upon a goat. Here, however, he is in a peaceful aspect and his color is white rather than the usual red.[27] He is "in the guise of an ṛṣi," one of the divine sages who composed the Vedas.[28]

The text specifies the offerings: "ghee; firewood a span long that comes from the top of a milk-fruit tree, or wood smeared with scent, or rubbed with butter—whatever can be properly counted; black sesame; incense of white sandalwood, and so forth; sāl gum; white flowers, and so forth" [4.3]. These are supplemented with a variety of grains, grasses, and even store bought biscuits.

Several sets of offerings are burned in this phase of the ritual, in a complicated pattern of sevens and threes. The lama and assistant count out the offerings, often audibly. Solid offerings are transferred by hand from their trays to the plate that will carry them to the fire. The melted butter is doled out using a pair of ladles.[29] The smaller simpler ladle (*dgang gzar*) is used to fill the larger more symbolically complex ladle (*blug gzar*).

As in other Buddhist Burnt Offerings, after the offerings to the "mundane Fire God," a set of Buddhist deities is worshipped. This "transcendental Fire God" is Lord of the Dance accompanied by his entourage.

Throughout the festival, these deities have dwelt in the sand *maṇḍala* in the center of the chapel. Now their Wisdom Beings (*ye shes pa*, *jñānasattva*) must be brought from the *maṇḍala* to the courtyard to participate in the Burnt Offering.

The divine *déménagement* is done with appropriate pomp, a grand procession carrying the caravan of the gods. Several methods of accomplishing the transfer are known. Pinches of sand may be taken from the divine seats, or the reflection of the deities may be captured in mirror and carried outside in a miniature pavilion.[30] In Mani Rimdu, the device used is a "bouquet" or "configuration" (*tshom bu*).

Thami Rinpoche with Burnt Offering "bouquet," Thami 1983.

The bouquet is assembled on the base of a *maṇḍala* offering plate. It consists of a group of small white cones of dough, which correspond in number and position to the gods of the *maṇḍala*. The lama prepares the bouquet a few days in advance.[31]

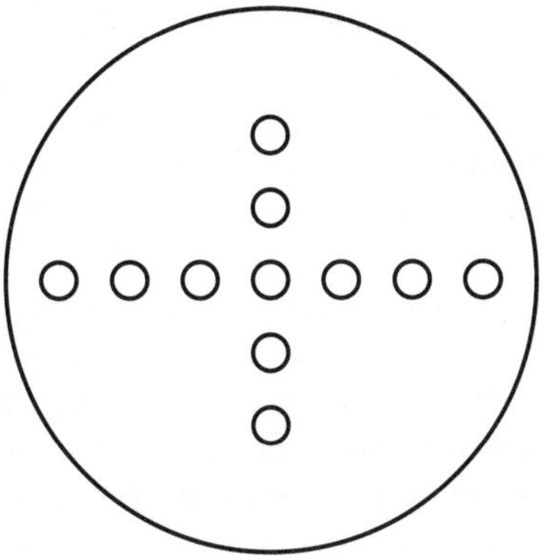

Bouquet, Seen from Above. Thami, 1983.

Once the monks have visualized the Lord of the Dance and his entourage in the fire, the bouquet is brought in. The procession, conches and oboes playing and incense burning, circumambulates the fire three times before it deposits the bouquet on the lama's table. A pair of pennants (*ba dan*) and a pair of victory banners (*rgyal mtshan*) accompany the bouquet on its tray. They are placed at the front and back of the side altar respectively.[32]

Saying the mantra of one of the gods, the lama breaks off the top of the corresponding cone and hands it to his assistant. The assistant brings it to the fire where the assembly has visualized the Pledge Beings. He tosses it in as he circles and returns immediately to the lama for the next. In this way, each Wisdom Being in turn is united with his visualized counterpart.

The bouquet is not mentioned in the *Burnt Offering* text, but in the *Precious Lamp*. This still attests, however, that it is a Mindroling practice rather than local innovation. Its absence from the *Burnt Offering* text might suggest that the custom is of a later date or perhaps came to Mindroling from a different source. Given Mindroling's tendency to separate elements of a ritual for the sake of secrecy, however, it is difficult to draw even such a small conclusion with much certainty.

Once the Wisdom Beings are in place, they are presented with a sequence of offerings similar to those for the mundane Fire God. In the midst of the offerings, we find a custom mentioned neither in the Burnt Offering text nor in the commentaries. A set of small scraps of paper are given to the lama. Each slip bears the name of someone who has died in the last year. The lama reads the names in silence, and then, using the large ladle transfers them to a plate already piled with other offerings. The assistant consigns them to the flames in the usual manner.

Before the worship of the transcendental fire-god concludes, one of the fire tormas is placed in the pyre. Thus placated, the assembly requests him to "perform the act of pacification" and to "cause us quickly to obtain Buddhahood." Each monk then visualizes that:

> Having thus made the request, the host of gods radiate a stainless light, like moon-beams from their bodies. It completely purifies all my spirits of sickness, sins and obscurations. [7b3]

They recite the Hundred Syllable Mantra of Vajrasattva and make a confession. The transcendental deities are recalled to the bouquet—half of each cone of dough has been left on the plate to receive them—and returned in procession to the indoor *maṇḍala* along with the banners and pennants.

Further offerings are made to the mundane fire-god, including the second fire torma, and he is requested to grant the customary boons.[33]

> Take this torma, worshipfully offered!
> Obtain for us yogis and our entourage:
> Health, life, dominion,
>
> And glory, fame and good fortune—
> Every enjoyment, vast and complete!
> And then bestow upon us true achievement
> Of the acts of pacification, extension and the rest!
>
> Guard us, O Sworn Ones!
> Be a friend who aids all true achievement!
> Make naught of untimely death and diseases
> And Malignancies and Obstructors!
>
> Make naught of bad dreams
> And bad signs and bad deeds!
> Make the earth pleasant, the crops good,
> The grain grow and the cattle grow!
>
> Fulfill all the desires in our hearts,
> The wellspring of everything virtuous and good! [PO 5b4]

The lama removes his crown and the entire assembly puts on ceremonial hats for the auspicious recitation. As instructed by the text, the assistant pours a glass of milk in a circle on the hearth to symbolically put out the fire.[34] The empty utensils and plates are passed over the flames. The lama removes his hat and the concluding prayers draw to an end. The monks rise, and without ceremony, mount the stairs and enter the assembly hall.

At one point or another in the latter sections of the offering, the monastery serves food to people as well as to gods. Formerly, monks, visiting clergy, and the patron's family were the only recipients, although more recently the few outsiders in the courtyard have also been served. The elders of the family are served in a style that rivals the treatment due to the lama. Their food is abundant and neatly arranged on their plates; their teacups rest in stemmed silver stands.

When the fire has died down, the villagers come to collect the coals and ashes. Having been the residence of the gods they carry a blessing, and in the Himalayas are sometimes placed beneath the foundations of houses.

Before the fire cools, the monks return to the chapel, where they continue the concluding segments of the Lord of the Dance rituals from where they left off before the Burnt Offering.

Once more it is time for "Taking the True Achievement."[35] The monastic orchestra begins to play as the bouquet is removed from the north side of the *maṇḍala* and given to the lama. He touches it to his head. He then breaks the remains of each cone, first off the plate and then into small pieces. He replaces the broken bouquet on the tray and puts a pinch of dough on his assistant's head. The assistant circles the chapel, placing a bit of the bouquet on each monk's head.

When they finish, the monks rise and don their ceremonial hats. The lama also rises and puts on his mitre and yellow *vinaya* robe. Still reciting Lord of the Dance's mantra, they leave the chapel to loosen the cordon of protection that they established on Day One.

RELEASING THE BORDERS—ERASING THE SAND

Considering the often intentionally obscure cast of Mindroling's commentarial literature, Dharmaśri's *Notes on the Practice of the Entire Accomplishment Worship of Great Compassion*, although typically incomplete, does give a fairly clear description of Releasing the Border (*mtha' sgrol*) and the rituals that follow it.[36] When I asked for a text of those rituals, the relevant passages of Dharmaśri's commentary were duly copied. The following description is based on the performance of the ritual at Chiwong, expanded with reference to Dharmaśri's text.

The first act is to circumambulate the monastery and free the borders, or release the Kings of the Four Directions who were set to guard the place of religious practice. As might be expected, in many ways the ritual mirrors the one it undoes. Similar trays of offerings are carried, and music is played in each direction. In each of the four directions, the image is sprinkled, an offering left and the Guardian King set to his "appointed task." Then, the victory banner that was set out for him is removed, and the procession proceeds to the next location. As they move from place to place, they are never silent. They recite Lord of the Dance's mantra continually.

When the procession reaches the door, a monk removes the shoulder blade icon placed there on the first day. The procession reenters the chapel and all but the lama and his assistants take their seats.

While the procession was busy outside, others dismantled the gazebo that encloses the sand *maṇḍala*, taking care not to disturb the delicate painting. The roof tiers and columns, even the foundation that supported the sand-painted tabletop have been put aside. The tabletop now lies directly on the ground.

The offerings have been taken from the surface of the *maṇḍala* and the magic daggers moved to its edge. The daggers, however, still maintain their relative positions symbolic of the ten directions.

The lama and assembly recite the "Four Hūṁ Mantra" over and over in unison: "oṁ vajra kīlaya utkīlāya sarvakīlā vajradharaṇa ajñāvaya hūṁ hūṁ hūṁ hūṁ phaṭ hoḥ."[37] As they recite, the lama removes the daggers, circling clockwise to take them from the intermediate directions, and counterclockwise for the cardinal directions.[38] He sprinkles the tips of the spikes and the spike stands with milk.

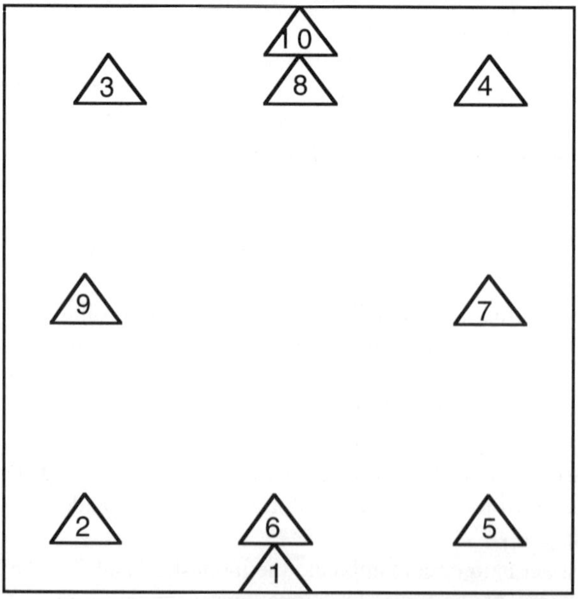

Order for Removing the Magic Daggers, According to TCU

Now the time has come to gather the residual power from the gods' seats and to erase the *maṇḍala*. The oboes play the stuttering notes that launch the orchestral accompaniment for the acts that follow. With a look of intense concentration, the lama takes a pinch of sand from each position and places it on his head. The words of the mantra he recites mean "Oṁ! The syllable A is first, because of the primordial non-arising of events. Oṁ āḥ hūṁ phaṭ svāhā."[39] Then, he places the point of his *vajra* in the sand in one corner and slices through the painting. His *vajra* cuts a spiral that loops inward though the doorways and the lotus petals, finally cutting to the very heart of the *maṇḍala*.

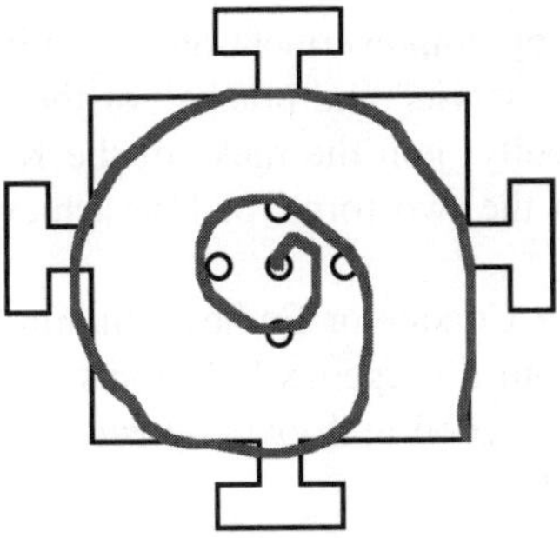

Reciting "Oṁ! The syllable A is first . . ."

When he is finished, the lama steps back. There is a moment's lull; all present—these include laymen some years—wait. Then, following the lama's gesture like an orchestra its conductor, the others descend on the *maṇḍala* and sweep it away with their hands. In a single minute, the magnificent painting born of a week's patient labor has returned to amorphous sand.

They sweep the sand into a pile and scoop it into a brass vase. When the vase will hold no more, a monk packages the remainder in slips of paper to distribute as a blessing. The vase is set on a tripod in the center of the barren *maṇḍala* table. The periphery is decorated with the usual series of eight offerings beginning with the "flower on the edge."

The rest of the monks return to their seats. The assembly puts on its hats, and the prayers continue. Dharmaśri's commentary instructs, "Do "[In] Heruka['s] Glorious . . ." and "[Consider me,] Lama, Tutelary . . .", the Dedicatory Prayer and the Auspicious Omens." This is the Dedicatory Prayer—

[May the turning of the feast circle]
In HERUKA's glorious city
[Make myself, others—all beings without exception,
Succeed in this single *maṇḍala*!]

Consider me, Lama, Tutelary and divine host!
I dedicate to great enlightenment
The virtue my striving has achieved here today,
Combined with the virtues I accrue and possess in the past, present and future! [38b6]

From now on, until I am in the heart of enlightenment,
May I be of good family, clear of mind, without egoism,
Very compassionate, and respectful to the Lama!
May I remain in the glorious diamond vehicle! [39.1]

May I be matured by empowerment and attentive to my vows!
May I complete the service and practice of the two sequence path,
And, without difficulty, join the ranks of the Knowledge Bearers!
May I easily attain the two forms of true achievement! [39.2]

It is certain that the Conqueror Endless Illumination
Prophesied birth from a gorgeous holy lotus
Into the Conqueror's good and joyous *maṇḍala.*
May I attain it! [39.4]

When I actually obtain there what has been prophesied,
May I, in a billion emanations,
Aid sentient beings greatly with my spiritual powers (*blo yi stobs*),
Wherever they may be in the ten directions! [39.5]

May the Conqueror's teaching spread far and wide!
May every goal its adherents explain be achieved!
May all contrary conditions be pacified for all who are born!
May they meet with spiritual and material wealth (*phun tshogs*)—whatever they wish! [39b1]

The oboists rise and play a recessional for the lama. The concluding series of the monastery's daily prayers drones on. Without the imposing structure of the *maṇḍala* house, the room seems empty.

19

Day Seventeen: Invitation to the River

According to Trulshik Rinpoche, the purpose of the Invitation to the River is simple:

> To pray to the king of the Serpent Spirits and his entourage that they take charge of the precious sand that has been blessed by the Tathāgatas; and to make offerings to them and put them to work at increasing and spreading perfect happiness and goodness in the world in general and in this place in particular.[1]

Consignment to the King of the Serpent Spirits is the common fate of *maṇḍala* sands. At Yung-ho-kung, Lessing tells us, they were placed in the "Well of the *Nāgas*," a structure in the temple's entrance courtyard that symbolized the "world ocean."[2] Dharmaśri's commentary advises us to seek out such places as:

> the bank of a river that flows continually without ever drying up, a pool in a river that descends to the ocean and a spring . . . .[3]

In Solu-Khumbu such places are typically small streams downhill from the monastery. At Chiwong, there is an ideal place for the purpose—a miniature waterfall in a tiny rivulet a half hour's walk down the mountainside.

This morning, there is no ritual in the chapel. The only preparation is to paint the white eight-petalled *maṇḍala* of the Serpent Spirits. This is done with colored powder on a *maṇḍala* plate. The plate is first coated with butter to keep the painting from being destroyed before it reaches the stream.[4]

The procession to the river starts in the late morning. It is even more elaborate than the usual form of this festive event. Before it gets under way, two monks mount the roof to play a booming chorus on the long horns. The sand is the star of this show, and the procession begins at the place where it now resides—the vase in the center of the *maṇḍala* table. The lama leads the way, holding a *vajra* and ringing a bell as he walks. Behind him is the Diamond Master of Chiwong. To him is entrusted the vase of sacred sand, covered with a folded altar cloth appliquéd with squares of silk. Three men carry flags on long poles. One monk bears the offering torma (*mchod gtor*) for the Serpent Spirits. Another holds a tray of offerings—the *maṇḍala* of the *nāgas*, the flask, a set of silver bowls and lamps for the offering set (*nyer spyod*), the lama's rice container and bowls of rice for the monks. Another monk carries a glass of milk. Milk is the offering par excellence for the serpents. When Trulshik Rinpoche officiated at a *klu* service in a nearby village, it was considered an auspicious sign when his mare gave milk when nearing the shrine.

For music, there is the obligatory oboe duet, and the Chant Leader of Thubten Chöling plays the cymbals. A monk with a censer follows along. Amidst all this, a villager leads the lama's gaily saddled horse. As usual in processions, the monks wear their ceremonial hats.

The procession stops at a place where the stream crosses their path. Above the trail, there is an embankment some two feet high. The stream forms a small pool atop the embankment before it falls to another small pool at the side of the trail. A flat stone lies over the waterfall, on which the assistant lays out the offerings, the torma, the sand, and the *nāga maṇḍala*.

The monks remove their hats, sit down on the embankment and begin to recite. Few have the manuscript for this ritual and they must look over each other's shoulders. They visualize an "ocean filled with jewels and flowers." "In the middle of it," they recite, "is a white eight-petalled lotus," symbolized by the miniature sand painting they have placed above the stream. In the center of the *maṇḍala*, the King of the Serpent Spirits and his consort appear. Around them on the petals are the eight lesser Serpent Spirits of his entourage. The assembly calls them all by name, praises and makes offerings to them. Finally, with the gift of the torma, the Serpent Spirits are enjoined with their task.

> Serpent King with your entourages—worship, as you have promised, these sands, precious in nature, recently blessed by the Tathāgatas, and increase and expand the perfect glory of pleasure and goodness, for the world at large and for this region in particular!

The monks put their hats back on for an auspicious recitation. They throw rice to represent a rain of flowers. After a few other small rituals, the monks send the Serpent King and his entourage back to their undersea paradise.

Sand in the River, Chiwong 1979

To a musical accompaniment, the offering torma is placed in the upper pool and the *nāga maṇḍala* washed off. Finally, the sand is carefully poured from its vase. The pool slowly turns a dark purplish hue as the water leaches the pigment from the sand. After a few moments, the colored water cascades over the falls, and begins its long journey to the sea.

The assistant rinses the vase and fills it with water. The lama washes his hands and face in the waterfall, paying careful attention to his eyes, ears, and mouth. Somewhat incongruously, given the ritual aspect of his ablutions, he uses a bar of soap, and for his teeth, a toothbrush. When he is finished, the senior monks follow suit, and after them, the others present.

The assembly makes its slow way uphill, the lama on his horse. There is no music until the procession is in sight of the monastery, then as the long horns greet them from above, the musicians begin to play.

With a green-leafed twig, the Diamond Master sprinkles water from the vase onto the path and the land surrounding it, to distribute good fortune. As he does so, the text instructs him to recite the mantra "Oṁ ruru sphuru jvala tiṣṭha siddhi locana sarva artha sādhani svāhā." He begins this auspicious cleansing at the stream and continues it even inside the assembly hall.

Back in their seats, the monks recite both dedications of merit, the ordinary one from the *Manual* and the longer one from the appendix, plus the long auspicious recitation.[5] After this, barring a few short interpolations, the rituals run as follows—

- the Auspicious Prayer from *Religious Practice* (RP f 180.6 ff);
- the Seven Branches (RP f 162.1–163.1).

At this point, it is the custom at Chiwong to thank Trulshik Rinpoche. To do this, a representative of Chiwong presents him with a *kha btags* reciting the "Maṇḍala Offering" from *Religious Practice* (RP f 21.3–22.4). The *maṇḍala* offering is an elaborate one, using the same set of symbolic objects used for that purpose during the public empowerment—the statue, book, and *stūpa*. Following the offering to the lama, a *kha btags* and a gift of money are distributed to all those who participated in the ritual. Even wood carriers and ethnographers are included in this largesse. The amount given is large by local standards. In 1983, the rank and file monks received ten rupees each.

The thanksgiving continues with the following special long-life prayer for the lama (*zhabs brtan*)—

The lama's body is a diamond body.
More beautiful to look at there is none.
Its qualities are inconceivable.
May the Lama's body endure!

The lama's speech is the song of Brahmā.
Its unstoppable lion's roar
Terrifies the Hindu deer.
May the Lama's speech endure!

The lama's mind is like the sky,
An empty realm—blissful, clear, and free from conceptualization.
It dwells within the three freedoms.[6]
May the Lama's mind endure![7]

This is followed by a small selection of prayers in general use in the monastery:

- the general long life prayer (*zhabs brtan spyi*) for all lamas from the Mindroling *Religious Practice* collection (RP f 90b2–91b2);
- a confession, also from *Religious Practice*[8]
- a series of short minor prayers so well-known and so thoroughly memorized that the Chant Leader of Thubten Chöling had no manuscripts for them.

The final act is a brief ritual in which the meditator visualizes that the lama in the form of Padmasaṁbhava bestows the four empowerments upon him.[9] That done, the lama stands to make his ceremonial exit. Without fanfare, the assembly follows him.

Mani Rimdu has come to an end.

Part Three

In Conclusion

20

Epilogue

In 1985, I returned to Solu-Khumbu with a film I had made about Mani Rimdu called *Lord of the Dance/Destroyer of Illusion.* It was the first time a film had been projected in any of these isolated villages and monasteries; indeed, our generator was the first electricity much of the district had seen. Our premiere was at Chiwong, late the night of the dances. About five hundred people huddled on the frigid flagstones of the courtyard. The projector whirred and the crowd fell silent.

The film begins in blackness, like the void out of which the visualizations of ritual arise. A small red point appears. As the camera pans downward, the point grows into a brilliant crimson triangle. It is not until the end of the shot that we understand what it is that we are seeing. The red triangle is Trulshik Rinpoche's hat; the first shot ends with his face filling the screen. When the audience, chilly and exhausted after their fourteen-hour theatrical marathon recognized that image, they broke into applause and cheers.

Until quite recently, Mani Rimdu and the village festival of Dumje were the Sherpas' only form of theater. They are still their most elaborate cultural performances. The heroic exploits of lamas have long been a part of Sherpa folklore. Every local Sherpa knows the story of how Serpa Dorjesangpo (Ser pa rdo rje bzang po) climbed the thousand-foot cliff to Chiwong using his magic dagger as a piton (Macdonald 1980). Today, despite changes on every hand, lamas are still the heroes of the Everest region.

FUNCTION

Mani Rimdu reaffirms this perception. The monks distribute magic pills to provide spiritual sustenance and physical well-being to all who take them. The fearsome deities with whom lama and monastery must deal are paraded before the public. The monks abandon their dull maroon uniforms and don the splendid brocades of tantric magicians, with *mudrās* and magic weapons matching the chaotic forces of the supernatural threat for threat. To the spectators, so great is the monks' mastery of the mysteries, that their mantras can prevent a sharp sword from penetrating human flesh. It is no wonder that when the need for discretionary ritual services is the greatest, at times of death or serious supernatural interference, the village turns to the monastery. This interdependence of the laity and the clergy, with the clergy providing spiritual services, and the laity, material support (*mchod yon*), is a key concept in Tibetan Buddhist societies.

The monk garbed as a magician is not just an outward symbol of a social relationship however. He expresses an inner truth. As we have seen, in the rituals themselves the monks constantly enact the role of spiritual hero: "I am Padmasambhava" they tell "the Great Stern One, God of the Plain" [Followers 12b1].[1]

This power to help others and to master enemies natural and supernatural, external and internal, comes from meditation on the deity. In tantra everything can be related to the deity. As 'Gyur med rdo rje, the fountainhead of the Lord of the Dance tradition stated,

> Whatever mantric practitioners do for their own sake and for the sake of others—all supreme and ordinary true achievements up to the subtle activities—is only using a particular ritual practice such as meditation and recitation to satisfy a god [BO 2.1].

But the self-creation of tantric yoga is more than simple instrumentality, although in the magical world view, the supernatural power of the divine is the most potent instrument possible. Through the ritual, the monks try to come into contact with the ultimate rightness of existence itself. Within the charmed circle of the ritual —

> The world outside becomes a divine palace.
> Its inhabitants are perfected as the gods of the circle.
> Sounds that resound are the mantra's own sound.
> The mind's memories and thoughts are the Body of Truth. [UB 18.5]

The rituals reinforce this perception and reaffirm a monk's compassionate duties: it is he, who for the sake of all beings, meditates on the infinite increase of the good, and takes on the responsibility of keeping the dangerous forces of the unseen world at bay.

The rituals, if they idealize the world, are also an all-embracing mirror of life. While working together on the manuscript of the *Playful Ocean*, Lama Tharchin once pointed out that in day-to-day life we never do one thing at a time. We may be eating a meal, but at the same time listening to music, thinking, and holding a conversation. Similarly, ritual engages all our senses at once. Drums boom, incense wafts in clouds. A monk's hands are rarely still: they roll in *mudrās*, ring bells, tell beads. As his voice chants, his mind's eye visualizes the ritual drama unfold. He dissolves the world into the blackness of emptiness and recreates it as paradise.

STRUCTURE

If Buddhism has classically tended to concentrate on the inner life, putting the emphasis on the achievement of Buddhahood and the conquest of psychological enemies, in our context conquest is often seen as twofold. In ritual one deals with external enemies (*dgra*) as well as the obstructive forces within the mind (*bgegs*). Whether they are internal or external, the process of dealing with "undesirables" is identical. When Trulshik Rinpoche assassinates the *lingka*, one cannot determine by the structure of the ritual whether "the ones imagined" are the spying ghosts that haunt monasteries or the five passions that poison living beings' hearts.

Some of these structures have their origins or at least their analogues outside of the Buddhist world. Buddhism is a religion of considerable tolerance. Lacking philosophical absolutism and a commensurate concept of heresy, it has been able to adapt symbols and assimilate traditions freely. In these pages, we have seen many analogues to shamanist belief and practice. Some doubtless existed in Tibet long before Buddhism came; others may have seeped in through its northern borders at a later date; yet others were already a part of Buddhism before it left India. To sort them out is tricky at best: as the dances of Dorje Drolö and Sharlung demonstrate, to distinguish a non-Buddhist tradition in Buddhist guise from a Buddhist tradition with non-Buddhist trappings may be a hopeless task.

Many of these common structures, the world-tree for one, are so widespread as to defy an attempt to determine their origin. That we find them in Mani Rimdu is no surprise; the world-tree is everywhere from the Maypole and the Christmas tree to the Yakut's tent. What is interesting is not their provenance, but how they function and interact within the festival. The rainbow-cord, which leads the shaman and the ancient Tibetan King to the upper storeys of the universe, and which connects god to god in a Tibetan *thang ka*, connects man to god in the daily mantra recitations. The row of poles that stretches from the courtyard to the chapel defines the *axis mundi* for each part of the festival: in the *maṇḍala* for the main ritual, in the torma for the empowerment, and in the courtyard for the dance. The crossed *vajra* is the foundation of the world as *maṇḍala*, and in the "Horse Dance," it presses down with the weight of the world-mountain on demons, or on our ordinary view of reality. Hollow tubes (the central channel, the magic dagger, the god's tongue) suck spiritual substance (be it of a man, a demon, or an offering) into another realm. Trulshik Rinpoche kills the ghosts and the passions and sucks their essence up through his magic dagger into a higher realm. Pelkidorje, one of Trulshik Rinpoche's previous incarnations, kills King Langdarma with an arrow—a device which shamans from Tibet to Siberia use to suck disease from a patient (Nebesky-Wojkowitz 1956: 544).

This type of analysis has its limits. Freud is said to have remarked that "sometimes a cigar is just a cigar." When Trulshik Rinpoche states that he chooses an arrow to bless the multitudes because it is a convenient length, we must grant him equal courtesy.

Other types of logic operate in a festival such as Mani Rimdu. We have seen the logic of the ordering of the festival and its degree of elaboration. Sometimes the boundary between order and randomness is arbitrary: there is a logic to the historical development and diffusion of the festival but also a random element. We can trace the steps that took a small private cult from a monastery in Central Tibet and made it the focal point of a rural festival in Nepal. They have the order and the randomness of the breaking balls in a game of billiards, ruled at once by physics and chance.

CHANGE

Today Tibetan and Sherpa culture are both at a crossroads. The terrible destruction of lives and culture that have taken place in Tibet under Chinese rule is well known; Rongphu itself lies in ruins. Fortunately, in our little corner of the Himalayas, the refugee monks of Thubten Chöling are, as the French say, *bien tombés*. Having fled Rongphu, their new monastery has assumed much of their former home's position of spiritual leadership in the Everest region.

The Sherpas, too, face drastic cultural change; gone are the days when the monastery was the principal means of education and social mobility. Sherpas today have government schools and many more options. In the previous generation, a young man cut out for something other than farming would more than likely become a monk. Today, the monastery must vie with the trekking agency and the other lucrative adjuncts of mountaineering and tourism. Sadly, with progress comes loss. More Sherpas can read and write than ever before, but in Nepali, the language of the governing elite, not in the Classical Tibetan of their own monasteries.

In both parts of our region there are other outside pressures: pressures toward Hinduization (more in Solu than in Khumbu, but everywhere through schools and radio), and toward Westernization (more in Khumbu than in Solu, but moving southward as tourism expands).

Everywhere, we see a deteriorating environment and an uncertain future. Caught between the pincers of overpopulation and deforestation; poised between China and India, Nepal is a potential trouble spot to say the least.

Tengpoche Rinpoche once asked why I was making such a detailed study of Mani Rimdu. "Did I," he asked, incredulously, "plan to perform Mani Rimdu in the United States?" I countered his question with another. Did he think Mani Rimdu would be performed in another fifty years? In another hundred? His answer was "probably not" to the former and "definitely not" to the latter. "Well," I said, "this way people will know how it was done." The lama looked at me, straight and hard. "What you said is very good," he replied, and as if to prove it, a manuscript that I had asked to copy but that previously could not be found, that probably did not exist, materialized within a half hour.

Although migration to Kathmandu (and even New York!) has emptied many villages of their young adults in recent years, Sherpas fortunately retain a positive sense of the value of being a Sherpa and an interest in preserving their own heritage. The people of the Chiwong area, for example, are now embarked on a restoration of their exemplary but long neglected monastery. Sherpa language classes have sprung up in Solu's schools.

We have spent several hundred pages discussing a small festival in an out of the way place. Such a mass of material often has a chilling effect on future research, but truly we have just scratched the surface. We have introduced propitiation literature, but have scarcely given it the attention it deserves; nor have we even tried to plumb the depths of tantric yoga. The dance *qua* dance and the theatrics of Day Fifteen were but barely mentioned. Buddhist sermonizing, seen in passing on Day Fourteen, was hardly addressed. As much as we have spoken about art and iconography, we have not been exhaustive. The list could go on. Thus, this is an epilogue, not a conclusion.

William Blake said that one can see the world in a grain of sand. In Mani Rimdu we have an entire *maṇḍala*.

In closing, then, it seems fitting to recall the words of the Lord of the Dance *Manual*,

> Here, in the Union of the Blissful *maṇḍala*,
> We, through our shameless ignorance,

Have erred in view, meditation and behavior, and have gone astray.
The creation sequence was unclear; the spells recited, too few.
The ritual was impure; the remainder, mixed up.
The substances offered won't do. We have been lazy and indolent.
These and any other failings there may be,
We confess. Please be patient with us! [38.3]

21

Outline of Lord of the Dance Union of the Blissful Text

1.0	The Preparations—arranging the necessary objects.	2b1
2.0	The Actual Method of Achievement	3.4
2.1	The Preliminaries	
2.1.1	General Preliminaries	
2.1.1.1	Going for Refuge	3.5
2.1.1.2	Generating the Aspiration	3b6
2.1.1.3	The Diamond Mind Meditation Recitation	4.3
2.1.1.4	The *Maṇḍala*	4b6
2.1.1.5	Guru Yoga	5.2
2.1.2	The Special Preliminaries	6b4
2.1.2.1	Expelling Demons	
2.1.2.2	Defining the Borders	7b1
2.1.2.3	Confession	7b5
2.1.2.4	Showering Blessings	8.4
2.1.2.5	Blessing the Things to be Offered	8b1
2.2	The Actual Practice	9.2
2.2.1	Meditation on the *Maṇḍala* of the Residence and the Residents	9.3
2.2.2	Blessing and Consecration	10b1
2.2.3	Inviting the Wisdom Circle	11b1
2.2.4	Entreating them to Stay	12b1
2.2.5	Salutation	12b3
2.2.6	Offerings	12b5
2.2.6.1	Outer Offerings	
2.2.6.2	Inner Offerings	15b4
2.2.6.2.1	Offering Medicine	

Appendices included in Thubten Chöling edition:
A Shower of Benefit and Pleasure.
The Auspicious Omens of Profound Path Union of the Blissful.
A Paradise of Benefit and Pleasure.
A Prayer for Lord of the Dance Great Compassion Union of the Blissful.
[END]

22

Outline of *Playful Ocean* Text

1.0	The Preliminaries	
1.1	Arranging the Equipment	
1.2	The Yoga of Self	3.1
1.3	Blessing the Offerings	4.1
1.4	Offering the General Torma to the Lama and the Tutelary Deity	4b5
2.0	The Actual Practice	
[2.1.0	The General Invitation to the Defenders of Religion from *The Guardians of the Word*	3b6-8b1]
2.1	The Sequence of Ceremonies of the Individual Sworn Ones	5b5
2.1.1	The Ceremony for Virtuous One	
	Entourage:	
	1. Krodhīśvārīma	6b3
	2. Karma Protector	
	3. Vajrakiṁkara	
	4. Malefactor/Benefactor	
	5. Rāhula	7.6
	6. Black Remati	7b3
	Invitation	8.5
	Plea to Stay	8b3
	Entrusting the Vow	8b5
	Salutation	9.2
	Offerings	

23

Outline of *Followers* Text

Notes

Sources and Methodology

1. Its 108 minute theatrical version, 56 minute television version (broadcast as *Destroyer of Illusion. The Secret World of a Tibetan Lama*), seventeen hours of archival film material, and seventy hours of archival audio were designed in part to serve as a resource for scholars. On the use of photography and film as data, see Collier 1967.

2. "The Descent of the Wisdom Beings," UB 2.3.3.1.1.2.2, f 25.5. *The Torma Empowerment* used on the fourteenth day of Mani Rimdu has a similar passage.

3. A brief biography of Trulshik Rinpoche can be found in *Chö Yang* 1991: 33–34.

4. This 'Gyur med rdo rje is not to be confused with the seventeenth-century Mindroling treasure master of the same name.

5. On the question of Indic and Tibetan cults, see for example: on *klu,* Macdonald, "The Coming of Buddhism," 1980: 141; on *gnod byin,* Snellgrove, *Buddhist Himālaya,* 1957: 291, n. 29; and Nebesky-Wojkowitz, *Oracles and Demons,* 1956: 280–281; on *srin po,* Nebesky-Wojkowitz 1956: 14; and in general, Tucci, *Religions of Tibet,* 1980: 163–64. On the value of fictitious etymologies, see Turner, *The Forest of Symbols,* 1961: 11.

6. I did, however, make one editorial decision in the transliteration: to render the Tibetan "ba" by "va" when appropriate. Thus, *vajra* appears in recognizable form instead of as "bajra". Similarly, tsa, tsha, and dza are given in accordance with the Basham system: ca, cha, and ja. The editorial "*sic*" when it appears, does not indicate deviation from correct Sanskrit (which is rife), but gross deviation from the texts' own system.

7. UB 2.3.3.1.1.2.1, "Undertaking the Vow," f 24b5. The term *Las byang* (Manual) is from *'phrin las gyi byang bu,* (chart of ritual actions). The term does not mean, as has sometimes been suggested, "karma purification."

8. "Essence of Tantra," in Tsong-kha-pa: 1977, pp. 17–18.

9. Beyer, *The Cult of Tārā,* 1973: 54.

10. SST interview 1/86.

Chapter 1: Introduction

1. Oppitz, "Myths and Facts," 1974: 232.

2. von Fürer-Haimendorf, *The Sherpas of Nepal,* 1964: 175. Also see Snellgrove, *Buddhist Himālaya,* 1957: 216; and Ortner, *Sherpas through their Rituals,* 1978: 11, and 1985. On cultural differences, see Miller, "Tibetan Culture," 1978.

3. See von Fürer-Haimendorf, *The Sherpas of Nepal,* 1964: 126 ff.

4. Rockhill, "The Lamaist Ceremony," 1890a.

5. See Nebesky-Wojkowitz, *Oracles and Demons,* 1956: chap. 27, "Some Notes on Tibetan Shamanism," pp. 538–553; Samuel, *Civilized Shamans,* 1993; and Stein, *Tibetan Civilization,* 1972: 191, "Tradition—the Nameless Religion." Also my see notes on the dance altar on Day 13 and elsewhere.

6. The monument of Nyingma tantric studies is Dudjom 1991. On Tibetan tantrism in general, the works of Professor Geshe Sopa of the University of Wisconsin, Jeffrey Hopkins, and others at the University of Virginia, Tulku Thondup, and several recent publications of the Library of Tibetan Works and Archives are also notable. See for example: Khetsun Sangpo, *Tantric Practice,* 1982; Cozort, *Highest Yoga Tantra,* 1986; Tsong-kha-pa, *Tantra in Tibet,* 1977, and *The Yoga of Tibet,* 1982; Dhargyey, *A Commentary on the Kālacakra Tantra,* 1985; and Mullin, *Meditations on the Lower Tantras,* 1983.

7. Eliade, "Methodological Remarks on the Study," 1959: 95.

8. On the tube, see Days Ø, 13, 15; on the descent of light, see Day 1: the reception, Days 6–12, 14; on the rainbow cord, Day 1: the reception, Days 6–12; on the world tree, Days 2–4: the main torma, Day 13, Day 15; and the cosmic sheep, Day Ø, Day 1: site, Day 13:3.

9. Trulshik Rinpoche: n.d.e.

10. John G. Neidhart, *Black Elk Speaks: Being the Life story of a Holy Man of the Ogalala Sioux.* (New York: William Morrow, 1932; Lincoln: University of Nebraska Press, 1961) bison ed., 42–43, cited in Campbell, *The Way of the Animal Powers,* 1984: 224.

11. Eliade, *Shamanism,* 1964: 107.

12. Henry Miller, *Black Spring.*

13. Campbell, *The Way of the Animal Powers,* 1984: 8.

Chapter 2: The Gods

1. Thus, *Lord of the Dance* was a natural choice for the title of my 1985 film about Mani Rimdu. To confuse the matter a bit, though, recently a quite unrelated Nyingma lama gave his English-language biography the same name.

2. Snellgrove, *Buddhist Himālaya,* 1957: 235–236. Snellgrove also mentions Lord of the Dance who he calls "Lotus-Lord of the Dance" or "Unity of All the

Blessed" on p. 255, where the name "Unity of All Blessed" occurs as an epithet of Padmasambhava in a *dKon mchog spyi 'dus* ritual; and on p. 259–261, where he describes the fierce form of the Burnt Offering associated with Lord of the Dance.

3. Snellgrove, *Buddist Himālaya,* 1957: 204.

4. The texts, UB f 10.2 and the *Daily Practice*, f 2b1, are somewhat ambiguous here: *phreng ba* can mean either rosary or garland. The details are evident in paintings of the god. The rosary counting gesture can be seen in many other forms of Lokeśvara: see Bhattacharyya *Indian Buddhist Iconography,* 1958: 401 ff.: figs. 3 (A), 6 (A), 11 (A), 12 (A), and so forth.

5. For more on Lord of the Dance's consort, see below, pp. 19–21.

6. Kapstein, "Remarks on the Maṇi bKa'-'bum," 1992b: 88.

7. Such beliefs are expressed in the *Ma ṇi bka' 'bum*, a *gter ma* compiled in the twelfth and thirteenth centuries. See Kapstein, Ibid., 1992b: 80; Tucci, *The Religions of Tibet,* 1980: 41; Stein, *Tibetan Civilization,* 1972: 38. Also see, among others, Dalai Lama II (1475–1542), *A Meditation on the Four-Armed Avalokiteśvara,* in Mullin, *Meditation on the Lower Tantras,* 1983: 50.

8. Snellgrove and Richardson, *A Cultural History of Tibet,* 1968: 130. Also see Kapstein, "Remarks on the Maṇi bKa'-'bum, 1992b: 85.

9. Kapstein, Ibid., 1992b: 83.

10. Stein, *Tibetan Civilization,* 1972: 174.

11. Bhattacharyya, *Indian Buddhist Iconography*, 1958: 126. See also Tucci, *The Religions of Tibet,* 1980: 170.

12. For some possible historical ramifications of this concept on the Lord of the Dance tradition, see chap. 5. On Ṣaḍakṣari-Lokeśvara, see Bhattacharyya, Ibid., 1958: 125 ff.; figs. 94–97 on pp. 173–174; and fig. 6 (A) on p. 402. According to Snellgrove, *The Hevajra Tantra,* 1959: 102, n. 3, Padmanarteśvara is also mentioned in Kaṇha's *Yogaratnamālā*, ms. belonging to Cambridge University Library, Add. 1699, p. 146, ll. 21–22, and in Tucci's, *Indo-Tibetica,* iii:2, p. 57.

13. Personal communication, August 1999.

14. Nor, for that matter, between Mani Rimdu and dance—Mani Rimdu is performed without dances at Thubten Chöling.

15. Das, *Journey to Lhasa*, 215.

16. *Followers*, f. 7.2. Also see Khempo Sangyay Tenzin and Gomchen Oleshay, "The Nyingma Icons," 1975 (*Kailash*, III/4): 371. The term also occurs in the name of at least one Bonpo deity, *gar dbang rta mgrin*, a Bonpo form of Hayagrīva. See Nebesky-Wojkowitz, *Oracles and Demons,* 1956: 23, note 2.

17. LT, instructions on the *mKha' 'gro thugs thig*, Santa Cruz, Ca., 7/87.

18. Canto 3: Rewalsar edition f 11b4; Ye shes mtsho rgyal 1978, p 13.

19. Section 2.7.1.6, "The Great God's Propitiation," f. 45b6 ff.; Section 2.3.6, "The Praise of the Great God, the Great Lord," f. 35b6 ff.

20. Section 2.1.6, "The Deeds of the Great God, the Great Lord," f. 22.3 ff.

21. "S'il existe des analogies indéniable entre Avalokiteçvara et Çiva, elles ne remontent pas à la période ancienne: textuellement et iconographiquement, elles ne semblent pas apparaître avant le Xe siècle au plus tôt," de Mallmann 1948: 115, translation mine. In her discussion of this question, pp. 111–115, de Mallmann summarizes and refutes the opposing view as stated by Kern, 1884, *Saddharmapuṇḍarīka*, Sacred Books of the East XXI. Oxford: p 407, n. 2; Foucher, 1900: *Étude sur l'Iconographie Bouddhique de l'Inde*, 1e partie, Paris: pp. 172–3; de la Vallée-Poussin, 1909, *Encyclopædia of Religion and Ethics*, Edinburgh-New York, II, Avalokiteśvara; and Przyluski, 1923: "Les Vidyârâja. Contribution à l'histoire de la Magie dans les sectes mahâyânistes," *Bulletin de l'École Française d'Extrême-Orient*, Chap. 23: 301–318, p. 314.

22. Tucci, "A propos Avalokiteçvara," 1951: 186, and note 2.

23. Snellgrove, *Buddhist Himālaya,* 1957: 187.

24. Interview with Pandit Vaidya Ashakaji Bajracarya, 10/9/83. Dr. Bajracarya, a *vajrācārya* of Patan, is a noted physician, and community leader as well as a scholar. According to him, there is also a two-handed form who holds a *vajra* and bell and two different six-handed forms, one sitting and one standing. Dr. Bajracarya says that when a *vajrācārya* dances, he holds the vajra and bell like the two-handed Padmanarteśvara. Amoghabajra Bajracarya (1979: 38) also gives an eight-handed form and lists Padmanarteśvara among the 108 forms of Avalokiteśvara (1979: 21).

25. Khetsun Sangpo 1982: 25–26, for example, says that the six-syllable mantra "overcomes the seeds of defilements that would cause rebirth" in each of the six realms.

26. For a photograph of the first, see Amoghabajra Bajracarya, *Nepāḥdeya,* 1979: 21.

27. For more on the relation between Padmanarteśvara and Minath, see Dowman, "A Buddhist Guide," 1981: 246–247.

28. This form of Padmanarteśvara, one of three mentioned in the *Sādhanamālā*, is described by Bhattacharyya, *Indian Buddhist Iconography,* 1958: 133 ff. Gordon, *The Iconography of Tibetan Lamaism*, 1939: 65, notes an interesting *yab yum* variety.

29. Ashakaji Bajracarya, interview 9/12/83. This song is published in his Newari work *Mallakālīna Kaṁ Pyākaṁ* (The Dance of the Aṣṭamātṛkā).

30. Ashakaji Bajracarya, interview 9/12/83.

31. David Gellner, interview 9/12/83. Also see Nepali, *The Newars.*

32. Shrestha, *Buddhist Ritual Dance,* 1986, p. 8–9.

33. Snellgrove, *Buddhist Himālaya,* 1957: 233. According to Kapstein (personal communication), however, "the peaceful deities are generally associated with the heart, and the wrathful with the head."

34. Snellgrove, Ibid., 1957: 235.

35. At Trakshindu, built around the time of Snellgrove's visit, there is a beautiful *maṇḍala* of Lord of the Dance on the ceiling of the chapel, however there is no worship of the god at that monastery at this time. Chiwong itself went through a period of decline since Snellgrove's visit; perhaps the god declined with it.

36. von Fürer-Haimendorf, *The Sherpas of Nepal,* 1964: 223.

37. Waddell says *bde gshegs kun 'dus gar dbang* and *thugs rje chen po.* Although he probably means our *bDe gshegs kun 'dus gar dbang thugs rje chen po*, it is possible that he does actually mean to indicate two deities (1) Lord of the Dance, and (2) the common white four-armed form of Avalokiteśvara sometimes called *Jo bo thugs rje chen po.* Waddell, *Buddhism of Tibet,* 1895: 182–183, n. 1.

38. This work may be quite similar to the *Manual* used at Mani Rimdu which has forty-one folios. (See below.) Waddell, Ibid., 1895: 182–183. Waddell also mentions (p. 175) a four-page manuscript of "The Collection of the Tathagatas" *maṇḍala* rituals that the monks were required to memorize for their examinations. Unless this is merely a confusion of numbers, the latter manuscript is possibly the Lord of the Dance Daily Practice text, the *Thugs rje chen po'i rgyun khyer zab lam snying po'i dril ba.* The xylograph edition of this work presented to me by Trulshik Rinpoche is three folia long.

39. On Pemayangtse, founded in A.D. 1705, see Waddell, *Buddhism of Tibet,* 1895: 285 ff., Nebesky-Wojkowitz, *Where the Gods are Mountains,* n.d.: 120; Surdev Singh Chib, *Sikkim*, p. 72; and so forth.

40. Waddell, *Buddhism of Tibet,* 1895: 173.

41. Waddell, Ibid., 1895: 173.

42. Followed by Gu ru drag dmar, sKu gsum thugs thig, and Byang gter drag mthing. Trulshik Rinpoche, 1980 interview.

43. This is based on estimates made for two recent years by Ngawang Norbu, manager (*phyag mdzod*) of Thubten Chöling.

44. UB f 41.

45. UB 2.1.1.3, f 4.3 ff. This is absent in the Vajrasattva practice described by Khetsun Sangpo 1982: 141 ff. A similar set appears within the heart of Vajrakīlaya. See *Herein Is Contained The Daily Yoga Of The GLORIOUS DORJE PHURBA Called The Compact Heart Essence*, Dorje Nyingpo (Paris, n.d.), 7:5. For another non-anthropomorphic deity, see the "Contemplation Hero."

46. van Gulik, *Hayagrīva* 1935: 10: "From the variants Aśvaśīrṣa, Hayaśīrṣa, Aśvamukha, Vaḍavāmukha it appears that in this case Hayagrīva ought to be translated as 'Horse-headed One.'" My discussion here follows van Gulik.

47. Eliade, *Shamanism,* 1964: 154.

48. See UB f. 37.5.

49. See the appropriate sections of Day One and Day Fifteen for a more detailed description.

50. UB 2.1.2.2, 10.5.

51. UB 2.1.2.2, f. 7b1 ff.

52. UB 10b1.

53. See *The Daily Yoga Of The GLORIOUS DORJE PHURBA*, cited in note 45.

54. Snellgrove, *Buddhist Himālaya,* 1957: 235–236. Also see, *The Hevajra Tantra,* 1959: 102, n. 3. Her name, usually given as Pāṇḍaravāsinī, means "The White Clad One." Her name leads Snellgrove to conclude that she is "probably [an] imaginative Buddhist creation," unlike many other deities who are "essentially non-Buddhist in origin." See Snellgrove, *Indo-Tibetan Buddhism* 1987: 150–151. According to Dowman, Sky Dancer (1985: 201; chap. 5, n. 7), her name relates to her position as the goddess of *gtum mo,* of psychic heat.

55. Snellgrove, *Indo-Tibetan Buddhism,* 1987: 150–151.

56. *Sādhanamālā*, p. 75, cited in Bhattacharyya, *Indian Buddhist Iconography* 1958: 134. The earliest known edition of the *Sādhanamālā* is dated 1165. See Bhattacharyya, Ibid. 1958: 385.

57. Tsong-kha-pa (Hopkins, transl. and ed.), 1981: 149.

58. I am indebted to Matthew Kapstein for this comment on consorts.

59. Mysterious Apparitions Canto 34: f 111.5–114. 5 in the Rewalsar edition, p. 219 ff. in Ye shes mtsho rgyal, 1978.

60. Tarthang's rendering has "teachings" for empowerment here.

61. Tarthang, *Kalacakra,* p. 221; Rewalsar ff. 112.5–12b1. I have modified the Toussaint / Tarthang translation somewhat. Parenthetical material is from the Rewalsar edition.

62. See the section entitled Four Sorceresses below.

63. This alone is too fragile a foundation on which to build an argument concerning the historicity of the Lord of the Dance tradition. For a summary of the long and complex evolution of the Five Buddha system, see Snellgrove, *Indo-Tibetan Buddhism,* 1987: 189 ff.

64. Snellgrove, *Buddhist Himālaya,* 1957: 66–67. I am indebted to Prof. David Germano of the University of Virginia for noting the absence of *'phrin las* in this chart.

65. Nebesky-Wojkowitz, *Tibetan Religions Dances,* 1976: 92, passim, prefers "witches".

66. UB 11.5.

67. UB 12.1.

68. LIS 126b5 ff.

69. UB 2.2.4, f. 12b2. Also see *Spying Ghosts;* S/R 3b1, and so forth. Beyer first made this structural connection between creation stage visualization and the creation of effigies. See Beyer, *The Cult of Tārā,* 1973: 101–102. Beyer has sketches of the *mudrās* on p. 102.

70. Among a heterogeneous list of terms nondescriptly styled "names originating in the tantras." *Mahāvyutpatti* (MV) 4234, 4284.

71. See for example, the "sorcerer" of the Trois Frères cave, c. 14,000 B.C. Campbell, *Way of the Animal Powers,* 1984: 76, fig. 132.

72. See Dehejia, *The Yoginī temples,* 1982, 1986.

73. Eliade, *Shamanism,* 1964: 37.

74. The story of Padmasambhava and the *ḍākiṇī* is given on page 20–21.

75. Nebesky-Wojkowitz, *Oracles and Demons,* 1956: 46-47 thinks, for I am indebted to Prof. David Germano of the University of Virginia for noting the absence of *'phrin las* in this chart.example, that the animal-heads of the goddesses in Four-Handed One's entourage may indicate "that they are Bon deities who have been assigned a minor position in the pantheon of Tibetan Buddhism."

76. See Fremantle and Trungpa, *The Tibetan Book of the Dead,* 1975: 65. Mindroling tradition includes the slightly rarer male form of this deity, see *Followers* [1], ff. 1b1–2b4.

77. Dowman, "A Buddhist Guide," 1981: 267–268.

78. Of the Chönyid Bardo. See Gordon, *Iconography of Tibetan Lamaism,* 1939: 101, who calls them the "Hlanmenmas," and Evans-Wentz.

79. See below, and for Vajrakīla, Nebesky-Wojkowitz, *Tibetan Religions Dances,* 1976: 92; for Union of the Precious Ones, Snellgrove, *Buddhist Himālaya*, 1957: 232. The Union of the Precious Ones tradition also has four directional sets of six goddesses each who preside over the four actions of pacifying, and so forth.

80. Bhattacharyya, *Indian Buddhist Iconography*, 1958: 316–317.

81. The specimen I describe is in the possession of Dr. David Gellner, and was purchased in the vicinity of Kwa Bahal in Patan. I am also indebted to him for the identification of the Goddesses.

82. The skull bowl usually forms a pair with the chopper. According to my notes, however, these goddesses hold only the skull bowl.

83. Bhattacharyya, *Indian Buddhist Iconography*, 1958: 385.

84. Fremantle and Trungpa, *The Tibetan Book of the Dead,* 1975: 67. See Bhattacharyya, *Indian Buddhist Iconography*, 1958: 364 for Vārāhī as she appears in the *Niṣpannayogāvalī.*

85. Fremantle and Trungpa, Ibid., 1975: 63 and note; quotation from Basham, *The Wonder that was India,* 1959: 318.

86. Bhattacharyya, *Indian Buddhist Iconography*, 1958: 196. Edgerton, *Buddhist Hybrid Sanskrit,* 1970: II, 346 simply defines the term as "ogress."

87. When I ask SST, however, if *phra men ma* are witches, using the Nepali term "bokshi," he agrees. He further states they are like *mkha' 'gro ma*, but a little lower. He does not know the etymology of the term, but agrees with Geshechodak's definition of "lha min srin po."

88. Or magicians—*"sna tshogs bstan [phyir] sgyu 'phrul,"* TR 12/2/83.

89. TR 12/2/86. Das, it should be noted, also gives *phra men ma* as a synonym of *'gyad ma*, "a goddess . . . that brings on division, dissention, or disunion." (D 295)

90. Ardussi and Epstein, "The Saintly Madman in Tibet," 1978: 329.

91. Ardussi and Epstein, Ibid., 1978: 329.

92. Basham, *The Wonder that was India*, 1959: 318.

93. Basham, Ibid., 1959: 168. It is also interesting to note, that like the *nāga*, the legendary *piśāca* seem to be based on a tribe living in India at the time. See p. 318.

Chapter 3

1. Dudjom Rinpoche's chapter on "the Resultant Vehicle of the Secret Mantra," 1991: v.1, pp. 243–372, is a superb summary of the Nyingma perspective on this crucial subject. Cozort, *Highest Yoga Tantra*, 1986: 65, *passim*, gives a detailed discussion of *rdzogs rim* and of the *anuttarayogatantra* system as a whole from the Geluk point of view.

2. Trulshik Rinpoche notes that the flask generation is unimportant if you are not doing a self-application (*bdag 'jug*) or an empowerment (*dbang*).

3. This threefold analysis and the discussion that follows are based on oral instructions of Lama Tharchin. Beyer, *The Cult of Tārā*, 1973: 68ff. also covers this material in a lucid way.

4. Robert Thurman has proposed the translation "archetype deity" much in this sense. The related term *dam tshig pa* also seems to have the signification of provisional, promised or potential. The *dam tshig pa* is the visualized deity which will be enlivened when the deity's wisdom essence (*ye shes pa*) descends during empowerment. UB 25.5.

5. LIS 123.5. Also see UB 2.2.7, The Praise, f 17.3.

6. The story of Rudra, perhaps the most fascinating episode of Tibetan mythology, may be found in cantos 5 and 6 of O rgyan gling pa's version of Ye shes mtsho rgyal's biography of Padmasaṁbhava. Also see Kapstein, "Samantabhadra and Rudra," 1992, and Davidson, "Reflections on the Mahesvara," 1991.

7. Khetsun Sangpo, *Tantric Practice in Nyingma*, 1982: 18–29.

8. Dudjom Rinpoche, *The Nyingma School*, 1991: 244.

9. PO 1.4, General Torma for the Lama and Tutelary Deity, f 5.2.

Chapter 4

1. Cf. UB f 5.6. Of course, the Hīnayāna and Mahāyāna conceive *nirvāṇa* differently. The rhetoric of ritual posits a *nirvāṇa* closer to that of the Hīnayāna, at least for emotional effect.

2. Donden, *Health through Balance*, 1986: 129.

3. Ekvall, *Religions Observances in Tibet*, 1964: 25, also see Nebesky-Wojkowitz, *Where the Gods are Mountains*, n.d.: 205 for a similar conclusion. It

should be noted that Ekvall's example does not refer to the high *dharmapāla*s but rather to local spirits subdued by Padmasambhava.

4. Ekvall, Ibid., 1964: 25.

5. The classic example is Sierksma's, *Tibet's Terrifying Deities. Sex and Aggression in Religious Acculturation*, The Hague: 1966. A more knowledgeable and respectful author once suggested to me that the protectors "are usually taken to represent unliberated karma."

6. Lessing, "Calling the Soul," 1951: 265.

7. That in Solu-Khumbu there are both native Sherpa and refugee Tibetan monasteries, should not confuse this issue. The statement holds true for each community.

8. 11/22/85. The following account is based on notes summarizing the interview, which was considerably longer than it appears here. Although these notes were written down immediately after the interview took place, it is a summary rather than a transcript, and contains omissions and possibly minor inaccuracies. Although some of the language is direct quotation, it is by and large paraphrase. Material in brackets, as usual, is my interpolation.

9. Listed under "Gter-bdag-gliṅ-pa 'Gyur-med-rdo-rje" in the Library of Congress catalogue. Others may now be found in the collected works of Gter bdag and Lo chen published by D. G. Khochhen Trulku in Dehra Dun, India. These were not available to me in connection with the present research.

10. PO 1.3, f 4.1.

11. *bDag gi rnal 'byor* 'Yoga of Self'—PO 1.2, ff. 3.1–4.1.

12. Snellgrove, *Buddhist Himālaya*, 1958: 242 gives a slightly different list of "the chief protectors" at "Chiwong and among the Nying-ma-pas generally." The list contains one or two small errors—Ekajaṭā should be sNgags srung ma, not Dur khrod lha mo; Vajrakumāra is better classed with the *yi dam* than with the *dam can*. If we wish a generic list of protectors, it might be better to examine painting of the Sworn Ones in Trulshik Rinpoche's collection—the only such *thang kha* I have seen in Solu-Khumbu. It consists of two long book-sized panels, each containing seven gods standing in a row. The first panel depicts the Protectors "that are prayed to often:" Son of Renown, Great God, Four-Faced One, Neuter, Mantra Guardian, Cemetery Grandmother, and Long Life Woman. All of these gods are among the Great Protectors worshipped at Mani Rimdu. The second panel shows deities who are "prayed to less often:" Good Diamond (rDo rje legs pa), Visṇu (Khyab 'jug), Four-Handed One, Virtuous One, Lion-Face (Seng gdong), Medicine Lady (sMan btsun), and Red Ts'iu (Ts'iu dmar po). These seven, with the possible exception of Ts'iu dmar po, are, for this tradition, derived from either the *Playful Ocean* or the *Followers*.

13. LLW 4.5–4b3. Detlef Ingo Lauf states that they were subdued by Milarepa in the eleventh century, who in turn attributed their first conversion to Buddhism to Padmasambhava. *mGur 'bum*, Canto 30, cited in Lauf, "Tshe-ring-ma," 1972: 260–261. Also see Mi-la-ras-pa 1989: 296–332.

14. The Followers and other minor deities are worshipped at this point.

15. In the "General Invitation," the request to act comes before the praise.

16. On this symbolic alphabet, see Tulku Thondup, *Hidden Teachings of Tibet,* 1986.

17. Each section of the *Followers* retains its colophon, which aids analysis considerably; the *Playful Ocean*, by contrast, has lost its colophons.

18. Stein (*Tibetan Civilization,* 1972: 192) remarks that in general, the structure which we find in the invocation of God of the Plain, which inquires as to the god's name in both the religion of gods and in the religion of men is indicative of "the ancient style of the songs." That alone among the Mani Rimdu rituals this prayer has been translated more than once is a tribute to the unerring instincts of Snellgrove and Nebesky-Wojkowitz. See Snellgrove, *Buddhist Himālaya*, 1957: 239–242; Nebesky-Wojkowitz, *Oracles and Demons,* 1956: 206, and n.d.: 32-33. Nebesky-Wojkowitz's passage is shorter and the text he used may not be identical to Snellgrove's and mine. For my full translation, see Lopez, *Religions of Tibet,* 1997: 387–394.

19. *sku lha'i yab smos pa.* 'O te gung rgyal, which Nebesky-Wojkowitz gives as 'Od de gung rgyal, 'O de gung rgyal, and 'O di gung rgyal, is the god of a mountain of that name in central Tibet. An old man dressed in silk and wearing turquoise bracelets, he carries a lance, a flag, and a cane-stick. According to Klong rdol bla ma, he is the father of eight mountain gods. See Nebesky-Wojkowitz 1956: 206, 208, 277, and 311. Stein (1962: 194) remarks that "Ode Kunggyel" is the god who descends to earth to become progenitor of the line of kings. Snellgrove translates his name, which he gives as 'Od gung rgyal as "Zenith Sovereignty of Light." Tucci (1980: 226) locates the mountain south of 'Ol kha.

20. 'Dam bshod snar mo (or 'Dam shod snar mo, viz. Nebesky-Wojkowitz) might be translated as Shivering Swamp Bottom, or following Snellgrove, "Oblong Lower Marsh." Das refers to a *'dam bshod sdar mo* as "one of the thirty-seven sacred places of the Bon," D 679.

21. Stein, *Tibetan Civilization,* 1972: 192.

22. According to Nebesky-Wojkowitz (n.d.: 32), "Nyen-chen Tang-la [is] the embodiment of the Trans-Himalaya, the mighty range of mountains that runs through the wilderness of Northern Tibet." Stein (1972: 192) equates him with a single holy mountain that bears the god's name—Nyenchen Thanglha, not the entire range. In later times, he is considered to be the god of "Potala Hill" (dMar po ri) in Lhasa. Nebesky-Wojkowitz, *Oracles and Demons,* 1956: 205.

23. Nebesky-Wojkowitz, *Where the Gods are Mountains,* n.d.: 32. For an example of a similar story, see Lauf, "Tshe-ring-ma," 1972: 259. Nebesky-Wojkowitz notes that Thang lha is worshipped in Sikkim as well as Tibet; it is probably there that he collected his data.

24. [44b3] The beribboned arrow appears again in the ancient *Mountain Incense Offering* performed on the days of the dance. See Day Thirteen.

25. On this subject see Campbell, *The Way of the Animal Powers,* 1984: passim. An excellent plate of a display *thangka* can be found in Thurman and Rhie #158.

Chapter 5: The Lord of the Dance Rituals

1. I am indebted to Matthew Kapstein for this precise date, a by-product of his long labors in Nyingma history. See Dudjom Rinpoche 1991, vol. 1, pp. 825–834. Dargyay, *The Rise of Esoteric Buddhism in Tibet,* 1979: 179, and n. 371, gives the date as the twenty-ninth day of the sixth Tibetan month. 'Gyur med rdo rje mentions Sha 'ug stag sgo in his *Biographical Prayer*, f. 2b3, although not specifically in connection with the Lord of the Dance Union of the Blissful cycle. 'Gyur med rdo rje has been called "one of the most essential links in the preservation of the entire Nyingma lineage of bKa-ma teachings of Mahā-, Anu- and Atiyoga." *Crystal Mirror, Journal of the Tibetan Nyingma Meditation Cente*r, vol. 5, Berkeley, 1985, 285.

The original *gter* ms. is preserved in the collection of Minling Trichen. A photograph of a part of it appears in Thondup, *Hidden Teachings of Tibet,* 1986: plate 16. On the discovery, also see LIS 223b5 and the note on Tulku Thondup's plate 6.

2. Prats, "Some preliminary considerations," 1980: 256. For short biographies of 'Gyur med rdo rje, see Dargyay 1979: 174–186 and Thondup, *The Tantric Tradition,* 1984: 81–83, and 1986, passim. Dargyay 1979: 174 gives his birth date as either 1634 or 1646. Dudjom Rinpoche (1991) has a more complete account. Portraits of 'Gyur med rdo rje may be found in Dudjom Rinpoche and in *Kailash* III, 4: 380.

3. Nebesky-Wojkowitz, *Tibetan Religions Dances,* 1976: 85; Snellgrove and Richardson, *A Cultural History of Tibet,* 1968: 196.

4. Snellgrove and Richardson, Ibid., 1968: 196. 'Gyur med rdo rje is generally credited with founding Mindroling in 1676. For more on Mindroling, see Ferrari, *mK'yen brtse's Guide,* 1958; Li-An-Chi, "rNying-ma-pa," 1948: 149–151; Waddell, *The Buddhism of Tibet,* 1895: 73, 175; Tucci, *To Lhasa and Beyond,* 1956: 146–147; Das, *Journey Lhasa and Central Tibet,* 1909: 304.

5. Mindroling and rDo rje brag pa were the two major monasteries of the Nyingma Sect (Waddell 1895: 277). On the fifth Dalai Lama's relations with the Nyingma Sect, also see Stein, *Tibetan Civilization,* 1972: 171–172; Tulku Thondup, *The Tantric Tradition,* 1984; and Dudjom Rinpoche 1991, vol. 1, pp. 683–4 and 821–4.

6. In 1647, at the age of thirty, the Great Fifth began work on his own *Dance Notes* (*'chams yig*), the basis of the text translated by Nebesky-Wojkowitz, *Tibetan Religions Dances,* 1976: 111–245. On the transmission of *'chams*, see Nebesky-Wojkowitz 1976: 85 ff.; on that of the Lord of the Dance tradition, see Thondup, *Hidden Teachings of Tibet,* 1986: n. on pl. 16.

7. Thondup, Ibid., 1986: caption to plate 16.

8. These are more what we might call resonances than one-to-one correlations or direct linkages. Among them are that Lord of the Dance is red, sexualized, secret, closely linked to the Nyingma protector µiva and with Hayagrīva, who although worshipped by all the Buddhist orders of Tibet, is himself closely linked to Padmasambhava.

9. The terma explains that Avalokiteśvara took his *bodhisattva* vow before Amitābha to help all beings, culminating in his incarnation as Dalai Lama. Stein, *Tibetan Civilization,* 1972: 84.

10. Snellgrove (1957: 235) also states that Lord of the Dance was the "special *yi-dam*" of Chiwong Monastery. Whatever the situation was in 1957, as I indicate, this is no longer the case. Lord of the Dance rituals at the monastery are now restricted to the once-a-year Mani Rimdu celebration.

11. See the discussion of Lord of the Dance under "gods" earlier in this section.

12. Waddell, *The Buddhism of Tibet*, 1895: 175, 182–183. See the discussion of "gods" earlier in this section for a summary of Waddell's account.

13. This and the estimates that follow are from a 1980 interview with Trulshik Rinpoche.

14. Jerstad, *Manc Rimdu,* 1969: 72. Tengpoche Rinpoche, however, in an 5/26/83 interview claimed Mani Rimdu was first performed at Tengpoche 65–66 years ago—or in 1917–1918, quite a number of years before the monastery was built!

15. von Fürer-Haimendorf, *The Sherpas of Nepal,* 1964: 135. Jerstad who ignores the rituals, characterizes the early Thami Mani Rimdus as "dances," stating that the 1950 performance was distinguished by having for the first time "the 'proper' dances in their order, and with the correct masks and costumes."

16. This tradition has also been revived at Thubten Chöling. In 1985, it was performed on the twenty-ninth day of the ninth month. Trulshik Rinpoche, interview, 11/11/85.

17. Based on "Tibet and Adjacent Countries," Snellgrove, *Buddhist Himālaya,* 1957.

Chapter 6: Tibetan Religious Dance

1. E.g., in Jerstad's *Mani Rimdu. Sherpa Dance-Drama.*

2. See the section titled "The Days."

3. Nebesky-Wojkowitz, *Tibetan Religious Dances,* 1976: 65.

4. Tucci, *The Religions of Tibet,* 1980: 233.

5. See Tucci, Ibid., 1980: 237.

6. According to oral tradition; see Nebesky-Wojkowitz, *Tibetan Religious Dances,* 1976: 32.

7. Nebesky-Wojkowitz, Ibid., 1976: 32.

8. There is some question as to whether Pelki Dorje was a lay tantric or a monk. Contemporary lay tantrics, such as LT, claim him as one of their own. Most sources identify him as a monk. As Matthew Kapstein points out (personal communication), monastic records from Dunhuang confirm that there was a famous monk by this name.

9. Nebesky-Wojkowitz, *Tibetan Religious Dances,* 1976: 43. Stein, *Tibetan Civilization,* 1972: 82.

10. Mindroling maintained a connection to the central government until the Chinese invasion as a place where officials went for education. The connection was

reconfirmed at least once in modern times through the medium of dance when Mindroling performed a special *'chams* for visit of regent Reting Rinpoche. Nebesky-Wojkowitz, Ibid., 1976: 66, n. 6.

11. Matthew Kapstein, personal communication, 1989.

12. The *Zhi khro'i rtsa 'chams* portrays forty-two peaceful and fifty-eight wrathful deities. Nebesky-Wojkowitz, Ibid., 1976: 12.

13. Nebesky-Wojkowitz, Ibid., 1976: 9.

14. Tucci, *The Religions of Tibet,* 1980: 237.

15. Perhaps covertly, or even unconsciously, this was also his way of asserting independence from the Rongphu tradition and its heir, Trulshik Rinpoche.

16. The Nyingma tradition adapted by the Gelugpa uses Vajrakīla and a Sakya version of a Vajrakīla *'chams yig* also exists. See sNgags 'chang chen po kun dga' rin chen (1517–1584) 1576.

17. Nebesky-Wojkowitz, *Oracles and Demons,* 1956: 402, note 5.

18. Trulshik Rinpoche 11/30/83. In lieu of one, Trulshik Rinpoche recommends a work on *'chams* in general, the *'Chams yig kun bzang rnam rol* or *rol mtsho.* This seems to have some relation to Nebesky-Wojkowitz's *'chams yig*, the *Kun tu bzang po'i 'chams kyi brjed byang lha'i rol gar*, Dalai Lama V, Ngag dbang blo bzang rgya mtsho, et al.: 1712. See Nebesky-Wojkowitz, *Tibetan Religious Dances,* 1976: 111–245.

19. My source here is unfortunately indirect, although a reliable informant. It was many years before I was to obtain a copy of this five folio work—the *'Cham[s] gyi tho dge*—alas, too late to include here. Translation and analysis of it will have to wait for a future publication.

20. Nebesky-Wojkowitz, *Tibetan Religious Dances,* 1976: 241.

21. Tengpoche Rinpoche n.d.: 7. Trulshik Rinpoche has also said that *Ngag dbang bstan 'dzin nor bu* adapted the traditions of several different monasteries in creating the Mani Rimdu dances. See descriptions of the individual dances, Day Fifteen.

22. Dalai Lama V, et. al. 1712 as translated by Nebesky-Wojkowitz in *Tibetan Religious Dances,*1976: 242–243.

23. Nebesky-Wojkowitz, Ibid., 1976: 242–243.

24. Sangyay Tenzin, interview.

25. Stein, *Tibetan Civilization,* 1972: 189. Stein also records a mask called "Black able-to-fly."

26. Nebesky-Wojkowitz, *Tibetan Religious Dances,* 1976: 51.

27. Cited in Stein, *Tibetan Civilization,* 1972: 190.

28. Eliade, *Shamanism*, 1964: 179–180. Emphasis is Eliade's.

29. Joshi, "The Living Tradition," 1987: 51–52.

30. I have observed this myself in Kathmandu as well as discussed it with several Newarists. To the ethnographer's chagrin, tape recorders and cameras are often seen as sacrilegious intrusions, and more than one has fallen to the sword of a god.

31. Or in some instances his allomorph, Hayagrīva, the Horse-Headed One.

32. Nebesky-Wojkowitz, *Tibetan Religious Dances,* 1976: 33 reports that the dancer who portrays the demoness bDud mo at the *bSam yas mdos chen* dances must spend a week in meditation beforehand. Although Nebesky-Wojkowitz does not specify the subject of the dancer's meditation, it is safe to assume that the yogi does not meditate that he is a demoness. Most likely he meditates on a *yi dam* to give him the spiritual strength to master the demoness, perhaps followed by a propitiation of her. Nebesky-Wojkowitz, 1976: 75 gives a series of "special rules" that dancers must obey in preparation for their performance. Among these is "meditation on those deities they will personify." In the absence of evidence to the contrary, it should be assumed that such meditation is self-creation *only* if the deity is capable of functioning as a *yi dam.* If the deity is a Sworn Protector or similar deity, logically, the meditation would be a propitiation of some sort.

33. PO 44b4; 3.1 ff.

34. Nebesky-Wojkowitz, *Tibetan Religious Dances,* 1976: 113.

35. Nebesky-Wojkowitz, Ibid., 1976: 240.

36. "yid lha gang dang gang gi nga rgyal brtan po 'dzin cing/." Translation, mine. Cf. Nebesky-Wojkowitz, Ibid., 1976: 112.

37. "yid kyi bzo ni lha'i bskyed rim gyi nga rgyal gsal snang dang ma bral bas so//." Translation, mine. Cf. Nebesky-Wojkowitz, Ibid., 1976: 241.

38. Nebesky-Wojkowitz, Ibid., 1976: 191.

39. Trulshik Rinpoche interview,11/27/83. Of course, in the dance of the *'chams yig*, the *yi dam* Vajrakīla himself appears. This, however, should not muddy the waters once we understand the principle involved—the exigencies of creation process yoga.

40. This structural similarity was noted by Stein, *Tibetan Civilization,* 1972: 188.

41. Interviews conducted by Ashok Kumar Gurung and Professor Dunbar Ogden of the Drama Department at University of California, Berkeley, at Chiwong Monastery, December 15–18, 1986. Unfortunately, as these interviews were conducted in Nepali and translated into English, it is unclear where the monks would place this theatrical type of visualization in the more formal conceptual framework of ritual, which is formulated in Tibetan.

42. Nebesky-Wojkowitz, *Tibetan Religious Dances,* 1976: 183.

Chapter 7: The Officiants

1. See for example S/P f 2b3.

2. "The Diamond Master's Empowerment," UB 29b4.

3. This occurs often enough in the course of a normal Mani Rimdu, especially for physically strenuous rituals such as carrying the sand to the river. When Trulshik Rinpoche was ill in 1984, Sang Sang Tulku came in his stead. That year and in 1985, when at my suggestion he attended the Mani Rimdu site rituals, he did all the work of the Diamond Master.

Chapter 8: The Days

1. von Fürer-Haimendorf, *The Sherpas of Nepal,* 1964: 212 has four days; Jerstad, *Mani Rimdu,* 1969: 162 has three.

2. Although a connection between the two festivals is unlikely, we might note in passing that the Nyingma monastery of Tshal gung thang in Tibet also traditionally performed a *'chams* on this date. The dance was "popularly known as the *Gung thang me tog mchod pa*, the (*Tshal*) *gung thang* flower offering." Nebesky-Wojkowitz, *Tibetan Religious Dances,* 1976: 30.

3. Tengpoche Rinpoche, 1/26/83 interview.

4. In 1984, for the purposes of our filming, the monks of Chiwong stuck to the traditional schedule—but in this instance, they asked us when we would like them to begin.

5. Discussions of the four actions abound. An unusual one can be found in Paul, *The Tibetan Symbolic World,* 1982: 72.

6. Trulshik Rinpoche interview, n.d.

7. Thubten Chöling is however, not "anti-dance." In 1985 (T9/29, November 11th), *gtor rgyab* and *gser skyems* dances traditionally performed at Rongphu in the twelfth month were performed at Thubten Chöling.

Chapter 9: Day Zero: Exorcism

1. In 1984, when I observed activating the *lingka* for the first time, I had invited Sang Sang Tulku to accompany me to Chiwong. As representative of Trulshik Rinpoche (and, by reincarnation, his father), Sang Sang Tulku was the ranking lama and thus officiated. The following account is based on an interview with him that took place following Mani Rimdu, and secondarily, on film material shot at during the ritual. See Kohn, *Lord of the Dance,* 1985.

2. "Le liṅga des danses masquées lamaïques et la théorie des âmes." Stein's interest in the subject continued, and he followed that article with one on the *phur-bu* in 1978, "A propos des documents anciens relatif au *phur-bu* (*kīla*)."

3. Stein, "Le liṅga des danses," 1957: 201. Stein cites MV "mtshan" and "rtags" as well as Filliozat. As Mark Tatz observes, these terms also can mean "primary sexual characteristic." Personal Communication, February 1988.

4. The individual *lingka* rituals will be discussed as we come to them in the festival and in the texts. One such discussions is found in UB f 22b3.

5. The rather cryptic one folio manuscript that SST uses to order the ritual, the *Thun daṁ sri* from the *Thun bzhi'i zin bris* gives several possibilities ranging from one to four days.

6. Yet another version of the *lingka*, and a particularly bizarre one at that, can be found in Rawson, *The Art of Tantra,* 1973, pl. 106. This is a carpet in the shape of a *lingka* in the pit. Its use is difficult to imagine.

7. In 1985, no other fabric coming readily to hand, Sang Sang Tulku used a piece of black drapery from our film équipe.

8. This consists of reciting the entire *Union of the Blissful Manual* up until "[Mantra] Recitation," including "Offering" (*mchod pa*) and "Praise" (*bstod pa*), and the "Exhortation" (*bskul*).

9. The *Knowledge Holders' Root Tantra (Rig 'dzin rtsa rgyud)* is found in *gTor zlog*, ff 4b1–6. The directions for customizing it for Lord of the Dance are found in PL f 2b5 ff, and in NP (*bDe kun*, vol. Wu), f 2.

10. The ritual is quite similar in form and content to the "Liberating" (*bsgral*) section (UB 2.3.3.3, f. 22.4) of the "Feast Offering" (*tshogs mchod*) in the main ritual.

11. *'brub khung,* according to Das is a synonym for the fire-pit used in the burnt offering (D 933).It would seem to derive from the verb *'brub pa* "to overflow, or gush forth." TR, however, says that this is not its meaning in the phrase *'brub khung*, which "is like a prison." "Once they are imprisoned in the pit, they cannot go anywhere, cannot spy. They may die or they may not."

12. PO 2.7.1.2, 42b3.

13. LT.

14. According to TR. The source cited by Stein, "Le liṅga des danses," 1957: 226 mentions "a variety of magical ingredients" (*thun rdzas sna tshogs [kyis] brab*), which "must be let fall on the body of the enemy-obstructor and reduce it to a powder." Also see Lessing's 1959 article "Senfkörner."

15. The Feast (*tshogs*), the Remains (*lhag ma*), and the Auspicious Omens (*bkra shis*).

16. GC 312 spells this name *nyul le* and defines it as "a gnome who interrupts religious practice." *bsgrub pa'i bar chad pa'i dam sri'i ming.*

17. Tucci, *The Religions of Tibet,* 1980: 193. Also see Beyer, *The Cult of Tārā,* 1973: 299.

18. S/P 4b4. This is also the opinion of the practitioners of the ritual. See notes on the *Spying Ghost* ritual, Kohn, *Mani Rimdu,* 1988: 522.

19. Nebesky-Wojkowitz, 1956: 300. Nebesky-Wojkowitz spends some time in *Oracles and Demons of Tibet*, discussing the *sri* in general and the *dam sri* in particular, although unlike our text, he never links them to the *nyul len* spirits. Other references can be found on pp. 119, 284, 302–303, and 469.

20. In his *Byang gter phur pa'i sri mnan yi dam drag po gang la'ang sbyar du rung ba'i lag len 'don 'gregs dkyus gcig tu bsdebs pa 'bar ba'i brjid gnon thog brtsegs zhes bya ba bzhugs so*, cited by Nebesky-Wojkowitz, 1956 300 ff.; 595.

21. Nebesky-Wojkowitz, *Oracles and Demons,* 1956: 300–301.

22. Nebesky-Wojkowitz, Ibid., 1956: 301–302. It is possible that in other accounts, the *dam sri* have a different bodily form. In a *lingka* for subduing the *dam sri* reproduced by Nebesky-Wojkowitz as figure 25 on page 518, the figure has the head of a bird rather than a pig.

23. Tucci, *Tibetan Painted Scrolls,* 1949: II: 715 cited in Nebesky-Wojkowitz, *Oracles and Demons,* 1956: 516, n. 15. Nebesky-Wojkowitz (301, n. 98) also directs us to Tucci's *Indo-Tibetica*, III/2, p 92. We should note that in this context *gshen* is a class of religious officiant and thus perhaps better translated as sacrificial priest.

24. Toussaint, *Le Dict de Padma,* 1933: 248, 193; cited by Nebosky-Wojkowitz, *Oracles and Demons,* 1956: 301, n. 98.

25. Nebesky-Wojkowitz, Ibid., 1956: 516.

26. Nebesky-Wojkowitz, Ibid., 1956: 516.

27. Nebesky-Wojkowitz, Ibid., 1956: 517.

28. Stein, "Le liṅga des danses," 1957: 205. Stein also notes that *rnam shes* (see below), which he translates as "âme," soul, has that significance in ordinary speech and in the Chinese and Mongolian lexicons (where *bla* is given as its synonym), "whatever else it might signify in orthodox dogma." According to some orthodox sources, however, it is the *rnam shes* that transmigrates.

29. See Dargyay, *The Rise of Esoteric Buddhism,* 1979: 114–115. We should add however that Chos dbang himself said that given the difficulty of finding human birth, to do the same for a human being would give rise to "unlimited evil" despite the benefits to the victim. See Dudjon Rinpoche 1991, vol. 1, p. 767. On the general question, also see Tucci, *The Religions of Tibet,* 1980: 186.

30. Eliade, *Shamanism,* 1964:183

31. Nebesky-Wojkowitz, *Where the Gods are Mountains,* n.d.: 250. A similar paper effigy, "wetted with the blood of a woman of ill-repute" is buried in a wild yak horn along with some of the victim's hair in a ritual of assassination practiced by the Bonpo of the Chumbi Valley. See Nebesky-Wojkowitz, Ibid., n.d.: 252.

32. Patrul Rinpoche, (Orgyan) 1994: 305–306.

33. Stein, *La Civilization Tibétaine,* 1981: 18.

34. For further discussion of Bon shamans as officiants of sacrifice, see Ekvall, *Religious Observances,* 1964: 30, and 38.

35. Bischoff and Hartman, "Padmasambhava," 1971; Stein, *La Civilization Tibétaine,* 1981: 167; Beyer, *The Cult of Tārā,* 1973: 44, and n. 83; Locke, *Karunamaya,* 1980: 209.

36. Cited in Stein, *Tibetan Civilization,* 1972: 152.

37. Or, as SST explains it, his body is cooked and offered to the Union of the Blissful *maṇḍala* gods. The phurbu itself can also be seen as "eating" the victim: as Stein (1977: 59) observes, ". . . d'une manière ou d'une autre, la guele du *makara* du *phur-bu* est censée «manger» les démons transpercés. La lame triangulaire sert sans doute de langue que absorbe par un canal intérieure." We will see more on this "canal" elsewhere. Its should be noted that a dancer impersonating Dorje Drolö will "eat" a torma with his dagger later in the festival. See Day Fifteen, Dance Three.

38. Yet another yogic level can be found in the Biography of 'Brugs pa kun legs. "I place the *lingka* of illusory (*'khrul pa'i*) karmic propensities / In the burnt offering pit of the Illusory Body (*sgyu lus*) / I strike it with the dagger of the unborn mantra / And reach the peak where enemies [and] obstructors are slain." "sgyu ma lus kyi hom khung du / bag chags 'khrul pa'i lingga bcug / skye med sngags kyi phur bus btab / dgra bgegs rtsed nas gcod pa'i yang rtse phyin /." Cited in Stein, "Le liṅga des dances," 1957: 160. I have retranslated the Tibetan text.

39. Beyer, *The Cult of Tārā,* 1973: 312.

40. Cozort, *Highest Yoga Tantra,* 1986: 98. On the model of the action of the *phurbu*, we could hypothesize a yoga in which the movement from the tip of the penis to the crown of the head is continuous and complete. RK.

41. See Stein, "Le liṅga des danses," 1957: 221–222; and my note on UB 23b3.

42. On this see Eliade, "Methodological Remarks," 1959: 100, and so forth. There is perhaps a hint of this in Mahāyāna Buddhist rhetoric when it speaks of the *dharmadhātu* as "the unborn state."

43. See UB f 36b4.

Chapter 10: Day One

1. In certain *'chams* traditions, similar rituals may be performed amidst the dances themselves. See Nebesky-Wojkowitz, *Tibetan Religious Dances,* 1976: 101–102.

2. *The Unabridged Recitations for the Site Ritual and Preparation for Great Compassion / Union of the Blissful* (S/P).

3. See "Drawing the *maṇḍala*" and S/P f. 7.5.

4. This pattern was mentioned by TCU; yet another example both of the detail with which Tibetan ceremonies are laid out, and of a good Chant Leader's knowledge of them.

5. The changes are: (1) "General Confession" (*spyi bshags*) (UB 8.5) is omitted; (2) in the "Descent of Blessings" (*byin dbab*), the three musical interludes (*brgyud gsum rol mo*) are replaced by single one; (3) the bulk of the outer offerings, such as water, flowers are glossed over (UB 12b6–15.5), and the monks proceed to the inner, tantric offerings; (4) the "Flask Practice" (*bum sgrub*) (UB 19b3–20.2) is omitted.

6. This is the *lhar ldang*, that is, the Gathering Sequence from the *Manual* (UB 38b2 ff.).

7. This hidden text (*gter ma*) was found by sPrul sku bzang po grags pa and transcribed by Rigs 'dzin rgod ldem, the pair who discovered the famous *Le'u bdun ma*. It is also known as Turning Back the Gnomes (*Sri bzlog*). In RP, the colophon reads "sPrul sku bZang po grags pa removed this from the treasure of rGyang yon po and gave it to the Knowledge Bearer rGod ldem."

8. SST interview 1984.

9. See UB 2.3.3.1.1.1.2.5: "Entering via the Four Doors and Salutation," f 24b1 ff. Also note that east vis-à-vis the *maṇḍala*, and east vis-à-vis the assembly hall are different, as in the previous illustration.

10. Or "Son of [the sage] Viśravas," see Snellgrove, *Indo-Tibetan Buddhism,* 1987: 333.

11. Based on a sketch from Chiwong. Offerings 4–7 completed from PL and TCU.

12. See text in Day 0.

13. The liturgy lists the range of deities, although the context of the Site [God's] Ritual complex tends to focus attention on the latter.

14. S/P 5.1.

15. *The Site Ritual* text differs slightly from the similar Spying Ghosts ritual employed during the rest of Mani Rimdu. Lord of the Dance and his entourage are included among the homages and "the unrighteous sentient beings, who are the family of *yama* gnomes" are substituted for "the ghosts who interrupt realization and lead it astray, who are the family of spying demons." S/P f 4b4.

16. S/P f 5.3.

17. In the *maṇḍala* offering, Meru also performs this function. See Lessing, "Miscellaneous Lamaist Notes," 1956 on the "Thanksgiving Offering," p. 66.

18. gShin rje'i gshed nag po. The god in question here, although called gShin rje'i gshed (Yamāntaka), by his function of protecting the door, his epithet "Lord of Religion," and his mantra "Oṁ vajra yamarāja . . . " is evidently the Lord of Death himself (Tib. gShin rje, Ssk. Yama). Lama Tharchin supports this conclusion. According to his exegesis, Yama (gShin rje) and Yamāntaka (gShin rje'i gshed) are the same. Yamāntaka is not the slayer of Yama, but the slayer of black magicians (*byad ma*). With this in mind, we can rethink the genitive particle, and read the name gShin rje'i gshed not as "The Slayer of the Lord of Death," but as "The Slayer who is the Lord of Death."

19. The Inner Yamarāja (gShin rje nang sgrub) has the head of a *rākṣasa* rather than a bull. See photograph D25 in Pal 1982, *A Buddhist Paradise,* which Pal incorrectly identifies as Mahākāla. On gShin rje nang sgrub, see Nebesky-Wojkowitz, *Oracles and Demons,* 1956: 82.

20. See, for example, Lokesh Chandra, *Buddhist Iconography,* 1988, #384.

21. Eliade, *Shamanism,* 1964: 257, n. 131.

22. See David Keightley's classic *Sources in Shang History. The Oracle Bone Inscriptions of Bronze Age China* (Berkeley: University of California Press, 1978).

23. Reindeer among the Chukchi (Bogoras, *The Chukchee*, 487 ff., cited in Eliade 1964: 257, n. 131); seal among the Koryak (Eliade 1967: 164).

24. Ekvall, *Religious Observances in Tibet,* 1964: 21.

25. Hoffmann, *Quellen zur Geshichte,* 1950: 193–195 refers us to the documents from Turkestan (Nºs 100 and 101) published in *JRAS* (1934): 488. See Ekvall, *Religious Observances in Tibet,* 1964: 263–264 on contemporary Tibetan shoulder bone divination.

26. Eliade, *Shamanism,* 1964: 116.

27. Eliade, Ibid., 1964: 164. See Bawden's 1958 article "On the Practice of Scalpulamancy . . ." for a Mongol lamaist scapulamancy text.

28. Nebesky-Wojkowitz, *Where the Gods are Mountains,* n.d.: 154.

29. Hoffmann, *Quellen zur Geschichte,* 1950: 193, 194–195; 1967: 82; Ekvall, *Religions Observances in Tibet,* 1964: 21.

30. Eliade, *Shamanism,* 1964: 164, n. 97 summarizes some of the vast literature. So wide is the distribution of scapulamancy that it has even been adduced in support of the Siberian landbridge theory. See Laufer, "Columbus and Cathay, and the meaning of America to the Orientalist," *JAOS*, LI 2, (June 1931): 87–103.

31. *Die Religionen der Jugra-Völker*, II, 335, cited in Eliade, *Shamanism,* 1964: 164.

32. Lessing gives a detailed list of good and bad omens taken from the weight, texture, smell, and taste of the bone. Lessing, "Calling the Soul," 1951: 275; Karmay, "L'âme et la turquoise," 1987: 97. For more on the ritual of "Calling the Soul," see Day 13.

33. Walter, "Scapula Cosmography," 1997.

34. Stein, *Tibetan Civilization,* 1972: 211. We will hear more about this skull and the interchangeability of sheep and goats, in the *Mountain Incense Offering*, a *bsangs* ritual performed on the days of the dance. See Day 13.

35. S/P 5b5. According to Trulshik Rinpoche, the Ten Magic Daggers are different from the similarly named deities that we will meet later in the *Followers* Ritual. These latter, the twelve Magic Dagger Guardians (*phur srung*), are the female Dog, Weasel, and Mistress spirits. If they resemble their names, they would be different even in appearance from the present deities (*Followers*, 3: f 3b3 ff.). Newar Vajrācāryas protects a sacred space with a Daśakrodha ritual employing ten *kīla* (see Locke 1980, 209). Although Locke identifies the *krodha* as the ones subdued rather than as here the subduers, a connection between the two rituals is evident.

36. SST Interview 1984.

37. This was noted by Stein, "Le liṅga des danses," 1957: 221–222.

38. LIS. See UB f 22b3. The dagger mantras in *The Spying Ghosts* and in *Erasing the Lines* use the phrase "Vajrakīlaya." The term *vajra* here is somewhat problematic. It may be used simply in a poetic sense, or in the broad sense of *vajrayāna*. Alternatively, it may indicate the intrusion of another tradition, in which the dagger is grouped with the *vajra* family instead of with the *padma* family, or it may invoke the deity Vajrakīla who wields the magic spike.

39. In Stein's text (1957: 221–222), Chos kyi seng ge's *rTsa gsum rab 'byams rgya mtshor mchod pa'i tshogs kyi 'khor lo'i rnam bshad bde chen rab 'bar,* the dagger is also visualized as Hayagrīva. "In rolling the dagger in his fingers, the force of the deities concentrates and melts into the *phur ba.* The white and red emissions of the five couples mix. This mixture melts into the crown of the head (the syllable *oṁ*) of the *phur pa* (who is Hayagrīva), then descends in succession first to the throat (*āh*), then to his heart (*hūṁ*). The rays of light coming from the letters transform into hooks, which draw in the soul (*bla srog*) of the enemy-obstructor in the form of a green syllable *nrī*, and join it to the breath [which incorporates it into the *phur pa*]. From the heart of the *phur pa* (the *hūṁ* place), it again mounts [united to the god] progressively in the *āh* (the throat) and the *oṁ* (the crown)." The officiant strikes the lingka and imagines that his life ("longevité") mixes with that of the enemy, and that he thus obtains "immortality as indestructible as a vajra." The five families send out waves of *amṛta* which bathe the enemy and purify his sins. "His *ālaya-vijñāna* and *kliṣṭamanas* rest in the form of a *nrī* in blood plasma." In turning the *phur pa,* (the soul) becomes black and loses consciousness. One thus radically severs the sins and the three bodies. After this "bath," "the nature of the Three Bodies (the Buddha nature inherent in the soul) is imagined as a white 'a'. This 'a' passes through the body of the *phur pa* (formed, below by the triangular blade and above by rTa mgrin), and melts, at the crown, into the palace of Bliss of the Akaniṣṭha heaven, in the figure of glorious rTa mchog rol pa ('Best of Horses,' a form of Hayagrīva), dwelling in the five wisdoms." It is interesting to note that the hollow blade of the *phur pa* resembles the hollow tongues of gods which ingest the offerings. Cf. UB f 29b1, SWT f 1b1, and so forth.

40. UB 2.1.2.2, f 7b1 ff.

41. PL 3b5. See S / P, the passage following f 6.3.

42. S / P f 6.4.

43. S / P f 6b2.

44. PL 3b5 ff.

45. AM 11b1 ff. Cited in note on S/P, f. 7.6, "Arranging the Ornaments."

46. *gzungs* in Sanskrit is *dhāraṇī.* A *dhāraṇī* is a type of mantra, often of considerable length.

47. Stein, *Tibetan Civilization,* 1972: 203; 224–225.

48. Eliade, *Shamanism,* 1964: 118. Sandscheiew mentions an interesting Buriat ritual in which a red string tied on one end to an arrow and on the other to a birch tree is used in a ritual of recalling the soul of an invalid. G. Sandscheiew, "Weltanshauung und Shamanismus der Alaren-Burjaten," *Anthropos:* 22–23, Posieux 1927–1928: 581, cited in Nebesky-Wojkowitz, *Oracles and Demons,* 1956: 551.

49. Eliade, *Shamanism,* 1964: 111.

50. Nebesky-Wojkowitz, *Oracles and Demons,* 1956: 551, also see Nebesky-Wojkowitz, "Die Tibetische," 1947: 59.

51. Eliade, *Shamanism,* 1964: 132.

52. Stein (1962: 224–225) has already noted the similarity between the death of a rainbow-bodied saint and of an ancient Tibetan king.

53. The colored strips of cloth on the edge of a thangka are also said to represent a rainbow that connects it to heaven. See Nebesky-Wojkowitz, *Oracles and Demons,* 1956: 551.

54. Here, *bhrūṁ*. S / P 6b3.

55. S / P 6b3.

56. UB 20.1–20.2. This structure holds for flask rituals irrespective of deity or sect. For a Kagyü example with the goddess Tārā, see Beyer, *The Cult of Tārā,* 1973: 409–415.

57. Chiwong, 1980.

58. Lessing, *Yung-Ho-Kung,* 1942: 129 notes that as is the case here, "If the stand is used for the maṇḍala of one definite deity only, permanent outlines for the maṇḍala are drawn in black on its platform."

59. Tsongkhapa is of a somewhat different opinion. In *sNgags rim chen mo*, he specifies that the *vajrācārya* meditate that he is the main deity and the other *grub thob,* who help draw the *maṇḍala* with the string, imagine themselves as Vairocana (system of Luchang) or bDud rtsi dkyil ba (system of Shendapa). Others: Lawapa, Nyimajungne, and so forth, state that the lama may use either his favorite deity or the main deity of the *maṇḍala* in question.

60. A short description of the process of preparing a sand *maṇḍala* at Yung Ho Kung, see Lessing, *Yung-Ho-Kung,* 1942: 128.

61. AM 9b4.

62. S / P 7.4.

63. AM 10.2 ff.

64. AM 10.2 ff.

65. AM 10.2 ff. Also see note in S / P following f 7.4.

66. One, it will be noted, is an extra axis. Whether this was a first attempt to solve the problem, or an inaccuracy in my own note-taking process is difficult to say. The difference between a man standing to the leftish part of the side of the *maṇḍala* and one standing to the rightish part of the corner may be nil, especially if that person is unsure of where he is supposed to be.

67. In my field sketch of 1983, the sixth line appears to be more in the center than on the edge. In 1980, however, the positions of the four edge lines were clear.

68. Chiwong: November 17, 1982.

69. The head monk of Chiwong did so in 1980; the monks of Namgyal monastery use quartz for the Kālacakra *maṇḍala*.

70. TCU interview. These directions suggest that at Chiwong the *maṇḍala* east is oriented to the compass south. See note a to p. 90 above and S / P 7.5.

Chapter 11: Days Two to Four

1. See Nebesky-Wojkowitz, *Oracles and Demons*, 1956: 363.

2. Also called "bab dra." Trulshik Rinpoche interview, 12/86.

3. See Beyer, *The Cult of Tārā,* 1973: 158 and passim.

4. Trulshik Rinpoche interview, 11/79.

5. See UB, passage following f 19b6 and note.

6. Trulshik Rinpoche interview, 11/79.

7. Cf UB 2.2.8, 18b3.

8. These mantras can be found in UB4, f 31.1 ff. "kāya . . ." is short for "kāya abhiṣiñca hūṁ," the mantra of the body empowerment. Since the mirror is associated in the ritual with the throat, the center of speech, rather than with the body per se, "kāya . . ." may be an error resulting from copying the mantras from the body empowerment text.

9. Tucci, *Tibetan Painted Scrolls*, 1949: 270. On the etymology of the word *dkyil 'khor*, see Haarh, "Contributions to the Study," 1959: 59 ff.

10. Called *blo blang dkyil 'khor*, examples can be found in the Potala in Lhasa and in the Library of Tibetan Works and Archives in Dharamsala. David Germano reports that a three-dimensional *maṇḍala* of the Peaceful and Wrathful deities exists at Penor Rinpoche's monastery in Byalakuppe, India. In the 1980's, a Tibetan woodworker was commissioned to make a three-dimensional *maṇḍala* in Japan. The same artist later created a similar *maṇḍala* at Khetsun Sangpo's monastery in Kathmandu. Personal communication, 1995.

11. There are exceptions to at least the former rule. The gods of the painted wood *maṇḍala* at Chiwong, like those of a sand painting, are represented symbolically rather than figuratively. I have never seen a figurative sand *maṇḍala*, however. Also see Lessing, *Yung-Ho-Kung*, 1942: 128ff.

12. Tucci, *Tibetan Painted Scrolls*, 1949: 270. On the *paṭa*, see Kapstein, "Weaving the World," 1995.

13. Snellgrove, *The Hevajra Tantra*, 1959: I.x.4; vol. I, p. 81; vol. II, p. 35. Snellgrove seems to arrive at the term "sacred writing-colours" from the Sanskrit text of the tantra: "divyena rajolekhena athavā madhyamena tu// pañcaratnamayaiś cūrṇair athavā taṇḍulādibhiḥ." It is clear that the Tibetan relates to this, however: "rdul mtshon dam pa'i tshon dang ni// yang na 'bring po nyid kyis te// rin chen lnga yi phye ma'am// yang na 'bras pa sogs pas so//" The phrase corresponding to "sacred writing-colours" is *divyena rajolekhena*, "divine writing powders."

14. Snellgrove, Ibid., 1959: I.ii.20; vol. I, p. 51.

15. For more on the sand, see the discussion under Day One. A detailed description of the sand painting process at Thami appears in my article "The Ritual Preparation of a Tibetan *Maṇḍala* ," in *Maṇḍala and Landscape*, edited by A. W. Macdonald (1997).

16. Conversation at Tengpoche, 1986.

17. The word is also given to a water offering to the hungry ghosts, a separate subject.

18. Das, *Journey to Lhasa*, 1909 calls this dye *smug rtsi* or *smug tshos*, and identifies the root from which it comes as *macretomia*.

19. Ekvall, *Religious Observances*, 1964: 28–29.

20. *gshen*. See Snellgrove and Richardson, *A Cultural History of Tibet*, 1968: 52. Descriptions of Tibetan royal sacrifices can be found in the biography of Yeshe Tsogyal. See Dowman's 1985 translation, *Sky Dancer*.

21. See PO 2.7.1.7, f 47.5 and Lama Tharchin's note; also f 41b3.

22. Ekvall, *Religious Observances*, 1964: 28–29, and n. 28; Hoffmann 1967: 72–73.

23. Basham, *The Wonder that was India*, 1959: 42, 81 ff.

24. Basham. Ibid., 1959: 81.

25. Horsch, "The Wheel," 1957: 63; citing Keith, "Religion and Philosophy of the Veda," *HOS*, 31, p. 67; quoting Weber, "Über den Vājapeya," pp. 20, 34. It is interesting to note that this cake was placed upon a pole. In present day tormas, as I show elsewhere, the pole, suggestive both of placement at the center of the universe and of a shift in planes of existence, is incorporated into the body of the torma itself.

26. See Locke, *Karunamaya*, 1980: 78–81 on Newar *bali*; see Singh, *Ajanta*, for the proto-torma.

27. Although in practice, the achievement torma is not eaten at Mani Rimdu. See discussion under "The Main Torma," below.

28. Stablein, "A Descriptive Analysis," 1978: 533. This visualization, however is not mentioned in our ritual texts.

29. The vertical pole inside a statue of a god is also called a *srog shing*. See Stein, *Tibetan Civilization*, 1972: 187. The fascinating subject of "life-trees" will be raised again on Day 13.

30. In the drawing, the *mtheb kyu* (buttons) are the three small ledges in the corners opposite the lotus petals. This term also refers to the similar small "ledges" on the backs of the protector tormas and to the finger-sized hand moldings of dough affixed to other tormas. Beyer, *The Cult of Tārā*, (1973: 324) describes "buttons" as "small tetrahedrons of dough placed around the base of the torma as an additional food offering." The term might be translated "crooked thumbs," which they sometimes resemble (cf. D 587, 608).

31. The actual motif used is a flame pattern with a familial resemblance to "Nepali design" (*bal ris*), the fill motif most common to Tibetan design.

32. Trulshik Rinpoche 12/4/83.

33. Trulshik Rinpoche 12/4/83.

34. The *Rong phu oyan mdo sngags bzung 'jug chos gling nges pa don gyi dga' ba'i tshal gyi chog khrid deb sa ther kun gsal me long*. A copy of this extremely rare manuscript reposes in the East Asian Library of the University of California, Berkeley.

35. Trulshik Rinpoche interview, 11/80. A similar situation seems to obtain in the Kagyü tradition; see Beyer, *The Cult of Tārā*, 1973: 403, 430.

36. See UB f 15b4 ff. The medicine and rakta are symbols of the male and female generative fluids respectively. According to Paul, *The Tibetan Symbolic World*, 1982: 87, "Through their magic sexual union, the deity will be generated as to be present in the ritual." Although this observation has logic, it is not found in the liturgy, nor have I found any Tibetan source that makes this connection.

37. TCU, 1983.

38. Tengpoche Rinpoche, 5/26/83 interview

39. The spelling of this alexical term was given by Ngawang Samten, the former Chant Leader of Chiwong.

40. PO f 24.5. This is the way the tormas appeared at Chiwong in 1980.

41. In 1980 there were twelve in 1983, sixteen. TCU speculated that in 1983, they may have added a torma for the local deity (*yul lha*) to the series, but could not even guess about the 1980 number. It is barely possible at Thami, where the monks are somewhat secretive, that I was never given an opportunity to see the Followers torma in its final form.

42. This was the form in which the torma appeared in the entourage of Planet at Chiwong in 1983. The 1983 tormas at Thami also had such a torma among them, but since their order and number was different, it is not absolutely certain that it was for this deity. At Chiwong among the Followers tormas per se, Good Diamond has had an ordinary triangular torma in all the years for which I have sketches.

43. See PO 39.2.

44. In 1983. In 1980, there were only nine. According to TCU, ten is the correct number.

45. Cf. "The General Torma," PO f. 4b6 ff.

46. PO f. 38b3 ff.

47. Chiwong, 1980, Day 2.

48. Trulshik Rinpoche, 6/87.

49. Charts of these schedules appear in the section on the protector rituals in the introduction.

50. Trulshik Rinpoche, 1980.

51. Paradoxically, the liturgy also prescribes an offering of "the enemies' flesh and blood" for the peaceful goddess Long Life Woman. LLW f 9.2.

52. Ngag dbang bstan 'dzin nor bu's *bDe kun tshogs la byor rung rgyu'i mkha' 'gro'i [b]sun bzlog*.

Chapter 12: Day Five

1. More informally, the cord may be tied to the flask, as was the case at Chiwong in 1980.

2. The string has been discussed at length in the Preparation Ritual on Day One. The mirror, in the discussion of the pills on Day Two.

3. Dingo Khyentse Rinpoche / Tulku Pema Wangyal, explanation of the Vajrakīla empowerment (Boulder, Colorado: 6/20/87). See Rockhill, "On the Uses of Skulls," 1890b for other interpretations.

4. See the sanctification of the ambrosia in PO 1.3, Blessing the Offerings, f 4.5.

5. See TE, Part Three (The Conclusion). Heat (Ssk. *tapas*) and spiritual achievement have, of course, been likened in India since the time of the Vedas.

6. I have eliminated the mantras here. They may be found in S/P 7b2 ff.

7. It is not clear where these skulls are to go, as they are not employed at Chiwong. They may be intended as receptacles for the arrows, especially as TCU notes that the skulls and arrows can be carried by the same person.

8. Although in 1983, I counted three instead of the requisite four.

9. Such was the arrangement in 1980. In 1983, the order was changed. According to former Chant Leader Ngawang Samten, the 1980 order was correct. Interview, 1983.

Chapter 13: Days Six to Twelve

1. Given how widespread this three-part analysis is, it is somewhat surprising that it is not generally applied to Mani Rimdu as a whole. For Trulshik Rinpoche's definition of the parts of the festival, see the discussion of the "Day Zero" rituals.

2. In Trulshik Rinpoche's short text, *Abridged Prayers for the Local Gods.*

3. According to Trulshik Rinpoche, as the protector of Rongphu, Sharlung is not necessary elsewhere, just as Tashi Palchen is not needed outside of Solu. (Interview 11/15/84.) The list of gods worshipped at Tengpoche was provided by Tengpoche Rinpoche in a series of interviews conducted in May 1983 (5/28–29/83). According to Trulshik Rinpoche, Zur ra rva skyes can be applied everywhere in Solu-Khumbu, since is a general protector of the region. Gesar, although not used at Chiwong, as a protector is "particularly powerful in this dark age" (TR interview, 11/15/84). Each of these deities has his own one to two folio liturgy. That of Khum bu yul lha, for example, is *The Offering Cloud for the Local God*, composed by rDza sprul Rinpoche.

4. My translation of this text can be found in Lopez, *Religions of Tibet*, 1997.

5. Tengpoche Rinpoche, interview 5/26/83.

6. The Union of the Blissful *Manual*, for example, requires "fierce sounding music" (*rol mo'i sgra drag po*) to expel obstructive spirits and (UB 7b1), and a

"longing melody" or "plaintive song" (*gdung dbyangs*) for showering blessings (UB 8.5).

7. The spelling *sbub 'chal* is uncertain. Nebesky-Wojkowitz, *Tibetan Religious Dances*, 1976: 27 gives it as above; Tucci, *The Religions of Tibet* 1980: 119 as *sbub chal;* D 937, and Jä 404 have *sbug chal* or *sbug chol;* and Jerstad, *Mani Rimdu*, 1969: 102 gives it as "Sbug 'cham." In Solu-Khumbu, I have always heard the term pronounced "buup chen." Nebesky-Wojkowitz calls the *sbub 'chal* "small cymbals," perhaps thinking of a version similar to those used in Mani Rimdu's dance of the Ging. Tucci's identification and sketch are correct.

8. For example, according to TCU a musical interlude is optional at the end of PO 2.7.3, "Requesting Action toward the Desired Goal," f. 51b6. At other junctures, (PO f. 40b4) music is only played if the monks take a toilet break.

9. Etymologically, *dung chen* means "big conch."

10. PO f. 25.4.

11. The *sbram* and *sbir sbram* of the Vajrakīla *'chams yig* is more than likely TCU's "bram" and "pi-pa-ram". Cf. Nebesky-Wojkowitz, *Tibetan Religious Dance*, 1976: 109, passim. Ibid., pp. 246–247 and note has a partial glossary of cymbal and drum terms used in the *'chams yig.*

12. At Chiwong, the conch prayer used is *Twenty-one Salutations and Praises of the Noble Tārā, using her Root Mantra* (*Āryātārāmantra-mūlastotra-nāmaskārekaviṁśatikanāma, 'Phags ma sgrol ma'i rtsa ba'i sngags kyis bstod cing phyag 'tshal ba nyi shu cig pa*), RP ff. 39b3–43.6.

13. Khetsun Sangpo, *Tantric Practice*, 1982, and Patrul Rinpoche, (O rgyan), 1994 are notable examples.

14. According to Das, *mthu,* "force or power of an inherent nature; innate energy; capacity, resource. Chiefly used for Magic Powers, but not invariably. . . . *mthu rtsal = mthu stobs,* Prabhāva, magic, witchcraft" (D 600). LT gives *nus pa* (capability) as a synonym for *mthu.* He says there are three types of *mthu:* outer, inner and secret. Outer power is the power to get rid of demons. Inner power is the power to get rid of hindrances. Secret power is the power to liberate the idea which perceives a self into the realm of selflessness ("bdag 'dzin gyi rtog pa bdag med pa'i dbyings su sgral ba'i mthu dan ldan pa"). Colloquially, *mthu rgyab,* "to strike with *mthu,*" means to curse in a magical sense.

15. The impure grasping ideas (*ma dag dngos 'dzin gyi rnam rtog*) in the minds of the worshipers, which are mental stains (*sems kyi dri ma*), are burned by the fire, scattered by the wind and washed by the water—TR. LIS 65.1 specifies that fire that emerges from *raṁ* burns away every impurity of the substances offered, the wind that emerges from *yaṁ* blows away every shackle of holding things to be real (*dngos 'dzin*), and the water that emerges from *khaṁ* washes away every stain of evil karmic propensities (*bag chags ngan pa*).

16. On the centrality of mantra recitation and for a fascinating critique of its abuses, see Patrul Rinpoche 1994: 274.

17. LIS 129.5 mentions that the mantras should revolve clockwise. LT notes that this is generally true for male deities. The mantras in female deities hearts circle counterclockwise.

18. Griffiths, *On Being Buddha*, 1994: 103.

19. Ibid., 1994: 104.

20. *Manual*, f. 9.2 ff.

21. Ibid., f. 20b5 ff.

22. The Entrance is divided into Entering the External Symbolic *Maṇḍala*, Making it Enter the Tools, and the Actual Entrance, which in turn consists of a Prayer, Taking Refuge, Adhering to the Special Vow, The Secret Mantra's Inner Generation of the Aspiration to Enlightenment, Salutation upon Entering via the Four Doors, and Entering the Inner Wisdom *maṇḍala*. This last is further subdivided into five parts: Undertaking the Vow, The Wisdom [Beings] Descend, Throwing and Fastening the Flower, Opening the Eyes, and Teaching to See.

23. The Flask Empowerments are: (1) the Five Ordinary Empowerments of Awareness, (2) The Diamond Master's Empowerment, and (3) the Empowerment of Body, Speech and Mind. The Highest Unelaborated Empowerments are: (1) The Secret Empowerment, (2) The Wisdom [Woman's] Innate Wisdom Empowerment, and (3) the Fourth Empowerment.

24. This passage comes from later in the empowerment—f. 31.5.

25. Spinner "The Painted Mind," 1979: 88. Beyer, *The Cult of Tārā*, 1973: 460 describes such a ritual.

26. Personal communication, Joy Wolf Shepherd on recarved temple struts.

27. See, for example, the discussion of Kaigen Kuyo, opening the eyes of Daruma, McFarland, *Daruma*, 1987: 64.

28. Eliade, *Shamanism*, 1964: 148.

29. Michael Oppitz, conversation, 6/10/83. Also his 1980 film, *Shamans of the Blind Country*. A still photograph can be found in Oppitz, *Shamanen im Blinden Land*, 1981:219.

30. *bya grub ye shes*. "Active," cf. Snellgrove, *Buddhist Himālaya* 1957: 67.

31. *chos ston bkra shis dung bus la/byang chub gnas du dbugs phyungs shig/* TR glosses this saying that the Diamond Master prophesies that his disciples will live in the home of the enlightened ones (*byang chub gnas*).

32. Like the blindfold, the mirror has an interesting history as a shaman's tool. Although, according to Eliade (1964: 153–154), it is "clearly Sino-Manchurian," in origin, its use is widespread, with its "magical meaning."

33. Cozort, *Highest Yoga Tantra*, 1986: 34. The sequence of empowerments, as understood in the Nyingmapa tradition, is surveyed inter alia in Dudjom 1991, vol. 1, pp. 346–372.

34. One of the two divisions of the Truth Body, *ngo bo nyid sku;* Ssk. *svabhāvikakāya*, could be translated many ways—Nature Body (following Hopkins), Existential Body, Essentiality Body, or Identity Body.

35. The schedules for both the Great Protectors and the Followers are given above in chart form at the end of the chapter on the Sworn Protectors in part 1.

36. For an overview of the imagery, structure, and literary style of protector rituals, see the section on the Sworn Protectors in part 1.

37. See page 57, and Dance Eight in Day Fifteen.

38. For example, the enormous painting belonging to the Musée Guimet reproduced in Rhie and Thurman #158.

39. At this point, a special confession to Virtuous One is performed, if it is a day on which that god is propitiated. Great God's Confession follows, and after it, the section called the Actual Confession.

40. The GING mentioned here are "almost the same as" (*gcig pa 'dra po*) those in the dance—TR. The commentary (LIS 193.1) speaks of the Eighteen Great GING, of which Nebesky-Wojkowitz (1956: 279) gives several different lists. SST states that the Langka are the same as Ghouls (*srin po, rākṣasa*). In light of this, it is interesting to note that (µri) Laṅkā in Indo-Tibetan myth was traditionally the home of the *rākṣasa* (cf. D 1205, 1290). Sorcerers = *phra men.* SST, defining *shugs* as "slowly" (cf. *shug shug la,* D 1239), tentatively identifies a Slow-Walker (*shugs 'gro*) as a being similar to a Sky Walker. Das 1240, however, defines *shugs 'gro* as a mule or a horse, and GC 882 as a mule (*dre'u*). Nebesky-Wojkowitz, *Oracles and Demons*, 1956: 92 lists a *shug sgrogs mgyogs byed* as one of the twenty-one Butchers (*bshan pa*) in the retinue of the god lCam sring. [An alternative explanation derives *shugs 'gro* from *shugs*, "power," and thus considers the term as equivalent to Ssk. *śakti.*—MK.]

41. SST seems to favor this interpretation. *Dam tshig rjes gcod* might also be taken to mean "you judge our vows."

42. The *Showering Blessings* here is not Ngawang Tenzin Norbu's separate ritual, but the similarly named section of the *Manual*, f. 8.4 ff.

43. "*I and all other living beings . . . ,*" *The Ocean Queen Prayer*, and "*The Three Jewels. . . .*"

Chapter 14: The Public Days

1. Lessing's article on the "Thanksgiving Offering" gives an account of a *maṇḍala* ritual performed at an audience with the Panchen Lama (1956: 60, n. 4). The photograph included, which Lessing says "resembles the golden mandala used at the audience," shows a more elaborate version of the gold *maṇḍala* plate than Trulshik Rinpoche employs. Both *maṇḍala* plates have metal representations of the *tshom bu* offerings affixed to their surface. On Trulshik Rinpoche plate, these metal fingers are uniformly

plain. In Lessing's, the fingers are capped with sculptural versions of the offerings they represent. The ritual he describes elsewhere in the article, however, calls for *tshom bu* made of rice.

Chapter 15: Day Thirteen

1. It is first found in von Fürer-Haimendorf, *The Sherpas of Nepal*, 1964: 213, then in Jerstad, *Mani Rimdu*, 1969: 100, and so forth.

2. Cf. *brgyugs,* D 342. One of the ex-Chant Leaders of Chiwong spelled the term for me as *'chams rgyid.* It is possible that *rgyid* is for *skyed,* "growth" (D 108), a close enough approximation to the way that he defined the term. Another term sometimes seen, *'chams dmar,* or "red dance," he had never heard before. This term is said to be derived from the red, or naked, unmasked faces of the dancers. Interview, 11/19/83.

3. This was corroborated by interviews conducted by Ashok Gurung, then a student at World College West, in the Chiwong Mani Rimdu of 1986.

4. TCU interview, 5/83. This was the case at Chiwong in 1982.

5. Stein goes so far as to say, "C'est dans ces rituels que se sont mieux conservés le style et le panthéon de la réligion ancienne." For more on this fascinating subject, see Stein's discussion of *bsangs* offerings and their history (1981: 180 ff.).

6. Lama Tharchin points out that the Vajrasattva meditation in its full form, and the cutting *(gcod)* ritual are other effective means of dealing directly with karmic creditors. As well as having a similar intent, all of these rituals have, in this respect, a similar structure.

7. Stein 1972: 199. Such rituals also seem to have a broad connection with *bsangs* rites. See Stein, *La Civilization*, 1981: 180.

8. SST. According to SST, in the Rongphu and Thubten Chöling method, some of the *Playful Ocean* is inserted. At Thubten Chöling, the *Unelaborated* is recited and then the torma and golden libation taken out.

9. Indeed the tormas are nearly identical in form. TCU, in a 1984 interview, identified it as belonging to the *Mountain Incense Offering,* which its appearance and disappearance at this moment confirms. The 1983 torma had the typical back arrangement of a gift torma—a large "shouldered" torma flanked by smaller triangular and round ones; and a front arrangement of four small red tormas. The first, second and fourth of these were identical: triangular in shape and decorated with a button. The third torma was phallic and decorated with a button and ball. Also see Days 2–4.

10. *Ri bo bsangs mchod mchod gtor ma*–TCU.

11. TR 1983.

12. Chiwong 1982. In any event, by the end of the *Mountain Incense Offering,* both sets of tormas and the golden libation are removed.

13. TCU interview, 5/83. Interview 12/6/83.

14. Its other name in Tibetan, *g.yang mda'*, "fortune arrow," also seems to link it to ceremonies such as the present. The most well-known use of the arrow is in the Tibetan marriage ceremony, where the matchmaker uses it to hook the bride and drag her away from her companions. See Lessing, *Yung-Ho-Kung*, 1942: 142–143 for a lengthy treatment of the physical appearance and symbolism of the beribboned arrow; and Lessing, "Calling the Soul," 1951: 283, n. 19 for a bibliography on the subject.

15. Chiwong 1983, 1984.

16. One is available from Orgyan Cho Dzong Nyingma Study and Retreat Center, P.O. Box 555, Route 81, Greenville, NY 12083. For a related text, see also Lopez, ed., *Religions of Tibet* 1997, pp. 401–406.

17. Lessing, *Yung-Ho Kung*, 1942: 139–147 has described a *g.yang 'gug* ceremony of the Gelugpa sect in some detail. This ceremony is somewhat different from ours. As an "orthodox" touch for a ritual to evoke prosperity, it involves Vaiśravaṇa, although it preserves some of the interesting pre-Buddhist elements of our ritual, such as the beribboned arrow. Also see note 14.

18. Like ours, Stein's version also has a beribboned arrow. Stein 1962: 199. For a photograph of the *g.yang dkar lugs,* a sheep head molded of *tsampa* and decorated with colored butter offered at the New Year, see Stein, *La Civilization*, 1981: 179.

19. Lessing, "Calling the Soul," 1951: 267–268, 274–275. The soul leg is used here in combination with the soul stone of human beings—the turquoise. When he recovers, the victim must put on the turquoises and eat the leg of mutton. On soul-stones, et al., see the introductory remarks on the *Playful Ocean,* and PO f 44b3, passim. For more on shoulder bones, see Day One: The Site Ritual and Walter, "Scapula Cosmography," 1997.

20. Tucci, *The Religions of Tibet*, 1980: 234.

21. Tucci, Ibid., 234.

22. Tucci, Ibid., 234–235.

23. Stein, *Tibetan Civilization*, 1972: 211.

24. In my sketches of the altar from 1980 and 1983, I labeled this item *chang.* In 1982 and again in 1984, my notes specify that milk is offered—in Solu-Khumbu the two often look identical. On a 1983 interview however, TCU corrected my impression. According to him, it is *chang.*

25. The cups and bottles of *chang* have a flame-shaped dot or smear of butter on their rims. As Nebesky-Wojkowitz, *Where the Gods Are Mountains*, n.d., 155 (among others) has observed, for the Sherpa, a smear of butter is a necessary part of formally serving *chang.*

26. In 1980, the courtyard altar arrangement was somewhat different:

> Upper shelf, front row (r, l): the "seven offerings"; upper shelf, back row (l, r): *tsampa* in a stemmed metal bowl; ambrosia; offering torma for the *Mountain Incense Offering* on a stemmed pedestal; *rakta;* the beribboned arrow in a stand; *chang* in a butter decorated glass. On other occasions, a bottle of *chang,* either the traditional wooden variety or the now ubiquitous

recycled glass bottle may be seen. Lower shelf: golden libation liquid in a metal ewer; the white and red tormas.

27. Jerstad, *Mani Rimdu* 1969: 100; von Fürer-Haimendorf, *The Sherpas of Nepal*, 1964: 214.

28. I have noted these canteens used at Thami. Sometimes, as at Chiwong in 1980 and 1983, they are omitted. The decorative tassels that tie up their robes and the rest of the regalia, however, remain. Rockhill, "Notes on the Ethnography of Tibet," 1971 (1893): plate 33, fig. 2 has an early photograph of one of these canteens.

29. The first, the Long-Life Man took an hour and the second, the Wise Man, three hours and twenty minutes.

30. The curtain dividing the porch and the temple used as a dressing room are both common features of *'chams*. Nebesky-Wojkowitz's *'chams yig* calls the dressing room the *"chas zhugs khang pa."* See Nebesky-Wojkowitz, *Tibetan Religious Dances*, 1976: 67; 105.

31. Chiwong 1983.

32. See Lessing, *Yung-Ho-Kung*, 1942: 143; Nebesky-Wojkowitz, *Oracles and Demons*, 1956: 365–383, passim.

33. Nebesky-Wojkowitz, Ibid., 365–368 lists three pages of such arrows.

34. Nebesky-Wojkowitz, Ibid., 543.

35. For a use of arrows in Siberian séances, see U. Harwa, *Die religiösen Vorstellungen bei den siberischen Völkern* (Stuttgart: 1925), 55, cited in Eliade, *Shamanism*, 1964: 175, n. 140.

36. Oppitz, "The Wild Boar and the Plough," 1983: 36.

37. Eliade *Shamanism*, 1964: 175, n. 140. Also see Nebesky-Wojkowitz, *Oracles and Demons*, 1956: 543. The use of arrows to expel demons is also seen in the exorcistic rituals of Tibetans and Sherpas. A prominent example of the latter is the Dumje festival performed in Junbesi and other Sherpa villages.

38. Nebesky-Wojkowitz, Ibid., 544.

39. Among the Vasyugan-Ostyak. See this book, Day One; Eliade, *Shamanism*, 1964: 164; and Karjalainen, *Die Religionen der Jugra-Völker*, II, 335.

40. Nor are the pole and the altar unique to Mani Rimdu; they seem to be a fixture of Tibetan sacred dance. Nebesky-Wojkowitz (1976: 24) reports that at the New Year's dance at Gangtok, the royal Sikkimese flag in the center of the dance court is replaced by an altar and two victory banners. Note that as at Thami, an old pole is replaced with a new one.

41. Nebesky-Wojkowitz, *Tibetan Religious Dances*, 1976: 67. It is interesting that in Nebesky-Wojkowitz the pole is connected specifically with the cult of the *dharmapālas,* who are by definition pre-Buddhist deities, although admittedly in the case of the major *dharmapālas*, mostly of Indic origin.

42. According to Michael Oppitz, the noted expert on Magar shamanism, the Magar have two cosmological schema. "The shamanic one is indeed vertical, the central pillar of the house and the life-tree [are] the most concrete representations of

this concept." Interestingly, the other schema is "a question of inside (a rock)—the side of the gods and outside." Personal communication, 9/19/87. The ritual birth of a Magar shaman, in which the initiate climbs the tree of life may be seen in Oppitz's film *Shamans of the Blind Country*. Oppitz's writings and film are an invaluable resource on Magar shamanism in particular and Siberian shamanism in general.

43. Eliade, *Shamanism*, 1964: 264.

44. Ekvall, *Religious Observances*, 1964: 19.

45. Nebesky-Wojkowitz, *Tibetan Religious Dances*, 1976: 67. Nebesky-Wojkowitz also notes that his *'chams yig* speaks of a first and second dance circle (*'chams skor*).

46. See Nebesky-Wojkowitz, Ibid., 65. Tengpoche Rinpoche states that the Mani Rimdu dances originated in the mediations of Ngawang Tenzin Norbu, the founder of the festival. Tengpoche Rinpoche n.d.: 7.

47. In some monasteries, the structure that supports the pole serves as an altar—a "square or rectangular base two to three feet high and made of stone or mud." (Nebesky-Wojkowitz 1976: 67). This arrangement would further heighten the similarity between the courtyard pole and the torma "life-tree" and "world-mountain" discussed previously. In Solu-Khumbu, however, the pole is anchored in the courtyard floor and a movable wooden altar employed.

48. Stein has developed these arguments persuasively. Stein, *Tibetan Civilization*, 1972: 210 ff, passim.

49. Stein, Ibid., 225.

50. Hoffmann, *Quellen zur Geshichte*, 1950: 19, cited in Nebesky-Wojkowitz, *Oracles and Demons*, 1956: 552. See Nebesky-Wojkowitz, Ibid., 552–553 for a good discussion of the life-tree in its various guises and in relation to the world-tree. Also see Nebesky-Wojkowitz, *Tibetan Religious Dances*, 1976: 73 on the "life-wood" of a thread cross.

51. Certain gods are also called *srog shing* (Life Tree). Four-Faced Mahākāla (GW f 6b5; PO 2.3.4, f 33b3) and RAHULA (PO 2.3.7, f 36b3) are called the backbone or life-tree of the Knowledge Bearers. Also see Nebesky-Wojkowitz, *Oracles and Demons*, 1956: 194. Son of Renown is called the "Fabulous tree who rains down everything desirable, whatever we wish!" (PO 2.3.8, f 37b6; GW f 7.5). Although, it is obvious for the god of wealth to be called a wish-granting tree (see PO 2.1.8, f. 26.3), we should not ignore that the wish-granting tree in Indian myth also leads from one plane to another—from the world of the demigods to the world of the gods.

52. Nebesky-Wojkowitz, *Oracles and Demons*, 1956: 552.

53. Kazi Dawa-samdup, *Shrīcakra Sambhāra Tantra*, 1919 [1987]: 114.

Chapter 16: Day Fourteen

1. Quoted by Ku śri bka' bcu siddhi in his commentary on Tsongkhapa's *The Foundation of all Excellence*, cited in Wangyal 1983: 285.

2. Basham, *the Wonder that was India*, 1959: 81; *Śatapatha Brāhmaṇa* v, 4, 3,4; v, 2, 2, 15. Cited in Basham 1959: 81 and notes 4 and 5. See Greenwold, "The Role of the Priest," 1978: 501 for some interesting remarks on the relationship between *dikṣa* and the *homa* sacrifice in the Newar priesthood.

3. My translation of the full text of the torma empowerment can be found in Lopez, *Religions of Tibet*, 1997.

4. Jerstad, for example, echoed Haimendorf's identification of the empowerment as a *tshe dbang*. Jerstad, *Mani Rimdu*, 1969: 102–103; von Fürer-Haimendorf, *The Sherpas of Nepal*, 1964: 215. In fairness to both men, it should be emphasized that this assertion can probably be traced to a Sherpa villager who served as an informant.

5. Beyer, *The Cult of Tārā*, 1973: 403, 430. On p. 430, Beyer describes a torma empowerment connected with White Tārā.

6. Trulshik Rinpoche 12/6/83. My translation of the text can be found in Lopez, *Religions of Tibet*, 1997: 225–233.

7. Chiwong, 1982—11 A.M.; 1983—10 A.M.

8. Chiwong 1983. In the mass of movement at this point, the exact order of the procession is difficult to ascertain.

9. This torma may occasionally be referred to as the *bdag bskyed*, or "self-creation." It is sometimes called the "tranggyen" (*'brang rgyan*—TCU; or *'brang rgyas*). I am somewhat uncertain of the etymology of this latter word. According to Das, *Journey to Lhasa*, 927, *'brang rgyas* means a woman's breast, and can refer to a round torma (*gtor ma zlum po*). Trulshik Rinpoche denies any such connection, at least in the torma's current significance. Interview 12/6/83. The resemblance of tormas in general to breasts, and Sherpa joking on the subject has been remarked elsewhere, prominently in the writings of Robert Paul; see Paul, *Sherpas and their Religion*, 1970: 352–353; 1982 passim. Das aside, the shape of the true achievement torma is not the one that Tibetans normally refer to as round. See sketch.

10. Trulshik Rinpoche, 12/6/83.

11. Chiwong 1982.

12. My outline follows TCU's description.

13. See Days Six to Twelve. A complete translation of the Torma Empowerment ritual can be found in Lopez, *Religions of Tibet*, 1997.

14. According to TCU. By way of confirmation, I found the torma in the gable above the courtyard two days later. 11/22/83.

15. Chiwong 1983.

16. In 1983, two hundred fifty by my count.

17. *Torma Empowerment* (TE), f 1b.

18. According to Sang Sang Tulku, who officiated at Chiwong in 1983. Beyer gives an example of the type of speech that many lamas give on the occasion of a public empowerment. Beyer, *The Cult of the Tārā*, 1973: 386. For an additional example, see Lopez, ed., *Religions of Tibet* 1997, pp. 355–368.

19. Noted in 1982 and 1983 respectively. Other details of the performance of the empowerment liturgy can be found in the notes to the translation of TE, and in the directions given by the text itself.

20. In 1986, after the Liberation Dance, Trulshik Rinpoche used the flat of his magic dagger to touch those who sought his blessing. Occasionally, when this researcher was being particularly obtuse, the lama would flick the recalcitrant ear with his finger, as we might tap a radio, television, or computer in hopes of improving its performance.

Chapter 17: Day Fifteen

1. Trulshik Rinpoche, 1986 interview.

2. According to TCU 1982 interview, except where otherwise noted.

3. Chiwong 1983.

4. TCU 1982, confirmed Chiwong 11/21/83.

5. Nebesky-Wojkowitz, *Tibetan Religious Dances*, 1976: 94–98 has a superb study of the costume of a black-hat dancer based on his study of the *'chams yig*. Jerstad's descriptions of the costumes and masks of the Tengpoche Mani Rimdu are by and large excellent, and without doubt the best feature of his work.

6. Nebesky-Wojkowitz, Ibid., 1976: 94 calls this a *stod le*. Jerstad, *Mani Rimdu*, 1969: 113 uses the term *rdor gong*.

7. *pang khebs*, see Nebesky-Wojkowitz, *Tibetan Religious Dances*, 1976: 94.

8. I have always heard the dance footwear referred to as *lham*, the ordinary word for boot. Nebesky-Wojkowitz, Ibid., 1976: 94 also uses this term. Jerstad, Ibid., 1969: 113 calls the dance boots *ras zom*.

9. This list has several spelling and punctuation errors, some of which effect meaning. For example, "Remainder Sword Dance" should be separated by punctuation and the "Drum Dance" appears as the homophonous "mantra dance." Verbatim, the list is: "*sngags pa/ging pa/rdo rje gro lo/sngags chams/mi tshe ring/dur bdag gnyis/dgral chams/mgon chen/mi nag/sha lung nga/mkha' 'gro/rtogs ldan/lhag ma gri chams/zor chams/chams sna/bkra shis//*"

10. Inasmuch as the sole function of the Ging is to herald Dorje Drolö, Dance Two is related at least indirectly to the feast.

11. TR 11/27/83. According to Trulshik Rinpoche, the Music Dance as practiced today "has some faults." The following description is taken from the 11/21/83 performance at Chiwong, except where otherwise noted.

12. Chiwong 12/1/82.

13. At Rongphu, there were a dozen music dancers. Trulshik Rinpoche 1986 interview.

14. "de nas ri bo bsang mchod dang 'brel ba'i chos skyong gi bskang rdzas chibs rta chibs g.yag la gzung gso." Thubten Chöling Chant Leader, Ngawang Tsundru

confirms that at Rongphu a horse and a yak were offered in connection with the *Mountain Incense Offering*, but says that at Chiwong sometimes they are given and sometimes not. Nebesky-Wojkowitz, *Oracles and Demons*, 1956: 541, and *Tibetan Religious Dances*, 1976: 23–24 describe the use of horse offerings in Sikkimese dances dedicated to Gangs chen mdzod lnga, the god of Mt. Kanchenjunga.

15. On pre-Buddhist *bsangs*, see Stein, *Tibetan Civilization*, 1972: 206–210. On animal sacrifices, see Stein, Ibid., 1972:117 passim. Also see the discussion of tormas as sacrifice in Days 2–4 above.

16. Sanskrit, *mantri*, literally, "those who use mantras" or "the tantrics." Nebesky-Wojkowitz's *'chams yig* refers to the *sngags pa* as *sngags 'chang*, *mantradhara*, "mantra holders" (1976: 115). Some of Nebesky-Wojkowitz's informants identified the character in this dance as a Bon priest. Nebesky-Wojkowitz agreed with his "more learned Tibetan informants" that black hat dancers are Tantrics. Nebesky-Wojkowitz himself notes no "striking similarity" between the dress of a Bonpo and the black-hat costume. Further, citing an account of Reting Rinpoche leading a black-hat dance, Nebesky-Wojkowitz finds it unlikely that so august a Buddhist dignitary lead a dance that portrayed Bonpo. See Nebesky-Wojkowitz, *Tibetan Religious Dances*, 1976: 80, and 93.

17. Nebesky-Wojkowitz devotes five pages (1976: 94–98) to a detailed description of the black-hat costume. There is also a lengthy passage in his *'chams yig* on the subject (pp. 115–118).

18. Jerstad's informants evidently subscribe to same theory—he calls this dance the *gser skyems*. Jerstad, *Mani Rimdu*, 1969: 112 ff. Tom Laird, a photo-journalist and former resident of Junbesi reports that Sherpa laymen also call it by the name *gser skyems*. 1982.

19. There is no evidence that it has any connection with Zur ra rva skyes or Samantabhadra as Jerstad (1969: 115) suggests.

20. The text, a customized version of the ritual found in the *Knowledge Holders' Root Tantra*, is found in Site Rituals: S/P 4b2 ff. The *Knowledge Holders' Root Tantra* (*Rin chen rtsa rgyud*) is from *gTor zlog*, ff. 4b1–6. The directions for customizing it for use with the Lord of the Dance cycle may be found in PL ff. 2b5 ff., or in NP f 2.

21. At Chiwong in 1986, the present and ex-Chant Leaders, standing and dancing next to each other, carried magic daggers. The other dancers held *vajras*. According to Trulshik Rinpoche, in a 1986 interview, at Rongphu there were eight to twelve Golden Libation dancers.

22. The replacement of the black-hat magicians' traditional *phurbu* and *bandha* (skull cup) by a stemmed libation cup in contexts where an offering is made to the local spirits was noted by Nebesky-Wojkowitz, *Tibetan Religious Dances*, 1976: 98.

23. My notes from 1983 state that a drum is also used here, while in 1985, I noted that the drum was only used when the dancers were in motion.

24. Detailed choreography is beyond the scope of this paper. An interesting symbolic analysis of one sequence of steps can be found in Jerstad, *Mani Rimdu*, 1969: 118.

25. Nebesky-Wojkowitz, *Tibetan Religious Dances*, 1976: 118–119. Nebesky-Wojkowitz's translation differs slightly from my own.

26. In 1985, the dancers at Chiwong had new hat cloths. The cloths were two of each color, and the dancers exited by color coordinated pairs. Exit Order: Blue, Red, White, and Pink.

27. G. A. Combe, *A Tibetan on Tibet*, London 1926, cited in Nebesky-Wojkowitz, *Tibetan Religious Dances*, 1976: 18.

28. Nebesky-Wojkowitz, Ibid., 1976: 119.

29. According to Jerstad, *Mani Rimdu*, 1969: 115–117, for example, the dance tells the story covertly, an example of what he calls "the 'hidden' discourse" of "symbolic, tantric language."

30. Stein, "Le liṅga des danses," 1957: 203.

31. Jamyang Norbu, former director of the Tibetan Institute for Performing Arts, interview, 11/85. Nebesky-Wojkowitz, *Tibetan Religious Dances*, 1976: notes that "the higher-ranking lamas personify the chief divinities of the dance and the leader of the Black Hats." 1976: 75.

32. See for example, Nebesky-Wojkowitz, *Oracles and Demons*, 1956: 34, 91, 95, 145, 147, 156, 157, 267, 278–80; *Tibetan Religious Dances*, 1976: 81; Tucci, *Tibetan Painted Scrolls*, 1949: 617. No doubt this variety of Ging is what convinced Jerstad (1969: 123) that the Guardians of the Four Directions were the Ging of Mani Rimdu. He seems to be alone in this conclusion. Jäschke's (68) essay at defining *ging:* "a little drum, or the beating of it, as an accompaniment in dancing" is possibly a confusion based on the fact that *ging* of dances often play drums. Das (219) repeats Jäschke's error, adding the *caveat* "probably".

33. Nebesky-Wojkowitz, Ibid., 1956: 278–80; Ibid., 1976: 81; Geshe Chodrak (dGe bshes chos grags. 1949):116; Beyer, *The Cult of Tārā*, 1973: 50. Beyer gives the etymology of *ging* as a shortened version of "*gingkara*" derived from the Sanskrit *kiṁkara*, "servant, attendant."

34. Trulshik Rinpoche, based on 11/27/83 interview and others. Also see Stein, *Tibetan Civilization*, 1972: 188. I have found no evidence to suggest they are connected with the *lokapāla* as Jerstad suggests (1969: 122–123).

35. The *Tshig bdun gsol 'debs* is also used in Dance Four (*rnga 'cham*).

36. Literally, "Highest and Ordinary True Achievements."

37. According to Trulshik Rinpoche. GC 116 defines *Ging po* and *Ging mo* simply as male and female servants (*g.yog po*, *g.yog mo*).

38. According to Trulshik Rinpoche and at Chiwong. Jerstad, *Mani Rimdu*, 1969: 121 gives a different schema.

39. These fans are also seen in the Lords of the Cemetery of Dance Six. There they are said to differentiate those deities from similar but lesser figures. Perhaps they perform a similar function in the iconography of the Ging, although this would seem to be contradicted by their single diadem. On these fans, see Dance Seven.

40. Khetsun Sangpo, *Tantric Practice*, 1982: 197.

41. Trulshik Rinpoche, 1986 interview.

42. See note 27 under Dance One and Nebesky-Wojkowitz, *Tibetan Religious Dances*, 1976: 1976: 6–7; 15, 81.

43. Some are evident in dances held at Bodhanath *stūpa* in Kathmandu, see Nebesky-Wojkowitz, Ibid., 1976: 30–31, citing M. Lobsiger-Dellenbach, "Recherches éthnologique au Népal," *Globe* 92–93 (1954–1956): 74–76; E. Maillart, *The Land of the Sherpas* (London, 1955), p. 42. The dance of the eight manifestations of Padmasambhava is described by Combe. A dance of the eight manifestations was founded in America in recent years, by Lama Tharchin at his center in Corralitos, California.

44. Lama Tharchin, lecture, "The Eight Forms of Padmasambhava," 10/7/87.

45. A new Dorje Drolö mask was introduced at Chiwong in 1983. The old one was similar, but had no earrings—at least in its last years.

46. Trulshik Rinpoche interview 11/27/83. The first and second feasts can be found in the Lord of the Dance *Manual*, ff. 21b4–22.3, i.e., UB 2.3.2.3.1 and 2.3.2.3.2. Jerstad notwithstanding, this liturgy contains neither praises of Dorje Drolö nor lists of the demons he destroyed. Cf Jerstad, *Mani Rimdu*, 1969: 126.

47. Tengpoche Rinpoche, interview 5/9/83. In a rival lama's opinion, this addition is rather "stupid."

48. Deities sitting to be honored is a feature of other *'chams*. In the Padmasambhava dances described by Combe, eight forms of Padmasambhava sit to be "receive homage." See Nebesky-Wojkowitz, *Tibetan Religious Dances*, 1976: 15–17.

49. See Stein "La Gueule du Makara," 1977: 59; Day Zero; and Dances Six and Eight.

50. According to informants, the "second feast," the one stanza confession that follows this offering is also read during the dance of Dorje Drolö. See UB f 22.3.

51. According to my notes of 1980, that year there were only four drum dancers—two with cymbals and two with drums. Chiwong 11/23/80.

52. Chiwong 12/1/82.

53. Trulshik Rinpoche interview 11/27/83.

54. Chiwong 11/21/83.

55. In the dance list posted at Thami and in a Chiwong monk's notebook, respectively.

56. Tengpoche Rinpoche, 5/29/83. Tengpoche Rinpoche called this dance "po drup." In Nebesky-Wojkowitz, such hats are sometimes called *bse thebs*.

57. According to some of Nebesky-Wojkowitz's informants, although the dance he himself witnessed was performed by Bhutanese soldiers as part of a royal wedding in the fall of 1951. See Nebesky-Wojkowitz, *Where the Gods are Mountains*, n.d.: 163, and *Tibetan Religious Dances*, 1976: 35–36.

58. Nebesky-Wojkowitz, Ibid., 1976: 98; also 107. The Vajrakīla *'chams yig* describes an elaborate drum dance in eight movements. See Nebesky-Wojkowitz, Ibid., 1976: 194–208.

59. See for example Jerstad, *Mani Rimdu*, 1969: 132. Jerstad cites an interesting tale from "one Buddhist informant" that the character of Hva Shang was imported from China by the 13th Dalai Lama from a monastery "outside Peking" that he visited during his stay there. Jerstad—or his informant—may have been thinking of the 13th Dalai Lama's exile in Mongolia (1904–1906), during which he had a dream leading to the importation of a similar figure from Mongolian dance—the *cagan ebügan* or *cagan öbö*, Tib. *rgan po dkar po* (the 'White Old Man'). As mentioned, the *cagan öbö* has some similarities to the Seer of Dance Ten. See Nebesky-Wojkowitz, *Tibetan Religious Dances*, 1976: 44, 83–84.

60. Nebesky-Wojkowitz, Ibid., 1976: 82. See Nebesky-Wojkowitz, Ibid., 1976: 82–83 for a general account of Hva Shang. Also 1976: 40 (at Hemis); 43–44 (the Potala); 48 (Tashilhunpo).

61. Nebesky-Wojkowitz, Ibid., 1976: 83. In the performance described by Jerstad (1969: 132 ff.), there is only one assistant, who is enlisted later in the act.

62. At Thami, the act is essentially the same. In 1980, the year my notes on this act at Thami are the fullest, I do not record a prostration lesson. Many of the other routines, however, are identical. I indicate a few of these similarities in the notes below.

63. According to Nebesky-Wojkowitz, these boys relate the figure to the "*arhat (gnas brtan) Ha zhang*." Nebesky-Wojkowitz, Ibid., 1976: 83; also see pp. 15–17, and 42–43.

64. At Chiwong in 1986, these proctors took a more active role. There were three, rather than the usual one or two, all young Sherpas recruited from other monasteries. Instead of merely bearing their traditional fringed hat and whip, they were masked and suited in black like minor spirits. Their boisterous improvisational slapstick became a show in itself at times interfering with the flow of the proceedings. The audience at the time responded enthusiastically, and their humor and élan made them unusually effective proctors. Nonetheless, afterwards some thought they had gone too far, and there is some doubt as to whether they will appear in future performances or become a part of the tradition at Chiwong. As an interesting sidelight, these young Sherpas showed evidence of exposure to Kathmandu "bideo" parlors—their steps often owed as much to the traditions of Kung Fu film as to those of Tibetan sacred dance.

65. Chiwong 11/21/83.

66. Chiwong 12/1/82; Thami 1980.

67. Chiwong 11/21/83.

68. One year, the Long-Life Man undercut his own success. After the first success, his arms still around his assistants shoulders, he led them not into a second prostration, but a Sherpa line-dance (*zhabs bro*). Chiwong 11/21/83.

69. Chiwong 11/21/83; Thami 1980.

70. *rten 'brel*, interview 11/27/83. Otherwise, the dance is "just play."

71. At Tengpoche, with the lama seated in the balcony, the *kha btags* presentation becomes a hilarious comedy of errors involving that universal device of slapstick, a ladder. See Jerstad, *Mani Rimdu*, 1969: 133.

72. Such was the case at Chiwong in 1982. Trulshik Rinpoche entered about an hour into the act, during the "torma offering lesson." Long-Life Man broke off the act, saluted the lama and exited.

73. To the "chief figures of the *'chams*," as Nebesky-Wojkowitz states somewhat vaguely. At Mani Rimdu it is to the lama. At Tashilhunpo, the spectators throw scarves at him. Nebesky-Wojkowitz, *Tibetan Religious Dances*, 1976: 83.

74. Nebesky-Wojkowitz, Ibid., 1976: 16.

75. Nebesky-Wojkowitz, Ibid., 1976: 62 after P. Labbé, *Chez les lamas de Sibérie* (Paris, 1909), pp. 177–89.

76. For such an account, see Nebesky-Wojkowitz, *Tibetan Religious Dances*, 1976: 83.

77. See Stein's classic 1957 article, "Le liṅga des danses masquées lamaïques et la théorie des âmes." As could be expected, Nebesky-Wojkowitz (1976) has numerous descriptions of this event, viz.: in eastern Tibet, citing Combe, 18–19; at Hemis, 40; at 'Gye mur, citing Pott, 40–42; at the Potala New Years, citing various sources, 44–45; at Tashilhunpo, various sources, 49; at Choni (Co ne), citing Rock, 49–50; among the Minyag, citing Stein, 54; at Kumbum, citing Filchner and Tafel, 57–58; in Mongolia, citing Lessing, 59; in Inner Mongolia, citing Haslund-Christensen, 60. In 1783, Samuel Davis made what is perhaps the earliest account by a European; see Aris, *Views of Medieval Bhutan*, 1982: 59.

78. Joshi, "The Living Tradition," 1987: 48, 50.

79. *Dur bdag gnyis*, Ssk., *Citipati;* see Nebesky-Wojkowitz, *Oracles and Demons*, 1956: 86. They may also be called *Zhing skyong*, *Kṣetrapāla;* see Nebesky-Wojkowitz, *Tibetan Religious Dances*, 1976: 78. According to Lama Tharchin, in some *'chams* they are simply called the *lingka-* carriers (*ling 'khyer*).

80. For others that appear in the dance, see Nebesky-Wojkowitz, Ibid., 1976: 78–79. For an example from the visual arts, see Tucci, *Tibet,* 1967: 122, fig. 4.

81. Namkhai Norbu, *Crystal and the Way*, 1986: 49.

82. Nebesky-Wojkowitz, *Oracles and Demons*, 1956: 95.

83. Nebesky-Wojkowitz, Ibid., 1956: 86.

84. *zhing dbyug* or *zhing rgam pa'i dbyug pa*. Trulshik Rinpoche 1983. These sticks are replaced from time to time. At Chiwong in 1980 they were two feet long, with one spade-shaped end and one spoon-shaped end. Each had a small ball-shaped lump midway and was unpainted. In 1983, the *zhing dbyug* were eighteen inches long, straight and one-ended (spade-shaped), and roughly painted with red diagonal stripes. These are reminiscent of the long "spotted sticks" of Mongolian *'chams* with which two subordinate skeleton dancers "put to flight the evil-natured raven who tries to

steal the linga." Nebesky-Wojkowitz, *Tibetan Religious Dances*, 1976: 78–79. In the Protector dance Ekajaṭī also brandishes a mummy-club, but it is far more detailed than the rudimentary props of the Lords of the Cemetery.

85. They are called *ru rang* in a Chiwong monk's own notes on the dance. He pronounces *ru rang* as "ru-tang." The term is no doubt derived from the classical Tibetan *rus-krang*.

86. According to TCU, 1982. See *Spying Ghosts* text.

87. Occasionally, snatches of liturgy are overheard. At Chiwong 11/21/83, I could distinguish the passage "the true words . . . the true words" at this point, confirming TCU's 1982 testimony.

88. I only recorded two times in 1983, however.

89. Stein reproduces a fascinating manuscript illumination showing a magician tying down a demon with a rope around his neck in just such a manner. See, *La Civilization*, 1981: plate facing p. 148. Jerstad, *Mani Rimdu*, 1969: 137 reports, interestingly, that he has heard the effigy "called a *bskang ba*, an offering to the Lord of the Dead."

90. Interview with Jamyang Norbu, former head of the Tibetan Institute for the Performing Arts, Dharamsala, 11/85. In 1982 with Trulshik Rinpoche presiding and again in 1983, when Sang Sang Tulku officiated, the entire dance was completed and the dancers had made their exits before the stabbing and burning took place on the dais. In 1980 and 1986, however, Trulshik Rinpoche disposed of the last feast and the paper effigy *before* the dancers' exit. Immediately after the burning effigy was placed on the ground, the Magicians danced and made their exit. The skeletons then enacted their play with the doll and made their exit. TCU, in describing the liturgy of this dance, also indicated that there were further dances after the ritual. The order of the dance I have chosen to describe here is that of 1982 and 1983, but details of the performance come from my notes of all four years.

91. The Vajrakīla *'chams yig* directs that "the liberation be done according to the *Manual*." (*las gzhung ltar bsgral*). Cf. Nebesky-Wojkowitz, *Tibetan Religious Dances*, 1976: 222-223.

92. Observed, Chiwong 11/21/83. Note that this is specified by the *Manual*. Cf. f 22b1

93. According to Jerstad, Tengpoche Rinpoche claims it is eaten by the *zhva-nag*. This assertion is so bizarre that it must be the result of a translation problem. See Jerstad, *Mani Rimdu*, 1969: 139.

94. According to TCU (1982), dance should follow burning the *lingka*. By this point in 1983, however, the dance had already finished and the Lords of the Cemetery had abandoned the doll. The assistant removed the doll and placed it under the altar. At Chiwong 12/17/86 a young monk ran out at another point and took the doll inside the chapel directly from where the skeletons had left it on the courtyard floor.

95. Nebesky-Wojkowitz goes so far as to say that "The cult of the *dharmapālas* includes the performance of religious dance." Nebesky-Wojkowitz, *Oracles and Demons*, 1956: 402.

96. Propitiation of Four-Faced One, PO f 44b4. Ironically, except in the last two years of Mani Rimdu at Rongphu, which had all ten Protectors, this is the only form of Mahākāla not portrayed in the Mani Rimdu dances. According to some informants, at Chiwong, where the form of Mahākāla danced is Four-Handed One, this section would not even be read during the dance.

97. Nebesky-Wojkowitz reports a Protector dance done at Mindroling itself in conjunction with the Padmasambhava *'chams*, but the group of deities is different—the so-called *Ma gza' dam gsum—Ma* mo Ekajaṭī, *gZa'* chen Rahu and *Dam* chen rDo rje legs pa. See, *Tibetan Religious Dances*, 1976: 14.

98. Trulshik Rinpoche. Accounts of the number originally presented at Rongphu differ. According to TCU in an 1983 interview, only eight were danced at Rongphu. There is also mention of nine protectors danced. The chart follows TCU's list.

99. Which of the *Playful Ocean's* four forms of Mahākāla is the "logical choice" is somewhat problematic, however. Virtuous One is sometimes considered the "chief of the protectors" (PO 40b2). In other ways, Four-Faced One seems the "best choice." If we look at the four groups of four deities used when performing the *Playful Ocean* piecemeal, Four-Faced One is the form of Mahākāla found in the list most closely resembling the group in the dance—that of "type four" days. As it is, the selection used in the dance corresponds to no known grouping. Again, in Trulshik Rinpoche's Protector *thang ka*, Four-Faced One, not Four-Handed One is found among the more frequently worshipped gods of the top row; and according to Beyer, Four-Faced One is the special protector of the Nyingma sect. A Nyingma iconography prepared by two noted Sherpa experts (Khempo Sangyay Tenzin, et al. 1975), however, lists every Mahākāla of the *Playful Ocean* except Four-Faced One. This is yet another example of the difficulty of extrapolating from one tradition to another in Tibet's dizzying pantheon of protectors.

100. Trulshik Rinpoche interview 11/27/83. TCU, who was hesitant about some of the later segments of the dance, stated in an 1982 interview that the propitiations of all the gods were recited. In his schema of 1983, adopted here, propitiations are only performed for deities actually danced. According to TCU, the confession is not performed.

101. The following description is taken primarily from the 1983 performance. The text selections were first identified by TCU in a 1982 interview. In 1983, we reviewed these field notes together to reconcile them with the fine points of the liturgy. According to Jerstad, the eight sections correspond to the number of Protectors danced. In his account, the positions of the dancers rotate, so that each deity stops in his dance in front of the lama as "a chant is intoned, invoking the protection of the particular deity who faces the Abbot at that time." Jerstad, *Mani Rimdu*, 1969: 147. Tengpoche Rinpoche once told me that the dance of the Protectors contains only the Propitiation rituals, which would be consistent with Jerstad's account. Unfortunately, I was not able to discuss the dance in sufficient detail with Tengpoche Rinpoche to confirm or deny Jerstad on this point. As noted below, there are some problems with TCU's account of the last movements which would be solved if we apply Jerstad's scheme to Chiwong.

102. This was the order in 1983. In 1980 and 1982, it was Four-Handed One, Cemetery Goddess, Great God, and Mantra Guardian.

103. Chiwong 12/1/82.

104. "Support substances" (*rten rdzas* = *rten pa'i dam rdzas*). LT explains this term in two ways. The first is that it means "things that make a god stay." Examples are the soul-stone and the life-wheel. In the second interpretation, the term means "holy substances of dependence," indicating that the yogi depends on, or resorts to the god. *rTen rdzas* include black yaks, and so on. *sKang rdzas* (propitiation substances).

105. *Playful Ocean* f 42.2 ff.

106. *Playful Ocean* f 43.3, "*chos kyi dbyings. . . .*"

107. *Playful Ocean* f 44b6 ff.

108. *spyan gzigs* (displays) are displays of wildlife; in modern Tib. = zoo.

109. *Playful Ocean* f 45b4,"*bshan pa srog. . . .*"

110. *Playful Ocean* f 45b6 ff.

111. *rang shar rang grol gnas lugs ji bzhin dbyings*. The three yogas each have a meditation on emptiness: Mahāyoga, that appearances are empty (*snang stong*); Anuyoga, that bliss is empty (*bde stong*); and Atiyoga (*rdzogs chen*), that knowledge is empty (*rig stong*). LT

112. *Playful Ocean* f 48.6.

113. *sgrub pa'i rig 'dzin mdo sngags chos gling sder*. "Sutra/Tantra Religious Island" is a common part of a monastery's name in Solu-Khumbu. The textual passage, *Playful Ocean* f 48b6 ff.: "*zhing skyong. . . .*" is, as usual according to TCU. My field notes from 1983, however, indicate that this dance is devoid of liturgy.

114. TCU does not indicate where this starts, but as Great God is worshipped in the dance, it would be logical to begin with his "*phrin las*," *Playful Ocean* f 50b6 ff. According to TCU, the confession that comes between the propitiations and the "request" is skipped. As mentioned above, Trulshik Rinpoche states that it is performed.

115. *gdon bgegs*. Any harm or decline produced by a non-human agent. There are twenty-one thousand classes of malignancies (*gdon rigs*) and eighty thousand classes of obstructors (*bgegs rigs*). LT

116. LT defines "free from extremes" (*mtha' bral*) as "free from elaboration's four extremes" (*spros pa'i mtha' bzhi dang bral ba*). In other words, not existence, not nonexistence, not both and not neither (*yod ma yin/med pa ma yin/gnyis ka ma yin/gnyis ka min pa ma yin*).

117. *Playful Ocean* f 53.2 ff. This seems confirmed by observation at Chiwong (see the following note), although Trulshik Rinpoche's account and observation at Thami place that ritual in the "Sword Dance." Also see Dance Twelve.

118. The removal of the torma was observed in 1980 and 1985. The timing is confirmed by TCU in our 1983 interviews. The other details in this paragraph are based on a single observation: Chiwong 10/29/85.

119. *Playful Ocean* f 54.4 through end.

120. The three secrets are of body, speech, and mind (*gsang ba gsum/sku'i gsang ba/gsung gi gsang ba/thugs kyi gsang ba*). LT

121. See for example the dance of Vaiśravaṇa at Shalu (Zhva lu), Nebesky-Wojkowitz, *Tibetan Religious Dances*, 1976: 34; the dance of Neuter (Ma ning) in eastern Tibet, Nebesky-Wojkowitz, Ibid., 1976: 17.

122. Witnessed by Nebesky-Wojkowitz, Ibid., on April 5, 1952. See Nebesky-Wojkowitz, Ibid., 1976: 36 ff. From its position in the line-up, the dance of the Ten Wrathful Ones (*khro bcu*) of the Eastern Tibetan monastery visited by Combe seems to represent a lower order of supernatural entities. See Nebesky-Wojkowitz, Ibid., 1976: 15.

123. See Jerstad, *Mani Rimdu*, 1969: 140 ff.

124. Gordon, *The Iconography*, 1939: 36. For the record, Gordon's list was: 1. Lha-mo, 2. Tshangs pa dkar po. 3. Beg tse, 4. gShin rje chos rgyal, 5. rNam thos sras, 6. mGon po, 7. rTa mgrin, 8. gShin rje gshed.

125. Jerstad, *Mani Rimdu*, 1969: 144.

126. Jerstad, Ibid., 1969: 146.

127. Fantin, *Mani Rimdu. Nepal.* 1976: 90–100. Although, to his credit he occasionally trusted his eyes enough to report a moment when Jerstad's account veered sharply from reality.

128. See Nebesky-Wojkowitz, *Tibetan Religious Dances*, 1976: 37, 75. To attempt to align Jerstad's observations to the *Playful Ocean* is a difficult and unrewarding task. For a chart correlating the deities of the dance with the *Playful Ocean*, see "Protector Dance Masks and Props," earlier in this section. To be fair to Jerstad and Fantin, the time and training necessary to untangle the skein of a ritual like Mani Rimdu are prohibitive. The account you are reading—as unsatisfactory as it is in many ways—is the product of nearly a decade of translation, field research, and interviews.

129. Nebesky-Wojkowitz, *Oracles and Demons*, 1956: 222. Nebesky-Wojkowitz lists several other miscellaneous *dge bsnyen* deities, including the important *dge bsnyen* Phying dkar ba (160–165); and Lha'i dge bsnyen, an outrider of the god of Mount bKra bzang zhing skyong in the Changthang "12 stages to the north of Shigatse" (220). In Tingri district, of which Rongphu is a part, Shar lung is also found as the name of a village, and there may be a relation between the two (see Aziz 1978: appendix I).

130. At Chiwong in 1980, one mask was black, one brown. According to TCU, at Rongphu the masks were black. At Thami, the Black Men wear animal pelts as belts.

131. According to Jerstad, *Mani Rimdu*, 1969: 155, they wear "everyday black woolen Sherpa boots."

132. At Chiwong 11/29/85, they used *kha btags*. In 1983, they used ropes.

133. Trulshik Rinpoche interview 10/27/85. Thami 5/23/83.

134. Trulshik Rinpoche interview 11/30/83. Body gods, LT explains, (*sku lha*, or, as here *lus lha*) are gods that protect your body. They are also often mountain gods. Thang lha, one of Tibet's more important autochthonous deities, for example, is "body god of Khri srong lde btsan" (Followers 12.2).

135. *dBen gnas rdza rong phu'i bka' srung shar lung dge bsnyen gyis mchod sprin sgrub pa'i re skong zhes bya ba bzhugs so*, from *Collected Propitiations* (*bsKang 'dus*), vol. Ja.

136. Some of Jerstad's informants identified him incorrectly as Khumbu yul lha. See *Mani Rimdu*, 1969: 157. For more on Khembalung, and secret valleys in general, see Bernbaum, *The Way to Shambhala*, 1980: 53 ff. For an illustration of Zur rva, see gTer ston Sans rgyas dbaṅ 'dus 1979: 592; the volume also contains a ritual dedicated to the god, #236 "gSang ba'i bdag Zu rwa ba'i 'phrin las 'dod pa'i dpal ster (Zu rwa)," pp. 200–217.

137. Interview, 11/27/83. TCU adds that he is the guardian of the door (*sgo srung*) of Khembalung—he does not let others in.

138. Tengpoche Rinpoche, 5/29/83, specifies that Zur ra's short (*sdu ba*) ritual be used.

139. Roerich, "The Epic of King Gesar," 1942: 289, 299. We should note that Gesar himself, in addition to his duties as an epic hero, is worshipped as a local protector. Indeed, he is a personal favorite of Tengpoche Rinpoche who has added him to the list of protectors worshipped during Mani-Rimdu at his monastery.

140. Those reported by Combe have both. Combe's *ḍākiṇī* dancers beat drums like those of the Ging, "but somewhat smaller" and "sing a short song of praise." See Nebesky-Wojkowitz, *Tibetan Religious Dances*, 1976: 16–17. In the dances that Nebesky-Wojkowitz himself witnessed in the Pedong Valley, two *pañcatathāgata*-crowned dancers accompanying themselves with *ḍamaru* and bells executed a "slow dance." See 1976: 37.

141. Nebesky-Wojkowitz, Ibid., 1976: 16–17; Fantin, *Mani Rimdu. Nepal.* 1976: 49. When in recent years, Lama Tharchin has mounted the first productions of *'chams* in the United States featuring his American students as dancers, women have danced the Sky Walkers with a singularly appropriate and beautiful effect.

142. Interview 11/27/83.

143. At Thami, the Sky Walkers are greeted by a formal procession, complete with incense and oboes. The procession reappears to see them out. Thami 5/23/83.

144. Trulshik Rinpoche explains the allusion to sexual yogic practice in the verse below, stating that "according to ritual" means "without desire, as opposed to in the manner of laymen."

145. Trulshik Rinpoche interview 11/27/83.

146. Trulshik Rinpoche interview 10/27/85.

147. Chiwong 12/1/82. Similarly, Sherpa villagers who have seen my film *Lord of the Dance/Destroyer of Illusion*, often ask with disappointment, "Where is the Tolden?" The answer best given is that it was too dark to shoot. That the Tolden's performance is three times the length of a feature film is staggering to contemplate for Sherpa and Westerner alike.

148. "*nga bka' rgyud grub thob yin*." Sherry B. Ortner has already refuted Jerstad's claim that the Seer is an Indian yogi and an object of ridicule in the eyes of the Sherpas. My own research bears out her statements. As Ortner says, "Most of the Sherpas I spoke to were not aware of this meaning, and were impressed by the Tolden's feats of spiritual strength." See Ortner, "The White-Black Ones," 1978b: 282; also Das, *Journey to Lhasa*, 539; Dargyay, *The Rise of Esoteric Buddhism*, 1979: 35; and Dowman, *The Divine Madman*, 1980: 61, n. 2. Allione, *Women of Wisdom*, 1986: pl. 26 shows a modern-day Tolden from Tashi Jong, in Northern India, also firmly identified as a Kagyü yogi: "These Yogis practice the Six Yogas of Naropa and wear only thin white cotton clothes, symbolizing that they have accomplished the yoga of inner heat *(tummo)* like Milarepa." Although Jerstad's assertion that the Seer represents a Hindu *sādhu*, and Fantin's interpretation of his name as "The Over-Confident Man" seem to be totally without merit, similar figures in other *'chams*, the *atsara*, may be so characterized with some justice. The question of the *atsara* will be dealt with later in this section.

149. Ortner, "The White-Black Ones," 1978b: 282.

150. Stein, *Tibetan Civilization*, 1972: 218.

151. My manuscript was copied by Agike, monk and former Chant Leader of Chiwong Monastery, from the Chiwong manuscript. I checked the copy with Ngawang Yonten of Chiwong, who plays the part of the Seer. Ngawang Yonten was servant and student of Ngawang Tsokdruk (Ngag dbang tshogs drug), one of Chiwong's first monks and until his death in 1981, head monk of Chiwong. The interpolations in brackets are Ngawang Yonten's. NY attributes the authorship of *The Seer* text to his teacher, whereas, several layman of Junbesi attributed it to the renowned painter O Leshe, also of Junbesi, adding that "many people say that." O Leshe was reputedly involved in the founding of Mani Rimdu at Chiwong. He is generally regarded by local Sherpas to have been a saint. For more on him, see Downs, *Rhythms of a Himalayan Village*, 1980, passim. According to Thami Rinpoche, there is also a small text for the Seer at his monastery, but I have not been able to compare it to the Chiwong edition.

152. The specific refuge that the Tolden recites comes from UB f. 3b3 ff.,

153. *ngo shes bya*. NY says that this consists of "my saying *'chape nang jung'* (Tib. "Welcome!") to [the late] Ngawang Tenzin Norbu, Trulshik Rinpoche, and so on, and then to the patrons of the monastery, and then to the monks."

154. According to NY, these are two books printed in Solu-Khumbu.

155. *chos 'chad* = "*chos thams cad kyi rtsa ba ni . . .*", see below. NY.

156. *mi rtags* (*sic*). NY says that there is no book for this. He simply extemporizes along these lines: "First you get married. Then a child is born. Then, you get sick. Then, a Lama comes and treats you, but you can't be cured and then, you die.

Then, the Lama transfers your consciousness ("*pho ba rgyab gyi red*"). Then, they bring your body out of the house."

157. See ff. 14–16b2. NY

158. *lha bsang*, that is, he recites a small passage from the *Mountain Incense Offering* (*Ri bo bsangs mchod*)—the first page. NY

159. NY says "any song is O.K. This year I sang Sherpa songs, Tibetan songs, and Nepali songs."

160. *'bras dkar*, for *'dre dkar* [pronounced drekar]. Although in my copy of the manuscript this line comes below, NY places it here instead, and says that after "Attracting Fortune," he did another *gcod*, and then the two Black Men (*mi nag*) entered with knives. In any event, the drekar is an itinerant Tibetan entertainer who gives humorous religious teachings. There is a "drekar" book, which NY knows by heart. However, he does not know where a copy of it could be found. During this segment, the Seer begs money from the audience. NY also sang the jesting song ("Dochire . . .") from the Nepali Tihar (Divali) festival at this point, which he categorizes as a "Nepali drekar." After the drekar, the Seer plays dice.

161. NY identifies the *Bro brdung* as a book belonging to the *gcod* (cutting off) the ego tradition. The part recited is the first eight lines beginning "*bdag nyid he ru ka ka pa la la 'di/*" and then "*de nas rnal 'byor. . . .*"

162. This semicomic empowerment is done with a Lama's hat, a Lama's boot, and the doll used elsewhere in the dances. NY.

163. *g.yang 'gugs*, (Attracting Fortune) probably indicates the verse that follows it. As will be remembered, however, there is a section dedicated to this ancient and popular pre-Buddhist Tibetan ritual in the *Mountain Incense Offering*. See note 14 and Day Thirteen.

164. NY says that he does not know what these ejaculations mean, but that Ngawang Tsokdruk, to whom he attributes the text, did.

165. I.e., the Auspicious Omens, f 17 ff, usually up to "*skyabs gnas. . . .*" NY.

166. *zhabs brtan ni bden pa'i 'jug tu/*. According to NY, the "Truths" is the evocation of the power of truth found in the Spying Ghosts ritual, etc.: "*sangs rgyas gyi bka' bden pa/chos gyi . . . /dge 'dun gyi . . .*" up to "Oṁ sumbhani sumbhani." Note, however, that the first stanza below is also an evocation of the truth. The "Long Life Prayer", begins "Oṁ svasti", below. NY continues his account as follows: first, the "*chos kyi ḍa ma ru*", four lines, then the *gCod yul mkha' 'gro'i gad rgyangs* from the *Klong chen snying thig*, pp. 571–586. The passage used begins "Phaṭ . . ." on p. 574, line 6, and continues to ". . . *shog/*", p. 578, line 4.

167. *ris 'brus 'grub par mdzod ris 'brus* should read *re 'bras*, (the result of one's hopes). NY.

168. The Fourth Guide (*rnam 'dren bzhi ba*) is the Buddha (RT). His spiritual son or disciple was Ānanda. Ngag dbang blo bzang mdo sngags, Trulshik Rinpoche, is considered Ānanda's reincarnation. Thus, this prayer is dedicated to the lama who presides, not only over the Chiwong Mani Rimdu, but the entire tradition.

169. In this prayer whenever the Seer says "I offer . . . this long life prayer!" (*zhabs brtan 'bul lo*), he falls on his sword. NY.

170. *Bu ram shing pa*, "Ikṣvāku, n. of the progenitor of the solar race, an epithet of Sākya Siṁha Buddha who was born of that race," from *bu ram shing*, (sugar cane plant) D 871. Also see MV 79.

171. I.e., Jambudvīpa: India, the known world. *Khyad par 'dzam gling yongs kyi bstan 'dzin mkhyen*, probably for *mkhan*, "those who." RT.

172. Sovereign Nyima Wözer = *mnga' bdag* Nyi ma 'od zer. Lama Sangyay = Bla ma sang [rgyas], the patron who built Chiwong. His family, the Lama clan of Phaphlu is said to be the lineage of Nyima Wözer, i.e., of the Nyang clan (NY). On Nyang Nyima Wözer, the great twelfth century *gter ston*, see Tulku Thondup, *The Tantric Tradition*, 1984: 151, and Dargyay, *The Rise of Esoteric Buddhism*, 1979: passim. See now also Dudjom 1991, vol. 1, pp. 755–759. Family panegyrics have long been a part of Tibetan festivals. See Stein, *Tibetan Civilization*, 1972: 193.

173. *sngon du ma bye na/*. The manuscript has *bye* for *byed*. RK

174. The text actually reads *slob dpon* (master). That phrase inverted, however, *dpon slob*, is an abbreviation for *slob dpon dang slob ma* (master and disciple).

175. Adams, *Tigers of the Snow*, 1996: 147.

176. Jerstad describes another sort of trick sword. In his account, the weapon is sharp, hard, and truly dangerous. The trick lies in a blade that retracts part way into the handle. Instead of bending the sword, the dancer "turns slightly to avoid the blade." *Mani Rimdu*, 1969: 153–154.

177. Chiwong 12/1/82.

178. On the *cagan öbö*, see Nebesky-Wojkowitz, *Tibetan Religious Dances*, 1976: 83–84; Berger and Bartholomew, *Mongolia*, 1995: 158.

179. Nebesky-Wojkowitz, *Tibetan Religious Dances*, 1976: 82.

180. Ibid., 1976: 17; 84.

181. Ibid 1976: 84.

182. Nebesky-Wojkowitz, *Where the Gods are Mountains*, n.d.: 211.

183. Ibid., 220.

184. Ibid., 217.

185. As Trulshik Rinpoche put it, uncharacteristically using the Nepali word. Interview 11/27/83.

186. TCU thus corrects me when I call them the "Black Men" (*mi nag*). There are, interestingly enough, a group of Bon deities called the *lhag ma bzhi*, although they have no relation to the present liturgy. See Nebesky-Wojkowitz, *Oracles and Demons*, 1956: 315.

187. I include here only the main recitation. The subsidiary passages and stage directions, can be found in UB 35.1 ff, Throwing out the Remains (*lhag ma gtong ba*).

188. *Langka* indicates the carnivorous *rākṣasa* demons who populate mythological µri Lanka. The exact significance of *langka tshar gsum*, which I have provision-

ally translated as "the three types of *langka*," however is not entirely clear. It might also be for *langka rtsa gsum*, "the [twenty-] three *langka*."

189. LIS 192b6–193.2. I take the text's *phra men* (Sorcerer) for *phra men ma* (Sorceress). On *shugs 'gro*, see note in Day 6–12, the first session.

190. Quoted by Jerstad, *Mani Rimdu*, 1969: 159. Jerstad's guess that the dancers are the goddesses Makaravaktrā and Siṁhavaktrā is just that—a guess—and not a likely one given that those goddesses have the heads of a crocodile and a lioness, respectively, a detail that would no doubt be reflected in their masks, were the goddesses present.

191. This may be the reason the Thami list, cited earlier in this chapter, does not separate it by punctuation from the Sword Dance that follows.

192. Chiwong 11/21/83.

193. I have only the word of TCU that the ritual is read at this particular juncture. I have never actually seen or heard it either at Chiwong or at Thami. The rest of this account is a composite of 1982 and 1983.

194. See Nebesky-Wojkowitz, *Tibetan Religious Dances*, 1976: 187.

195. This is asserted to be for purely practical reasons. We should note in passing that Ekajaṭī (known as Mantra Guardian in the *Playful Ocean*), whose mask is one used here for one of the liberation Ging, appears among a group of deities in a *gShin rje* dance of the Nyingma sect under the name of "liberation mother" (*sgrol yum*). Nebesky-Wojkowitz, Ibid., 1976: 14.

196. Although in Mani Rimdu the dancers enter the courtyard carrying their weapons, in other *'chams* the weapons are already on stage, either on the central altar or on a table next to the dough effigy. Nebesky-Wojkowitz, Ibid., 1976: 67.

197. At Chiwong 1983. The above account is summarized from that year.

198. I first observed these tormas at Chiwong in 1982, although was unable to identify them. In 1984, the Contract and Steadfast Women tormas were removed at this time. By all accounts (and the logic of the ritual), however, they should not be taken out until the next dance when the contract torma becomes a magic weapon.

199. Trulshik Rinpoche interview 11/27/83. In a similar vein, the Vajrakīla *'chams yig* refers to a liberation sword (*sgrol gri*). Nebesky-Wojkowitz, *Tibetan Religious Dances*, 1976: 193.

200. Jerstad does not mention the dough effigy in his brief account of the sword dance, although I witnessed it used at Thami in 1980 and 1983, and at Tengpoche in 1987. Cf. Jerstad, *Mani Rimdu*, 1969: 161.

201. TCU 1983.

202. TCU, examining my sketch from Thami, states that the figure used at Rongphu was made differently. The interpretations of the parts of the *lingka* are his. According to Nebesky-Wojkowitz, the dough effigy is called a "*zan ling*," as opposed to a "*shog ling*," a paper effigy. He indicates that it may also be painted dark blue or constructed of black flour, but at Thami and Tengpoche it is red. Nebesky-Wojkowitz, *Tibetan Religious Dances*, 1976: 106–107.

203. According to TCU. My sketch from Thami shows them straight.

204. Nebesky-Wojkowitz gives an elaborate list of magical additions to *lingka*-figurines and to scapegoats (*glud*) that allow them to magically stand in for those whom they represent. Nebesky-Wojkowitz, Ibid., 1976: 106.

205. *dgra bgegs kyi gzugs brnyan*. Cf. Nebesky-Wojkowitz, Ibid., 1976: 203.

206. Nebesky-Wojkowitz Ibid., 1976: 193.

207. There is a plate of feast in front of the torma, it is possible, though less likely that it is the object of these attentions, since it remains untouched for the rest of the evening.

208. Based on observation at Thami 5/23/83.

209. In an interview on 11/27/83, Trulshik Rinpoche said that the Protector ritual used is the *Chos skyong spyi la gtor ma 'bul*. Although this designation is ambiguous, it almost certainly indicates the "Feeding the Tormas," *Playful Ocean* f 53.2 ff. The relevant field observations I possess confirm this. In addition to the above from Thami in 1983, when I was first at Thami in 1980, I overheard part of the offering mantra, ". . . *khahi khahi*," and noted that a torma was sprinkled and removed at this time. This data conflicts with TCU's account in which the "Feeding" was already done during the Protector Dance and the liturgy of the *Playful Ocean* long since concluded. It is possible that the two monasteries differ on this point. If we grant this, and assume that the Thami practice is closer to the Rongphu system, we can explain the discrepancies between the two accounts. TCU, who performs the rituals of both Dance Seven and Twelve at Chiwong, would tend to describe the present-day practice of Chiwong. Trulshik Rinpoche, who by contrast leaves the dais before Dance Twelve is performed, would be more likely to describe the "official" Rongphu system.

210. *Playful Ocean* f 53b4.

211. TR interview, n.d. The Vajrakīla *'chams yig* goes so far as to indicate the syllables of liturgy on which certain dance steps are to be executed. See for example, Nebesky-Wojkowitz, *Tibetan Religious Dances*, 1976: 221: "The step taken with the left foot should correspond to the final stanza of the *bsgral śloka*, but, should the *śloka* not accord with the movements, one should correlate the final word with the left foot step in the direction of walking." Also see 1976: 205 ff.

212. Nebesky-Wojkowitz, *Where the Gods are Mountains*, n.d.: 237; also see Tucci, *The Religions of Tibet*, 1980: 155.

213. Nebesky-Wojkowitz has written widely about one such performance in the Sikkimese Kangchenjunga dance. It is performed immediately after the overture to "drive away lingering evil forces," the dancers entering the courtyard shouting a Tibetan war-cry—"*kyi hu hu!*" Some movements of this dance—among the few dance movements named anywhere in Western literature—mimic swordsmanship: "unsheathing the sword" (*gri 'khor*), "sharpening the sword" (*gri rdar*), and "lifting the sword" (*gri 'phyar*). See Nebesky-Wojkowitz, *Oracles and Demons*, 1956: 404; n.d.: 235; and 1976: 23. For a dance performed by soldiers, see my notes on Dance Four.

214. This is part of a ceremony called *lo re'i gsol kha*. See Nebesky-Wojkowitz, *Tibetan Religious Dances*, 1976: 27. We have already seen the relation between oracles and swords above in Dance Ten.

215. Trulshik Rinpoche interview 11/27/83.

216. Neither the *Manual* nor commentaries name this *mudrā*. The description in my notes is reminiscent of the "opening gesture" (*dbye rgya*) used to open the doors of the *maṇḍala* during the daily self-empowerment. Why such a gesture should be employed here is another matter entirely.

217. Chiwong 1982. Although, checking in 1983, I could not hear the recitations.

218. UB f 37.2.

219. In eastern Tibet, the *gtor rgyab* is also performed by black hats. On *gtor rgyab* see Nebesky-Wojkowitz, *Tibetan Religious Dances*, 1976: 19; on *zor* and other magic weapons, see Nebesky-Wojkowitz, *Oracles and Demons*, 1956: 354-358.

220. It was reputedly introduced there by the first Dharmarāja of Bhutan. See Nebesky-Wojkowitz, *Tibetan Religious Dances*, 1976: 35. Nebesky-Wojkowitz 1965: 404 also refers to the *zor 'chams* as a dance step related to the diamond walk (*rdo rje 'gro*).

221. LIS 193b6.

222. Lit., "varied dance." It is also called the "*log 'chams*," the "Return Dance," or perhaps the "Expulsion Dance." Tengpoche Rinpoche also calls it the "*mtha' 'chams*," the "Final Dance" (Tengpoche Rinpoche 5/29/83). At Chiwong in 1982, the Magicians held *vajras*. In 1982, the "Black Men" carried the props that represent the "enemy's heart"; in 1983, their hands were empty.

223. Tengpoche Rinpoche 5/29/83.

224. Trulshik Rinpoche, 1986 interview.

225. At Thami, in 1983, I noted that the dancers all do the hook *mudrā*, as they stand during the liturgy.

226. Tengpoche Rinpoche (5/29/83) specifies this passage (UB 39b2 ff) as the Auspicious Omens text used at this point. There are other "Auspicious Omens" used in Mani Rimdu, such as that of the *Manual* appendix and the one in *Religious Practice*. Similar recitations are found at the end of most complicated Tibetan ritual sequences. According to TCU (1982), all the *Manual* between the Horse Dance and the Auspicious Omens is read. At Chiwong in 1983, I heard rituals recited consonant with his identification.

227. When grain is thrown indoors at an analogous moment it represents a rain of flowers, Lama Tharchin 6/84.

228. Trulshik Rinpoche interview 11/27/83, see Day Ø.

229. "Mais il s'y attache aussi pour les spectateurs un intérêt pratique. . . . Parmi les images terribles surgissent surtout dans le bardo les divinités protectrice démoniaques. L'un des but des danses culturelles consiste à les faire connaître aux

croyants, à familiariser ceux-ci avec leur physionomie à fin que, parvenirs à l'état intermédiare, ils ne se dérobent pas devant leurs saveurs." Bleichsteiner, *l'Église Jaune*, 1937: 219. In Solu-Khumbu, this observation has been confirmed as recently as 1986 by A. Gurung.

Chapter 18: Day Sixteen

1. TCU interview, 1982.

2. The outline is based on TCU's 1983 revision of his 1982 account. I was able to corroborate it in nearly every detail at Chiwong, 11/22/83.

3. The name TCU used here was *bsDus gsol*, evidently for *gSol bsdus*, the *Abridged Prayer*, i.e., Trulshik Rinpoche's *Abridged Prayers for the Local Gods* (*gNas bdag gsol bsdus*).

4. TCU did not mention this latter, but it was used Chiwong 11/22/83.

5. In 1983, the *'bul gtor* had gifts for four deities: Four-Faced One, Mantra Guardian, Great God, and Cemetery Grandmother. TCU judged the addition of a sub-torma for Mantra Guardian an unimportant error. It was not reflected in the liturgy.

6. 12/10/82, 11/22/83. In 1983, at the end of the day the following tormas remain in the torma cabinet: the Great Protectors, the food, the fierce food, the flower of the senses.

7. TCU notes that because on the Burnt Offering day there are no flasks (*las bum, rnam rgyal bum pa*), instead of starting at RP151.1, "SVABHVA . . ." you need the *mudrā* and mantras found on f 150b6–151.1—the Diamond Malefactor/ Benefactor gesture with "Oṁ vajrayakṣa hūṁ," and the diamond fire gesture with "Oṁ vajra jvalayanala hana daha paca mathabhañjaraṇa hūṁ phaṭ." See *Three-Part Torma* text, in Lopez, *Religions of Tibet*, 1997.

8. *Kun bzang rnam rol mchod pa'i tshogs. . . .* UB 38.2 requires repetition of an earlier passage—"the clouds of inner and outer worship offered in common" from The Outer Offerings, f 15.5–15b6.

9. See Day Six.

10. See Greenwold, "The Role of the Priest," 1978: 493.

11. Lessing, for example, describes a peaceful Burnt Offering of the god Saṁvara, in his book, *Yung-Ho-Kung*, 1942: 151–160. Beyer describes a peaceful Burnt Offering of Tārā in, *The Cult of Tārā*, 1973: 264–275. Snellgrove describes a Lord of the Dance Burnt Offering of the fierce type performed on an ad hoc basis at Chiwong, *Buddhist Himālaya*, 1957: 259 ff, and plate 39b. Also see Skorupski's contribution to Staal, *Agni*, 1983.

12. BO 3b6.

13. The pull to reconcile the facts of practice with the theories of commentary is a strong one. TCU attempts to reconcile the Chiwong schedule with the *Precious Lamp*. He observes that the commentary antedates the invention of Mani Rimdu, and

therefore does not take the days of dance into account—in the *Precious Lamp*, the empowerment and Burnt Offering fall on the same day. Thus, the commentary must be adjusted to fit the necessities of the festival.

14. My notes from Chiwong 1983 indicate that a mantra beginning "Oṁ sarvabighanaṁ . . ." is also recited, although neither BO nor S/P mentions such a mantra. PL 6b6 states that the Sky Treasury mantra (*nam mkha' mdzod sngags*) should be used here: "Namaḥ sarvatathāgatebhyo viśvamukhebhyaḥ sarvathākhaṁ utgate sparaṇa imaṁ gaganakhaṁ svāhā" (cf. S/P 3.2). It is quite possible that I misheard it.

15. PL 7.1; Chiwong 1983.

16. In 1983, SST used his left hand although the *vajra* is typically wielded in the right.

17. BO 4.1. For more on the geometry and construction of Burnt Offering *maṇḍalas*, see Beyer, *The Cult of Tārā,* 1973: 250; 265–266; 268.

18. *mTsho bdun ri bdun.* TCU calls these elements of Buddhist cosmology the seven rivers and seven mountains—*chu bdun ri bdun.* Stein's photograph from Ghoom shows the syllable, minus the rivers and mountains, painted directly on the fire wall. Lessing's version also has merely the syllable. See Stein, *La Civilization*, 1981: 68, top; Lessing, *Yang-Ho-Kung*, 1942: 153.

19. Ortner has written on the status implications of seating at some length. Ortner, "Sherpa Purity," 1978: 61, 74 ff, fig. 1 on p. 75.

20. By 1993, the family's position during the dance had moved to the side balcony, a less convenient but more easily defended location. This in itself shows a change in the relations between the leading family and the surrounding community. In the early 1980s, interlopers in the "private box" could and would be informed of their gaffe by most any Sherpa. In the mid-1980s one occasionally saw a lone interloper refuse to move and his presence finally be accepted with a shrug. In 1994, non-family members casually edged into the private domain en masse, despite the presence of police officers charged to block their way.

21. The chronicles give examples of this practice as early as the eighth century in the reign of 'Khri srong lde'u btsan. See Stein, *Tibetan Civilization*, 1972: 142.

22. This actually happened in 1980. With changes that are now in the wind, it is interesting to speculate what would happen were the incident to be repeated some years hence. In 1987, for example, the family's privileged seating at the public empowerment simply ceased to exist.

23. Other Sherpas sometimes state with a mixture of pride and resentment that their forebears built Chiwong too. The pride is in the accomplishment. The resentment is twofold: (1) that their forebears' labor was conscripted by the all-powerful Sangyay Lama, who provided the capital and took all the credit; (2) that despite the contribution of others, his descendants persist in regarding Chiwong as their own private property. Ortner, "Sherpa Purity," 1978: 76 gives a sketch of the movements in clan hierarchy that surrounded the building of Chiwong, although she disguises the names as usual. The interloper in the example below, was not to my knowledge a descendant

of one of these conscripts, but merely from a village too far distant to appreciate the situation. There is some evidence that the perception of Chiwong as a "private" monastery is now changing, but to what extent only the future will tell.

24. Lessing's physical description of the preparation of the sticks accords with the practice at Chiwong. According to Lessing, the wood symbolizes the Bodhi tree and "is offered in order to obtain early illumination." See, *Yung-Ho-Kung*, 1942: 152, 157. Judging by its leaves, it is perhaps a variety of bay or even willow.

25. For a drawing of this, see Lessing, Ibid., 1942: 153; for a photograph, Stein, *La Civilization*, 1981: 68, top.

26. These are also used in the self-administered empowerment, UB 22b6. Lessing (1942: 154–155) describes such regalia in detail.

27. See Bhattacharyya, *The Indian Buddhist*, 1958: 362; Lessing, Ibid., 1942: 158

28. BO f 4b5.

29. Beyer, *The Cult of Tārā*, 1973: 167 has a sketch of these ladles.

30. Lessing, *Yung-Ho-Kung*, 1942: 160-161.

31. See note in BO following f 6.1. The concept of a configuration of "heaps" on this plate is also present in the *maṇḍala* offering ritual. In that context, Lessing translates *tshom bu* as "little heap of offering stuff." See Lessing, "Miscellaneous Lamaist Notes," 1956: 60; and 66, n 16.

32. Chiwong 1980.

33. I.e., GW 19b3–20.2. See PO 1.4, f 5b4 ff.

34. Just how symbolically was evidenced in 1980, when wood was added to the pyre *after* it had been "put out" with the milk. The wood was presumably added so that the fire would stop smoking.

35. Cf. Day Fourteen. The following description was taken from Chiwong 11/24/80. Interview subjects did not discuss this repetition of the "true achievement" in specific, but by its character and from its position vis à vis the other ritemes, the identification is self-evident. At Tengpoche, where the "true achievement" torma is elaborately shared out at this point, its presence is even more conspicuous.

36. NP f 11 ff.

37. "Erasing the Lines" and SR f 2b2.

38. Chiwong 1980; also cf. note in "Erasing the Lines."

39. Oṁ akāro mukhaṁ sarvadharmānāṁ ādyanutpannatvāt oṁ aḥ hūṁ phaṭ svāhā. The translation is from Beyer, *The Cult of Tārā*, 1973: 146. The gesture recalls Lessing's account of transferring the wisdom beings via pinches of sand during the Burnt Offering.

Chapter 19: Day Seventeen

1. "rDul tshon chu bor spyan 'dren pa'i dgos pa ni klu'i rgyal po 'khor dang bcas pa rnams la de bzhin gshegs pa rnams kyis byin kyis brlabs pa'i rdul tshon rin

po che'i rang bzhin can de bdag gir mdzad par gsol nas mchod pa dang/ 'jig rten gyi khams spyi dang/ khyad par sa phyogs der bde legs phun sum tshogs pa 'phel zhing rgyas pa'i phrin las bcol ba'i dgos pa dang phan yon pa red." Trulshik Rinpoche, personal communication.

2. Lessing, *Yung-ho-Kung,* 1942: 6, 161.

3. NP, f 11.

4. Dharmaśri avoids this problem by directing that the *maṇḍala* be created at stream side. See NP.

5. The longer dedication is *A Paradise of Benefit and Pleasure;* the auspicious recitation, *A Shower of Benefit and Pleasure*. This and the rituals that follow were identified by TCU in 1982, the list incorporates several emendations that he made in 1983. Thus, the account is well considered to say the least, although I have never been able to corroborate the texts by independent observation.

6. *rnam thar gsum*, probably for *rnam thar sgo gsum*, "the three doors of liberation": emptiness, the sign-less, the wish-less. Cf. D 759.

7. This prayer is said to be an adaptation of a praise from *Religious Practice.* TCU gives it as: "bla ma'i sku ni rdo rje sku// mdzes zhing blta bas chog mi shes/ / bsam gyis mi khyab yon tan ldan// bla ma'i sku la zhabs brtan 'bul// bla ma'i gsung ni tshangs pa'i dbyangs// 'gag med seng ge'i sgra dang ldan// mu stegs ri dwags skrag mdzad pa// bla ma'i gsung la zhabs brtan 'bul// bla ma'i thugs ni nam mkha' 'dra// bde gsal mi rtog stong ba'i ngang// rnam thar gsum la legs gnas pa// bla ma'i thugs la zhabs brtan 'bul."

8. "Desire, anger . . . " following the "Seven Branches," RP f 163.1–b6.

9. "Namo guru . . . ", RP 52.2–54b6.

Chapter 20: Epilogue

1. My translation of this prayer can be found in Lopez, 1995.

Bibliography

Adams, Vincanne. 1996. *Tigers of the Snow and Other Virtual Sherpas. An Ethnography of Himalayan Encounters.* Princeton: Princeton University Press.

Addiss, Stephan. 1985. *Japanese Ghosts and Demons. Art of the Supernatural.* New York: George Braziller.

Allione, Tsultrim. 1986. *Women of Wisdom.* London, Boston, and Henley: Arkana.

Ardussi, John, and Lawrence Epstein. 1978. "The Saintly Madman in Tibet." In *Himalayan Anthropology.* Ed. J. Fisher, pp. 327–338.

Aris, Michael, and Aung San Suu Kyi, ed. 1980. *Tibetan Studies in Honour of Hugh Richardson. Proceedings of the International Seminar on Tibetan Studies.* Oxford: 1979. New Delhi: Vikas Publishing House Pvt., Ltd.

Aris, Michael. 1980b. "Sacred Dances of Bhutan," *Natural History*, 79, no.3: 38–47.

———. 1982. *Views of Medieval Bhutan. The Diary and Drawings of Samuel Davis. 1783.* New Delhi: Roli Books International.

———. 1988. *Hidden Treasures and Secret Lives. A Study of Pemalingpa (1450–1521) and the Sixth Dalai Lama (1683–1706).* Dehli: Motilal Banarsidass.

Aziz, Barbara N. 1976. "Reincarnation Reconsidered: or The Re-incarnate Lama as Shaman." In *Spirit Possession in the Nepal Himalayas.* Ed. J. Hitchcock and R. Jones, pp. 343–360 Warminster: Aris and Phillips.

———. 1976b. "Views from the Monastery Kitchen," *Kailash. A Journal of Himalayan Studies*, IV, No. 2: 155–167.

———. 1978. *Tibetan Frontier Families. Reflections of Three Generations from D'ingri.* New Dehli: Vikas Publishing House.

Aziz, Barbara, and Matthew Kapstein, eds. 1985. *Soundings in Tibetan Civilization.* Proceedings of the 1982 Seminar of the International Association for Tibetan Studies held at Columbia University. New Delhi: Manohar.

Bacot, Jacques. 1957. *Zugiñima.* Cahiers de la Société Asiatique XIV. Publiés avec le Concours du Centre National de la Recherche Scientifique. Paris: Imprimerie Nationale.

Bagchi, P. C. 1933. "A note on the word Parāvṛtti," *Calcutta Oriental Journal*, I, 1, (No. Oct. 1933).

Bajracarya, Amoghabajra. 1979. *Nepāḥdeya Kanakajaityamahāviharayā Aṣṭottarasata Lokeśvara Parijaya.* Nepal: Lokeśvara Saṁgha.

Bajracarya, Pandit Vaidya Ashakaji. 2039 (N.E.). *Mallakālīna Kaṁ Pyākaṁ.* (*The Dance of the Asthamatrika*). Kathmandu.

Basham, A. L. 1954. *The Wonder that was India.* New York: Macmillan; Reprint, Grove Press, 1959.

Bawden, C. R. 1958. "On the Practice of Scapulamancy among the Mongols," *Central Asiatic Journal* IV: 1–31.

Beresford, Brian C., trans. and ed. 1980. *Mahāyāna Purification. The Confession Sūtra with commentary by Ārya Nāgārjuna and the Practice of Vajrasattva. Supplemented by verbally transmitted commentaries from Geshe Ngawang Dhargyey, Geshe Rabten, Gegen Khyentse, Thupten Zopa Rinpoche.* Dharamsala: The Library of Tibetan Works and Archives.

Berger, Patricia and Terese Tse Bartholomew. 1995. *Mongolia. The Legacy of Chinggis Khan.* New York and London: Thames and Hudson in association with Asian Art Museum of San Francisco.

Bernbaum, Edwin. 1980. *The Way to Shambhala. A Search for the Mythical Kingdom beyond the Himalayas.* Garden City, N.Y.: Anchor Books.

———. 1994. "The Dancer's Sleeve," in *Parabola*, (Fall).

Beyer, Stephan. 1973. *The Cult of Tārā. Magic and Ritual in Tibet.* Berkeley: University of California Press.

———. 1974. *The Buddhist Experience: Sources and Interpretations.* Encino, Ca.: Dickenson Publishing Company.

———. 1977. "Notes on the Vision Quest in Early Mahāyāna." In Lancaster (ed.), *Prajñāpāramitā and Related Systems.* Berkeley: University of California Press.

Bharati, Agehananda. 1965. *The Tantric Tradition.* London: Rider and Company; reprint. Bombay: B. I. Publications, 1976.

Bhattacharyya, Benoytosh. 1958. *The Indian Buddhist Iconography.* 2nd Ed. Calcutta: Firma K. L. Mukhopadyay; Reprint, 1968.

Bischoff, Friederich A. 1966. "Theater in Tibet." In *Asian Drama: a collection of festival papers.* Edited by Vermillion: University of South Dakota Department of Speech and Dramatic Arts. Henry Wells, 149–54.

———. 1978. "Padmasambhava est-il un personnage historique?" In *Proceedings of the Csoma de Körös Memorial Symposium*, L. Ligeti, ed., 27–33.

Bishoff, Friedrich A. and Charles Hartman. 1971. "Padmasambhava's Invention of the Phur-bu Ms. Pelliot Tibétain 44." In *Études Tibétaines Dédiées à la Mémoire de Marcelle Lalou.* Paris: Librarie d'Amérique et d'Orient Adrien Maisonneuve.

Bleichsteiner, Robert. 1937. *l'Église Jaune.* Paris: Payot (1950 ed.).

British Museum. 1982–1985. *The Art of Central Asia: the Stein Collection in the British Museum.* 2 v. Tokyo: Kodansha International in cooperation with the Trustees of the British Museum.

Campbell, Joseph. 1984. *The Way of the Animal Powers. Historical Atlas of World Mythology. Vol. 1.* London: Times Books.

Chö Yang (Chos dbyangs*). "The voice of Tibetan religion & culture."* Year of Tibet Edition, 1991. Dharamsala, India: Council for Religious and Cultural Affairs of H.H. the Dalai Lama.

Clark, Walter E. 1937. *Two Lamaistic Pantheons.* Harvard-Yenching Institute, Monograph Series, III, IV. Cambridge, Massachusetts.

Collier, John Jr. 1967. *Visual Anthropology: Photography as a Research Method.* Studies in Anthropological Method. New York: Holt, Rinehardt and Winston.

Combe, G. A. 1926. *A Tibetan on Tibet.* [Sherap, Paul, b. 1887. *A Tibetan on Tibet; being the travels and observations of Mr. Paul Sherap (Dorje Zodba) of Tachienlu; with an introductory chapter on Buddhism and a concluding chapter on the devil dance, by G. A. Combe.* London, T. F. Unwin, Ltd.; New York: D. Appleton.

Combs-Schilling, M. E. 1989. *Sacred Performances. Islam, Sexuality, and Sacrifice.* New York: Columbia University Press.

Coomaraswamy, Ananda Kentish. 1980. *Yakṣas.* 2nd ed. New Dehli: Munshiram Manoharlal Publishers Pvt., Ltd.

Cozort, Daniel. 1986. *Highest Yoga Tantra. An Introduction to the Esoteric Buddhism of Tibet.* Ithaca, N.Y.: Snow Lion Publications.

Dalai Lama II (dGe 'dun rgya mtsho, 1475–1542). n.d. "A Meditation on the Four-Armed Avalokiteśvara," Extracted from "Concerning the Meditational Deity Practices" (*yi dam sgrub skor*), Collected Works. Vol. II, Drepung Edition. In *Meditation on the Lower Tantras.* Ed. G. Mullin, 47–50.

Dargyay, Eva M. 1979. *The Rise of Esoteric Buddhism in Tibet.* 2nd Rev. Ed. Dehli: Motilal Banarsidass.

Das, Sarat Chandra. 1909. *Journey to Lhasa and Central Tibet.* Edited by the Hon. W. W. Rockhill. New Edition. London: John Murray.

Davidson, Ronald M. 1991. "Reflections on the Maheśvara Subjugation Myth: Indic Materials, Sa-skya-pa Apologetics, and the Birth of Heruka," *The Journal of the International Association of Buddhist Studies*, 14, No. 2: 197–235.

Dehejia, Vidya. 1982. "The Yoginī temples of India: A preliminary Investigation." *Art International*, (March–April), 6–28, and p. 97.

———. 1986. *Yoginī Cult and Temples. A Tantric Tradition.* New Dehli: National Museum.

Dhaky, M. A. n.d. "Bhūtas and Bhūtanāyakas: Elementals and their Captains." In *Discourse on Śiva. Proceedings of a Symposium on the Nature of Religious Imagery.* Ed. M. Meister, 240–256. Bombay: Vakils, Feffer and Simons, Ltd.

Dhargyey, Geshe Lharampa Ngawang. 1985. *A Commentary on the Kālacakra Tantra.* Translated by Gelong Jhampa Kelsang (Allan Wallace), Coordinating Editor: Ivanka Vana Jacic. Dharamsala: The Library of Tibetan Works and Archives.

Donden, Dr. Yeshe. 1986. *Health through Balance. An Introduction to Tibetan Medicine*. Edited and Translated by Jeffrey Hopkins. Co-edited by Dr. Lobsang Rabgyay and Alan Wallace. Ithaca, N.Y.: Snow Lion Publications.

Dowman, Keith. 1981. "A Buddhist guide to the power places of the Kathmandu valley," *Kailash. A Journal of Himalayan Studies*, vol. 8, No. 3–4: 183–291.

———. 1985. *Sky Dancer. The Secret Life and Songs of the Lady Yeshe Tsogyal*. London: Routledge and Kegan Paul.

Dowman, Keith and Sonam Paljor. 1980. *The Divine Madman. The Sublime Life and Songs of Drukpa Kunley*. London: Rider and Company.

Downs, Hugh R. 1980. *Rhythms of a Himalayan Village*. San Francisco: Harper and Row.

Dudjom Rinpoche, Jikdrel Yeshe Dorje (bDud 'joms 'jigs bral ye shes rdo rje). 1991. *The Nyingma School of Tibetan Buddhism. Its Fundamentals and History*. Translated and edited by Gyurme Dorje with the collaboration of Matthew Kapstein. Boston: Wisdom Publications.

Duncan, Marion. 1932. "The Tibetan Drama," *China Journal* 13, No. 3: 105–111.

Edgerton, Franklin. 1970. *Buddhist Hybrid Sanskrit Grammar and Dictionary*. Delhi: Motilal Banarsidass.

Ekvall, Robert B. 1964. *Religious Observances in Tibet: Patterns and Function*. Chicago and London: University of Chicago Press.

Eliade, Mircea. 1959. "Methodological Remarks on the Study of Religious Symbolism." In *The History of Religions. Essays in Methodology*. Ed. Mircea Eliade and Joseph M. Kitagawa, 86–107. Chicago and London: The University of Chicago Press.

———. 1964. *Shamanism. Archaic Techniques of Ecstasy*. Translated from the French by Willard R. Trask. Bollingen Series 84. Princeton: Princeton University Press. 1967.

Fantin, Mario. 1976. *Mani Rimdu. Nepal. The Buddhist dance drama of Tengpoche*. New Dehli: The English Bookstore.

Ferrari, Alfonsa. 1958. *mK'yen brtse's Guide to the Holy Places of Central Tibet*. Completed and edited by Luciano Petech. With the collaboration of Hugh Richardson. Serie Orientale Roma XVI. Roma: Instituto Italiano per il Medio ed Estremo Oriente.

Filliozat, Jean. 1937. *Étude de Démonologie indienne, Kumāratantra de Ravaṇa*. Cahier de la S.A., IV, Paris.

Fisher, James F., ed. 1978. *Himalayan Anthropology. The Indo-Tibetan Interface*. The Hague, Paris: Mouton.

Fremantle, Francesca and Chögyam Trungpa, trans. 1975. *The Tibetan Book of the Dead. The Great Liberation through Hearing in the Bardo. By Guru Rinpoche according to Karma Lingpa. A new translation from the Tibetan with commentary Francesca Fremantle and Chögyam Trungpa*. Boulder and London: Shambhala.

Funke, Friedrich W. 1969. *Religiöses Leben der Sherpa*. Khumbu Himal. Munich and Innsbruck: Universitäts Verlag Wagner.

von Fürer-Haimendorf, Christoph. 1955. "Pre-Buddhist Elements in Sherpa Belief and Ritual," *Man*, No. 61: 49–52.

———. 1958a. "The Religious Life in a Nursery of Climbers: A Buddhist Revival in the Shadow of Everest with a Strange Economic Background," *London Illustrated News*, (November 29, 1958): 940–943.

———. 1958b. "Images and Offerings Made Mainly of Yak Butter: A Report on Little-Known but Fascinating Requisites of Buddhist Ritual," *London Illustrated News*, (December 13, 1958), Supp. I & II: 1041–42.

———. 1964. *The Sherpas of Nepal. Buddhist Highlanders*. London: John Murray; Reprint. New Dehli: Sterling Publishers, 1979.

———, ed. 1964b. *Contributions to the Cultural Anthropology of Nepal. Proceedings of a Symposium held at the School of Oriental and African Studies, University of London, June/July,1973*. Warminster, England: Aris and Phillips.

———. 1984. *The Sherpas Transformed. Social Change in a Buddhist Society of Nepal*. New Dehli: Sterling Publishers.

Gammerman and Semicov. 1963. *Dictionary of Tibetan Medicinal Plants*. Ulan-Ude (USSR).

sGam po pa (1079–1153). 1959. *Jewel Ornament of Liberation*. Translated by Herbert V. Guenther. London: Rider and Company.

Geertz, Clifford. 1973. *The Interpretation of Cultures*. New York: Basic Books.

Gellner, David N. 1992. *Monk, Householder, and Tantric Priest. Newar Buddhism and its hierarchy of ritual*. Cambridge and New York: Cambridge University Press

Getty, Alice. 1928. *The Gods of Northern Buddhism, their history, iconography and progressive evolution through the Northern Buddhist country*. Trans. J. Deniker. Oxford: Clarendon Press.

Godwin-Austin, Captain H. H. 1895. "Description of a Mystic Play in Ladak, Zanskar, &c," *Journal of the Asiatic Society of Bengal (Calcutta)*. Vol. 34, Pt. I, 71–76.

Gordon, Antoinette. 1939. *The Iconography of Tibetan Lamaism*. New York: n.p. [Rutland, Vt.: Charles E. Tuttle, 1959].

———. 1963. *Tibetan Religious Art*. 2nd Ed. New York: Paragon Book Reprint Corp.

Greenwold, Stephan Michael. 1978. "The Role of the Priest in Newar Society." In *Himalayan Anthropology*. Ed. J. Fisher, 483–504.

Griffiths, Paul J. 1994. *On Being Buddha. The Classical Doctrine of Buddhahood*. Albany: State University of New York Press.

van Gulik, R. H. 1935. *Hayagrīva. The Mantrayānic Aspect of the Horse-Cult in China and Japan*. Internationales Archiv für Ethnographie, vol. 33, Supplement. Leiden: E. J. Brill

Gurung, Ashok Kumar. 1987. "The 'Mani Rimdu' Ritual: Performer and Audience at Tibetan Buddhist Dance-Drama. At Chiwong Monastery, Solukhumbu, Nepal, December 15–18, 1986." Guided Independent Project for World College West, Petaluma, Ca.

Haarh, Erik. 1959. "Contributions to the Study of Maṇḍala and Mudrā," *Acta Orientalia* 23: 57–91. (Soc. Orient. Danica Norvegica Svecica).

Harper, Katherine Anne. 1989. *Seven Hindu Goddesses of Spiritual Transformation. The Iconography of the Saptamatrikas.* Studies in Women and Religion, Vol. 28. Lewiston [NY]/ Queenston [Ontario]/ Lampeter [Wales]: The Edwin Mellen Press.

Herrmann–Pfandt, Adelheid. 1992. *Ḍākiṇīs. Zur Stellung und Symbolik des Weblichen im tantrischen Buddhismus.* Bonn: Indica et Tibetica Verlag.

Hoffmann, Helmut. 1950. *Quellen zur Geshichte der Tibetishen Bon-Religion.* Wiesbaden: Abhandlungen der Akademie der Wissenschaften und der Litteratur im Mainz, geistes- und sozialwissenschaftliche Klasse 4.

———. 1967. *Symbolik der Tibetischen Religionen und der Schamanismus. Symbolik der Religionen. Herausgegeben von Ferdinand Herrmann. XII.* Stuttgart: Hiersemann.

Hopkins, Jeffrey. 1984. *The Tantric Distinction. An Introduction to Tibetan Buddhism.* Edited by Anne C. Klein. London: Wisdom Publications.

Horsch, Paul. 1957. "The Wheel: an Indian Pattern of World Interpretation." In *Liebenthal Festschrift.* Ed. Kshitis Roy, 62–79. Sino-Indian Studies 5, nos. 3–4. Santiniketan, Visvabharati.

Hulton-Baker, Robert. 1987. *Tibetan Buddhist Drama.* Dissertation Abstracts International 48(05):1059, University Microfilms ADG87–12490. Ph.D. diss. New York University.

Huntington, John C. 1975. *The Phur-pa. Tibetan Ritual Daggers.* Ascona, Switzerland.

Huntington, Susan L. 1985. *The Art of Ancient India. Buddhist, Hindu, Jain.* New York and Tokyo: John Weatherhill, Inc.

Huntington, Susan L. and John C. 1990. *Leaves from the Bodhi Tree: The Art of Pāla India* (8th–12th centuries) *and its International Legacy.* Seattle and London: The Dayton Art Institute in Association with the University of Washington Press.

Imaeda, Yoshiro. 1979. "Note préliminaire sur le formule Om dans les manuscrits tibétaines de Touen-houang." *Contributions aux études sur Touen-houang*, 71–76. Geneva/Paris: Librarie Droz.

———. 1981. *Histoire du Cycle de la Naissance et de la Mort. Étude d'un texte Tibétaine de Touen-houng.* Centre de Recherches d'Histoire et de Philologie de la IVe Section de l'École pratique des Hautes Études. II Hautes Études Orientales 15. Geneva/Paris: Librarie Droz.

Jäschke, H. A. 1865. "Translation of a Manuscript obtained in Ladak regarding the Dancing on the Tenth Day of the Fifth Month, a Great Holiday," *Journal of the Asiatic Society of Bengal (Calcutta)* 34, Part I 77–79.

Jerstad, Luther G. 1969. *Mani Rimdu. Sherpa Dance-Drama.* Seattle and London: University of Washington Press.

Jest, Corneille. 1981. *Monuments of Northern Nepal.* Paris: Unesco.

Jig-me Ling-pa. 1982. *The Dzog-chen Preliminary Practice of the Innermost Essence. The Long-chen Nying-thig Ngon-dro with the original Tibetan root text composed by the Knowledge-Bearer Jig-me Ling-pa (1729–1798).* Translated with commentary by Tulku Thondup, edited by Brian C. Beresford. Dharamsala: The Library of Tibetan Works and Archives.

John Sanday Consultants International. 1982. *The Repair–Conservation of the Chiwong Gompa in Solu Nepal. A Report Commissioned by Christoph Giercke for the Chiwong Gompa Conservation Committee.* December 1982. (Limited Distribution).

Joshi, Tulasi Diwasa. 1987. "The Living Tradition of the Astamatrika Dance-Drama in the Kathmandu Valley, Nepal." Offprint from *International Symposium on the Conservation and Restoration of Cultural Property—Masked Performances in Asia.* Tokyo: Tokyo National Research Institute of Cultural Properties.

Kalff, Martin. 1977. "Ḍākīṇīs in the Cakrasaṁvara Tradition," in *Tibetan Studies presented at the Seminar of Young Tibetologists, Zurich, June 26–July 1, 1977.* Edited by Martin Brauen and Per Kværne, 149–162. Zürich: Völkerkundemuseum der Universität Zürich.

Kapstein, Matthew. 1983. "Sherpas: Religion and the Printed Word," *Cultural Survival Quarterly*, 7, No. 3, (Fall): 42–44.

———. 1992. "Samantabhadra and Rudra: Innate Enlightenment and Radical Evil in Tibetan Rnying-ma-pa-Buddhism." In *Discourse and Practice*, Frank Reynolds and David Tracy, eds. Albany: State University of New York Press.

———. 1992b. "Remarks on the Maṇi bKa'-'bum and the Cult of Avalokiteśvara in Tibet." In *Tibetan Buddhism. Reason and Revelation.* Ed. Steven D. Goodman and Ronald M. Davidson. Albany: State University of New York Press.

———. 1995. "Weaving the world: The Ritual Art of the *Paṭa* in Pāla Buddhism and Its Legacy in Tibet," in *History of Religions* 34/3: 241–262.

Karmay, Samten G. 1975. "A General Introduction to the History and Doctrines of Bon," *Memoirs of the Research Department of the Toyo Bunko (The Oriental Library),* No. 33: 171–218.

———. 1987. "L'âme et la turquoise: un rituel Tibétain. The Soul and the Turquoise: A Tibetan Ritual." *L'Ethnographie*, 83, 100–101: 97–130.

Katz, Nathan. 1977. "Anima and mKha'-'gro-ma: A Critical Comparative Study of Jung and Tibetan Buddhism." *The Tibet Journal*, 2, No. 3 (Autumn): 13–43.

Kazi Dawa-samdup, ed. 1919. *Shrīcakrasambhāra Tantra. A Buddhist Tantra.* Vol. 7 of Tantrik Texts under the general editorship of Arthur Avalon. Calcutta: Thacker, Spink & Co.; Reprint. ed. by Lokesh Chandra, New Dehli: Aditya Prakashan, 1987.

mKhas grub dge legs dpal bzang po (1385–1432). 1968. *Fundamentals of the Buddhist Tantras.* Trans. F. Lessing and A. Wayman. The Hague: Mouton.

Khempo Sangyay Tenzin and Gomchen Oleshay. 1975. "The Nyingma Icons. A Collection of line drawings of 94 deities and divinities of Tibet." Trans. Keith Dowman. *Kailash. A Journal of Himalayan Studies*, 3, No. 4.

Khetsun Sangpo Rinbochay. 1982. *Tantric Practice in Nyingma.* Translated and Edited by Jeffrey Hopkins. Co-edited by Anne Klein. Ithaca, NY: Snow Lion.

———. 1986. *Bod kyi rabs sa 'og nas bsnyes pa'i dum bsgrigs rna ba'i bdud rtsi zhes bya ba bzhugs so.* (*A Nectar for the Ear. An Early History of Tibet Edited from the Findings Unearthed at the Dunhuang Caves.*) Kathmandu: Nyingmapa Wishfulfilling Center for Study and Practice.

Kinsley, David Robert. 1986. *Hindu Goddesses: Visions of the Divine Feminine in the Hindu Religious Tradition.* Berkeley, London: University of California Press.

Kirkland, J. Russell. 1982. "The spirit of the mountain: myth and state in pre-Buddhist Tibet." *History of Religions* 21:257–71. From Beyer 1992.

af Kleen, Tyra. 1924. *Mudrās. The Ritual Hand-Poses of the Buddha Priests and the Shiva priests of Bali.* London: London, K. Paul, Trench, Trubner & Co., Ltd.; New York; E. P. Dutton & Co. Reprinted 1970, New Hyde Park, N.Y., University Books.

Klein, Anne. 1987. "The Birthless Birthgiver: Reflections on the Liturgy of Yeshe Tsogyal, the Great Bliss Queen." *The Tibet Journal*, 12, No. 4: 19–37. Reprinted in Willis 1989.

Kohn, Richard. 1988. *Mani Rimdu. Text and Tradition in a Tibetan Ritual.* Dissertation Abstracts International 49-06A, University Microfilms 8809033. Ph.D. diss. University of Wisconsin–Madison.

———. 1991. "Shakyamuni Buddha Attaining Parinirvana," "Guhyasamaja Akshobhyavajra Father-Mother," and "Paramsukha–Chakra–samvara and Vajravarahi," in Rhie and Thurman.

———. 1993. "Trance Dancers and Aeroplanes: Montage and Metaphor in Ethnographic Film," in *1942–1992: Fifty Years after Balinese Character. Yearbook of Visual Anthropology. Published under the Auspices of the Commission on Visual Anthropology (IUAES). Vol. 1.* Firenze: Angelo Pontecorboli Editore.

———. 1994. "Paramsukha-Chakrasamvara and Vajravarahi" and "Seated Vairocana with Attendants," in *Asian Art Museum: Selected Works*, Seattle and London: University of Washington Press, with Terese Tse Bartholomew.

———. 1997a. "The Ritual Preparation of a Tibetan Maṇḍala." In *Maṇḍala and Landscape*, ed. A. W. Macdonald. Delhi: DK Printworld. 1997.

———. 1997b. "A Prayer to the God of the Plain." In *Religions of Tibet in Practice.* Edited by Donald S. Lopez, Jr., Princeton: Princeton University Press.

———. 1997c. "A Rite of Empowerment." In *Religions of Tibet in Practice.* Edited by Donald S. Lopez, Jr., Princeton: Princeton University Press.

———. 1997d. "An Offering of Torma." In *Religions of Tibet in Practice.* Edited by Donald S. Lopez, Jr., Princeton: Princeton University Press.

———, dir. 1985. *Lord of the Dance. Destroyer of Illusion.* (16 mm film, 108 minutes, color; Franz-Christoph Giercke, prod.; Sky Walker International Productions). Also *Garwang Tojay-Chenpo. Le Dieu de la Danse*; *der Herr der Tänze. Zerstörer der Illusion.*

———, dir. 1987. "Lord of the Dance," National Geographic Explorer, WTBS, November 22, 1987. (Cable Television Magazine Segment).

———, dir. 1988. *Destroyer of Illusion. The Secret World of a Tibetan Lama.* KTEH/ The Learning Channel, broadcast 1990. (56 min television film; Richard Kohn, dir., script and translations; Richard Gere, v.o.; Franz-Christoph Giercke and Barbara Becker, prod.; Sky Walker International Productions.)

———, dir. n.d. *Lord of the Dance. Destroyer of Illusion. Archival material.* (Work-prints, out-takes and sound track. 17 hours one-inch video + 50 hours audio). London: Meridian Trust.

Kramrisch, Stella. 1981. *The Presence of Śiva.* Princeton: Princeton University Press.

Kruger, John R. and E. D. Francis, comp. 1966. *Index to F.D. Lessing's Lamaist Iconography of the Peking Temple. Yung-Ho-Kung.* Assisted by Schuyler van R. Cammann and Alex Wayman. Bloomington, Indiana.

Kyabje Yonzin Trijang Dorje Chang Losang Yeshe Tenzin Gyatso Pal Zangpo. 1982. "The Significance of the Six-Syllable Mantra OM MANI PADME HUM." *The Tibet Journal* 1, No. 4 (winter): 3–10.

Lalou, Marcelle. 1932. "Un traité de Magie bouddhique." In *Études d'Orientalisme publiées pa le Musée Guimet à la mémoire de Raymonde Linossier,* 303–322. Paris. Tôme II.

Lauf, Detlef Ingo. 1972. "Tshe-ring-ma, die Berggöttin des langen Lebens und ihr Gefolge," *Ethnologische Zeitscrift Zürich*, Nr. 1, Zürich: 259–283.

———. 1976. *Tibetan Sacred Art. The Heritage of Tantra.* Berkeley and London: Shambhala Publications.

———. 1979. *Eine Ikonographie des tibetische Buddhismus.* Graz, Austria: Akademische Druck -u. Verlagsanstalt.

Laufer, Berthold. 1917. "Origin of the Word Shaman," *American Anthropologist*, 19: 361–371.

———. 1919. *Sino-Iranica. Chinese Contributions to the History of Civilization in Ancient Iran. With Special Reference to the History of Cultivated Plants and Products.* Pub. 201, anthropological series., Vol. 15, No 3. Chicago: Field Museum of Natural History; Peking 1940.

———. 1931. "Columbus and Cathay, and the meaning of America to the Orientalist," *JAOS*, 51, 2, (June): 87–103.

Lerner, Lin. 1983. "Two Tibetan Ritual Dances: A Comparative Study." *The Tibet Journal*, 8, No. 4 (Winter): 50–57.

Lessing, Ferdinand Diederich. 1942. *Yung-Ho-Kung. An Iconography of the Lamaist Cathedral in Peking. With Notes on Lamaist Mythology and Cult.* Reports from the Scientific Expedition to the North Western Provinces of China under the Leadership of Dr. Sven Hedin, 8, I. Stockholm.

———. 1951. "Calling the Soul: a Lamaist Ritual," *Semitic and Oriental Studies*, U.C. Publications in Semitic Philology, 11. Ed. Walter Joseph Fischel. 263–284. Berkeley: University of California Press.

———. 1956. "Miscellaneous Lamaist Notes, I. Notes on the Thanksgiving Offering," *Central Asiatic Journal*, 2: 58–71. The Hague: Mouton.

———. 1959. "Miscellaneous Lamaist Notes, III. Senfkörner," *Central Asiatic Journal* 4, No. 2: 143–144.

Lévi-Strauss, Claude. 1963. *Structural Anthropology.* New York: Basic Books.

Li-An-Chi. 1948. "rNying-ma-pa, the early form of Lamaism," *Journal of the Royal Asiatic Society*, (1948): 142–163.

———. 1948b. "Bon: the Magico-religious Belief of the Tibetan speaking peoples," *Southwestern Journal of Anthropology* (Albuquerque) 4, 1: 31–42.

Lincoln, Bruce. 1989. *Discourse and the Construction of Society: Comparative Studies of Myth, Ritual and Classification.* New York: Oxford University Press.

Ligeti, Louis, ed. 1978. *Proceedings of the Csoma de Körös Memorial Symposium Held at Mátrafüred, Hungary, 24-30 September 1976.* Bibliotheca Orientalis Hungarica, vol. XXIII. Budapest: Akadémiai Kiadó.

Lobsang Dorje. 1984. "Lhamo: The folk opera of Tibet." Translated from the Tibetan by C. B. Josayma and Migmar Tsering. *The Tibet Journal* 9, No. 2 (Summer): 13–22.

Locke, John K., S.J. 1977. "Newar Buddhist Initiation Rites." In *Contributions to Nepalese Studies*, Tribhuvan University. Kirtipur, Nepal 2, No. 2.

———. 1980. *Karunamaya. The Cult of Avalokitesvara-Matsyendranath in the Valley of Nepal.* Kathmandu: Sahayogi Prakashan/CNRS.

Lokesh Chandra. 1965. *Three Hundred Gods.* New Dehli: s.n.

———. 1988. *Buddhist Iconography.* 3rd Rev., and enlarged ed. 2 vols. New Dehli: Aditya Prakashan.

Lopez, Donald S. Jr., ed. 1997. *Religions of Tibet in Practice.* Princeton: Princeton University Press.

Luneau, Georges. 1974. *Musique Sacrée tibetaine.* OCORA OCR71, record/ disc. (Recordings from Mani Rimdu at Thami. Also see Peter Crossley-Holland, review in *Ethnomusicology*, (1974): 341–343.)

Macdonald, Alexander W., ed. 1971. "Çar-pa'i čhos-byuṅ sṅon-med chaṅs-pa'i dbyu-gu," *Documents pour l'étude de la Religion et de l'Organisation Sociale des Sherpas.* Junbesi/Paris-Nanterre.

———. 1979b. "On the Writing of Buddhist History in Nepal." In *History of Buddhism.* Edited by A. K. Narain. 121–131 Dehli.

———. 1980. "The Coming of Buddhism to the Sherpa Area of Nepal," *Acta Orientalia Hung.*, Tomus XXXIV, Fasc. 1–3, Budapest, 139–143.

Macdonald, Alexander W. and Anne Vergati Stahl. 1979. *Newar Art. Nepalese Art during the Malla Period.* New Dehli: Vikas Publishing House, Pvt., Ltd.

Macdonald, Ariane. 1962. *Le maṇḍala du Mañjuśrīmūlakalpa.* Paris: Adrien-Maisonneuve.

Mackerras, Colin. 1988. "Drama in the Tibetan Autonomous Region." *Asian Theater Journal* 5, No. 2:198–219.

de Mallmann, Marie Thérèse. 1948. *Introduction à l'Étude d'Avalokiteçvara*. Paris: Civilizations du Sud.

———. 1964. *Étude iconographique sur Mañjuśrī*. Publications de l'École Française d'Éxtrême-Orient, vol. LV. Paris: École Française d'Éxtrême-Orient.

———. 1968. *Hindu Deities in Tantric Buddhism*. Translated from the French by Simon Watson Taylor. Bonn: Zentralasiatische Studien.

———. 1975. *Introduction à l'iconographie du tāntrisme bouddhique*. Paris: Bibliothèque du Centre Recherches sur l'Asie Centrale et la Haut Asie, I.

March, K. S. 1977. "The Iconography of Chiwong Gompa," *Contributions to Nepalese Studies*. 5. No. 1 82–92: Tribhuvan University, Kirtipur, Nepal.

Martin, Dan. 1987. "On the Origin and Significance of the Prayer Wheel According to Two Nineteenth-Century Tibetan Literary Sources." *The Journal of the Tibet Society* 7. Bloomington, IN.

Mayer, Robert. 1990. "Tibetan Phurpas and Indian Kīlas," *The Tibet Journal* 15, No. 1, (Spring). Also in *The Buddhist Forum*. London: SOAS.

McFarland, H. Neil. 1987. *Daruma. The Founder of Zen in Japanese Art and Popular Culture*. Tokyo and New York: Kodansha International.

Meisezahl, Richard O. 1980. "L'étude iconographique des huit Cimetières d'après le traité µmaśānavidhi de Lūyī." In *Geist und Ikonographie des Vajrayāna-Buddhismus*. Beiträge zur Zentralasienforschung: Bd. 2. 4–119. Sankt Augustin: VGH Wissenschaftsverlag.

Migot, André. 1958. "Notes sur le Théatre Tibétain," *Revue de la Société d'Histoire du Théatre*, I, Paris.

Mi-la-ras-pa. 1989. *The Hundred Thousand Songs of Milarepa*. Translated and annotated by Garma Chen-chi Chang. Translation of mGur 'bum. 2 vols. Reprint of 1977 ed. Boston and Shaftbury: Shambala Publications.

Miller, Beatrice D. 1978. "Tibetan Culture and Personality: Refugee Responses to a Culture-Bound TAT," in *Himalayan Anthropology*, Ed. J. Fisher, 365–393.

Mullin, Glenn H. (Compiled and Edited). 1983. *Meditations on the Lower Tantras. (A Stairway for Ascending to Tusita Buddha-field.) From the Collected Works of Previous Dalai Lamas*. Dharamsala: The Library of Tibetan Works and Archives.

Mumford, Stan R. 1989. *Himalayan Dialogue: Tibetan Lamas and Gurung Shamans in Nepal*. Madison: University of Wisconsin Press.

de Nebesky-Wojkowitz, René. 1947. "Die Tibetische Bon-Religion," *Archiv für Völkerkunde* II: 26–68.

———. 1956. *Oracles and Demons of Tibet. The Cult and Iconography of the Tibetan Protective Deities*. 's-Gravenhage: Mouton and Co.

———. 1976. *Tibetan Religious Dances. Tibetan text and annotated translation of the 'chams yig*. Edited by Christoph von Fürer-Haimendorf. With an appendix by Walter Graf. The Hague: Mouton.

———. n.d. *Where the Gods are Mountains. Three Years among the People of the Himalayas.* Translated from the German by Michael Bullock. New York: Reynal. (also London: Weidenfeld and Nicholson, 1965; «Wo Berge Götter sind», Stuttgart: Deutsche Verlags-Anstalt, 1955).

Norbu, Jamyang, ed. 1986. *Zlos-gar: performing traditions of Tibet.* Dharamsala: Library of Tibetan Works and Archives.

Norbu, Namkhai. 1986. *The Crystal and the Way of Light. Sutra, Tantra and Dzogchen.* The Teachings of Namkhai Norbu. Compiled and Edited by John Shane. New York and London: Routledge and Kegan Paul.

Nyang ral Nyi ma 'od zer [1124–1196]. 1990. *Dakini Teachings. Padmasambhava's Oral Instructions to Lady Tsogyal.* Recorded and concealed by Yeshe Tsogyal. Revealed by Nyang Ral Nyima Oser and Sangye Lingpa. Translated by Erik Pema Kunsang. Boston and Shaftsbury: Shambhala.

O'Flaherty, Wendy Doniger. 1976. *The Origins of Evil in Hindu Mythology.* Berkeley: The University of California Press.

———. 1981. *Śiva. The Erotic Ascetic.* Oxford: Oxford University Press.

———. 1984. *Dreams, Illusion and Other Realities.* Chicago and London: The University of Chicago Press.

Olshak, Blanche Christine. 1973. *Mystic Art of Ancient Tibet.* In collaboration with Geshe Thubten Wangyal. London: George Allen and Unwin.

Oppitz, Michael. 1968. *Geschichte und Sozialordnung der Sherpa.* Khumbu Himal. Munich and Innsbruck: Universitäts Verlag Wagner.

———. 1974. "Myths and Facts: Reconsidering some Data concerning the Clan History of the Sherpa." In *Contributions to the Cultural Anthropology of Nepal.* Ed. C. von Fürer-Haimendorf, 232–43.

———, dir. 1980. *Shamans of the Blind Country.* (*Shamanen im Blinden Land*). Wieland Schultz-Kiel + Westdeutscher Rundfunk. (16 mm film, color).

———. 1981. *Shamanen im Blinden Land. Ein Bilderbuch aus dem Himalaya.* Frankfurt am Main: Syndicat.

———. 1983. "The Wild Boar and the Plough. Origin Stories of the Northern Magar." Unpublished ms.

———. n.d. *Materials on the Making of an Ethnographic Film: Shamans of the Blind Country.* Kathmandu: Goethe Institute.

Ortner, Sherry B. 1973. "Sherpa Purity," *American Anthropologist* 75: 49–63.

———. 1978. *Sherpas through their Rituals.* Cambridge Studies in Cultural Systems. Cambridge: Cambridge University Press.

———. 1978b. "The White-Black Ones: The Sherpa View of Human Nature." In *Himalayan Anthropology*, Ed. J. Fisher.

Pal, Pratapaditya. 1969. *The Art of Tibet.* New York: The Asia Society, Inc.

———. 1982. *A Buddhist Paradise. The Murals of Alchi. Western Himalayas*. Basel: Ravi Kumar for Visual Dharma Publications, Ltd., Hong Kong.

———. 1984. *Tibetan Paintings. A study of Tibetan Thankas Eleventh to Nineteenth Century*. Basel and London: Ravi Kumar and Sotheby Publications.

———. 1985. *Art of Nepal. A Catalogue of the Los Angeles County Museum of Art Collection*. Berkeley, Los Angeles, London: Los Angeles County Museum of Art in association with University of California Press.

———. 1990. *Art of Tibet. A Catalogue of the Los Angeles County Museum of Art Collection*. Expanded Edition. Los Angeles: Los Angeles County Museum of Art.

———. 1991. *Art of the Himalayas. Treasures from Nepal and Tibet*. New York: Hudson Hills Press in association with The American Federation of Arts.

Patrul Rinpoche (O rgyan 'jigs med chos kyi dbang po, dPal sprul, b. 1808). 1994. *The Words of My Perfect Teacher. Kunzang Lama'i Shelung*. (Kun bzang bla ma'i zhal lung). New York: HarperCollins.

Paul, Robert. 1970. *Sherpas and their Religion*. American Ph.D. Dissertations X1970, page: 0015. Ph.D. Diss. University of Chicago.

———. 1982. *The Tibetan Symbolic World. Psychoanalytic Explorations*. Chicago: University of Chicago Press.

Pott, P. H. 1965. "Some Remarks on the 'Terrific Deities' in Tibetan 'Devil Dances.' " In *Studies of Esoteric Buddhism and Tantrism in Commemoration of the 1150th Anniversary of the Founding of Koyosan*. Edited by Yukei Matsunaga, 269–278. Koyosan: Koyosan University Press.

———. 1966. *Yoga and Yantra. Their Interrelation and their Significance for Indian Archaeology*. The Hague: M. Nijhoff.

Prats, Ramon. 1980. "Some preliminary considerations arising from a biographical study of the early *gter ston*." In *Tibetan Studies in Honour of Hugh Richardson*. Ed. M. Aris et. al., 256–261.

Przyluski, Jean. 1923. "Les Vidyārāja, Contribution à l'histoire de la magie dans les Sectes Mahāyānistes," *Bullétin de l'École Française d'Extrème Orient* (*B.E.F.E.O.*), Hanoi. Tôme 33: 301–318.

———. 1926. *Le Concile de Rājagṛha, introduction à l'histoire des canons et des sectes bouddhiques*. Paris: P. Geuthner.

Rawson, Philip S. 1973. *The Art of Tantra*. London: Thames and Hudson.

Rechung Rinpoche, The Ven. Jampal Kunzang. 1973. *Tibetan Medicine. Illustrated in Original Texts*. Berkeley and Los Angeles: University of California Press.

Rhie, Marylin M. and Robert A. F. Thurman. 1990. *Wisdom and Compassion. The Sacred Art of Tibet*. New York: Asian Art Museum of San Francisco and Tibet House, New York in association with Harry N. Abrams, Inc.

Rockhill, William Woodville. 1890a. "The Lamaist ceremony called 'making the *maṇi* pills,'" *Proceedings of the American Oriental Society* (New Haven) (1888), 24–31.

———. 1890b. "On the Uses of Skulls in Lamaist Ceremonies," *Proceedings of the American Oriental Society*, 22–24.

———. 1895. "Notes on the Ethnography of Tibet Based on the Collections in the United States National Museum," *Smithsonian Annual Report, June 30, 1893*. Washington: Government Printing Office. Facsimile reproduction, Seattle: The Shorey Bookstore, 1971.

Roerich, George N. 1942. "The Epic of King Gesar of Ling," *Journal of the Royal Asiatic Society of Bengal. Letters*. Vol. 8, Article No. 7: 277–311.

Sacherer, Janice. 1979. "The High Altitude Ethnobotany of the Rowaling Sherpas," *Contributions to Nepalese Studies. Journal of the Research Centre for Nepal and Asian Studies*. Tribhuvan University. Kirtipur, Nepal. Vol. 6, No. 2, (June 1979): 45–64.

———. 1981. "Recent Social and Economic Impact of Tourism on a Remote Sherpa Community." In *Asian Highland Societies in Anthropological Perspective*. Ed. C. von Fürer-Haimendorf, 157–169. New Dehli: Sterling.

Sammlung fur Volkerkunde (Saint Gall, Switzerland). 1989. *Tibetische Kunstschätze im Exil. Ausgewälte Kultgegenstände aus der Sammlung S. H. des Dalai Lama in der Library of Tibetan Works and Archives, Dharamsala, Himichal Pradesh, Indien.* Sammlung für Völkerkunde. Mai bis Oktober 1989. [Ed., Roland Steffan]. St. Gallen: Stiftung St. Galler Museen.

Samuel, Geoffrey. 1978. "Religion in Tibetan Society: A New Approach. Part One: A Structural Model," *Kailash. A Journal of Himalayan Studies* 6, No. 1: 45–66.

———. 1978b. "Religion in Tibetan Society: A New Approach. Part Two: The Sherpas of Nepal: A Case Study," *Kailash. A Journal of Himalayan Studies*, 6, No. 2: 99–114.

———. 1985. "Early Buddhism in Tibet: Some Anthropological Perspectives." In *Soundings in Tibetan Civilization*. Eds. B. Aziz and M. Kapstein, 383–397.

———. 1993. *Civilized Shamans: Buddhism in Tibetan Societies*. Washington and London: Smithsonian Institution Press.

Schechner, Richard. 1985. *Between Theater and Anthropology*. Forward by Victor Turner. Philadelphia: University of Pennsylvania Press.

Schmid, Toni. 1967. "Shamanistic Practices in Northern Nepal." In *Studies in Shamanism. Based on Papers read at the Symposium on Shamanism held at Åbo on the 6th–8th of September*, 1962. Ed. Carl-Martin Edsman. Scripta Instituti Donneriani Aboensis. Stockholm: Almquist and Wiskell.

Schmidt-Thome, Marlis and T. T. Tingo. 1975. *Materielle Kultur und Kunst der Sherpa*. Khumbu-Himal. Munich and Innsbruck: Universitäts Verlag Wagner.

Schubert, Johannes. 1954. "Das Reis-maṇḍala: Ein tibetischer Ritual-text herausgegeben, übersetzt, und erläutert." In *Asiatica: Festschrift Friedrich Weller*. Leipzig: Otto Harrassowitz.

Sestini, Valerio and Enzo Somigli. 1978. *Sherpa Architecture*. Geneva: Unesco.

Sharpa Tulku and Michael Perrot. 1985. "The Ritual of Consecration," *The Tibet Journal. A publication for the study of Tibet published by the Library of Tibetan Works and Archives*, 10, No. 2: 35–49. (Summer). Dharamsala: The Library of Tibetan Works and Archives.

Shrestha, Rajendra. 1986. *Buddhist Ritual Dance*. Kathmandu: Kala-mandapa.

Singer, Milton. 1958. "The Great Tradition in a Metropolitan Center: Madras." In *Traditional India*. Ed. Milton Singer. Philadelphia: American Folklore Society.

Skorupski, Tadeusz. 1983. *The Sarvadurgatipariśodhana Tantra, Elimination of all Evil Destinies. Sanskrit and Tibetan Versions with an English Translation*. Delhi: Motilal Banarsidass.

Snellgrove, David. 1957. *Buddhist Himālaya. Travels and Studies in quest of the origins and nature of Tibetan Religion*. Oxford: Bruno Cassirer.

———. 1959. *The Hevajra Tantra. A Critical Study*. 2 vols. London: Oxford University Press.

———. 1966. "Toward a Sociology of Tibet," *Central Asiatic Journal*.

———. 1968. *A Cultural History of Tibet*. In collaboration with Hugh Richardson. New York: Praeger.

———. 1987. *Indo-Tibetan Buddhism. Indian Buddhists and their Tibetan Successors*. Boston: Shambhala.

bSod nams rya mtsho and Musashi Tachikawa. 1989. *The Ngor Mandalas of Tibet. Plates*. Bibliotheca Codicum Asiaticorum 2. Tokyo: The Centre for East Asian Cultural Studies.

Soothill, William Edward and Lewis Hodus. 1937. *A Dictionary of Chinese Buddhist Terms. With Sanskrit and English Equivalents and a Sanskrit Pali Index*. London: Kegan Paul, French, Trubner and Company, Limited. [Taipei: Ch'eng Wen Publishing Company, 1970.]

Sopa, Geshe Lhundup. 1976. "An Excursis on the Subtle Body in Tantric Buddhism (Notes Contextualizing the Kālacakra)," *Journal of the International Association of Buddhist Studies*. 6, No. 2.

Sopa, Geshe Lhundup, and Jeffrey Hopkins. 1976. *Practice and Theory of Tibetan Buddhism*. New York: Grove Press.

Spinner, Stephanie. 1979. "The Painted Mind," *Quest 79* [Ambassador International Culture Foundation] 3, No. 4 (June 1979): 86–88.

Spiro, Melford E. 1967. *Burmese Supernaturalism*. Englewood Cliffs, N.J.: Prentice-Hall.

———. 1970. *Buddhism and Society: A Great Tradition and its Burmese Vicissitudes*. New York: Harper and Row.

Staal, Frits. 1983. *Agni. The Vedic Ritual of Fire*. In collaboration with C.V. Somayajipad and M. Ravi Nanabudin. Berkeley: Asian Humanities Press.

Stablein, William. 1978. "A Descriptive Analysis of the Content of Nepalese Buddhist Pūjās as a Medical-Cultural System with References to Tibetan Parallels." In *Himalayan Anthropology*. Ed. J. Fisher, 529–537.

Stein, Rolf Alfred. 1957. "Le liṅga des danses masquées lamaïques et la théorie des âmes." In *Liebenthal Festschrift*. Ed. Kshitis Roy. Sino-Indian Studies 5, Nos. 3–4: 200–234. Santiniketan, Visvabharati.

———. 1972. *Tibetan Civilization.* Translated by J. E. Stapleton-Driver. London: Faber and Faber. [*La Civilization Tibétaine.* Paris: Dunod, 1962.]

———. 1977. "La gueule du makara: un trait inexpliqué de certains objets rituels," *Essais sur l'art du Tibet*, Ariane Macdonald et al., 52–62. Paris: Librarie d'Amerique et d'Orient.

———. 1978. "A propos des documents anciens relatif au *phur-bu* (kīla)." In *Proceedings of the Csoma de Körös Memorial Symposium Held at Mátrafüred, Hungary, 24–30 September 1976.* Ed. Louis Ligeti. Bibliotheca Orientalis Hungarica, 23: 427–444. Budapest: Akadémia Kiadó.

———. 1978b. "Le théâtre au Tibet." in *Théâtres.* Paris: Centre National de la Recherche Scientifique.

———. 1980. "Une mention de Manichéisme dans le choix de Bouddhisme comme réligion d'état par le Roi Tibétaine Khri-sroṅ lde-bcan." In *Indianisme et Bouddhisme, Mélanges offerts à Mgr. Étienne Lamotte*, 329–37. Louvain: Institut Orientaliste.

———. 1981. *La Civilization Tibétaine. Réedition revue et augmentée de l'édition de 1962.* Ouvrage publié avec le concours du Centre National des Lettres. Paris: le Sycomore/ l'Asiathèque.

———. 1985. "Tibetica Antiqua II. A propos du mot *gcug-lag* et de la religion indigene," *Bullétin de l'École Française d'Extrème Orient* (*B.E.F.E.O.*). Tôme 74, 84–133.

Steinkellner, Ernst. 1978. "Remarks on Tantristic Hermeneutics." In *Proceedings of the Csoma de Körös Memorial Symposium*, L. Ligeti, ed., 445-458.

Sutherland, Gail Hinich. 1991. *The Disguises of the Demon. The Development of the Yakṣa in Hinduism and Buddhism.* SUNY Series in Hindu Studies. Albany: State University of New York Press.

Tambiah, Stanley Jeyaraja. 1970. *Buddhism and the Spirit Cults in North-East Thailand [by] S. J. Tambiah.* Cambridge: Cambridge University Press.

Tarthang Tulku. 1971. *Kalacakra. The Cycle of Time.* Berkeley: Dharma Press.

Taube, Erika and Manfred. 1983. *Schamanen und Rhapsoden. Die Geistige Kultur der alten Mongolei.* Wein: Edition Tusch.

Tengpoche Rinpoche. n.d. *Information on Khumbu Sherpa Customs, on Sherpa Religion, on Tengpoche Monastery, and on Mani Rimdu.* Compiled by the Tengboche Reincarnate Lama. Translated by Sherry B. Ortner. n.p.: n.p.

Toussaint, Gustave-Charles. 1933. *Le Dict de Padma. Padma Thang Yig ms. de Lithang.* Bibliothèque de l'Institut des Hautes Études Chinoises. Vol. III. Paris: Librarie Ernest Leroux.

Trungpa, Chögyam. 1978. "Some Aspects of Pön." In *Himalayan Anthropology.* Ed. J. Fisher, 229–308.

Tsong-kha-pa. 1977. *Tantra in Tibet. The Great Exposition of Secret Mantra*. Introduced by H. H. Tenzin Gyatso, the Fourteenth the Dalai Lama. Trans. and Ed. by Jeffrey Hopkins. London: George Allen and Unwin.

———. 1982. *The Yoga of Tibet. The Great Exposition of Secret Mantra—2 and 3*. Introduced by H. H. Tenzin Gyatso, the Fourteenth the Dalai Lama. Trans. and Ed. by Jeffrey Hopkins. London: George Allen and Unwin.

Tucci, Giuseppe. 1949. *Tibetan Painted Scrolls*. Rome: Librario Dello Stato.

———. 1951. "A propos Avalokiteçvara," *Mélanges chinois et bouddhique*, vol. 9: 175–219. Brussels: l'Institut Belge des Hautes Études Chinoises.

———. 1956. *To Lhasa and Beyond*. Trans. Mario Carelli. Rome: Istituto poligrafico dello Stato.

———. 1961. *The Theory and Practice of the Maṇḍala. With Special Reference to the Modern Psychology of the Subconscious*. Trans. Alan Houghton Broderick. New York: Samuel Weiser.

———. 1967. *Tibet. Land of Snows*. Trans. J. E. Stapleton-Driver. New York: Stein and Day.

———. 1980. *The Religions of Tibet*. Trans. Geoffrey Samuel. London and Henley: Routledge and Kegan Paul.

Tulku Thondup. 1984. *The Tantric Tradition of the Nyingma. The Origin of Buddhism in Tibet*. Marion, MA: Buddhayana.

———. 1986. *Hidden Teachings of Tibet. An Explanation of the Terma Tradition of the Nyingma School of Buddhism*. Edited by Harold Talbott. Buddhayana Series I. London: Wisdom.

———. 1989. *Buddha Mind. An Anthology of Longchen Rabjam's Writings on Dzogpa Chenpo*. Edited by Harold Talbott. Buddhayana Series: III. Ithaca, NY: Snow Lion.

Turner, Victor Witter. 1967. *The Forest of Symbols. Aspects of Ndembu Ritual*. Ithaca, N.Y.: Cornell University Press.

———. 1977. *The Ritual Process. Structure and Anti-Structure*. Chicago: Aldine Publishing Co. Reprint, Ithaca, N.Y.: Cornell Paperbacks, 1977.

Vallée-Poussin, Louis de la. 1932. "Une Dernière note sur le nirvāṇa." In *Études d'Orientalisme publiées par le Musée Guimet à la memoire de Raymonde Linossier*, tôme. II: 329–54, Paris.

Vergati, Anne. 1986. "Quelques remarques sur l'usage du *maṇḍala* et du yantra dans la vallée de Kathmandu, Népal," 37-61 in *Mantras et diagrammes rituels dans l'Hindouisme*, André Padoux, ed. Paris: Éditions CNRS.

Vogel, Jean Phillippe. 1926. *Indian Serpent Lore; or, the Nāgās in Hindu Legend and Art*. London: A. Probsthain.

Waddell, L. Austine. 1895. *The Buddhism of Tibet, or Lamaism. With its Mystic Cults, Symbolism and Mythology, and its Relation to Indian Buddhism*. London: W. H. Allen; Reprint, New York: Dover, 1972.

Walter, Michael. 1997. "Scapula Cosmography and Divination in Tibet." Paper presented at the American Academy of Religion Annual Meeting, San Francisco, California, November 23, 1997.

Wangyal, Geshe. 1973. *The Door of Liberation.* New York: Maurice Girodias.

Wang Yao. 1985. "Tibetan Operatic Themes." In *Soundings in Tibetan Civilization.*, Edited by Aziz and Kapstein, 186–196.

Wayman, Alex. 1955. "Notes on the Sanskrit Tern Jñāna," *Journal of the American Oriental Society* 75, No. 4: 253–62.

———. 1959. "Studies in Yama and Māra," *Indo-Iranian Journal*, 3, No. I: 44–73.

———. 1971. "Contributions on the Symbolism of the Maṇḍala Palace." In *Études Tibétaines Dédiées à la Mémoire de Marcelle Lalou.* Paris: Librarie d'Amérique et d'Orient Adrien Maisonneuve.

Williams, Paul. 1989. *Mahāyāna Buddhism. The Doctrinal Foundations.* London and New York: Routledge and Kegan Paul.

Willis, Janice Dean. 1987. "Ḍākīṇī: Some Comments on its Nature and Meaning." *The Tibet Journal*, 12, No. 4: 56–71.

———, ed.. 1989. *Feminine Ground: Essays on Women and Tibet.* Ithaca, N.Y.: Snow Lion Publications.

Wylie, Turrell V. 1959. "A Standard System of Tibetan Transcription," *Harvard Journal of Asiatic Studies* 22: 261–67.

———. 1978. "Reincarnation: a Political Innovation in Tibetan Buddhism." In *Proceedings of the Csoma de Körös Memorial Symposium*, L. Ligeti, ed., 579-586.

Yamasaki, Taikô. 1988. *Shingon. Japanese Esoteric Buddhism.* Translated and adapted by Richard and Cynthia Peterson. Edited by Yasuyoshi Morimoto and David Kidd. Boston and London: Shambhala.

Ye shes mtsho rgyal. 1933. *Le Dict de Padma. Padma Thang Yig ms. de Lithang. Traduit du Tibétain par Gustave-Charles Toussaint.* Bibliothèque de l'Institut des Hautes Études Chinoises. Vol 3. Paris: Librarie Ernest Leroux.

———. 1978. *The Life and Liberation of Padmasambhava.* Translated into French as *Le Dict de Padma* by Gustave-Charles Toussaint; translated into English by Kenneth Douglas and Gwendolyn Bays. 2 vols. Berkeley: Dharma Publishing. (O rgyan gling pa, b. 1323.)

———. 1993. *The Lotus-Born. The Life Story of Padmasambhava.* Translated by Erik Pema Kunsang [Schmidt]. Shambhala: Boston and London. (Nyang ral nyi ma'i 'od zer, 1124–1192).

Zimmer, Heinrich. 1946. *Myths and Symbols in Indian Art and Civilization.* Edited by Joseph Campbell. The Bollingen Library. New York: Pantheon. Harper Torchbook edition, 1962.

Tibetan Sources

dGe bshes chos grags. 1949. *dGe bshes chos kyi grags pas brtsams pa'i brda dag ming tshig gsal ba bzhugs so.* Lhasa. Reedition, Beijing 1957.

Ngag dbang bstan 'dzin nor bu 'gyur med chos gyis blo gros, a.k.a. rDza sprul Waginḍa. (1867–1940). 1897. *Thugs rje chen po bde gshegs kun 'dus kyi sgrub thabs chog khrigs zab lam gsal ba'i nyin byed ces bya ba bzhugs so.* [The Sun that Makes the Profound Path Clear. The Practice (*sādhana*) of Union of the Blissful Great Compassion Arranged in Ritual Form.] Short Title: *bDe kun las byang* [Union of the Blissful Manual]. xyl. Rongphu/ Thubten Chöling. (UB).

———. n.d.a. *Gar dbang thugs rje chen po bde gshegs kun 'dus kyi smon lam phan bde'i ljon pa zhes bya ba.* [A Paradise of Benefit and Pleasure. The Lord of the Dance Great Compassion Union of the Blissful Prayer.] Short Title: *sMon lam* [Prayer]. xyl.

———. n.d.b. *bsTan bsrung bkra shis tshe ring ma'i cho ga yid bzhin 'dod 'jo.* [The Wish Granting Cow—A Ritual of the Guardian of the Teaching, Auspicious Long Life Woman.] Short Title: *Tshe ring ma* [Long Life Woman]. xyl. (LLW)

———. n.d.c. *bDe kun tshogs la 'byor rung rgyu'i mkha' 'gro'i [b]sun bzlog bzhugs so.* (Union of the Blissful *ḍākiṇī* torma offering). xyl.

———. n.d.d. *bDe kun ril sgrub byin 'bebs sprin phung zil mngar la ldeb bzhugs.* [Illustrated as a Sweet Dewy Mass of Clouds. The Shower of Blessings for the Union of the Blissful Pill Practice.] Short Title: *Byin 'bebs* [Shower of Blessings]. xyl. (SB)

———. n.d.e. *sPros med rang bab so ma'i gtor bsngo bzhugs.* [The Unelaborated Self Descending Soma Torma Dedication.] Short Title: *gTor bsngo* [Torma Dedication]; a.k.a. *sPros med* [The Unelaborated]. xyl.

———. n.d.f. *Zab lam bde gshegs kun 'dus kyi bkra shis phan bde'i char 'bebs zhes bya ba.* [A Shower of Benefit and Pleasure. The Auspicious Omens of Profound Path Union of the Blissful.] Short Title: *bKra shis* [Auspicious Omens]. xyl.

Ngag dbang brtson 'grus and Ngag dbang blo gros, comp. 1984. *Thugs rje chen po bde gshegs kun 'dus kyi sa cho ga dang/ sta gon gyi ngag 'don dkyus gcig tu bkod pa bzhugs so.* [The Unabridged Recitations for the Site Ritual and Preparation for Great Compassion Union of the Blissful.] ms. (S/P).

Ngag dbang blo bzang mdo ngag bstan 'dzin, Trulshik Rinpoche XI, a.k.a. Wāgindra Dharmamati. (b. 1923 or 24). n.d.a. *Kho bo kun rmongs Wāgindra dharma ma ti'i skyes rabs dang rnam thar gsol 'debs su btags pa dad pa'i 'jug ngogs zhes bya ba bzhugs so.* [The Ford of Faith. The History of the Births and Biography of Me, the Completely Confused Wāgindra Dharmamati.] Short title: *sKye rabs* [History of Births]. xyl.

———. n.d.b. *Thog mtha' bar du gnas lugs kyi gtam ston gyi pad tshal rkang pa drug pa'i glu chung zhes pa yod.* [This is called "A Little Song in Six Parts—A Lotus Garden which Tells the Tale of How Things Are from Beginning to End."] xyl.

———. n.d.c. *gNas bdag gsol bsdus.* [The Abridged Prayers for the Local Gods.] xyl.

———. n.d.d. *Lha sman sras gcig bkra shis dpal chen ni.* [The god and medicine spirit, the only son, Great Auspicious Glorious One.] (Prayer to bKra skis dpal chen). xyl.

sNgags 'chang chen po kun dga' rin chen (1517–1584). 1576. *rDo rje phur bu dngos grub char 'bebs kyi 'chams kyi brjed byang snang ba 'gyur thub. 'Khon lugs phur pa'i rnam bśad ['chams yig brjed byaṅ]. The Vajrakīla rites as practiced by the 'khon lineage of Sa-skya being the detailed exegesis of the sādhana and gtor zlog of 'Jam-mgon A-myes-zabs Kun-dga'-bsod-rnams and the notes on the sacred dance ('chams) of Sṅags-'chan Kun-dga'-rin-chen. Reproduced from manuscript copies of the ancient Sa-skya xylographic prints by Ngawang Sopa.* New Delhi: Ngawang Sopa, 1973.

Gter ston Sans rgyas dbaṅ 'dus. 1979. *Padma'i gsaṅ thig dgoṅ 'dus* or *Rtsa gsum gsaṅ thig dgoṅ 'dus.*

gTer bdag gling pa 'gyur med rdo rje. (1646–1714). 1695–96. *Zab lam bde gshegs kun 'dus kyi sbyin sreg gi cho ga 'dod don myur 'grub ces bya ba.* [The Profound Path Union of the Blissful Burnt Offering Rite, entitled "Quickly Achieving the Desired Goal."] Short title: *sByin sreg* [Burnt Offering]. xyl. Rongphu. (BO).

———. n.d.a. *Chos spyod kyi rim pa thar lam rab gsal zhes bya ba las/ gTor ma cha gsum gyi rim pa.* ["The Three-Part Torma Process" from *The Elucidation of the Path of Liberation: the Process of Religious Practice.*] In RP. (TPT).

———. n.d.b. *gTer chen chos kyi rgyal po'i rnam thar gsol 'debs zhal gzungs ma.* [The Recitation called the Biographical Prayer of the Righteous King, the Great Treasure Master.] Short Title: *gSol 'debs* [Prayer]. xyl. (BP).

———, ed. n.d.c. *bsTan pa skyong pa'i dam can chen po rnams kyi phrin las dngos grub rol mtsho.* [The Playful Ocean of True Achievement. The Ceremonies for the Great Sworn Defenders of the Faith.] Short Title: *sMin gling dngos rol* [Mindroling Playful [Ocean of] True [Achievement]. xyl., from the Rong phu blocks stored at Thubten Chöling. (PO).

———. n.d.d. *Thugs rje chen po bde gshegs kun 'dus kyi cho ga'i lhan thabs snying po'i mdzas rgyan zhes bya ba.* [The Accompanying Methods for the Great Compassion Union of the Blissful Ritual, entitled, "The Ornament which Beautifies the Essence."] Short title: *Lhan thabs* [Accompanying Methods]. xyl. (AM).

———. n.d.e. *Thugs rje chen po'i rgyun khyer zab lam snying po'i dril ba.* [The Heart of the Profound Path. The Daily Practice of Great Compassion.] Short title: *rGyun khyer* [Daily Practice]. xyl. (DP).

———. n.d.f. *Dam can spyi'i gtor ma'i cho ga nyung ngur bsdus pa.* [Condensed Torma Ritual for the Sworn Ones in General.] xyl. Thubten Chöling. (SO).

———. n.d.g. *rDul tshon chu bor spyan gyi cho ga.* [The Ritual of Inviting the Sand to the River.] xyl. (ICSR)

———. n.d.h. *rDo rje'i chos skyong rnams kyi las byang dngos grub rol mtsho'i rjes 'brang gi 'phrin las bye brag pa rnams phyogs gcig tu [b]sdebs pa dang skabs so sor brtan gsol bsdus pa thang lha bcas bcug pa.* [The Special Ceremonies for the Followers of the Diamond Defenders of the Faith Manual [called] "The Playful Ocean of True Achievement," Arranged in One Place, with the Addition, in their Respective Places, of the Short Prayers for the Steadfast Women [and for] God of the Plain.] Short Title: *rJes 'brang* [Followers]. xyl., from blocks stored at Thubten Chöling.

sMin gling lo chen Dharmaśri. (1654–1717). 1696. *Thugs rje chen po bde gshegs kun 'dus kyi sgrub thabs rnam bshad de kho na nyid snang ba'i 'od ces bya ba.* [The Light which Illumines Suchness: A Commentary on the Practice of Great Compassion Union of the Blissful.] Short title: *sGrub thabs* [Practice (*sādhana*)]. xyl. Rong phu edition. (LIS).

———. n.d.a. *Chos spyod kyi rim pa thar lam rab gsal zhes bya ba bzhugs so.* [The Sequence of Religious Practices called, "The Elucidation of the Path to Freedom."] Short title: *[sMin gling] chos spyod.* [[Mindroling] Religious Practice]. xyl. from Rong phu blocks stored at Thubten Chöling. (RP).

———. n.d.b. *Thugs rje chen po'i sgrub mchod dkyus ma tsam gyi phyag len zin bris.* [Notes on Doing the Complete Ritual Practice of Great Compassion.] In *bDe kun*, vol. *wu.* (Union of the Blissful Collection). xyl. Mindroling. (also Gyantse edition in the collected works of Dharmaśri, vol. *tsa*, p. 255 ff., Dehra Dun; and Rongphu edition.) (NP).

———. n.d.c. *Tshogs mchod cho ga'i phyag deb gsung rgyun ma rin chen sgron me.* [The Precious Lamp. A Handbook of the Complete Recitation of the Feast Offering Ritual.] ms. (PL).

Pha bong kha ['Khon ston dpal 'byor lhun grub]. (1561–1637). n.d. *dPyid gyi rgyal mo.* "The Song of the Queen of Spring." From *Bla ma'i mchod pa* [Worshipping the Lama].

sPrul sku bzang po grags pa and Rigs 'dzin rgod [kyi] ldem ['phru can]. (1337–1408). n.d. *'Khor lo 'bar ba zhes bya ba'i sgrub thabs*, a.k.a. *Sri bzlog.* ["The Blazing Wheel"— A Practice, a.k.a. Turning Back the Gnomes.] In RP.

rDza sprul ngag dbang bstan 'dzin 'jigs bral dbang phyug chos kyi rgyal mtshan. n.d. *rDza sprul ngag dbang bstan 'dzin 'jigs bral gyi skyes rabs rag bsdus dad pa'i snang 'byed.* Kathmandu: Dzatrul Rinpoche.

Ye shes mtsho rgyal. (8th cent.) 1972. "Slob dpon padma 'byung gnas kyi skyes rabs chos 'byung nor bu'i phreng ba (rnam thar zangs gling ma.) (Hagiography of Padmasambhava) Rediscovered by Mnga'-bdag Nyang-ral Nyi-ma-'od-zer." In *The Life of Lady Ye-shes-mtsho-rgyal.* Tashijong: The Sungrab Nyamtso Gyunphel Parkhang Tibetan Craft Community, pp. 361–613.

———. 1985. *O rgyan gu ru padma 'byung gnas kyi skyes rabs rnam par thar pa rgyas par bkod pa padma thang yig. The life of the precious Mahaguru Padmasambhava revealed from its place of concealment by gTer-chen O-rgyan-gling-pa. Reproduced from an illustrated and recently calligraphed manuscript made at the behest of H. H. Phuntsok Choeden by Golok Trulku.* Rewalsar: Shesrab Gyaltsen Lama and Āchārya Shedup Tenzin Zigar Drukpa Kargyud Institute.

Rin chen rnam rgyal a.k.a. Ratnabīja. n.d. *'Dir snang zin med kyi bya ba dang sgrib lus skye bar zlos pa'i rabs mdor bsdus tshigs su bcad pa byin rlabs myur 'jug ces bya ba.* [An Abridged Chronicle in Verse of the Unsuccessful Actions of the Life and Birth of this Obscured Body, called "Quickly Bestowing Blessings."] xyl. (QBB).

Lha btsun nam mkha' jigs med (1597–1655). n.d. *Rig 'dzin srog sgrub las ri bo bsang mchod.* [Mountain Incense Offering from *The Life Practices of the Knowledge Bearers.*] xyl. Thubten Chöling edition. (MIO).

Oḍiyāna (?= mKhan chen Oḍḍiyāna, aka O rgyan bstan 'dzin rdo rje, b. late 17th c., son of rGyal sras Rin chen nam rgyal, grandson of 'Gyur med rdo rje). n.d. *Thugs rje chen po bde gshegs kun 'dus kyi gtor dbang gi mtshams spyor ngag 'don bdud rtsi'i nying khu zhes bya ba.* [The Utterance that is the Essence of Ambrosia: The Annotated Torma Empowerment of Great Compassion Union of the Blissful.] Short title: *gTor dbang* [Torma Empowerment]. xyl.

bKa' rdzogs pa chen po yang zab dkon mchog spyi 'dus dang de'i cha lag zhi khro nges don snying ba'i las byang don gsal khyer bde bsgrigs pa pad ma'i dgongs rgyan. [Union of the Precious Ones Manual.] xyl. 'Ja' sa (Jalsa) edition.

'Chams gyi tho dge. (Mani Rimdu Dance 'Counting Book'). ms. Chiwong.

dBen gnas rdza rong phu'i bka' srung shar lung dge bsnyen gyis mchod sprin sgrub pa'i re skong zhes bya ba bzhugs so. ["The Fulfillment of the Practitioner's Hopes: A Cloud of Offerings for the Word Guardian of rDza rong phu Hermitage, Shar lung Upāsaka."] Short title: *Shar lung*. In *bsKang 'dus* [Collected Propitiations], Vol. Ja. xyl. n.d.

Thugs rje chen po bde gshegs kun 'dus kyi cho ga dang 'brel bar srung ma spyi dang bye brag gi mchod gtor 'bul ba'i ngag 'don gyi rim pa. [The Sequence of Recitations for the General and Particular Torma Offerings Connected with the Great Compassion Union of the Blissful Ritual.] Short title: *bKa' srung* [Guardians of the Word]. xyl. n.d. (GW)

Thun mtshams mka' 'gro gtor 'bul gzhugs so. [Herein lies the Sky Walker Torma Offering for the Break in the Session.] ms. n.d. (SWT)

De bzhin gshegs pa dang thugs rje dam la gnas pa rnams kyis brjod med kyi bshags pa. bShags pa'i rgyud dri med pa'i rgyal po las/ Ye shes lha dang 'khon gcugs pa ste le'u bzhi ba khol du phyungs pa'o. (The Inexpressible Confession Spoken by the Tathāgatas and Those Who Abide in Vows of Compassion. From *The Stainless King Confession Tantra:* an extract culled from the fourth chapter, "Confessing Strife with the Wisdom Gods.") In *Religious Practice*, ff 109–112.

Rong phu o-rgyan mdo sngags bzung 'jug chos gling nges pa don gyi dga' ba'i tshal gyi chog khrid deb sa ther kun gsal me long. (Mindroling ritual implements according to the early Rong phu system). ms. [Rong phu].

bSangs kyi cho ga bde legs kun 'byung rgyags ba rngan dang bcas pa. [Bulinasa (Solu) Edition].

Index